Missionary Atlas

A Manual of
The Foreign Work
of
The Christian and Missionary Alliance

Prepared by the Foreign Department

Under the direction of

ALFRED C. SNEAD, D.D., *Foreign Secretary*

Published by

CHRISTIAN PUBLICATIONS, Inc.

Third and Reily Sts., Harrisburg, Pa.

Credit is gladly given to

MARIE A. FRELIGH

Missionary in French West Africa for her valuable editorial ministries so joyously rendered during furlough in the preparation of this Atlas.

The mark of vibrant faith

CHRISTIAN PUBLICATIONS, INC.

Copyright, MCML

(Printed in the United States of America)

Table of Contents

Index of Fields

Index of Maps

INTRODUCTION

It has been our purpose to prepare an historical and descriptive Atlas of the mission fields of The Christian and Missionary Alliance. Items of general information are given concerning the Land, its Area and Population, People and History, Government, Climate, Physical Features, Resources, Progress, Currency, Languages and Religions. These are followed by the history of Missionary Occupation in general, and then by a description in detail of the work of the Alliance in the various areas.

As to terms used in connection with our work, every place where a missionary resides is listed as a *mission station*. Every place where there is a church with a resident native pastor, either ordained or licensed to serve Communion, is a *church center*. Thus a given place may be both a mission station and a church center. All places where services are held regularly by workers or lay members, but which are not listed as mission stations or church centers, are *outstations*.

An *organized church* is one with 10 or more members, and organized at least to the extent of having deacons and a church committee. Churches or groups without such organization, and those having less than 10 members, whether organized or not but holding regular services, are listed as *unorganized churches* or groups. One who has expressed a desire to become a Christian, and who follows up that initial step of prayer and faith by attending religious services and classes when possible, but who is not yet baptized, is considered an *inquirer*.

Since our last Atlas was published in 1936, rapid political changes have altered the names and boundaries of many countries, cities and towns. This has made the task of preparing maps particularly difficult. For example, because of unsettled conditions in the Near East, no definite boundaries can be given to Israel or to Arab-Palestine. For the present, because of the uncertain political situation, we are listing the Near East fields in three sections: Israel, Jordan and Syria. However, we do not consider them as three separate fields, although we realize that Israel will no doubt continue as a separate field but we are hoping that the Arabic sections, including Jordan and Syria, can be joined as one field.

Siam has again been officially changed to Thailand, but by the government and in common usage in Siam, both names are used so we are continuing to use the name Siam, although Thailand has official sanction.

The mainland of China is now under Communist control with the exception of the Province of Sikang in the far west. The description of conditions in China and of our mission fields there deal primarily with conditions prior to China's coming under the Communist regime.

In regard to the exchange value of the currency of the various countries, it is impossible to give information of lasting significance. The exchange values quoted in this Atlas were in effect at the time of going to press.

The Birth and Growth of the Alliance

The Alliance movement was born in prayer in Old Orchard, Maine, in August, 1887, when Dr. A. B. Simpson and a little company of God's children assembled there for fellowship. In that year was organized the *Evangelical Missionary Alliance,* and in 1889 it was incorporated under the name, *The International Missionary Alliance. The Christian Alliance* was incorporated in 1890, and in April, 1897, the two organizations were united under the present name, *The Christian and Missionary Alliance.*

The Alliance was not founded to establish another denomination, but to promote fellowship with all like-minded believers in foreign missions. Because of its long history and great growth, the Alliance has taken on some aspects of a denomination. Nevertheless it is still primarily a missionary movement, for the membership (over 80,000) in our various mission fields is greater than our membership (under 53,000) in the United States and Canada combined.

Alliance schools for training men and women for Christian service include: The Missionary Training Institute, Nyack, N. Y.; The St. Paul Bible Institute, St. Paul, Minn.; Simpson Bible Institute, Seattle, Wash.; Western Canadian Bible Institute, Regina, Sask., Canada; Toccoa Falls Institute and Bible College (Associated), Toccoa Falls, Ga.; and Mullen Bible Training School (Colored), Uree, N. C.

Not only in Bible Schools in the homeland are potential missionaries being trained, but also in the homes and schools maintained in various fields for the education of the children of our missionaries. A hostel is maintained for South China and other China fields in Kowloon, Hongkong, and the children are day pupils at the local government English school. Combined homes and schools are established in India, French West Africa, Indo-China, Indonesia, the Philippines and Ecuador. Largely as a result of such schools, we have in Alliance mission fields today nearly 50 second generation missionaries, while many more children of our missionaries are at present enrolled in Bible Schools and Colleges in America, in training for definite Christian service.

The work in the homeland, with the exception of the Bible Schools and publication work, is related to the Board of Managers through the Home Department. The Bible Schools and publication work at home are related to the Board through the Education and Publication Departments respectively. The foreign fields and all phases of ministry therein are related to the Board through the Foreign Department. There are at present 25 Bible Schools being carried on in our mission fields abroad, and an extensive translation, editorial and publication work in a number of the fields.

When Dr. Simpson went to be with Christ in 1919, the Alliance in its foreign fields was witnessing the gospel message in 24 languages and principal dialects. In 1940, the number had risen to more than 110, and today the message is being given by missionaries, native workers and members in our fields in 151 languages and principal dialects.

One in every 29 of the people of earth, or over 79,800,000 souls, live within the areas of Alliance responsibility in our 20 foreign fields. Of the 590 missionaries in active service at the end of 1949, 495 were on the field or enroute thereto. In the five years, 1945 to 1949 inclusive, more than 250 new missionaries sailed to our foreign fields.

Our foreign work is supported by the sacrificial gifts, not only of those who are members of our movement in the United States and Canada, but also of individuals, groups, churches, and church conferences who desire to share in world evangelization through Alliance channels. The Christian and Missionary Alliance rejoices in the prayer fellowship and cooperation of all Christians who share in this ministry of worldwide missionary work. Funds sent through the general missionary treasury in 1948 from Alliance churches and adherents only, revealed a per capita giving of $33.62, and represented over 90 per cent of our total income for missionary work.

The words of our Founder, Dr. A. B. Simpson, apply as truly today as when they were uttered:

"What do we ask of our people?

"First, that each one of them will become imbued with the missionary spirit, which means simply the Holy Spirit and the spirit of the Risen Christ. . . .

"Again, we ask our people to recognize the fact that the missionary interest is the chief business of every Christian. . . . Let us unite in a great missionary crusade. . . . Let everything be merged in this. Let our churches exist for this. . . . Let our business men carry on their business for this. Let all of us sacrifice for this. Let our homes be furnished and our wardrobes be purchased with reference to this. . . .

"And finally, this work can be done only by men and women who are filled with faith, armed with prayer, and baptized with the Holy Spirit. Mere human enthusiasm will wither and die. . . . Only when the church at home rises to a full realization of its responsibility and trust will the thought of God for this lost world be realized, and its evangelization will be not only possible but practicable in a single generation."

A PERSONAL WORD FROM THE EDITOR

We are grateful to the Lord of the harvest for the growing interest in our foreign missionary work. We praise God for the increased prayer ministry and for the widespread desire for information concerning the foreign fields. This third edition of the Atlas is the answer to many requests for present day facts concerning our mission fields.

The descriptions in this Atlas concerning Alliance fields and the work therein have been prepared in their final form from information furnished by the Chairmen and other missionaries for their respective fields. The major portion of the general research and the detailed editorial work was done by Miss Marie A. Freligh during an extended furlough from French West Africa. Others in the Foreign Department and in the fields gave assistance of great value in research, editing and in preparation of the manuscript for the printer. Heartfelt thanks are due and are hereby given to all of those mentioned above and to all who have rendered such untiring service in the preparation of the material in these pages.

All who read this Atlas are urged to share in making known to others the foreign missionary work of The Christian and Missionary Alliance. Mission Study Classes should be organized and Prayer Groups formed in every Alliance church and branch.

The Foreign Department sends out a monthly letter to many prayer groups, giving latest items of interest and prayer requests from the fields. A *Prayer Manual,* listing the names of fields, stations and missionaries, also excellent free literature concerning the work in the fields are available from Christian Publications, Inc., Third and Reily Streets, Harrisburg, Pa. Books describing certain fields can also be purchased. The *Alliance Weekly,* which is issued at $2.00 a year, is a very valuable source of missionary information including opportunities for investment of life and money in the mission fields in fulfilment of the Great Commission.

May God cause these facts of information to be set ablaze by the fire of inspiration through His Holy Spirit's ministry in the minds and hearts of all who read these Atlas pages until their lives shall be aglow with holy fervor and fiery zeal for the glory of God, the salvation of men, and the building of the Church of Christ among all the tribes of earth, in readiness for our Lord's return.

A. C. SNEAD.

Missionary Statesman, Intrepid Pioneer, Editor and Publisher, mightily used of God in manifold ministries in South China, Indo-China and Indonesia

Edited and published the Bible Magazine in Chinese and in Malay, thus ministering in large measure to the entire Church in China and Indonesia

REV. R. A. JAFFRAY, D.D.

A Missionary Atlas

INDIA

India's culture is so *old* that its scholars were already speculating about the soul of man when the inhabitants of the British Isles were still painting their bodies blue with dyestuff. India's area is so *vast* that, although it is a part of Asia, it is called a sub-continent. Of the three peninsulas in southern Asia, India is the middle one, shaped like a protruding tongue. The land is over 2,000 miles wide from east to west, by airplane, and nearly as long from north to south. It has over 4,000 miles of coastline, bordering the Arabian Sea, the Indian Ocean and the Bay of Bengal. From Baluchistan, where that country borders Persia on the west, the land frontiers of this sub-continent, including Burma, extend eastward in a serpentine line for more than 4,000 miles to China, Indo-China and Siam. In between these extremities, the frontiers of India, Pakistan and Burma touch Afghanistan, Turkestan, Tibet, Nepal and the tiny state of Bhutan.

Area and Population

Burma separated from India in 1937 and became the Union of Burma, a Republic. India and Pakistan became separate Dominions of Great Britain in 1947. The total area of India and Pakistan, including the independent Indian states which have acceded to them, is 1,581,410 square miles, an area as great as the United States east of the Rocky Mountains. According to the census of 1941, the total population of what is now India and Pakistan was 388,997,955. Since the partition, the various sections have been estimated as follows:

	Area	*Population*
Dominion of India	614,781 sq. mi.	250,000,000
States	598,272 " "	95,500,000
Dominion of Pakistan	368,357 " "	79,000,000
	1,581,410 sq. mi.	424,500,000

Between the years 1931 and 1941 the population of India increased at the rate of five millions annually, a total of 51 millions, or 14.7 per cent. Imagine three times the population of the United States living in three-fifths of its present area, and you have India's predicament, for there are more than 260 people to the square mile. In England 80 per cent of the population is in cities; and in the United States, over 56 per cent; but in India only about 13 per cent of the people live in cities. A large percentage of India's population is being drawn to the cities, attracted by the ever-increasing industrial opportunities, but India still has a tremendous rural population for there are only 58 cities in the country with a population of over 100,000.

People and History

The dates of India's ancient history are legendary. It may have been about the time Abraham migrated to Canaan, that the great Aryan race, living northwest of India, and akin to the Persians, moved southeastward to a new land which they named Hindustan. That was the beginning of the first period of Indian history, known as the National or Hindu period, and dating from about 2000 B. C. to 1001 A. D. The Aryan invaders were proud of their fair complexion and some his-

torians think that the caste system may have originated in their desire to keep their race unmixed with the flat-nosed, darker people whom they subjugated. The aborigines, of mixed blood now, and found today in the jungles and hill country of India, are relics of the very earliest inhabitants.

During that first period of Indian history, Gautama Buddha was born, reputedly in 557 B. C.; and Alexander the Great was in India during that same period, in 327 B. C. He was resolved to add the Punjab and Sind to his empire but his dream was never realized.

Of all those who have ruled India, the names of Asoka and Akbar stand out most prominently. Asoka (of the Hindu period) did much to propagate the Buddhist religion, sought to rule by kindness, and his benign edicts are still visible on carved pillars. By the fifth century A. D., the Hindus were flourishing in arts and religion. They claim to have invented chess and the decimal system; and vaccination may have been used in India twelve centuries before its use in Europe in the 18th century.

The second or Moslem period of Indian history lasted until 1757. To this period belongs Akbar the Great, Emperor of Hindustan from 1556 to 1605 A. D. Although a Moslem, Akbar founded a religion of his own and strove to get Hindus and Moslems to work together for the good of India as a whole. He was a great king, the equal perhaps of his contemporaries in Europe, Elizabeth of England and Henry IV of France. Shah Jehan, also a Mogul emperor, as was Akbar, built for his favorite wife, in the city of Agra, the famous Taj Mahal, the mausoleum in marble called the jewel of all architecture. The Mogul Empire was in its decline in 1739 when the Persian Nadir Shah invaded India. Soon many portions of India became independent states, and Hindu and Moslem adventurers established their own kingdoms in various places.

The third period of Indian history, the period of European Dominion, lasted from 1757 to 1947 A. D. The Venetians, the Genoese, the Portuguese and the Dutch had, by turns, traded with India. In 1602 the English appeared on the scene and for a long time the East India Company had a powerful hold upon the politics and commerce of India. Although founded for commerce, the Company was resolved to permanently establish English dominion in India. So well did the plan succeed that, by 1818, the British had become masters of most of India except the Punjab and Sind. After the Sepoy Mutiny in 1857-58, the British Viceroys consolidated the dominion during a period of peace and progress.

The early years of the twentieth century were disturbed by the rising tide of Indian nationalism but, on the outbreak of World War I, India gave allegiance to the Allies. In 1920 Gandhi started his policy of non-coöperation. The Round Table Conference in London, in 1931, closed with a pledge of Indian autonomy. Some progress was made toward this end, but members of India's Congress Party opposed entering the war (1939) and withdrew from participation in the government. In August, 1942, their leaders were interned; however, over two million Indians joined the colors in World War II. In 1946 when the interned political leaders of India were released negotiations were again opened for Home Rule. The Moslem League, led by Mr. Jinnah, insisted on founding Pakistan, a separate country designed to embrace those provinces where Moslems are in the majority. Despite the factions in the country, the British government announced its plan to withdraw from India. On August 15, 1947, after nearly 200 years of British rule, and after more than forty years of India's struggle for independence, the transfer of power took place, and the Union Jack was replaced by the national flags of India and Pakistan. Mr. Jinnah became Governor-General of the Dominion of Pakistan, with Mr. Liaqat Ali Khan as the Prime Minister. Lord Mountbatten became Governor-General of the Dominion of India, appointed by the Crown. In June, 1948, Lord Mountbatten retired, and C. J. Rajagopalachari of Madras took his place. Even in India they by-pass the new Governor-General's lengthy name and refer to him as "C. R." He is a Brahman but has always showed compassion for the Depressed Classes, and his daughter broke caste in order to marry Gandhi's son, who is a lower caste Hindu.

The States—variously referred to as Native States, Independent States, and Princely States—presented another problem in the new government. They had been in existence since the 18th century when various princes were rebelling against Mogul supremacy. The East India Company made alliances with many of these independent rulers, and when authority was transferred to the British Crown, most of the princes were already more or less subservient to the Company. The Crown, little by little, confirmed these rulers or Rajas in their hereditary rights. There were more than 550 of these States, with an irregularity of boundary that was as confusing as their respective sizes were irrational. With the withdrawal of the British from India, some of the princes strove to have their dominions recognized as independent States. Their subjects opposed them, and now the States have acceded to the central government. The smaller ones formed mergers, and these larger units have also become a part of India. The few States within the confines of Pakistan are expected to accede to that government. The leaders of the new government, in Delhi, have shown political sagacity in effecting within a year the integration of these States into the Indian Union. The State of Kashmir is still in a state of confusion, however, for the ruler is a Hindu, whereas 85 per cent of the population is Moslem. Hyderabad acceded in October, 1948, and there the ruler is a Moslem while seven-eighths of the population are Hindus. The new order in India has not been established peacefully. There have been riots and massacres and mass migrations; Hindus and Sikhs leaving Pakistan, and Moslems leaving India.

In spite of troublous times, there is now a new, self-reliant spirit in India. The new Cabinet, formed soon after independence was gained, reflected the government's avowal of equality for all. Of the fourteen members, including the Prime Minister, only six were caste Hindus. The other members included Moslems, Christians, one Sikh, one Parsi, and two Harijans (outcastes). One of the last two, Dr. Bhimrao Ambedkar, Minister of Law, is the long-time leader of the Scheduled Classes. The present Governor of Bombay Province, Sir Maharaj Singh, is a Christian. Pandit Jawaharlal Nehru, the Prime Minister, has been an outstanding political figure since 1929. He was educated at Cambridge, and is a Socialist but not a Communist. He is so opposed to dictatorship that he once refused to see Mussolini. His sister is at present Ambassadress to the United States. Another of India's women also gained political prominence; the renowned poetess, the late Mrs. Sarojini Naidu, was the first governor (or governess) of the United Provinces.

Great Britain has left the Indian scene but she has left behind eloquent testimony to long years of development and of service to India. She is still in India in her factories, railways, schools and—her cricket bat, now an established part of Indian life.

Government

Under British rule the two divisions of India were British India and the Native States. Then came the political division on religious lines into Hindustan and Pakistan, the name India being recognized as an English translation of Hindustan. Each had Dominion status with liberty to sever the connection with Great Britain if they so desired. In January, 1950, India broke her last symbolic bonds to Britain and became a sovereign democratic republic, declaring January 26 Republic Day. Pakistan, with its capital at Karachi in Sind, includes: Baluchistan, Northwest Frontier Province, Sind, West Punjab, a small part of Assam, and East Bengal. The rest of the country, including East Punjab and West Bengal, is the Dominion of India, with its capital at New Delhi. The provinces are similar to our states in their power to pass certain laws independent of the central government.

Moslem Pakistan desires a constitution based on Islamic law and religion, as set forth in the Koran. India has a democratic constitution with a Bill of Rights patterned after the American model. Drafted early in 1948, this new Constitution has a list of Fundamental Rights which prohibit discrimination on the grounds of religion, race, caste or sex; and it abolishes untouchability, making its practice a punishable offense. The Constitution provides for legislative bodies in the provinces and at the capital. The Union Parliament must meet at least twice a year and is made up of two bodies: the Council of States, elected by the provincial Legislatures; and the House of People, composed of 500 members elected directly by the people. The Head of the Union of India is elected by the Union Parliament. He appoints the Premier and the Cabinet. The chief political party in India is the Indian National Congress. Labor is represented by the Trade Union Congress. Communism is trying to work its way into this party, and is making headway among the common people.

Climate

Headline news each year is the report of the first monsoon rains, bringing relief from temperatures that rise to 120° in the shade during the hottest months. The monsoons are seasonal winds. The southwest monsoon strikes India early in June and brings 90 per cent of the rainfall. The northeast, or returning monsoon, brings rain to South India in the fall months. A moderate amount of rain falls on the hot plains (30 inches a year at Akola, Berar), but where the monsoon is checked by mountains, the rain falls in torrents. The heaviest rainfall in the world is on the slopes of the Himalaya Mountains. The climate of the country as a whole is tropical, but much cooler in the mountain regions. Prosperity or famine is India's lot according to the measure of rainfall; the condition of the crops determines whether the people will eat or starve.

In the areas where the Alliance Mission is working, the rainy season extends from June until September or October. The dry months following become increasingly cool and pleasant through February. From that time on it grows ever hotter until the rains arrive late in June. The hot season temperatures of our Marathi area stations are scarcely surpassed elsewhere in India. The Gujarat area, low-lying near the sea, endures both heat and humidity. The dry cool season is the best time to tour the districts and minister in villages that are more difficult of access.

Physical Features

The skyscrapers of India are its mountains. The highest mountain in the world borders it—Mt. Everest, "neighbor of the sky." No one has ever scaled it. It rises to an elevation of 29,141 feet, which is more than two miles higher than the highest of the Rockies in the western United States. The entire Himalayan system extends for 1,600 miles along the north of India, and boasts many mountains 25,000 feet high, which can be crossed only by passes at 17,000 to 19,000 feet. The Khyber Pass gives entrance into Afghanistan; the Bolan Pass into Baluchistan. During the recent war air fields were constructed in Bengal and Assam for flying "over the Hump" into China. The higher slopes of the Himalayas are devoid of vegetation, but some of the mountain valleys are wide and fertile, and in Kashmir they are unexcelled for climate and beauty.

The natural divisions of India and Pakistan are: (1) the high mountain areas of the north; (2) the river plains; (3) the peninsula proper, including the southern plateau. These three geographical divisions also indicate, to some extent, divisions in language, race and characteristics of the people.

The chief provinces of the river plains are: Bengal, the United Provinces, the Punjab, Rajputana and Sind. India's densest population and richest agriculture is on the alluvial lands of these sections. The principal rivers are the Indus, the Ganges and the Brahmaputra. The Indus rises on the northern slopes of the Himalayas, sweeps around the western extremity of the range and finally empties into the Arabian Sea. The Brahmaputra also rises on the northern slopes of the Himalayas, and enters India at the extreme eastern point of the ranges. It mingles with the Ganges before the two together finally enter the Bay of Bengal. The sacred Ganges is formed by the confluence of the streams which drain the southernmost slopes of the Himalayas.

The southern plateau comprises the Provinces of Bombay and Madras, the Central Provinces and the states of Hyderabad and Mysore. Part of this region was formerly called the Deccan, which simply means, the south. To the north are the Vindhya Mountains, the Narbada and Tapti Rivers. On either side of the plateau are mountain ranges, the eastern and the western Ghats.

Resources

Tea was first introduced into China from India, according to a Chinese legend. It is a fact that tea has been found growing wild only in Assam. Tea, jute and cotton manufactures head the list of India's exports. Great quantities of unrefined sugar are now being made from palmyra juice. Rice, wheat, millet, peanuts, spices and tobacco are also important agricultural products. Date and coconut palms and mango trees provide fruits. About 20 per cent of the land is forested, providing fragrant sandalwood, cedar, teak, ironwood and sal. Cotton, jute and oil seeds are important crops; shawl and carpet weaving are important industries. India has the largest bovine population in the world, due to the Hindu reverence for the cow, but the vast number of cattle are a decided drain on the land and the food supply. India is the main source of mica and manganese, has important iron deposits, and produces coal and gold in considerable quantities. In volume of trade India now ranks fifth in the world and is beginning to manufacture many articles previously imported.

Progress

Three provinces of India went dry in October, 1948: Madras, the Central Provinces and Berar, and the Northwest Frontier Province. Madras has forbidden newspapers and magazines published within its borders to carry liquor advertisements. In the United Provinces where prohibition has been in force for more than a year, both foreign and local liquor is banned, as well as opium and other poisonous drugs.

The first India-built aircraft of high performance made test flights in May, 1948. India has 22 internal air routes servicing about 25,000 miles daily, and also overseas service. The Indian sub-continent holds the world's first place in irrigation with its nearly 80,000 miles of canals irrigating some 70 million acres; yet this utilizes only six per cent of the country's water wealth. An Institute of Nuclear Physics has been founded at Calcutta University. When tempted to boast of the transcontinental railroads of the United States, remember that India's railway system is second only to ours. There are 24,565 miles of railway lines in India, and 6,748 miles in Pakistan. Only the steel mills of Pittsburgh surpass the Indian iron and steel works in the Province of Bihar. There are 264,605 miles of roads throughout the country, of which 95,000 miles are surfaced.

In spite of the fact that over 340 millions of India's people are still illiterate, nearly 4,000 Indian language newspapers are published; their circulation is four millions; and perhaps five times that many people read them. In 1935 the Government of India Act gave the right to vote to six million women. Today, Indian women may be seen driving their own cars, or doing picket duty in strikes. Recently a bill was passed in Madras making it illegal to dedicate girls to temples, a custom which long sold innocent children into a life of prostitution.

The richest man in the world is said to be the Nizam of Hyderabad in southern India. But in India's villages the people still live in one-room houses with earthen floors and walls plastered with a mixture of clay and cow manure. Their homes have no chimneys, the door being the only outlet for the smoke of their cooking fires. Their water supply comes from stagnant pools, open wells, or polluted streams. Great hydro-electric projects are under way in India, but as yet no better housing projects for the inhabitants of India's 700,000 villages.

Currency

The money of India is reckoned in rupees, annas, pice and pies. Pies resemble our one cent piece in size and appearance; are now seldom seen in circulation, but are still mentioned in reckoning. Three pies make one pice; 12 pies or four pice make one anna; and 16 annas, one rupee. At present an anna is worth a little less than one and one-half cents and the rupee about 21 cents in U. S. currency. There has been much discussion in the press on the question of discarding the present system of reckoning for the decimal system which is more generally used by the people.

Languages

Sanskrit was an old language when Latin was still new. Hindu mythology says that it was the language of the gods. Most Indian languages have absorbed large numbers of Sanskrit words. Under British rule, English was the court language of the country. Hindi will now be the dominant language in India, and Urdu in Pakistan. Hindustani is not a distinct language but may refer either to spoken Hindi or Urdu. There are not only 225 distinct languages and innumerable dialects spoken in India, but, to complicate matters, they are written in no less than eleven scripts, some reading from right to left, and others from left to right.

The following table shows the languages which are spoken

by five million or more people each, and also which Scripture portions are available in those languages:

Language	People (Estimate)	Bible Translation
Eastern Hindi	7,800,000	Bible
Lahnda	9,850,000	New Testament
Malayalam	10,500,000	Bible
Gujarati	12,400,000	Bible
Oriya	12,870,000	Bible
Kanarese	12,880,000	Bible
Rajasthani	15,900,000	New Testament
Punjabi	18,200,000	New Testament
Tamil	23,450,000	Bible
Marathi	24,000,000	Bible
Bihari	30,000,000	Portions
Telegu	30,000,000	Bible
Bengali	61,000,000	Bible
Western Hindi or Urdu ...	80,000,000	Bible

The entire Bible is available also in Assamese, Garo, Kashmiri, Khasi, Mundari, Nepali, Sanskrit, Santali, Burmese and Sinhalese; the New Testament in 24 other languages; and portions (an entire Gospel or other book of the Bible) in over 60 minor languages. The circulation of the Scriptures reached over 57 million copies during the 140-year period between 1804 and 1944.

The Directory of Churches and Missions in India (1947), shows the publication of the Scriptures in the languages of India, Pakistan, Burma and Ceylon as follows: entire Bible, 27; New Testament only, 23; Scripture portions, 51; total, 101 languages. The above report is for language groups of 5,000 or over.

When we remember that of the more than 200 distinct language groups in India, only 27 have the entire Bible in their native tongue, and only 74 others have the New Testament or some Scripture portion, it is evident that a great work yet remains to be done in making the Word of God available in all the languages of the people of India, and in teaching them how to read it.

Alliance missionaries and Indian workers are witnessing in the following languages: Marathi, Gujarati, Hindi and Urdu.

Religions

Hinduism. In India one can often tell by a man's headgear where he comes from and what his religion is. The distinctive twist of a turban can indicate whether a man is from the south of India or the Punjab; whether he is a peasant, a Sikh, or a Rajput. India has always been a land of many religions; it has been unique in its caste system, which is the outstanding institution of the Hindu religion. Caste has made sheep out of its followers; there is no place for initiative or personal preference. Caste tells the individual what his name shall be; the kind of food he may eat, and where; the kind of work he may do; whom he may marry, and when.

Caste has been one of the greatest hindrances to missionary effort, and a distinct hindrance to national unity in India. No non-Hindu, Moslem or otherwise, could rent a lodging in certain Hindu sections of even such a cosmopolitan city as Bombay. The system of cast is at least 2,400 years old. Some castes are more like trade-guilds; others are akin to religious sects. Underneath all the laws of caste are the exacting laws of ceremonial purification and defilement. According to tradition the origin of caste goes back to the time of Brahma, when the Brahmans supposedly sprang from his head, the Kshatriyas from his arms, the Vaishyas from his thighs, and the Sudras from his feet. The Brahmans are venerated to the point of worship; the Kshatriyas are the warriors from whom the Rajputs claim descent; the Vaishyas are the merchants; and the Sudras are the farmers and lowly laborers, but are not considered "untouchables."

There are many subdivisions of castes, each with its own particular taboos; and beyond the four principal castes with their many subdivisions, are the outcastes, numbering 28 to every 100 caste people. They are variously called the Depressed Classes and the Scheduled Castes. Gandhi championed their cause and changed their name from outcaste to Harijan (Children of God). Hinduism has considered it a religious duty to scorn them, teaching that because of sins committed in some previous incarnation, they were destined to the lot of outcastes.

Some modification of the ideas of defilement by proximity to outcastes first became necessary with the coming to India of railways and other modern inventions. Democratic ideas from the "Satanic West" also helped to bring about a change; Christian teaching and practice have done still more; but there is still another reason—the Hindus want the vote of the Scheduled Castes. When it became known that some 700,000 outcastes in Travancore State were thinking of becoming Christians, permission was granted to them to enter temples. The Indian government is endeavoring to abolish caste, and at least on the statute books, there is legislation granting them equal rights to public wells, schools, temples and restaurants. But it will take a long time to eliminate caste in practice.

It is from the Scheduled Classes that a large proportion of the Christians have been won. They are neither mentally nor spiritually inferior to other people. A few members of the higher castes have broken caste to follow Christ, but the number of converts from among them is lamentably small.

Hinduism is still supreme in India, the religion of over 60 per cent of the population, but Hinduism has never gained permanent, extensive power in any land outside of India. It was once influential in Burma, Siam and Ceylon, but lost its influence in those countries to Buddhism.

The Vedas, written in Sanskrit, are the sacred literature of the Hindus. They reveal a worship of the personifications of the powers of nature. "In India everything is god but God." The Hindu pantheon consists of some 330 million gods and goddesses. Hinduism is a highly metaphysical pantheism, with many systems of philosophy, among them the well known yoga; it is so full of contradictory beliefs that it harbors both atheists and polytheists. It teaches a triad of the Supreme Being, represented as Creator in Brahma, as Preserver in Vishnu, and as Destroyer in Shiva. Hindus say that it is not possible to know God, and since one can only speculate, no one religion is better than another. The Hindu believes in rebirth; there are said to be about 1,850,000 reincarnations in all. Eternal bliss is conceived of as the extinction of personality by its absorption into the Supreme Being; this attainment or state is called *nirvana*.

Islam. About 100 million people in India and Pakistan are Moslems. Islam, the name of their religion, means "submission to the will of God." In a sentence, the Moslem creed is: There is no God but Allah, and Mohammed is his prophet. Their sacred book, the Koran, is, they believe, a revelation from God through Mohammed. To them, Jesus is a lesser prophet. Jesus promised His disciples that another Comforter would come. Moslems claim that Mohammed is that Comforter. They deny the Trinity of God. They believe that in the final resurrection and on the Day of Judgment, Mohammed will be exalted in position above Jesus. Orthodox Moslems abstain from eating pork, drinking intoxicants, or using tobacco. Their regular fast days are obligatory; they fast from sunrise to sunset, and turn the nights into orgies of feasting and revelry. From the mosque towers a muezzin (crier) calls the faithful to prayer five times daily; they pray facing Mecca, at the mosque when possible, or by the roadside when traveling. A Moslem is proud of the spot of dust on his forehead, evidence that he has just come from prostrating himself in prayer. Moslems believe that a woman can enter paradise only on the merits of her husband. A Moslem is permitted to have four legal wives; there is no assurance that he can gain entrance to paradise for his concubines. Salvation, to the Moslem, means access to a paradise of sensual indulgence.

Islam abhors idolatry, yet the worship at the tombs of reputed saints approaches idolatry. It is democratic, in that it says all believers are equal, yet a *hadji,* one who has made the pilgrimage to Mecca, is greatly venerated. In India, in spite of the Koranic teaching of equality of believers, a certain amount of caste spirit has crept into the religion.

The law of apostasy in Islam, which enjoins the destruction of those who forsake that faith, has never been repealed, but an impartial government can hinder its operation. To the Moslem there is only one religion, Islam. If a Christian will not accept it, he is better out of the way. One who knows has said that the problem in dealing with Moslems is, "To persuade the proudest man on earth to accept a gospel he detests from a people he despises."

Zoroastrianism. Zoroastrianism, the religion of the Parsis of India, was the religion of Persia before it accepted Islam. The Parsis are descendants of Persian refugees who fled to India from Moslem persecution. They form the most exclusive society of any in India—no one can become a Parsi, he must be one by birth.

Zoroaster taught that the lord of light and goodness is continually at war with the author of darkness and evil, and that the good will ultimately triumph. The Parsis are for the most part a highly cultured people, and their women are given a place of high regard in the family life, and freedom in the affairs of the community.

Sikhism. Sikhism is a Hindu sect founded by Guru Nanak, who was a contemporary of Luther. *Guru* is a title of esteem given to a teacher; the word *sikh* means a disciple. The sect appeared in the Punjab about 1500 A. D., later changing from a religious reform to a great military organization. Orthodox Sikhs do not cut their hair, and always keep it covered in public. Sikhs believe in one god, prohibit idolatry, pilgrimages and charms; they abolish caste and refute the doctrine of the supremacy of the Brahmans.

Buddhism and **Jainism.** These two religions appeared about 550 B. C., both outgrowths of Hinduism. They both reject the authority of the Vedas and the idea of the supremacy of the Brahmans; both respect every form of animal life and refuse all blood sacrifices. In spite of so many similarities, the two religions differ considerably in doctrine and practice. Both revere the "Three Jewels" but, to the Buddhists, the term signifies: the Buddha, the Law, and the Order of Monks; to the Jains the term signifies: Right Faith, Right Understanding, and Right Morals. The founder of Jainism was Mahavira, a young nobleman who became dissatisfied with Hinduism and organized a society of friars to promulgate his new religion. Gautama Buddha (Buddha, from *bodhi,* meaning supreme knowledge or enlightenment) was a contemporary of Mahavira for a number of years. Gautama the Buddha, also a nobleman, became bored with the pleasures of court life and taught what was a philosophy rather than a new religion. He chose to ignore the existence of Deity rather than deny it. He was a moralist, urging his disciples to strive for holiness and truthfulness; and from moralist and philosopher, Buddha was elevated to the place of a savior. About seven centuries ago Buddhism died out in India, the land of its birth, and Buddha became one of the incarnations of the Hindu system. The Brahmans always opposed both Buddhism and Jainism, and Moslem conquest also helped to overthrow Buddhist influence. Today there are less than half a million Buddhists in India and Pakistan, but it flourishes in Burma, Ceylon, Siam, Cambodia, Laos, Nepal and Tibet, Mongolia, China and Japan. (Lamaism is the form of Buddhism found in Tibet and Mongolia.)

Hinduism, Jainism and Buddhism were the three religions of northern India. Their foe in the south was animism, the demon worship of the aboriginal Dravidian or Tamil nations (the former name of Tamil country was Dravidia). The census of India lists over 25 million aboriginal tribespeople, but most of them have become Hindus. About 5,500,000 of them are still animists. The following table shows the populations of India by religions as given in the 1941 census:

Hindus, including outcastes	266,053,000
Moslems	101,910,000
Christians	7,250,000
Sikhs	5,700,000
Jains	1,500,000
Buddhists	469,000
Parsis	114,000
Jews	22,000
Animists	5,541,000
Others	439,000
	388,998,000

Since, in the last census, people were enumerated according to origin and community rather than religion, the figure for Christians is considered much too low. It is estimated that by 1947 there were about 10 million Christians of various sects in India; approximately five millions of them Protestants; three and one-half million Roman Catholics; and one and one-half million Syrian Christians. Some 400,000 Christians are in Pakistan, and have remained there while Moslems and Hindus have been feverishly on the move to establish themselves in territories where their particular religion dominates. The general upheaval has thrown many of these Pakistan Christians out of employment, and they have been turned from a hard-working community into a poverty-stricken, sometimes starving group of people.

The population of India has been increasing annually by about five millions, yet the total number of Protestant Christians in the land today is no larger than the rate of population increase. Four hundred million people in India still look for salvation in another—not in Christ.

Missionary Occupation

It cannot be proved but it is probable that the fire of Pentecost carried the gospel to India even before it was taken to England. The Mar Thoma Christians of Southwest India claim that the Apostle Thomas went to India about 52 A. D., and that their community of Christians is descended from his converts. Some writers think that he had previously visited what is now known as the Punjab about the year 48 or 49. The story of Thomas' arrival in India may be mere legend, but it is a fact that Pantaenus of Alexandria went there about 190 A. D. in response to an appeal for Christian teachers. He found Christians already there who possessed a copy of St. Matthew's Gospel in Hebrew. For many centuries the Thoma or Syrian Christians (so called because of Syrian colonists who joined them) were considered to be a part of the Nestorian Church. Through the zeal of Nestorian Christians, there were about 350 churches in India in the fourth century. At one period of their history, many Mar Thoma Christians were won over by Jesuits to the Church of Rome. Some later shook off that yoke, and the church is now divided into three branches with a total membership of over one million. The Mar Thoma Christians have never been missionary-minded, but the Reformed branch of their church is showing signs of being more evangelistic.

Francis Xavier went to India in 1540 under the Jesuits, a Catholic order which is one of the bitterest enemies of the Protestant faith. Yet Xavier himself showed such a self-denying passion for the souls of men as to make his ministry an example of zeal and loyalty. He labored in South India for several years, where he won thousands of converts; he later pressed on to the Malay peninsula and eventually as far as Japan.

Christian Frederic Schwartz went to India in the year 1750, and labored for 48 years with such piety and zeal that, after his death, the adopted son of an Indian Raja wrote to the Board in England, "O gentlemen, that you were but able to send missionaries here who should resemble the departed Schwartz!" Others followed in his train, and all the missionaries of the Danish-Halle Mission left an effective impress as the first Protestant missionaries to India, but the place of Schwartz in the hearts of men was unique.

William Carey called himself "not a shoemaker, just a cobbler, a mender of other men's old shoes." In 1793 Carey sailed for India with his wife and a companion. They were obliged to travel on a Danish ship because the East India Company was so hostile to missionary work that it would not permit them to travel on an English ship. For years Carey supported himself and his family while mastering several languages, preaching daily, and translating the Scriptures. He cobbled shoes for a living, raised flowers for sheer delight, and for love of souls set as his goal to translate at least the New Testament into all the languages of India. He did not then realize how numerous were those languages, but he, with the aid of his coworkers, produced six translations of the complete Bible, twenty-three of the New Testament, and smaller portions of the Scriptures in five other languages. He also compiled dictionaries in Bengali and Marathi, and grammars in these and three other languages. The shoe cobbler became one of the greatest linguists of the world, and was appointed by the Governor-General of India as teacher of Bengali, Marathi and Sanskrit in Fort William College, Calcutta.

Alexander Duff was a gifted orator but was never content to remain at home in Scotland to labor for Christ. At the age of twenty-four he went to India where his burning zeal and overflowing energy immediately began to make an impress. At home as well as in India his influence was felt, for he moved hundreds of others to go and thousands to give for the advance of Christ's cause.

Reginald Heber survived only four years in India, but he became the second bishop of Calcutta and left an undying memory by his life and hymns. Adoniram Judson was driven out of India into Burma, and there translated the entire Bible in Burmese, and won thousands to Christ. The names of Taylor, Scudder and Thoburn belong to the long list of missionary heroes in India, as do also some of India's own women—namely, Mrs. Sorabji, wife of one of the first Christian converts from the Parsis; and Pandita Ramabai, the only woman in India to be accorded the title of Pandita (the learned). Her ministry for Christ to India's womanhood continues in the Mukti Mission which she founded.

Among the leaders in the churches of India today are those whose forefathers were won to Christ by Carey, Duff and their contemporaries. An Indian Moslem official once said, "I do not envy the nations of the west their armies and navies, their cultural advances, nor the high state of civilization to which they have attained, but I do envy them their missionaries."

The Directory of Churches and Missions for 1947 gives the number of foreign missionaries on the sub-continent as follows:

India	4,794	(including Pakistan)
Burma	126	
Ceylon	120	
	5,040	

Since about one-sixth of the missionary staff is on furlough at any given time, the active working force in India is about 4,000. There are just over 1,800 mission stations, and the ratio of occupation shows two workers (either national or foreign, men or women) for every 100,000 people. For India and Pakistan 22,747 Sunday schools are reported, with 43,532 teachers and 894,343 pupils. Under the old regime, missionary work was not permitted in some of the native States—one reason why about 500 of them were not occupied.

Missions are carrying on nearly all the work being done for sufferers from leprosy, and a large proportion of the tuberculosis institutions are also operated by missions. Mission schools include: 36 colleges, 308 high schools, 151 industrial schools, 138 teacher-training institutions, 130 seminaries and Bible schools, 284 hospitals and 343 dispensaries, a total of over 2,650 institutions. The Indian church is growing in numbers and in the ability to handle its own affairs, but with the church only 25 per cent literate, and Christians of all churches numbering only about two per cent of the population, the scope for missionary labor is still unlimited.

How does the present government of India view the presence of the Christian missionary? It restricts missionary activity in schools by barring religious instruction by the State or by any educational institution subsidized by the State. Nevertheless, the new Constitution declares that, "subject to public order, morality and health . . . all persons are equally entitled to freedom of conscience and the right to profess, practice and propagate religion."

The Christian and Missionary Alliance

In the year 1874, a godly British official and his wife, stationed in Berar, India, were so burdened for the two and one-half million souls in that province that they spent New Year's day in fasting instead of feasting. In answer to their prayers and those of others in America, the North Berar Faith Mission was founded in 1882 under Rev. and Mrs. Mark B. Fuller. The newly organized Alliance movement sent to India four missionaries—one each year—between the years 1887 and 1890. Those missionaries associated themselves with the North Berar Faith Mission which, in 1892, was merged with The Christian and Missionary Alliance. The British official mentioned above, when about to retire to England, deeded his property in Akola, and a bungalow in Chikalda, to the Alliance. The Akola property is the headquarters of Alliance work in India.

To the little group of missionaries in India, in the beginning of the work, were added seventeen new missionaries in 1892, while twelve new stations were opened. During the next five years, seventy-seven missionaries were sent by the Alliance to India. "By 1897 our far-flung stations were established . . . so strategically were they located that they remain substantially our chain of stations today. . . . With the advent of the motor car a few stations have been combined and a few new stations have been opened. One or two centers have been turned over to other societies, but otherwise the list of stations of 1897 is identical with the list today." So runs the account of those early days of the work.

Although the Alliance Mission in India is a unit administratively, its work is in two distinct languages and areas of Bombay Province, and in Central Provinces and Berar. Both areas are in the Dominion of India; we have no work in

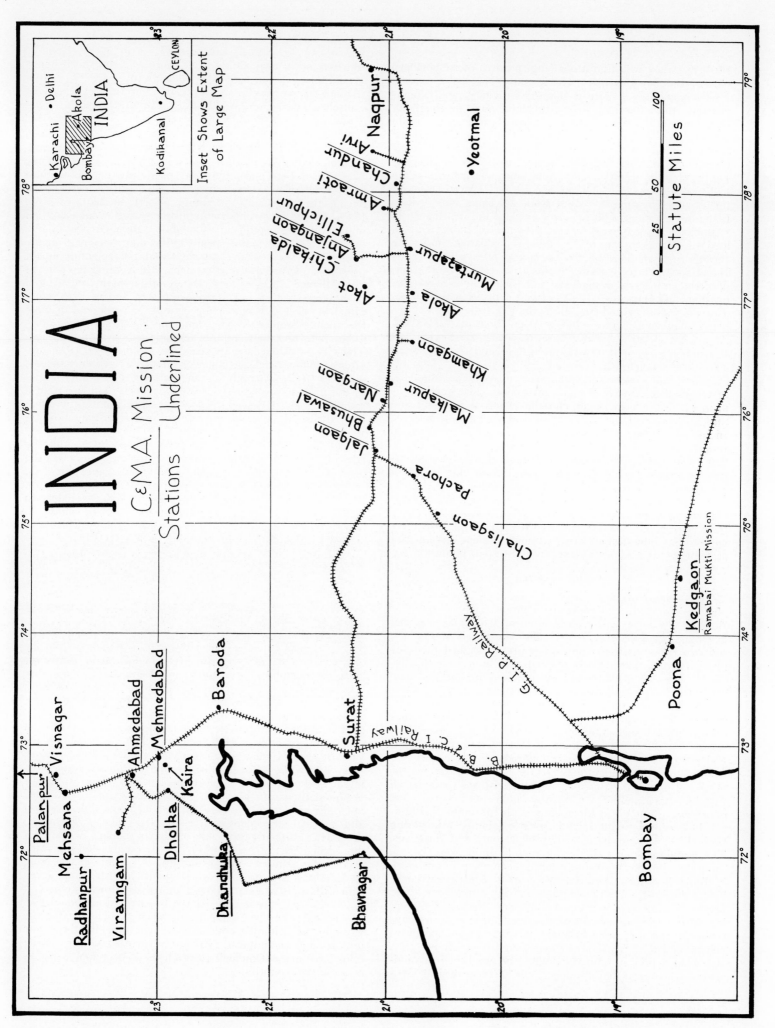

INDIA

C&M.A. Mission

Stations Underlined

Statute Miles

Inset Shows Extent of Large Map

INDIA

Karachi · Delhi
Akola
Bombay
Kodikanal
CEYLON

Naqpur

Arvi

Chandur

Amraoti

Yeotmal

Ellichpur

Anjangaon

Chikalda

Akot

Murtazapur

Akola

Khamgaon

Malkapur

Nargaon

Bhusawal

Jalgaon

Pachora

Chalisgaon

G.I.P. Railway

Kedgaon
Ramabai Mukti Mission

Poona

Bombay

Surat

B. & C.I. Railway

Baroda

Mehmedabad

Ahmedabad

Kaira

Dholka

Dhandhuka

Bhavnagar

Viramgam

Mehsana

Visnagar

Palanpur

Radhanpur

13

Moslem Pakistan. Gujarat is a language area in the northern part of Bombay Province. The Marathi language area is in East Khandesh, a district of Bombay Province; and extends also into the adjacent province of Berar and one county of the Central Provinces. There has long been excellent train service between the principal stations in both areas of the field, but much of the district work formerly had to be done traveling by ox-cart or horse tonga (a two-wheeled vehicle). During recent unsettled conditions, our missionaries again had to resort to those slow modes of travel. Even yet gasoline is strictly rationed. More roads are being improved so that now an automobile is a real asset in the district work.

Bombay is the second largest province in India, with an area of 84,600 square miles, and a population, including Baroda State of 23,704,850. There are 750 foreign and 184 Indian missionaries working in this area besides several hundred Indian pastors, evangelists, and Bible women of various missions and churches. The Christian population is 370,000. The Central Provinces and Berar have a little smaller area than Bombay Province, and a population of 16,813,000. Among all societies working here, there are 439 foreign and 109 Indian missionaries, in addition to other Indian workers. The Christians number 52,283.

Alliance missionaries in India meet in conference annually, in October or November. The missionaries are accepted as members of the local Indian churches where they reside, and thus are a part of the Christian and Missionary Alliance of India, that indigenous body composed of "all residents in India who accept the doctrines and principles of The Christian and Missionary Alliance of India." This body administers its affairs through Church Councils and other bodies of church representatives. As the work in India is now church-centric rather than station-centric, the mission stations of the various areas are here presented (in bold-face type) under their respective Church Councils. At the close of 1948 there were 15 mission stations (two without resident missionaries at the time); 20 church centers; and 65 outstations.

Gujarati Area

The Alliance work in Gujarat is in the Ahmedabad and Nadiad (formerly called Kaira) administrative districts of Bombay Province, with a population of about two and one-half million people. Our responsibility is nearly one million souls in these districts; and other areas assigned to us by mission comity, but not yet occupied, greatly increase this figure. The people speak many languages but Gujarati predominates. In Gujarat, Kathiawad and Cutch, even the resident Moslems speak Gujarati, an advantage which has never been properly exploited in dealing with them. Pioneer missionaries of the Alliance entered Gujarat in 1893. This area was severely affected by the famine of 1900. The orphanages at Kaira and Dholka cared for hundreds of those sufferers through four long nightmare years. Laboring among the dead and dying, the missionaries moved·wearily, "doing all that love and intelligent sympathy could do, and using the opportunity thus given for gaining souls for Christ." Physical destitution brought spiritual gain to many. Ministering to the body does not necessarily produce only rice Christians. The foundations of today's churches in India were laid in those dreadful days. The first large ingathering in our work in India came from Gujarat. "In 1900, 495 persons were baptized (mostly from Gujarat, but many from Berar) and our total membership reached 1,303. Moreover, we were left with 1,185 famine orphans. From those orphans have come the cream of our Christian workers, pastors and evangelists, and the main body of our church membership. . . . But what a price was paid. Weary and weakened missionaries worked until they dropped. Six of them died in 1900,

and four missionary children. Others were invalided home. Mrs. Fuller was one who died that awful year."

The Gujarat Synod divides the area into the following four Church Councils: *Ahmedabad, Dholka-Viramgam, Mehmedabad,* and *Kaira-Matar.*

Ahmedabad Church Council

Ahmedabad   Ahmedabad, the Manchester of India and the second largest city in the province, now numbers a million or more souls, owing to industrial expansion during the war, and the influx of Hindu refugees from Pakistan. It is an important railway junction and its chief industry is the manufacture of cloth. Refugees working in the mills may be found spending the night sleeping on the sidewalks. The housing shortage and the spirit of unrest present a picture of complete, crowded confusion. Of the two Alliance churches here, the Simpson Memorial Church is the largest of all our Indian churches, and in 1926 it became our first self-supporting church. By the end of 1947 the membership was 547, and the Christian community (Christians and their children) numbered almost a thousand. The city of Ahmedabad, opened as a station in 1894, still offers an unparalleled challenge, for to this center come the villagers of the surrounding districts to earn higher wages in the mills and offices. There is hardly a family within a radius of many miles which does not have relatives working in Ahmedabad. One-half of our Gujarat Christians now reside here.

In 1931 another congregation was formed in the mill district of Ahmedabad; and in the residential suburb of Maninagar, Christians of several denominations have united to build a church, in which Alliance preachers often minister. The Irish Presbyterians, the Methodists and the Salvation Army also have congregations in this city. The church at *Shantipur* (Village of Peace) is in a farm colony which was settled with Christians after famine days.

Visnagar   Visnagar, north of Ahmedabad in the *Mehsana* district, has been a mission station, but is at present unoccupied.

Dholka-Viramgam Church Council

Dholka   Thirty miles from Ahmedabad is Dholka with a population of over 17,000. It is best known in the Alliance because of the boys' orphanage located there ever since the opening of the station in 1897. At one time over 600 boys were cared for in the orphanage. Many of them have become faithful witnesses for the Lord in various localities, and a number of them are Indian pastors and evangelists, trained at the Bible School which was carried on first in Dholka and later in Mehmedabad. The first funds for the support of the Bible School were contributed by the orphans, who went without meals in order that the money thus saved might be used for the Bible School needs. The orphanage is now a preparatory school where students may be trained not only by a secular education but also by Bible teaching and spiritual experience to live for God. The Girls' School at Kaira, also an outgrowth of the orphanage work, was moved in 1934 to Dholka, where the two schools are operated at a saving of money and of the time of the missionaries and staff. Along with practical work and Bible instruction, seven standards of studies are taught in coeducational classes.

Dholka is the center of a large county with a population of 118,000. This station has also been responsible for the work in an adjoining county in which there has been one outstation at Dhandhuka. Pressure of work and war restrictions have made it difficult to reach the 270 or more villages in these two counties.

Dhandhuka Formerly an outstation, Dhandhuka, a county seat 40 miles distant from Dholka, was chosen by the 1949 Missionary Conference as a center for missionary residence. Thus the evangelization of this large area will be hastened.

Ashapur (Hope-town) is the largest of the four Christian villages in our Gujarat area. The Christian community numbers over two hundred. At Sanand is a small group of Christians who are connected with the Viramgam Church.

Viramgam Sixty miles from Ahmedabad is Viramgam, terminus of the railway line from Bombay, and a mill center with a population approaching 50,000. Here we have a thriving church, self-governing and supporting its own pastor. There is also a group of Christians here from the sweeper caste. The district around Viramgam is comparatively wealthy with surprisingly few low-caste people. Together with Sanand County the total population is over 200,000. Work was begun in Viramgam in 1897, and in Sanand in 1900. To the north are a number of states of various sizes, destitute of the Gospel. To the northwest lies Cutch, a state which our missionaries have long desired to enter.

Radhanpur In November, 1949, the missionary conference
Palanpur voted to enter areas north of Viramgam which had been native states, but are now part of India. The cities of Radhanpur and Palanpur were chosen as strategic centers for this pioneer work. In February, 1950, a house was rented in Palanpur and it was hoped that property could be secured in Radhanpur or some nearby town soon.

Mehmedabad Church Council

Mehmedabad Twenty miles by rail from Ahmedabad is Mehmedabad, famous in fiction as one of the homes of the infamous Bluebeard. It is now the center of a growing gospel ministry, and the church here has developed steadily ever since the station was opened in 1897. Besides Mehmedabad, the Church Council includes the churches of Akalacha, Hebron and Mahij. For many years the district has had more churches within its boundaries than any other district in the Alliance work in Gujarat. Mehmedabad is a center for great Christian gatherings, and the Gujarat Bible Training School for men is here. The recent war and subsequent upheaval and rationing made it necessary to discontinue temporarily the holding of large conventions.

Kaira-Matar Church Council

Alindra, Daroda, Kaira, Navagam, Vansar and *Vasna* are the churches of this Council and are all in the western part of this area, while the churches of the Mehmedabad Council are in the eastern part of the same area. Many of the famine waifs, gathered in during the early years, later married Christian girls from the Kaira school and were settled in farm colonies. These colonies formed the nucleus of the present churches throughout the area of these two Church Councils.

Marathi Area

Northeast of Bombay, the Gateway of India, runs the Great Indian Peninsula Railway to Delhi, Nagpur and Calcutta. Two hundred and fifty miles from Bombay on this line we enter Alliance territory, which extends over 200 miles across the entire Province of Berar, and on into the western end of the Central Provinces proper. The thirteen talukas (counties) constituting this missionary responsibility cover an area of 7,900 square miles and embrace a population of over two millions. The Calcutta Mail roars through this area in seven hours; but to visit each of the 3,000 towns and villages would require days of weary travel by train, car, bullock cart and on foot. No other societies are working here; the responsibility for all these souls is upon the missionaries and the Indian Church of the Alliance.

The Marathi Synod divides the area into four Church Councils: East Khandesh, Central Berar, North Berar, and East Berar.

East Khandesh Church Council

Traveling from Bombay northeastward, the towns of Chalisgaon and Pachora are passed, where Alliance missionaries pioneered for forty years. Hearts there have been much like the stony soil of East Khandesh, with only occasional fruit. These two stations are now manned by another evangelical Mission.

Jalgaon This city, opened as a mission station in 1895, is the capital of East Khandesh, a district of Bombay Province with a total population of 1,327,772 (1941 census). The population of Jalgaon County is 138,000; of the city, 50,000. It is an administrative center with some industries. Missionaries labored here for many years and saw a church erected, mainly from the gifts of Indian Christians who now partly support their ordained pastor. No missionaries reside here at present.

Bhusawal Sixteen miles farther east is Bhusawal, a railway junction with a population of 40,000. Our heritage here is the English Church founded by Bishop William Taylor in the 1870's. For more than forty years (since 1896) this church for the English-speaking population has been our responsibility. Many railway employees who were enlightened here carried the light farther on when they were transferred to other posts. Political changes are responsible for the departure of many of the English and Anglo-Indian people, but there is a continuing ministry to educated Indians who do not understand Marathi. The Indian Church in Bhusawal largely supports its pastor, who ministers to Marathi, Hindi and English-speaking Christians. Bhusawal County, which includes Nargaon, has a population of 164,000.

Nargaon This is the home of the Marathi Bible Training School for men, opened in 1908. Through the years it has provided well trained workers for our own Mission and for others also. Although Nargaon is a rural center, there are 25 villages that can be reached within a radius of five miles, and to them the Bible School students go to preach. The Bible School offers a three-year course but it requires five years to graduate, for, following a plan which was first used in the Tourane Bible School, Indo-China, studies occupy the first, third and fifth years, and practical service the second and fourth. Incompetent workers are thus weeded out, and the graduates are experienced men ready to take responsible places in the Lord's work. The Nargaon school works in affiliation with the Biblical Seminary, operated by the Free Methodist Mission in Yeotmal, where high school graduates can take studies of college level to fit them for places of greater responsibility. Neither the Bible School nor the Seminary is as yet an inter-mission institution, but several Missions coöperate by sending teachers and students to both schools.

Malkapur Malkapur, in Berar Province, has always been a battleground. The difficulty of work in this town of many Moslems is attested by the fact that not until 1922 were the first two converts baptized. There have been some baptisms since, and the people are friendly, but the Christian conquest is yet to be accomplished in this town where work was first started in 1896. Malkapur today has a population of 20,000 in the town, and almost 200,000 in the county.

Central Berar Church Council

The county of *Jalgaon (Berar)* is northeast of Malkapur, and off the railway line. Indian evangelists and pastors gave money to build an outstation in the county seat, a center for almost 100,000 people, but preoccupation with other needs has hindered from seeing much work done here. The census shows only 13 Christians among the many thousands.

Khamgaon   This city of 26,000 (county population over 150,000) has one of the largest cotton markets in India, but its most important output is trained Christian women. In 1893 a Girls' Orphanage was opened; it has been succeeded by the Girls' Preparatory School and the Bible Training School for women, both conducted here now. In the Preparatory School are some girls newly rescued from heathendom, and these are supported by gifts from America. Side by side with them in the classroom are other girls whose grandmothers were saved here when the school was an orphanage. These granddaughters of Christians are supported in school by the sacrifice of their parents, who must save carefully in order to pay the school fees that will give their daughters a Christian education. In the Bible Training School the girls are fitted to become Bible women and teachers. Also in the Bible School one may find older women from the villages, illiterate Christians who desire to read their Bibles and become grounded in the faith in order that they may go back and witness in their own villages.

Balapur has no workers at present. This county adjoins Khamgaon. The town has a population of 12,500; the county with its 200 towns and villages has over 115,000 inhabitants.

Akola   This city, 363 miles from Bombay, has a population of 65,000 and a county population of 200,000. Akola is important because of its government institutions, large factories, and an Arts college. It is important to us as the place of beginnings of the Alliance work in India (1892), and as the present headquarters of our entire India Mission. It was in Akola that the North Berar Faith Mission placed its property and work in the hands of The Christian and Missionary Alliance. The large structure housing the Mission Headquarters offices, also serves as a receiving home for new missionaries. Summer school sessions for Indian workers, inter-mission gatherings, Synod sessions, and the annual Mission Conference all make use of the facilities provided here. The Fuller Memorial Church in Akola is the largest of the Marathi churches and the oldest, having celebrated its golden jubilee in 1940. It has a membership of nearly 350, and the Christian community numbers 750. Two miles from the city is the Santa Barbara Preparatory School for boys, so named for the city of the early donors. In another direction from the city is the Christian settlement of Khadani.

The Akola church is self-supporting and is developing the work in a commendable way. Four Sunday schools are conducted in as many centers. There are permanent outstations in the district at Borgaon and Pailpada, centers of Christian village groups which are increasing in numbers. A hostel is maintained, in connection with the Santa Barbara School, for young men attending high schools in the city. They have a daily trek of six or seven miles between the hostel and the high school. Many of our Marathi pastors and evangelists have come from this mission enterprise.

Murtazapur   Thirty miles from Akola is Murtazapur, a railway junction and cotton center, with a population of several thousand; the county has a population of over 136,000. The station was opened in 1893. It was here and in the neighboring county of Daryapur that the first great break came in the villages of the Marathi area. The revival began after a period of unusual burden for souls, and after special daily periods set aside for prayer. Within five years seven hundred village people from this and other counties were baptized, after careful instruction. From family to family the gospel has continued to spread. Although not large enough to be called a mass movement, the revival has certainly been a group movement, confined mainly to one segment of the outcaste Mahars. A number of young men from this movement have gone to Bible school and are now working as catechists and evangelists.

North Berar Church Council

Anjangaon   Anjangaon is the center of the counties of Daryapur and Akot, which have a combined population of over 300,000 in 500 villages and towns. At first, Anjangaon was superintended from Murtazapur but a mission bungalow was built in Anjangaon in 1923 and it became a separate station. There are permanent outstations at *Akot, Telhara, Panori, Hingni, Daryapur, Nardoda, Surji, Sukli, Shingnapur* and *Kauta*. In 1947 there were 636 adult church members in good standing, and a community of over 1,000 scattered in 124 villages. The Bheel tribespeople of this area are showing an interest in the gospel. The growth in this our most fruitful area has been a natural one—the fruit of the gospel manifest in the changed lives of Indians in the community. About one-half of our present staff of Indian workers have come from this section of the country. Printed above the pulpit in the large Anjangaon Tabernacle, dedicated in 1945, is the verse: "Jehovah lifteth up the poor out of the dust to set them among princes."

East Berar Church Council

Amraoti   Thirty-five miles from Murtazapur is Amraoti, a large cotton market and government and educational center which vies with Akola in size. The population of the county is dense (210 to the square mile), and large—over 275,000. Work was begun here in 1893, and one of our earliest churches was built here. Its present pastor oversees the work in Badnera also, a mill center near by. The village groups show spiritual life, and there are outstations at *Mhaisapur, Donad, Watoda* and *Nandgaon*. Excellent work has been done in the children's meetings for non-Christians in Amraoti and Badnera. The Amraoti Sunday School observes missionary Sunday once a month, and their offerings have gone to various corners of the globe.

Chandur   Chandur was visited by Dr. Simpson when he was in India in 1893. He assigned missionaries to the station which was opened in 1894. Some converts were baptized here during the famine days, and there has been fruit in the villages in recent years. The county has a population of 173,000.

Arvi, east of Chandur, and therefore not in Berar, is a county of 163,000 people. The Alliance recently took it over from another Mission which had never developed the work; hence it is virgin territory. Shortage of workers has hindered us from doing much work in this area, but it presents an open door, with the usual adversaries.

Hill Stations and Children's Home   In the hills overlooking the plains of Berar, at an elevation of 3,600 feet, is the little town of *Chikalda*, where there is a small rest home which has recently served also as a home for missionaries' children, with a missionary matron in charge. However, most of the children of our missionaries go to school in *Landour* and *Ootacamund,* in both of which places we have property used as rest homes for the necessary recuperation during the hot season. There are also two mission bungalows in *Kodaikanal.* The elevation of these latter places is over 7,000 feet; they afford fresh vegetables and fruit; and they offer the needed escape from the heat of the plains.

The Ramabai The work which the late Pandita Ramabai
Mukti Mission founded in Kedgaon, Poona district, is still being continued as a work of faith along the lines laid down by the founder. Before her death Pandita Ramabai provided in her will that The Christian and Missionary Alliance should be asked to assume responsibility for such oversight and direction of the work at Kedgaon as would insure its remaining true to the principles which had characterized its history under the blessing of God. The Ramabai Mukti Mission, however, continues to function as a separate body under an Executive Committee and is represented in America by the American Council of the Ramabai Mukti Mission, through whose efforts people in various denominations and church groups are made acquainted with the work. Funds are provided through these channels and also through interested groups in Canada, Great Britain, Australia and New Zealand for the support of the valuable Christian ministries at Kedgaon for needy women and children of India. One or two experienced missionaries of the Alliance are often assigned to the work in Kedgaon as a contribution of the Alliance to the Ramabai Mukti Mission.

Translation and Publication Work

Complete Bibles are available from the British and Foreign Bible Society in Gujarati, Marathi, Hindi and Urdu, the languages used in Alliance areas in India. The need, therefore, is rather for Christian literature. There are two monthly magazines being published in Gujarati, and two in Marathi. One in Marathi is under the management of an inter-mission association of which the Alliance is a member. The second in Marathi is especially prepared for the newly literate. These magazines contain Sunday school lesson notes, young people's topics for study, sermons, articles and mission news. At present it is difficult to secure paper, but the *Fourfold Gospel,* by Dr. Simpson, and the *Life of Dr. Simpson* are both available in Gujarati; *Faith and Self Life,* by Dr. Simpson, is available in Marathi; and *Religion Weighed,* written to combat false teachings, is available in both Gujarati and Marathi.

The Chairman of the field writes: "Rather than many translations, we need books, in both Marathi and Gujarati, written from the Indian viewpoint."

Schools and Literacy Campaigns

There are two Bible Schools for men: for the Marathi area, at Nargaon; for the Gujarat area, at Mehmedabad. The Marathi Bible School for women is at Khamgaon, where there is also a Girls' Preparatory School. At Dholka in the Gujarat area are preparatory schools for both boys and girls. Near Akola is the Santa Barbara Preparatory School for boys. The above are all boarding schools. There are also two hostels with an enrollment of 15, and six primary village schools, total enrollment 139 (1948). The primary schools cover standards one to seven in Marathi and Gujarati, and standards one to three in English. The Hindi language is also compulsory now in schools.

Adult literacy classes are being conducted in the villages to enable older believers to learn to read their Bibles. The enrollment in 1948 was 134, and over 100 of those enrolled have become literate. In the same year three Workers' Institutes were held in the various Church Council areas, with 40 enrolled.

The church in India, on the whole, is weak as regards Christian education. The number and difficulty of the scripts of Indian languages is partly to blame, but too many Indian Christians still cannot read their Bibles. As late as 1944, only 25 per cent of all Christians in India were literate, which was an improvement of only ten per cent over the literacy situation in India as a whole. In 1941 only 12 per cent of the population over five years of age were literate enough to be able to read a letter and write the answer. The government of India hopes to achieve adult literacy within ten years.

The Church and the Challenge

The Christian and Missionary Alliance of India came into being with a new Constitution in 1931. Since that time, as a self-governing church, it has been taking its responsibilities cheerfully and is proving worthy of the confidence placed in it. It is officially registered, thus becoming incorporated and entitled to hold property; in fact, it was one of the first religious organizations in India to become incorporated as a purely Indian church.

Our Mission is known as The Christian and Missionary Alliance *in* India, thus distinguishing it from The Christian and Missionary Alliance *of* India, the indigenous body which administers its own affairs through local churches, Church Councils, Synods and a General Assembly. At least three churches are required for forming a Church Council, which is composed of the ministers and representatives from the churches within its defined area. Each Church Council appoints representatives to the Synod, which meets annually. The Gujarat Synod and the Marathi Synod are composed of four Church Councils each. The Synod has power to ordain, appoint, transfer, discipline or dismiss ministers of the gospel. Ordained pastors are paid from a Central Pastors' Fund. In the Gujarat Synod the Pastors' Fund is entirely supported by the churches although it should be increased so that some additional pastors could be appointed. In the Marathi Synod the Mission still gives a subsidy to help in the Pastors' Fund. For the evangelistic work in their areas, both Synods draw subsidies from the Mission.

The General Assembly is the highest authority in the India Alliance, and meets once in three years with representatives from the eight Church Councils. The General Assembly determines the minimum qualifications for ordination; coöperates with the Synods in Christian work; settles appeals; and is responsible for comity and coöperation with other societies. The general church rules include the following: Only those members of established Christian character and who have been baptized Christians for two years or more may hold office; a pastor must be at least twenty-five years of age, and must have been a baptized Christian for at least seven years; any church member who contracts a marriage with a non-Christian, or participates in such a contract in the case of his or her child, will be liable to discipline by the church. Missionaries are members ex-officio of the Church Council in whose area they reside, but any office held in this or in higher bodies must be by election. As the missionaries are in the minority, there is little danger of foreign domination in the Indian church.

Eight different Missions working in the Marathi language area, all of them fundamental in faith and practice, have formed an association known as the Berar-Khandesh Christian Council. The work done by the Young People's Committee of this association has been outstanding. Their united rallies have been attended by nearly a thousand people, with blessing to many young lives. The corresponding association in Gujarat is the Gujarat Regional Christian Council. Both Councils are associated with the National Christian Council for the purpose of representation to the government. *Sabhas* or *melas* are an interesting feature of Indian church life. To the Hindu, a sabha is any assembly; a mela is a larger gathering, a religious fair. To Christians the words have come to mean a camp meeting. Village groups sometimes go to the more distant of these annual gatherings on foot in pilgrim bands, singing as they go. Usually one service of the gathering is given over to a parade through the local town, with cymbals, drums and singing. By their testimonies and by the selling of Scripture portions, the company gives a witness to their faith. The Christian and Missionary Alliance of India is moving forward. The following table of comparisons is evidence of the growth:

	1936	1948
National workers	96	123
Church members	1,996	3,059
Church offerings	Rs. 9,825	Rs. 25,627
Baptisms	89	139
Christian communities, population	3,884	6,100
Sunday schools	68	71
Sunday school scholars	2,397	2,118
Boarding school students	247	392
School fees paid	Rs. 4,058	Rs. 15,534
Organized churches	....	36
Self-supporting churches	8	17
Bible school students	nil	58

In Berar, during the year 1948, the government imposed a law requiring those who desired to change their religion to secure a permit from the magistrate. The restriction was later lifted, but as it was in effect for most of the year, the number of baptisms was understandably smaller than it would have been under normal conditions.

Our churches are weakest along the line of self-propaga-tion. They need prayer that their slogan may be Augustine's words, "What I live by, that I impart," and that Paul's warning, "Woe is unto me, if I preach not the gospel," may stir them until they cannot rest while portions of India still wait for the gospel.

The Alliance responsibility in India is five million souls. In East Khandesh and Berar (Marathi areas) no other missions are working in the counties we are endeavoring to occupy, except in Bhusawal, and also in a small portion of Chandur which has been turned over to the Free Methodists. In the northern part of the Gujarat area, and extending over into the Hindi language area, lies a great expanse of unoccupied territory with a population of some 300,000. The area is well covered with railways, making many centers readily accessible. Other sections can also be reached, but over difficult roads. India has far too many unreached villages at the end of difficult roads. In the East Mehsana district some impression has been made through work in Visnagar, where missionaries resided for a time, and a few Indian workers have visited that region, but much of it is virgin territory. An earnest plea has recently been received from our Mission in India for missionary reinforcements so that not only East Mehsana but also the former native states of Radhanpur and Palanpur may be entered and occupied for Christ. Still beyond this lies Rajputana, a province largely desert, and rather sparsely populated, but one whose spiritual condition is more barren than its soil. Canadian Presbyterians are working along the border, but the need is great in the interior. Rajput means "king's son." Our King should have a heritage of sons from this land. Alexander McLeish, in *The Evangelization of India*, World Dominion, says:

Recent study of the field confirms the statement, which I made elsewhere, that, if we took up all the missionaries and removed them from the sphere of the Indian church, we could set the whole five and a half thousand to pioneer new areas, and new peoples, and having completed that could still repeat the process.

Students from Ntoroso Bible School witnessing in the Habbe tribe, French West Africa

Evangelistic Band from Village Church in Gujarat, India

AFRICA

Africa, the second largest continent, lies south of Europe and east of the Americas. Although the Atlantic Ocean separates Africa from the Western Hemisphere, it is a flight of only four or five hours from Dakar, westernmost point of Africa, to Natal, easternmost point of South America. Africa is separated from Europe by the Strait of Gibraltar and the Mediterranean Sea; is joined to Asia on the east by the Isthmus of Suez; and is bounded on the east by the Red Sea and the Indian Ocean, the latter bounding it on the south also.

Area and Population

Africa is more than three times the size of the United States, with a maximum length from north to south of 5,000 miles and a maximum breadth of 4,650 miles. Africa's area of 12,563,807 square miles covers more than one-fifth of the earth's land surface, but the estimated population of 175,-869,488 (World Almanac, 1949) is less than eight per cent of the world's total, for vast desert and semi-arid regions cover about 3,900,000 square miles of the continent.

The European population of Africa was usually estimated at about 5,000,000 up to the outbreak of World War II, but many more Europeans are seeking their fortune in the dark continent since the close of the war.

People and History

Africa is known as the home of the black man, and *Sudan* is an Arabic word meaning black, but there are many variations in color between the inhabitants of North Africa and the Negroid tribes of Central Africa. The North African races vary in color from olive-brown to dark brown, and include the Copts of Egypt, the Berbers of Northwest Africa, and the Tuaregs of the Sahara Desert. The Negroid races include all dark-skinned inhabitants of tropical and subtropical Africa. The purest Negro types are found in the great bulge of the northern half of West Africa, south of the Sahara. The pure Negro "blondes" are a dark brown, their "brunettes" a sooty-black.

The Bushmen of the Kalahari Desert and Southwest Africa are sometimes called the aborigines of Africa. There are probably less than 10,000 of them today. The Hottentots, unimportant numerically, are also found in the southwest.

Pygmies were known to early Egyptians and to the Greeks of Homer's day. Varying in height from four feet to four feet nine inches, Pygmies are the African Negritos, while the under-sized, black aborigines of the Philippine archipelago and Malaysia are classified as Oceanic Negritos. African Pygmies are found today in the forests of the equatorial belt. They are nomadic, have a low culture and one skill—hunting.

The Bantu-speaking tribes are found south of a line running from west to east across the continent, beginning at the British Cameroons on the west, and running to Mombasa on the east coast. They vary in color from black to yellowish brown. The classification is really linguistic rather than racial, for there are common features in all the languages of the tribes classed as Bantu, which are not common in the languages of the Negroes north of the Bantu line.

General Faidherbe, France's "Colonial Napoleon," said: "The black man is naturally good, with an intelligence comparable to the white man's. But he is lacking in will power, prevision, perseverance, so that he will always be at the mercy of races better endowed in those respects."

The known history of Africa goes back to 480 B. C., the year that Hanno, a navigator from Carthage, reached the west coast of the continent. He wrote that it was almost inaccessible because of the heat. Greek and Roman writers referred to Africa as Libya. The Arabs were acquainted with the country south of the Great Desert in the 7th century A. D. In the 15th century the Portuguese made discoveries along the northwest coast as far south as Sierra Leone and the Congo. The Cape of Good Hope was discovered a few years before Columbus discovered America, and a few years later, Vasco de Gama discovered the Cape route to India.

As time progressed, Britain, France, Portugal, Spain, Holland and Germany all competed for possessions in Africa. When the conquests closed in closer and closer in territories claimed by the British and the French, those two nations decided to meet, in 1890, and designate their respective spheres of influence. In West Africa Britain received Nigeria, the choicest part of the Lower Niger valley. France received the vast savanna land lost quickly in desert sands. At the conclusion of the agreement, the French General Galliéni remarked dryly, "The Gallic cock has plenty of sand to scratch."

Soon most of Africa was claimed by various European powers, and the subjugation of the colonies continued until now there are fairly well settled conditions and stable governments throughout the whole continent. In many instances European traders and officials inflicted terrible cruelties upon the Africans, but in general the condition of the natives has been greatly improved under these governments.

Government

Almost all of Africa is under the control of European governments. In recent years some of these governments have given the right to vote to large numbers of people just emerging from a primitive way of life. Many of the Africans themselves are confused as to the issue, and there is the story of the district chief who went to cast his vote, returned home and told proudly of how he had voted for *three* governors.

Three countries only are independent: Egypt, Ethiopia and Liberia. (The Union of South Africa is a self-governing Dominion within the British Commonwealth of Nations.) The Anglo-Egyptian treaty (due to expire in 1956) permits England to maintain armed forces at the Suez Canal, and Ethiopia has retained British advisers. In Liberia the economic aid rendered by the presence of the Firestone Plantations Company, puts Liberia under that company's influence to some extent.

The area and population of each of the three independent countries are as follows:

Country	Area	Population
Egypt ...... (estimated)	386,000 sq. mi.	(census, 1947) 19,090,048
Ethiopia	350,000 " "	(est. 1947) 15,000,000
Liberia	43,000 " "	(est. 1946) 1,600,000

The following map and table show how Africa is partitioned among the European powers. We are indebted to the *New York Sun* for the privilege of reproducing this map of which the status has changed somewhat since World War II, at which time Italy lost her African colonies. The deputies of the Allied Council of Foreign Ministers appointed a commission, in 1947, to investigate conditions in those colonies—Libya, Eritrea and Italian Somaliland—and to ascertain the sentiment of the local populations. The four powers—Britain, France, the United States and the U.S.S.R.—failing to come to a mutual agreement, the deputies decided (September, 1948) to refer the question to the United Nations General Assembly. In November, 1949, the United Nations

General Assembly decided that the former Italian colony of Libya (population, 1,120,000) shall be independent in 1952. Until that time a U. N. commission and advisory council will govern the country. The Assembly voted that Italian Somaliland (population, 915,000) should be placed under a ten-year Italian trusteeship, to be followed by full independence. A U. N. commission was appointed to make a first hand study of Eritrea, which Ethiopia would like to annex. The Big Four had agreed in a peace treaty with Italy that they would accept the recommendations of the U. N.

Country	Area	Population
Great Britain	3,776,972 sq. mi.	68,599,378
France	4,283,299 " "	45,382,156
Belgium	902,082 " "	10,425,235
Portugal	792,901 " "	9,174,729
Italy's former Colonies	889,112 " "	2,788,974
Spain (mere estimates)	134,536 " "	925,000

(Note: The above figures are from the World Almanac, 1949.)

Climate

How hot does it get in Africa? It has been proved that the hottest latitude is not the equator but the areas about ten degrees north of the equator. Temperatures in the Belgian Congo are not nearly so high as in Somaliland or the Sudan. It is not hot at all in Capetown, South Africa, where the average temperature is 62 degrees. In East Africa the Ruwenzori Mountains (Ptolemy's "Mountains of the Moon") and Mount Kenya, almost on the equator, are covered with perpetual snow. However, three-fourths of the total area of the continent lie within the tropics and under the vertical rays of the sun, producing perpetual summer with definite seasons of rain and drought. In tropical Africa the variations in temperature are due to rainfall, altitude and prevailing winds. It is a drastic transition from the steamy heat and "indirect lighting" of the dense forest areas to the sudden, unmitigated glare of the savannas where the hot winds are like a blast from a furnace.

Physical Features and Animal Life

Africa is an enormous plateau, shaped like an inverted saucer. Corresponding to the ridged base of the saucer is the escarpment of the plateau, which is divided from the sea by a strip of lowland of varying width. This escarpment was the obstacle to early exploration of Africa's interior. Wood-burning engines have had to pull trains up steep grades in order to reach the plateau, and vessels trying to ascend Africa's rivers have had to eventually conquer rapids or waterfalls. The continental plateau averages 2,000 feet above sea level, and there are three distinct mountain systems: the Atlas Mountains of the northwest; the west coast mountains, principally the Cameroon and the Kong Mountains; and the east coast system with ranges and peaks varying in elevation from 11,000 to nearly 20,000 feet. The highest peak is Kibo, Kilimanjaro, in British East Africa (elevation, 19,587 feet).

There are two great deserts: the Sahara in North Africa, the largest desert in the world; and the Kalahari in the south. The most important rivers are the Nile, the Congo, the Zambesi, and the Niger.

There are no tigers in Africa; the rare okapi is found only there; leopards, lions, hyenas, and all kinds of apes and monkeys are plentiful. The zebra and the giraffe are found in the east and southeast; the elephant, rhinoceros and buffalo, especially in the equatorial forest belt; and the hippopotamus in all the larger rivers. There are deadly snakes, but insects are Africa's greatest pests and killers; the jigger the most annoying, the mosquito and tsetse fly the most dangerous. The mosquito is responsible for malaria and yellow fever, and the tsetse fly for sleeping sickness.

Resources

Some writers declare that the Negroes were the first people to develop iron smelting and working. For exportation, however, Africa's supply of manganese is more important than the iron ore. Africa also produces gold, copper and coal; is the world's largest producer of chromium ore; produces 98 per cent of all diamonds; is progressing in the production of wild and plantation rubbers; produces 75 per cent of the world's supply of palm oil, and over 70 per cent of the cocoa.

Olives, figs, oranges and grapes are grown in the Mediterranean region of North Africa; the date palm is grown in Egypt and in the oases of the desert; and citrus fruits are being developed throughout tropical Africa. Egypt produces an abundance of cotton, wheat, flax, maize and rice; coffee is an important product of Ethiopia; and other parts of Africa produce the same products in lesser quantities. The Sudan is primarily cattle country; sheep and goats are plentiful, and hides are an important export. Horses and cattle are scarce or non-existent in the forested regions because of the tsetse fly. Maize and grain-yielding sorghums—durra (guinea corn) and pearl millet, as well as rice, are an important food supply. Shea butter (the white fat from the seeds of the shea tree) is to the Sudan what olive oil is to Italy, and is an important export. Palm oil and coffee are plentiful in the forest belt, from which are also exported ebony, mahogany, ivory, rubber and bananas.

Progress

A hundred years ago, Timbuktu (Fr. Tombouctou) on the buckle of the Niger River at the edge of the Sahara Desert, was a thriving trade center, "the meeting point of the camel and the canoe." It had a population of 85,000, but is reduced today to a mere 8,000, for Gao, farther east on the Niger, has taken its place as the gateway from Central Africa to the Mediterranean. The Trans-Saharan Company operates regular bus and air service across the desert; and a trans-Saharan railway is under construction, but progress is extremely slow. Unofficially this railway is known as the peanut-line, because it has been proposed to operate the engines with vegetable fuel oils.

Africans have always been classed among the more backward of the peoples of the world, but when we accuse the native of tropical Africa of having no inventive ability and little ambition, we are prone to forget that his body is the prey of debilitating malaria, dysentery and sleeping sickness. Add to this the fact that life in the tropics is fairly easy. One need not worry about a winter supply of fuel; shoes are not a necessity, and every family raises its own food on its own farm. Moreover, there is no incentive to lay up for the family future for most of the children die in infancy; or another pestilence may wipe out most of the population of the village.

In the far interior of Africa today, the people are in the bewildering stage of seeing modern civilization brought to their primitive doorsteps. Laborers may be hired to clear the grass and bushes from several acres of land, yet the unpredictable white man does not follow up this labor by farming the cleared area. The mystery is solved when one day a "sky-boat" floats down out of the blue and uses the cleared area as a landing field. In one inland city where native women still wear only aprons of leaves, stands an impressive white stucco railway station with graceful, lancet-arched windows.

Liberia is one of the most backward of African countries, with no railroads and few motor roads, but a new road has recently been completed, connecting Liberia with French Guinea. Africa's regular coastline boasts many fine seaports, Dakar being the best equipped one on the west coast. In the past few decades, the governments and commercial interests of various European countries have greatly developed the transportation facilities of inland Africa. Railway lines, internal air routes and thousands of miles of motor roads made possible the mobilization of an immense army of trained African soldiers for overseas service in the recent war. Africans from Madagascar to the Sudan met on the battlefields of Europe, and the African's horizon is no longer the sea, beyond which, he believed, no land existed.

Religions

Animism. More than forty per cent of the people of Africa are animists. Webster defines *animism* as "the belief that all objects possess a natural life or vitality or are endowed with indwelling souls. The term is usually employed to denote the most primitive and superstitious forms of religion." Some animists believe that souls or spirits dwell not only in men and animals, but also in plants, stones or even tools, and most animists believe in the activity of spirits of the deceased.

The widely used charms are to Africans just what a horseshoe or a rabbit's foot are to some Americans. Fetishes are supposed to be more powerful and are greatly feared. A fetish is a material object supposed to possess supernatural power to make the designs of the owner succeed, to preserve from danger, or to cure disease. The owner of a fetish is therefore a man to be respected, and those who would benefit by his fetish must bring the proper gifts. The fetish itself may be a natural object, as the tooth or claw or hair of an animal; or it may be artificial, as a carving in wood or bone. It is the supposed dwelling of a supernatural power or spirit, and is usually stained with the blood of many sacrifices.

Animism, in Africa, includes ancestor-worship. All unseen spirits, spirits of enemies or spirits of one's ancestors, are to be feared, consulted, appeased. Some believe that God is benevolent, therefore they give Him little thought. But the devil and his spirits are ever wanting to harm them, therefore they must be appeased. In some parts of Africa, Satan is believed to be the mediator between man and God. The "owner of heaven" is known to have created all things, even Satan himself, but they believe it is Satan who bears their requests to the Creator and beseeches Him to give benefits to the children of men.

Certain fetishes are said to demand particular sacrifices; some, the blood of dogs; another the blood of a white chicken; and to some must be offered human blood. To secure the human blood, a stranger, lodging for a night in the village, may be attacked. He may or may not recover from the wounds inflicted on him; many do not. This practice may have given rise to the story that cannibalism still exists, and among some tribes it probably does, but because of the watchful eye of the governments in control, the rite would need to be done in such secrecy that proof would be difficult. Cannibalistic practices probably grew out of the belief that one could partake of the courage of a fearless man by eating his flesh.

For the animist, nothing ever happens. When a babe is seized with convulsions, it is because a certain bird flew over the house. A man may be taken violently ill from eating tainted meat; to the African, an enemy is to blame. He may have poisoned the food, they say, or, by witchcraft, may have shot the poison through the air from a distant village. A land where animism reigns is a land of fear where the people spend much of their meager store, and engage in endless effort to obtain the proper charm to close up all the cracks of their houses and lives against the misfortune that lurks about them.

Islam. (See *Religions, India.*) Islam predominates in North Africa, and it has brought millions of people under its sway in East and West Africa also. The followers of Mohammed in North Africa are the more fanatical, for, south of the Sahara, there are many who are Moslem in name but animist in practice. The hundreds of tribes still in the depths of paganism should be given the gospel message before Islam lays its deadly hand upon them. After a tribe has accepted that religion, it is like hammering on granite to try to win them for Christ.

Roman Catholicism. (See *Religions, Latin America.*) The people of both Belgium and France are predominantly Catholic and therefore in the immense African colonies of both these nations, Catholicism has considerable influence, with more adherents than the various Protestant Missions.

The World Almanac, 1949, gives the religious population of Africa as follows:

Greek or Orthodox Catholic	5,868,089
Roman Catholic	6,866,072
Protestant Christians	2,782,864
Jews	542,869
Moslems	55,538,211
Others (mostly pagan tribes)	76,301,961

However, this makes a total considerably less than the present estimated population of Africa. According to the statistics of The Society for the Propagation of the Faith, the Roman Catholic figures are much too low. Their report for the year 1948 shows:

Native Catholics in Africa and insular Africa.	10,363,411
White Catholics in Africa and insular Africa.	641,564

Missionary Occupation

There were 900 churches and a missionary training school in North Africa by the end of the second century after Pentecost. The apostasy of those churches was followed by the advance of Islam, and soon the crescent took the place of the cross in North Africa. Moslem zealots carried their religion across the Sahara Desert and won over some of the tribes of the Sudan centuries before the first Christian missionary penetrated that part of Africa. However, missionaries finally did go in, and to their explorations the world owes most of its knowledge of inland Africa.

The Moravians were the pioneers of Protestant Missions in Africa. Their first missionary went to South Africa in 1737, was ordered home in 1743 by the hostile Dutch authorities, and it was half a century before Protestant work was resumed.

During the past century many missionary societies from Europe and America have labored in Africa, among them: the Church Missionary Society of England, the North Africa Mission, the American Mission (United Presbyterian), Egypt General Mission, Abyssinia Frontiers Mission, South Africa General Mission, Africa Inland Mission, United Brethren, Wesleyan Mission, Sudan Interior Mission, Sudan United Mission, several Baptist Missions, two Paris Societies, the Methodist Episcopal, Presbyterian, and Christian Churches, Mennonites, the Gospel Missionary Union, the World Evangelization Crusade, several German and Scandinavian Missions and The Christian and Missionary Alliance.

The former Italian colonies, Libya, Eritrea and Italian Somaliland, are perhaps the least occupied of all African territories, for Roman Catholic influence in Italy hindered Protestant missionary effort there. The same influence also blocked missionary effort in French West Africa and French Equatorial Africa until after World War I, when, by the terms of the Treaty of Versailles, Protestant missions were free to work in the French colonies.

Belgian Congo has been occupied many years longer and has over 1,500 Protestant missionaries for its population, variously estimated at from 10 to 13 millions. French West Africa (in May, 1948) had only 240 Protestant missionaries on the field, with perhaps 30 per cent more on furlough, for its total population of over 16 millions.

The Christian and Missionary Alliance has had work in the Belgian Congo, near the mouth of the Congo River since 1884; in the Portuguese enclave of Cabinda since 1907; in French West Africa since 1918; and in Gabon in southern French Equatorial Africa since 1934.

Africa, with its 700 languages, many of them still waiting to be reduced to writing, demands missionaries with linguistic gifts as well as spiritual power. The roster of pioneers and statesmen of the dark continent includes missionaries of high caliber, namely: Robert Moffatt, David Livingstone, John Mackenzie, Barnabas Shaw, François Coillard, James Stewart, Alexander Mackay, Dr. Robert Laws, S. T. Studd and Mary Slessor. Today, with African races clamoring for knowledge and power, making them an easy prey for Communism, Africa needs more Moffatts and Livingstones, men of keen intellect, high statesmenship and spiritual wisdom and strength.

FRENCH WEST AFRICA

French West Africa occupies most of the great bulge in the northern half of West Africa. On the map the three French Africas seem to be united, but they retain their individualities and are known as: French North Africa, which includes Morocco, Algeria and Tunisia; French West Africa, which is separated from North Africa by the Sahara Desert; and French Equatorial Africa, which bounds French West Africa on the east from Lake Tchad to Libya. On the south, French West Africa is bounded by the Gulf of Guinea, the Gold Coast and Nigeria. On the west it touches the Atlantic Ocean except where indented by the small enclaves of British Gambia, Portuguese Guinea, Sierra Leone and Liberia.

Area and Population

French West Africa is more than half the size of the United States, and comprises eight colonies, the mandate territory of Togo, and the district of Dakar and Dependencies, which is distinct, somewhat like our District of Columbia. For some years the Upper Volta was dissolved and apportioned to adjacent colonies. It has now been reinstated as a separate colony. A colony is any territory directly ruled by another Power. A mandate is one of the colonies formerly belonging to the German and Turkish Empires, turned over to the victors after the First World War, to be governed by them until the inhabitants should be ready for self-government.

Colony	Area, Sq. Mi.	Population	Capital
Senegal (including Dakar district)	81,817	1,755,996	St. Louis
Mauritania	278,671	499,405	St. Louis
French Guinea	109,737	2,145,024	Conakry
Ivory Coast	128,610	2,243,248	Abidjan
Upper Volta	123,200	2,528,522	Ouagadougou
French Soudan	308,109	2,878,469	Bamako
Niger	499,432	1,945,970	Niamey
Dahomey	43,688	1,474,751	Porto Novo
Togo (Mandate)	22,147	922,509	Lomé
	1,595,411	16,393,894	

(1948 Official Guide of French West Africa.)

The district of Dakar and Dependencies covers an area of 60 to 68 square miles. Besides several villages, it includes the city of Rufisque, population 30,000, while Dakar itself, the capital of all French West Africa, has a population of over 200,000, of whom some 16,000 are French and 5,000 are foreigners.

History

To primitive Africans historical events are interesting tales to relate around the campfire, or useful for comparing ages, for no birthdays are recorded. If one man says, "When the Bobos rebelled, I was old enough to blow the bellows in the blacksmith shop," another may establish his superior age by replying, "But at that time I was wearing my first trousers." Which, being interpreted, means that the first man was about seven years old when the Bobos rebelled, and the second about twelve (at which age trousers are added to the loincloth wardrobe). Only European records can give us definite historical data.

A French ship reached the River Gambia in the sixteenth century. In 1677 the French took the island of Gorée, just off the coast of Dakar, from the Dutch. Gorée was then a thriving center for the slave trade. The house, the rotting chains, and the door through which the victims were dragged to waiting boats, can still be seen there. Many ships called at the little island and slaves from Central Africa were detained there until other ships picked them up.

By the beginning of the 18th century France had opened up the country of the Senegal, but Mungo Park preceded by fifty years the company of great explorers of the interior. A Scotsman engaged by an African Society to explore the Niger River, he set sail for Gambia on the west coast in 1795, but after two years had not attained his goal. Again in 1805 he began an expedition, and this time he reached the rapids of Boussa beyond the buckle of the Niger, and there he and his men lost their lives. Richard Lander reached Mungo Park's goal, the mouth of the Niger, but not until 1830. Frenchmen reached Timbuktu (French, Tombouctou) in 1822, but René Caille was the first man to enter the city (1827-1828) and emerge alive. Dr. Barth, in 1853, brought the first definite information concerning the Niger valley and Timbuktu.

The French began their occupation of the Niger valley when they captured Bamako, over 700 miles inland from Dakar, in 1883. Their most dangerous enemy was the native chief Samory, whose kingdom covered 250,000 square miles, with a population of two million inhabitants. He had won his kingdom by force, pillaging villages, taking captives and selling them to slave traders. He specialized in little children. Travelers have recorded what they actually saw—little children in chains, their small bundles on their heads, trudging across the burning plains. Captives too weak to sell were slain, and the march of Samory across French West Africa left the trails littered with skeletons. For fifteen years the French were fighting this man before they finally captured him in 1898.

During this same period, an expedition was sent against Timbuktu, which was held by the nomadic Tuaregs. Colonel Bonnier and his army occupied Timbuktu in 1894, then pursued the Tuaregs on into the desert. At one point where the army made camp and slept, feeling sure no enemies were near, the Tuareg Chief Chabon and his warriors came out of hiding and attacked. Colonel Bonnier and most of his troops were slain in the mad stampede. Again in 1895 Timbuktu was occupied and the tricolor of France has flown over the forts there ever since. Today a troop of camel cavalry patrols the desert regions and keeps the nomadic tribes under control.

An uprising in 1916 among the Red Bobos spread through the Upper Volta and the Soudan. Telegraph wires were cut, and the government was obliged to send troops to disarm the people and establish peace.

For many years French West Africa was of interest only to the government that controlled it, and to the missionary-minded. During the recent war, however, its capital, Dakar, came out of the unknown and became a household word overnight. With only 1,620 miles to fly between Dakar and Natal, Brazil, a distance less than from New York to Denver, the world suddenly realized that South America could be bombed if an enemy power got control of Dakar. Events in French West Africa are henceforth of vital interest to the Western Hemisphere.

Government

The best appraisal of French colonial government is the remark of an African: "Our wives can now go in safety to neighboring villages. Before the French came they dared not go alone."

French West Africa is administered under a Governor-General, now called the High Commissioner of the French Republic, and his Council at Dakar. Over each colony is a Governor, and over each district thereof is an Administrator, or Commander of the "Cercle," as the districts are called. The circles are something like our counties. Within each circle, the groups of villages are under "medal" or paramount African chiefs, and over each village a local man is appointed as chief who is responsible for the local government of his village, and the collection of taxes. There is an annual recruitment of young men for three years of compulsory military training. The standing army of Africans includes infantry, motorized artillery, parachutists, and engineers.

Citizenship was accorded to natives of Dakar, Gorée, Rufisque and St. Louis in 1875. It has been extended to the inhabitants generally, in all of French West Africa, since May, 1946. A strong nationalistic spirit is manifest in all the cities, and particularly throughout the Ivory Coast. Labor unions, strikes, and the influence of Communism have combined to produce a spirit of unrest that makes the future unpredictable.

Climate

French West Africa is in the Torrid Zone, lying roughly between 5° and 20° north of the equator. In the southern forest areas it is only moderately hot, but the extreme humidity is enervating. In the grasslands of the Soudan and Upper Volta it rains only between June and the first of October, the climate closely resembling that of the plains of India. The months of December and January are pleasant with cool nights and mornings. The burning heat increases relentlessly from the middle of February until the middle of June when the rains begin to bring some relief. In the Guinea and Ivory Coast there are both grasslands and forests with corresponding variations in climate. The Fouta Djallon mountains in western Guinea offer the best climate. There a hill station at Dalaba with an elevation of 4,000 feet affords relief to the missionaries who spend a few weeks there annually.

Physical Features

French West Africa, traveling from north to south, goes from desolate desert to burning plains to humid forests and picturesque mountains. The two great rivers are the Senegal and the Niger. The Niger rises on the border of Sierra Leone and flows for 1,000 miles northeast to the border of the Sahara. There it buckles to the east and south to the Atlantic Ocean, covering more than 2,500 miles in its entire course. It is so sluggish that high floods at its source require almost a year to reach its mouth in the Gulf of Guinea. The Niger is a veritable river of life to this whole section. Besides irrigating the farm lands along its course, it abounds with fish, crocodiles, hippopotami, ducks and geese—all food for Africans; and the antelope and other animals that feed on its banks also provide game for the hunter.

Resources

Fruits, palm nuts and oil, shea butter, rubber, cotton, cocoa, lumber and peanuts are the most important exports from French West Africa. On the docks at Dakar are literally mountains of peanuts. In 1947 French West Africa exported to France over 174,000 tons of shelled peanuts, 32,000 tons of bananas, 19,800 tons of mahogany and other valuable woods, 18,500 tons of cocoa, 36,800 tons of coffee, 37,000 tons of palm kernels (for oil), besides diamonds, gold, cola nuts and hides. Rice is the principal grain in the Guinea, and various kinds of Indian millet in the Soudan and Upper Volta. Great herds of cattle, sheep and goats are raised in the grassland areas north of the forest belt.

Progress

When the first Protestant missionaries reached the interior of French West Africa, they found Waterman's ink and Heinz catsup already displayed in the stores. French, British and American commerce flourished there before the war, and the war-time empty shelves are once again being filled.

Four lines of railroad carry into the interior everything from passengers to gaudy cotton prints, automobiles and refrigerators. The line from Dakar to Bamako is the longest, with over 1,000 miles of rails. Shorter lines serve the Guinea, Ivory Coast and Dahomey. There are over 63,000 miles of graveled motor roads, of which nearly 17,000 miles are open the year round. When the water is high, the Niger River is navigable for small steamboats for over 1,200 miles except for two places where there are rapids and these are overcome by railway or motor road. Airplanes serve the principal cities of the interior, while from Dakar there are flights five times a week to Paris, twice a week to South America, four times a week to and from New York, and frequent service to all the world's capitals. In the Air France hotel at Dakar, sleep is interrupted every hour of the night by the steward tapping on some door calling a guest to be ready for a certain flight. The Sahara desert has been conquered by regular autobus and air service which connects with airplanes from central Africa. The Trans-Saharan Railway is under construction—slowly. The semi-desert areas northwest of the Niger are being reclaimed by the irrigation project near Segou in the Soudan. A dam over one mile long and two canals are being constructed, and the populations of entire villages are being moved there to cultivate the land.

Hospitals, only a few of which are fully equipped, have been built in the principal cities where there is a large European population. However, for French West Africa's population of 16 million, there are less than 22,000 hospital beds available for Africans. The European medical personnel includes about 450 doctors, dentists and nurses. In the African personnel there are over 650 doctors, midwives and nurses, and other medical assistants to the number of 3,500. Government doctors are fighting sleeping sickness, which periodically decimates the population of many forest villages. Early in 1949, 26,000 cases of this disease were being treated in the Kissi and Gueckedou districts alone, in French Guinea. There are a few agricultural colonies for persons suffering from leprosy, and the various clinics treat all who wish to come regularly for treatment. The one leprosarium, equipped for research as well as treatment, is located near Bamako in the Soudan. The total number officially known to be suffering from leprosy (Government reports of Dec. 31, 1946), in all French West Africa, was 102,207. In districts where there are no nurses or clinics, a large majority of the infants die before they are one year old. There is practically no provision for the insane. Such unfortunates may be seen in bush villages with their feet in stocks.

The French government has established an excellent school system providing for elementary, secondary and professional education. Elementary schools number 87 in Guinea, 132 in the Soudan, and 148 in the Ivory Coast, besides 20 mobile schools for the nomads of the Sahara. The government schools are able to care for only 7.7 per cent of the children between the ages of seven and twelve.

The Moslems conduct Koranic schools for the children of their followers. Passages from the Koran are learned by rote, although the children often do not understand what they are reading or repeating. A few advanced Moslem schools have been provided by the government where instruction in Arabic is given in theology, history and law, by Moslem professors.

The museum of African arts and crafts, in Bamako, is also a school to which artisans of any tribe may go and be taught how to improve their crafts in leather, weaving or metals.

Currency

The official currency is French but the Bank of French West Africa issues its own colonial notes in denominations of from 5 francs to 1,000 francs. The circulation of copper and aluminum coins of lesser value is still tolerated. Cowrie shells, probably brought in by East Indian traders long ago, were formerly much in use for barter in the country markets of the Soudan, but since the drop in value of the franc, the shells are worth so little that they are disappearing from the markets except for use as ornaments and charms. Late in 1949 the franc of French West Africa (franc C. F. A.) was worth twice as much as the franc of France (franc metropole). One dollar U. S. purchased about 175 French colonial francs, or about 350 francs in France.

(See cowrie shells under *Currency, Indonesia.*)

Languages and Tribes

A native of French West Africa remarked, "If you can speak Bambara and Foula you can get a drink of water anywhere in this country." In all there are 17 different major languages and 100 different tribal dialects in French West Africa. A few of the languages are used over very wide areas. The Mandingo dialects, which include Maninka (also known as Malinke), Bambara and Dioula, as a group are used by about 2,875,000 people, with two or three million more people understanding them to a limited degree throughout the Guinea, Soudan and Ivory Coast. The two dialects (Fouta Djallon and Macina) of the Foula language are used by over 1,800,000 people in the Guinea, Soudan, Ivory Coast and Niger colonies. The Foulas, a pastoral people, also called Peuhls and Foulbes, the latter being their word for "scattered," are not negroid in feature except where they are of mixed blood. Their origin is obscure, and has been variously declared to be Libyan, Egyptian or Semitic. The Mossis, another great tribe, found mostly in the Upper Volta, number over a million and a half. The approximate populations of the smaller tribes follows:

Senoufo (Soudan, Ivory Coast)	600,000	Sonhrai (Soudan, Niger)	240,000
Baouli-Agni (Ivory Coast)	550,000	Habbe (Soudan)	200,000
Bobo (Ivory Coast, Upper Volta, Soudan)	360,000	Mianka (Soudan)	172,000
		Kissi (Guinea)	150,000
Sousou (Guinea)	260,000	Tuareg (Soudan, Niger)	130,000
Gouro (Ivory Coast)	250,000	Gberese (Guinea)	120,000
		Samogo (Upper Volta)	91,000
		Toma (Guinea)	85,000

The languages used in Alliance work in this field are as follows:

Languages Used by Missionaries		Additional Languages Used by Native Christians
French	Habbe	Gouro
Maninka	Senoufo	Fanti
Sankaran	Bambara	Andos
Yalounka	Dioula	Ashanti
Foula	Black Bobo	Yokuba
Kissi	Red Bobo (two	Appoloni
Toma	dialects)	Djimini (above, all in the
Kpelle (Gbere-	Sonhrai	Ivory Coast)
ses' language)	Macina Foula	Gwen
Baouli	Tamachek (Tuar-	Mianka
Agni	egs' language)	Samogo, also Pana, Marka, Nounouma in same area.

Religions

Islam has a strong foothold in many sections of French West Africa, especially in Upper Senegal, along the Niger River, and in all the larger cities. The Foula and Maninka tribes are almost solidly Moslem. Roughly speaking half the population of the entire country is Moslem and the other half animist, for the number of professing Christians, Catholic and Protestant, is still a minority group. In reality, perhaps only one-tenth of the population is Moslem, for in both Moslem and Catholic converts the old animistic practices often remain, camouflaged with the outward ceremonials of a new religion. Catholicism does not change a man's morals; Islam permits him to continue in polygamy; true Christianity demands complete repentance and makes an economic hardship in the loss of the labor of plural wives. However, during the past years thousands have turned to God from paganism, and a few from Islam, and have given evidence that they are indeed new creatures in Christ Jesus.

Missionary Occupation

The total number of Protestant missionaries (May, 1948, report) for French West Africa's population of over 16 million was 240, actually on the field, while the number on furlough would add about 30 per cent more to that total.

The Roman Catholics report, for the year 1948, over 800 foreign priests, religious brothers and nuns in French West Africa, where they conduct over 850 schools and claim a total of 380,276 native Catholics and 18,931 white Catholics.

Several Protestant Missions are represented in French West Africa. The Paris *Société des Missions Évangéliques* has churches in Dakar and St. Louis in the Colony of Senegal, and in that same colony the World-wide Evangelization Crusade has work at Velingara. The above mentioned places represent the total of Protestant effort throughout all of Senegal with its area of more than 81,000 square miles and a total population of more than a million and a half. The Protestant population of Dakar itself may be about 400 non-Africans, of whom about 200 are connected with the French Protestant church there. There are also about 200 African Protestants, but practically all of them are from other parts of Africa, mainly from Dahomey and Togoland.

Construction has been begun on the building which is to provide an Evangelical Protestant Headquarters and Receiving Home in Dakar for the many missionaries of all societies who must pass through that city in order to reach their various fields of labor. This home will also be an evangelistic center for reaching Dakar's African and European population totalling more than 200,000. Of this *Fédération des Missions Protestantes de l'Afrique Occidentale Française*, the International Review of Missions (January, 1949) says: "The definite appointment to Dakar of a representative of French Protestant Missions, in the person of Monsieur Jean

Keller, has great strategic importance. Dakar occupies a key position not only as a port of disembarkation, but also as the headquarters of the government; and as the centre of higher education for all French West African Colonies, it offers a sphere where much useful work in presenting the Christian religion can be accomplished."

The Church of England works among the Sousous of western Guinea. The Gospel Missionary Union occupies a large area surrounding Bamako, among the Bambara-speaking people. The Assemblies of God Mission is responsible for the great Mossi tribe and the Gurunsis. The Sudan Interior Mission and the African Christian Mission have work farther east in Upper Volta and Niger Colonies; the English Wesleyans, the Paris Tabernacle Church Mission, and the Worldwide Evangelization Crusade all have work in the Ivory Coast, the latter also working among the Lobis of Upper Volta. The Conservative Baptists have entered a great unoccupied area in the northern part of the Ivory Coast. The Christian and Missionary Alliance has missionary centers in widely scattered areas in the colonies of Guinea, Soudan, Upper Volta and Ivory Coast, with a responsibility for about five millions of the total population of French West Africa.

The Christian and Missionary Alliance

In 1890 a party of missionaries sailed for West Africa and began work in Sierra Leone with the hope of reaching the Niger valley in the western Soudan. Within six months five of that band of nine were dead, victims of the climate. In 1896 Dr. Simpson wrote: "From the Soudan comes another forward cry. Our Mission has been reinforced by six new workers. . . . And now, a double advance movement is proposed, pushing northeast to Timbuktu and eastward across the Niger toward Lake Tchad. These advance lines in the Soudan will need at least 100 men."

The vision tarried, but Dr. Simpson and others held steadfast in praying and believing, and the first Alliance mission station in French West Africa was established at Baro in 1918, the year before his homegoing.

Early in the history of the Sierra Leone work, one of the missionaries went to Paris to interview the French government regarding permission to enter French territory, but after long delay the reply was "No."

Not until the fall of the year 1917 was prayer answered. Some Alliance missionaries, sailing for Sierra Leone on a French ship, met a friendly French official. Through him an interview was gained with officials at Conakry, and the final outcome was a reconnaissance trip into French Guinea, and later the establishment of the first station at Baro. All French West Africa lay before them, almost completely virgin territory as to the gospel.

In the fall of 1921 there was new encouragement when the Foreign Secretary visited Sierra Leone and French West Africa as a deputation from the Board of Managers. While present at a missionary conference at Makump in Sierra Leone, the subject of discussion was the transfer of a number of the Sierra Leone staff to the new field in French West Africa. Already two or three, formerly from Sierra Leone, were laboring at Baro. A map of West Africa lay on the table, and one missionary placed his thumb on the portion of Sierra Leone where the Alliance Mission was working, whereas the vast interior of unoccupied territory in French West Africa could not be covered by his outstretched hand.

The Foreign Secretary's journeys carried him through portions of Guinea and Soudan, and to Conakry, capital of the Guinea, to see about purchasing property in Siguiri, the second station to be opened. During this deputational visit it was decided that the headquarters should be established at

Kankan. The report of the deputation and the appeal of missionaries on furlough brought a ready response. Within a few years a large force of new missionaries was on the field and many stations were opened. The line of spiritual lighthouses reached all the way to Timbuktu but with immense gaps between. The gaps between our 27 mission stations of today are still too wide.

French Guinea

Baro   Although Baro had the distinction of being the first station opened in the Niger Valley (1918), it was not the first to show a harvest. The village, remote from highways, remained asleep until the fall of 1931. A church sprang forth almost in a day. A nucleus is still there but the advance has not been continuous. The Moslems are supreme in Baro. Today Baro is the home of a Girls' Bible School, with students from many tribes of the Guinea in attendance. Some of the older girls are endeavoring to translate certain portions of the Word into their tribal dialects and have done creditable work.

Kankan   The headquarters of the Mission is located here. A splendidly situated property conveniently near the business section was purchased and occupied in 1922. Kankan, the terminus of the 400-mile railway from Conakry, and now boasting an airport, has grown to be a city with a population of 20,000 Africans and 450 foreigners. There are French elementary schools and a normal school; three doctors care for the needs of the sick; and a number of French and Syrian stores are stocked with both African and European goods. The African community is for the most part staunchly Moslem but there is a cosmopolitan floating population of pagans and among them souls have been won from many tribes. Night classes are conducted at the Mission for these new converts, and a Sunday school class in French has been held for African students from the government school. Kissiens, Gbereses, Tomas, Foulas, Sousous, Miankas and Senoufos have been converted and baptized at Kankan, and today they are scattered throughout their various tribes, giving forth a witness to their own people.

The office of the field Chairman is at Kankan; the annual Missionary Conference is held here, the first one having been held in 1926. Scripture translations, primers, hymnbooks and all vernacular literature for the many tribes and languages of the entire field are printed here, except those books which have been printed by Bible Societies. A multigraph, mimeograph and hand press operated by trained Africans under missionary supervision have printed the vast amount of material being used by our missionaries and African Christians.

Siguiri   For several years this station has been manned by a native worker. Situated in the heart of the gold mining district, it is a town of over 10,000 inhabitants with a large proportion of them a floating population from many tribes. The chapel, situated near the market place, attracts many of these strangers and a number have been converted. The settled population of the town is strongly Moslem and unyielding to the gospel.

Mamou   This is the site of the school for missionaries' children. As the town is situated at an altitude of over 2,600 feet, the climate is much cooler than on the plains. A well-equipped home and school overlooking the town and beautiful hills provide a place of quiet and freedom for the children. The supply of water and light is still a serious problem, however. An adequate reservoir or pumping system and an electric light plant are greatly needed. Already three chil-

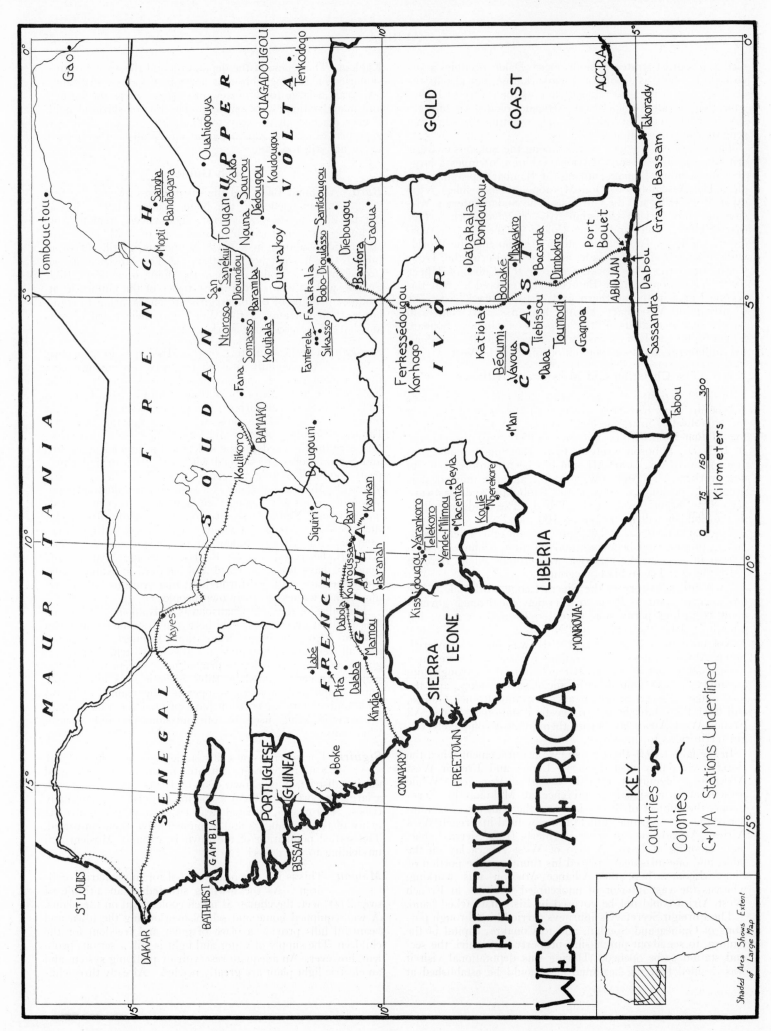

FRENCH WEST AFRICA

MAURITANIA

FRENCH SOUDAN

St. LOUIS

DAKAR

SENEGAL

BATHURST
GAMBIA

PORTUGUESE
GUINEA

BISSAU

Boke

CONAKRY

FREETOWN

SIERRA
LEONE

FRENCH GUINEA

Kindia
Mamou
Dalaba
Pita
Labé

Dabola
Kouroussa
Baro
Kankan
Siguiri

Faranah

Kissidougou
Yarankoro
Telekoro
Yende-Milimou
Macenta
Beyla
Koulé
Nzérékoré

LIBERIA

MONROVIA

Tombouctou

Gao

Kayes

Koulikoro
BAMAKO

Bougouni

Fana

Ntorosso
San
Sanékui Tougan
Dioundiou Nouna
Somasso Baramba Sourou
Kouhala
Sikasso
Fantérela Farakala
Bobo-Dioulasso
Bampla

Sangha
Mopti
Bandiagara

Ouahigouya
Yako
Dédougou
Koudougou
OUAGADOUGOU
Tenkodogo

UPPER VOLTA

Ouarakoy
Santidougou
Diebougou
Graoua

GOLD COAST

ACCRA
Takorady
Grand Bassam
Port Bouet
ABIDJAN
Dabou
Sassandra

IVORY COAST

Ferkessédougou
Korhogo

Dabakala
Bondoukou
Katiola
Béoumi
Mbayakro
Bacanda
Dimbokro
Bouaké
Yavoua
Daloa Tiebissou
Toumodi
Man
Gagnoa

Tabou

300
150
75
0
Kilometers

KEY

Countries ⌒
Colonies ⌒
C&MA Stations Underlined

Shaded Area Shows Extent
of Large Map

26

dren educated at Mamou have returned to Africa as missionaries. The investment of missionaries and money for operating this school has not only been necessary but worth while.

The evangelistic opportunities at Mamou include the town's population of 5,000 Africans and the district population of 121,000. Almost all the people are Foulas (Fouta Djallon dialect), and fanatical, unbending Moslems. The few who have become interested in the gospel are afraid to make an open confession because of the fierce persecution which is sure to follow.

Dalaba Dalaba is 38 miles from Mamou and about 4,000 feet above sea level. In 1924 the Mission chose a beautiful hillside site overlooking a wide valley. Terracing made it possible to erect grass-roofed huts and bungalows on several different levels. Fruit trees are now bearing; water has been piped from a spring; and recreation facilities are varied. To this ideal place, free from mosquitoes, our workers can go annually for a month to regain their strength. The government, seeing the advantages of our location, opened a much larger place for convalescents and tourists, within two and a half miles from our concession, and this has opened to us postal and telegraph services.

Labé Situated 90 miles north of Mamou, Labé is in the heart of the fanatical Moslem Foula tribe. This Fouta Djallon branch of the tribe is estimated to number from 800,000 to 1,000,000, and the Labé circle is the most densely populated district of French Guinea, with about 354,000 inhabitants spread over an area of nearly 9,000 square miles.

When the mission station at Labé was opened in 1923, the Moslem teachers boasted that, though the gospel should be preached there one hundred years, none of their number would ever yield to Christ. As in most Moslem work, it has been a hard field but preaching, faith and prayer have brought about a changed attitude and some advance has been made. The pastoral Foulas are scattered in tiny villages which are often no more than a cluster of huts and itinerating among them means much tramping over the hills. Quantities of gospel tracts have been scattered over many parts of the district and hundreds of Gospels in the Foula language, written in the Arabic script, have been sold. Recently about 50 Scripture portions were sold in each market visited by the missionaries. It is a victory when a Foula accepts Christian literature. The entire New Testament has been translated into Foula and is being revised for printing. The first draft of the entire Old Testament has also been translated. At the outstation of *Netere* there is a small band of believers, descendants of slaves of the Foulas.

Kissidougou The Kissi tribe, a purely pagan people, was a mighty challenge, and work was opened in the town of Kissidougou in 1926. The African converts built the first chapel in 1929, and this was replaced by a larger building in 1931. Souls began to be saved in the district also, turning to the Lord in such numbers that it was necessary to send them native teachers to instruct them. Much translation work has been done for the Kissiens, and the trade language, Maninka, has also been widely used among them. In order to better reach the large groups of Christians and the still untouched pagans hidden deep in the forests, the station at Kissidougou was sold in favor of three stations opened in different sections of the forest, namely: **Yarankoro, Telekoro,** and **Yende-Milimou,** all with the same post-office address, Kissidougou. These three stations all carry on an intensive program, winning and training new converts, preparing them to go to the central Bible School

of Telekoro. In three nights of meetings at one of the stations, nearly 100 people stepped out and signified their desire to become Christians. The entire district of Kissidougou has a population estimated at from 95,000 to 110,000, in an area of 3,700 square miles.

Telekoro This site, a few miles from Kissidougou, was chosen for the Guinea Bible School. During the year 1948 the 20 students enrolled represented the Kissi, Gberese, Toma and Sankaran tribes. The systematic training of native workers is the only way through. We can never hope to have a sufficient number of foreign missionaries to cover the Kissien country, while Gberese country farther south, and the Toma tribe represent a mission field in themselves. Maninka, the trade language, is used in the Telekoro school. Translations will be made in the tribal languages but the higher training must be done in Maninka for the students of the Guinea as a whole.

The well organized church at Telekoro is an encouraging feature of the work. Numbers of Christians from five or six near-by villages walk in to attend the services.

Faranah The usual routine was followed in establishing the station at Faranah—opposition from the enemy, trying to make a home, first in an old shack rented from a merchant and next, living in a native hut, followed finally by the granting of permission from the government to build a permanent station. Here, as on many other stations, the completed adobe bungalow with corrugated iron roof and cement floors, set in a garden of flowers and fruit trees, is an oasis in the desert all the more appreciated because of the first trying days of living in hovels.

Three languages are spoken in Faranah: Kuranko, Sankaran and Yalounka, all with some similarities and many differences. Of the three tribes the Yalounkas, notable for their energy and stability, have responded most readily to the gospel. Many have been baptized and are being instructed in the Word. An outstation has been built at *Yatia,* among the Yalounkas, where there is a goodly number of believers. Faranah is the only Protestant center within an area of 14,000 square miles having a population of 123,000.

Macenta Cova, a young Toma man, was converted and became burdened for his forest people. He repeatedly asked, "Is there no one who can go to tell my people the way of life?" As the call became more insistent, the Mission decided, in 1930, to undertake the responsibility for one more tribe for the Lord. Macenta district, covering 6,000 square miles, and with a population of nearly 98,000, is in the mountainous forest belt about 180 miles south of Kankan. When Cova heard that a missionary couple had been appointed to go to his people, he gave up his position as clerk and offered to accompany them. As usual the missionaries' first home was in poor, rented quarters with a leaky roof. Permission had not yet been granted to hold religious services, but groups gathered in the missionaries' living room and the message bore fruit. Permission finally was granted and a chapel was built, seating more than 200. From 1933 until 1947, Cova held this post alone except when assisted from time to time by another native worker. A missionary couple is now in residence at Macenta and the work is making definite progress.

Koulé This station, also situated in the mountainous forest belt, is the farthest south of all the Guinea stations, almost touching the border of Liberia. The station was opened in order to reach the Gberese tribe, variously estimated at from 120,000 to over 200,000 in number, in the Guinea area alone. Fetish worship holds strong sway among the forest tribes, but service among them is bringing fruit. There were from 25 to 30 inquirers and believers enrolled in the literacy classes held here in 1948. Our aim is to save them from the advance of both Islam and Catholicism. Rome has 20 priests located in this tribe while we have had only one missionary couple, and no one to replace them when they left on furlough early in 1949.

French Soudan

Sikasso This is the center of the Senoufo tribe and the first station to be opened in the French Soudan (1923). Its beautiful setting, in a natural basin surrounded by rolling hills, makes it also one of the hottest pockets, shut in as it is from the breezes of the plateau. The town has a population of 13,000 Dioulas, Foulas and Senoufos, the Senoufos being in the majority. The district covers nearly 8,000 square miles with a population of about 200,000. The early years saw some converts but it was not until 1931 that a break came. Four missionaries stationed there at that time were all stricken with yellow fever, and in less than a week only one of them was still living. Two of those who went to be with the Lord had spent several months in the district at Fanterela, 25 miles from Sikasso, and had seen signs of an awakening there. The seed corn cast into the ground to die, brought forth fruit. Shortly after the laying down of those three lives at Sikasso, 20 young men stepped out for the Lord in Fanterela, and the tide turned also in other parts of the Soudan and in far distant parts of French West Africa. In the years that have followed Sikasso has often seen pitched battles between the powers of light and darkness. Ntoroso Bible School students have been ministering at Fanterela and the outstation of Farakala in recent years. One of them gave as his verdict, "Sikasso district is Satan's headquarters." A new missionary couple has recently been appointed to that area, bringing the number of missionaries up to four. Once again the sword of God's Word is being lifted up against the enemy, and new villages are responding to the gospel message.

San San was occupied by our missionaries in 1926, but the increase realized was not great until that eventful year of 1931. The town presents almost a solid Moslem front. The district of 5,850 square miles and a population of nearly 160,000 is mostly pagan. Many a pagan boy attending the government French school at San has found Christ at the mission and then prepared the way for the missionaries in his distant village. The Red Bobo tribe, the Mianka tribe, and the Bambaras of this district have all shown a response to the Gospel. The district of San includes the mission stations of Ntoroso, Sanekui and Dioundiou. There is no resident missionary in San at present.

Ntoroso Ntoroso is the name given to a cluster of Bambara villages twenty miles from San in a district where many first turned to the Lord in 1931 and 1932. Two thatched huts were the first missionary residence and classroom here in 1933. Out of the night classes for teaching new converts, and the short-term Bible Schools, has come the establishment at Ntoroso, since 1936, of the Soudan Bible School, which trains men and women from eight or nine different tribes, from the Soudan and the Upper Volta, some of the students coming a distance of 500 miles to attend school. The course of study covers four years, eight months of each year. After two years of study, the student usually spends a year preaching in his own district before completing his studies. All classes are taught in Bambara. The fact that more of the Bible is available in the Bambara language than in any other tribal language of French West Africa, makes

it worth while, when necessary, for students to spend several months learning that language. The term of school held during the farming season (1948) had an enrollment of 69 men and 46 women (wives of students), and the dry season term had an enrollment of 102 men and more than 50 women. These figures represent the usual enrollment.

Sanekui This station was opened in 1936 when a French couple joined our ranks. The schoolboy Panca, previously converted while in government school at San, had gathered a group of new converts about him and they were being hard pressed by the pagans of the village. Their prayers were answered with the coming of the missionaries to help them and the work grew rapidly, but a Roman Catholic stronghold situated not many miles distant soon made its opposition felt. Permission had already been granted to our missionaries to occupy a plot of land and they had begun building without delay. It was a fortunate move, for the Catholics carried their complaints to the authorities, where their influence was so strong that, only because the construction of the Sanekui house had already been begun, was a permit granted by the government for a permanent concession there. The persecution that followed the new believers, everywhere in the Red Bobo district, was one factor in developing a strong church. Each new convert was urged to learn to read and nowhere on the field has a literacy campaign been carried on more diligently. Many of the Christians went to the Ntoroso Bible School for further training with the result that, within the last five years, the number of villages in the Sanekui district having groups of Christians, has increased from 35 to over 100. During the year 1948, three short-term Bible Schools were conducted; a group of girls was sent to the Baramba school, and over 30 men went to the Ntoroso school.

Red Bobo Christians crossed over and reached a group of Black Bobos living in their district. Language barriers were overcome, and the Black Bobos responded by first learning to read in the Red Bobo language, then in Bambara, in order that they might attend Bible School. Those Black Bobos are now making a strong appeal for a missionary to live among them. A new mission station is planned among the Red Bobos to the east at Djibasso, between the towns of San and Dédougou.

Dioundiou Opened in 1937, Dioundiou is the newest station of the San circle. It is in the southern section of the district where the population is predominantly Mianka. Hot-headed but intelligent and quick to respond to the gospel, the Mianka tribe has produced some stalwart Christians and capable workers. This tribe has some affinity with the Senoufos and Mianka teacher-evangelists are serving in the Sikasso district, where they are adjusting themselves to the Senoufo language without too much difficulty.

Koutiala A government post on the highway between Sikasso and San, this town has a district of about 8,000 square miles with a population of 181,000. Koutiala (opened 1935) has no resident missionary now as the real work of the district is carried on from the stations of Somasso and Baramba, both in the Koutiala circle. The Mianka tribe predominates in all this area but many of them understand the trade language, Bambara.

Somasso This village was first heard of through a Mianka lad looking for work in Kankan. From the first visit of the missionary there was a response, and the first chapel was built there in 1934. Today, besides the regular church work, a French school covering the first four grades, is being taught by an African Christian and supervised by the missionaries. The majority of the 80 pupils in attendance (1948) accepted Christ before the end of the school year.

Baramba Since 1937, this has been the home of the Girls' Bible School for the Soudan and Upper Volta, and it is also the center for evangelism in the surrounding Mianka villages. Strong native churches are going forward in this area and their offerings for the year 1948 were more than double those of the preceding year. From forty to fifty girls are in training here, and additions are being made to the buildings which will enable the workers to care for a still larger enrollment.

Sangha Missionaries began work at Sangha among the Habbe people in 1931. The Habbes, a tribe of some 200,000 people, build their houses high on the rocks and on the sides of steep cliffs. To live, they must cultivate the sandy soil of the valleys and every fertile pocket among the rocks. If the rain fails to come in due season, the burning sun dries up every vestige of verdure and plunges them into deep despair. A few years before the arrival of the missionaries, a famine swept over this tribe and numbers died. The bones of the victims can still be seen in the Habbe "mausoleums"—crevices and caverns in the rocks. That these people were strong fetish worshippers was clearly proved by their numerous altars on the hilltops and in their yards. Soon after the missionaries settled at Sangha, a crisis came that proved to be God's opportunity to open Habbe hearts. Men came to the station asking if prayer to God in Jesus' name would bring the needed rain and save their crops. All their sacrifices to the fetish had failed to bring results. The missionaries spent two hours in prayer, and less than an hour later the rain was falling. Soon forty men and six women had been converted. Many churches throughout the district, and many students in the central Bible school are the fruit of the work that is still growing. Hundreds of Christians from 34 towns attended the native conferences held in the district the past year.

Mopti This is the center of the great district of which Sangha forms a part. Mopti is situated on the Bani and Niger Rivers, and in the rainy season is surrounded by water when the rivers overflow. Missionaries entered Mopti in 1924. Work among the Macina Foulas in this district proved exceedingly difficult. The haughty Moslems refused to yield although convinced of the truth. Fruit was meager, but Mopti proved to be the key for opening the Habbe country. At present Sangha is the only occupied mission center in the entire Mopti district of 450,000 souls. Although no missionaries are now residing at Mopti, native Christians have given a witness there.

Tombouctou The first trip by Alliance missionaries
(Eng. Timbuktu) to Tombouctou was made in 1924, and two young men were sent to occupy it in January, 1925. By the fall of 1932 our missionaries noticed a softening of the granite of Islam there. Moslems not only came to the meetings, but remained for prayer. At the first baptismal service in December, 1932, five were baptized. Persecution followed and some fell away.

Work was also begun among the Moslem Tuaregs, the veiled nomads of the desert. Some of them visited the missionaries and listened intently to the Gospel. One precious soul has been redeemed from among them, Lamin, the first of this tribe to be baptized, so far as is known. Some translation work was done in Tamachek, the language of the Tuaregs, and the New Testament in Sonhrai has been printed. Sonhrai, with variations of dialect, is the language of about 240,000 people from Tombouctou down to the Niger colony.

Gao Early in 1928 the missionaries at Tombouctou divided their forces to open another Sonhrai center at Gao, farther east at the buckle of the Niger. Gao proved to be a more important commercial center than Tombouctou, linked as it is with the Mediterranean by Trans-Saharan auto and airplane service, and with the rest of French West Africa by river, motor roads and air service. The first baptismal service in Gao was held in 1932. Six men were baptized near the public wharf, each in turn publicly acknowledging the Son of God as his Savior. The Moslems spread a report that the American had bribed each man who had been baptized. Persecution inevitably followed, but not all fell away. One young man used to go up on his housetop regularly to announce the Christian services, and to preach a sermonette. Today one Sonhrai couple from Gao are in the Soudan Bible School, the Moslem wife having accepted the Lord since going to Ntoroso.

No missionaries reside at present in Mopti, Tombouctou or Gao. The Chairman of the French West Africa field has said, "We have made strategic withdrawals which have proved through the years to be wise moves. Concentration in pagan areas has brought forth a bountiful harvest. It may be necessary to still further shorten our lines in some sections so that we can properly care for the existing work." These Moslem centers should eventually again be occupied but it is imperative to concentrate on the pagan areas before the Moslems move in and do their deadly work among them.

Upper Volta

Bobo-Dioulasso This station in the pagan Black Bobo tribe was opened in 1923. The Black Bobos are an entirely different race from the Red Bobos both in physiognomy and language. These names have been given to both tribes by outsiders and are not their own tribal names. The Black Bobos are unusually backward about accepting any innovations of civilization or religion. Many of the women still wear only aprons of leaves. Up to 1932 only a few Bobos had knelt in prayer, although there were several from other tribes who had been converted there at the Mission. The Bobos themselves are beginning to leave the town of Bobo-Dioulasso since civilization has made so many inroads on their age-old customs. The town is now the terminus of the Ivory Coast railway; boasts several hotels, a movie theater, and a monument in the public square. Among the large floating population of traders and clerks are some Christians from more civilized tribes to the south, and they attend the services at the Mission. The evangelistic opportunities in Bobo-Dioulasso are those of a crossroads of civilization. Along with primitive Bobos have worshiped men from the Gold Coast, Ivory Coast, and even from Liberia, the latter, internes studying at the Sleeping Sickness Institute conducted at the hospital. Tri-lingual services are conducted in French, English and the vernacular.

Covering an area of over 16,000 square miles, the district of Bobo-Dioulasso has a population of nearly 300,000, which includes a number of numerically small tribes. The population of the Black Bobo tribe has been estimated at 60,000, of whom perhaps 5,000 have turned to Islam.

Santidougou The first real encouragement among the Black Bobos came in 1933 when about 25 natives from one village came desiring to be instructed. It was at this time that it was decided to establish a station at Santidougou nearer the villages and customary rural life of the people. Prior to this two towns had been opened to the gospel and there were interested individuals in other villages, but since that time there have been evidences of a more general awakening in the tribe. A short term Bible School of six weeks' duration and literacy classes have been a part of the regular program at Santidougou.

Banfora This station, opened in 1937, was closed during the war and, because of a more urgent need for the missionaries on another station, could not be reopened until 1947. A local Christian, converted years before at Bobo-Dioulasso, and now a carpenter working for the government in Banfora, had made an effort to hold the believers together, meeting in the chapel constructed there in 1938. A missionary couple is once more stationed in this area and a mission station is being built at Seniena, six miles from Banfora. Banfora, which is a subdivision of the Bobo-Dioulasso circle, has a total population of 150,000, which includes three pagan tribes: the Gwens, Karaboros and the Turkans. There are believers or inquirers in each of these three tribes, numbering about 28 in all.

Dédougou Dédougou was opened in 1927 in the heart of the eastern branch of the Red Bobo tribe, the independent, warlike race that rebelled against the French in 1916. While the Bobo race predominates in this section, there are also many Dafin (or Marka) people. Both tribes are largely pagan and both have responded to the gospel. The need is great for native workers in the large district. One faithful worker is trying to reach 15 villages on foot, besides holding classes and services at his own post. The nationalistic spirit, which has been called thinly veiled Communism, is unusually strong in the Dédougou area and the desire for independence and money has lured away some of the former teacher-evangelists. However, at a recent native conference, 200 delegates attended from 10 different villages.

Sourou This station in the hitherto unreached Samogo tribe was opened early in 1947. An abandoned caravansary provided living quarters for the missionaries. Rubber sheets, stretched as a ceiling, kept off some of the rain that poured through the leaky thatched roof. Dismal living quarters did not stop the teaching program. New converts came regularly to study at night after working all day on their farms. Classes continued as long as the missionaries could keep awake. The Samogos seem to be above the average in intelligence. After six months of teaching some were able to use their New Testaments and the majority of them could read their Bible-based primers and hymnbooks intelligently. Every week new inquirers came and many villages not yet visited by the missionaries had groups of believers, thanks to the Bible School students who had come to help evangelize the Samogo tribe. Seventeen new towns were reached during the year 1948.

The enemy has seldom allowed God's servants to penetrate new territory without a battle and Samogoland was no exception. Soon after our Mission began to build at Sourou, Roman Catholic priests arrived and laid a false claim to land immediately across the road from the concession the government had granted to us. The priests began to build and threaten. Even the elements seemed to be in league with our enemies. Unseasonable rains destroyed thousands of newly made sun-dried bricks. When the first building was finally up and roofed, a tornado struck before the corrugated iron roofing could be securely anchored, and roof and timbers were broken and scattered over the landscape. The missionaries carried on with the tenacity of termites and within a month the roof was repaired. By 1949 a missionary residence, classroom and chapel were built. The gospel continued to bear fruit; the priests remained and continued their threats. But priests, tornadoes, rains, shortage of funds and weak bodies were all outweighed by the joy of hearing men,

women, boys and girls reading the New Testament and singing hymns of praise.

There are only two missionary couples in all the district of Tougan, which covers an area of over 6,700 square miles, with a population of nearly 150,000 including people of the Samogo, Red Bobo, Marka and several smaller tribes.

Ivory Coast

Bouaké A tour of the lower Ivory Coast was made in 1925 to visit the churches which were an outgrowth of the Prophet Harris mass movement. It was found that the English Wesleyan Mission had entered the territory and planned to develop the entire district affected by this remarkable movement. Hearing that great areas in the interior were still unoccupied, an investigation was made in 1929. It was learned that no society had planned definitely to evangelize the Baouli tribe, now numbering, according to one government official, about 750,000, and the Gouro tribe of 250,000, and so Bouaké was opened in 1930. This city of growing importance with a population of 25,000, has a district population of 350,500, predominantly Baouli. The Word of God has been fruitful throughout this section, which has 38 outstations and 50 villages where there are groups of believers. The work among the Dyimini people to the north is supervised from Bouaké. No missionary is yet available to minister in the Dyimini district where groups of Christians are found in the towns of Cairo, Tiengedougou, Yevroso and Gorla.

Bouaké is the site of the central Bible School for the Ivory Coast, and also of a mission French school covering all the elementary grades. In 1948 there were 27 students in the Bible School and 140 in the French school, some of whom walked about nine miles daily to attend classes.

The Ivory Coast is the richest colony of French West Africa. The French language is spoken by so many of the natives that it may almost be said to be the trade language of the Ivory Coast. The people of this colony are in danger from their wealth, not from their poverty. Cocoa and coffee plantations yield a good income. Young men are loath to leave their sure income to become native pastors with a small salary and many burdens to bear. It means real consecration but some are responding and the prospects are bright.

Mbayakro This station, in the Bouaké district, 56 miles from that center, was opened when the Bouaké church became missionary-minded, sent one of their leaders to work there and contributed to his support. The people responded readily to the gospel, built a chapel, and two missionaries were stationed there to further instruct the Christians. The work continues to prosper in Mbayakro and the surrounding villages.

Béoumi Béoumi is a newly opened station, west of and a subdivision of the Bouaké district. A movement toward God began in this section during the year 1948, with many decisions for Christ. Though Albert, one of the native workers, has gone to be with the Lord, his widow is there and has won seven women to Christ. Word was sent for the Christians to gather recently for a special service when the Chairman of the field visited there, and about 150 people responded, representing 15 different groups of Christians.

Toumodi Missionaries took up residence in Toumodi in 1934 when a permanent residence and chapel were built. At a recent conference held there, a small band of workers (African) were gathered who represented sixty churches in three districts. Toumodi represents a district of 137 villages. It is a subdivision of the district of Dimbokro.

Dimbokro The entire district of Dimbokro, including Toumodi, covers over 7,000 square miles, and has a population of about 163,000. Bocanda, another subdivision of Dimbokro, has 124 villages, and is the section where the Alliance hopes to establish a new center for the preparatory training of future Bible School students. Dimbokro, long occupied by the native lay preacher, Julius the cobbler, is now occupied by a missionary couple.

Churches have multiplied in the Ivory Coast faster than workers could care for them, with a total of 5,000 Christians reported for the entire Baouli section, but there is a lack of preparatory schools as feeders for the Bible School. The greatest need of the hour in the Ivory Coast is for intensive evangelism, Scripture translations, and Bible teaching. Many converts are in grave danger of falling away to strange doctrines and the wiles of Satan. A resurgence of fetish practices, and the presence of Seventh Day Adventists and Jehovah's Witnesses make the danger grave.

Translation and Publication Work

The New Testament has been printed by Bible Societies in three different languages where the Alliance is working, namely: Maninka, spoken by over 600,000 people; Bambara, spoken by about 850,000; and a dialect of the Sonhrai for a population of about 154,000. Alliance missionaries translated the New Testament into the Maninka and Sonhrai languages; a missionary of the Gospel Missionary Union at Bamako translated the New Testament, and more recently has completed the entire Bible in Bambara. He is now perfecting and revising the translation before submitting it for final printing. Several of the Old Testament books have been translated into Maninka also, and these and tentative printings of Old Testament books in Bambara have been printed at Kankan and are widely used. Some portion of the Scriptures has been or is being translated in all the languages used by our missionaries. The printing department at Kankan has printed, and often in several editions, Gospels and other books of the Bible, besides portions, in French, Kissi, Red Bobo, Black Bobo, Toma, Bambara, Maninka, Foula, Habbe, Sonhrai, Baouli, Yalounka and Kpelle (Gbereses' language). Bible stories, primers and catechisms have been printed in all the languages in which our missionaries are working. The Gospel of Matthew has been translated into Tamachek, the language of the Tuaregs. A native scribe cut the stencils for the Scripture portions and Gospels written with Arabic characters in Foula and some other languages used by Moslem tribes.

Schools and Literacy Campaigns

The report from one station in French West Africa reads: "The day a Bobo repents he receives a primer lesson sheet and is inducted into school. His schooling continues until he is able to read the Word of God and has studied all the available Scripture portions translated in his language. The aspiration of nearly every healthy Christian Bobo is to reach the place where he will be accepted as a student at the central Bible school."

This is the aim and program on most mission stations, where evening classes for reading, writing and Bible study are a common sight. Short-term Bible schools provide further training when Christians from many villages gather in one central place for an intensive program of study and fellowship for a few weeks each year.

Two elementary French schools are located respectively at Bouaké and Somasso. These provide a Christian education for the children of converts, although non-Christian children are also welcomed. In government schools the children would be constantly under Moslem or Catholic influence unless a Christian hostel were maintained to give them Christian training outside of school hours. Such a hostel is planned for Warakoy, a center near the Dedougou mission station.

Bush schools in the vernacular are carried on daily in villages where there are groups of Christians, providing the village is fortunate enough to have a resident teacher-evangelist. The children, and any adults who care to come, are taught to read and write, to sing hymns, to memorize Scripture and learn Bible stories. The wooden slates are made by the local blacksmiths. Letters of the alphabet are learned by molding them from clay as well as by writing. In the year 1948, 49 primary schools were conducted with a total enrollment of 1,604.

There are two Girls' Bible Schools at present, one at Baro for students from the Guinea, and one at Baramba for the Soudan and Upper Volta. Plans are being discussed for the establishment of a third girls' school at Béoumi in the Ivory Coast.

There are three central Bible Schools with a total enrollment (1948) of 176: one school at Bouaké, Ivory Coast; one at Telekoro, Guinea; and one at Ntoroso, Soudan.

The Church and the Challenge

When a convert has been won to Christ, the missionary's responsibility to him has only begun. Every missionary must be a teacher as well as an evangelist and pastor. The diversity of French West Africa's more than 100 languages and dialects is one of the greatest hindrances to a rapid advance. The missionary has the colossal task of reducing a language to writing and then translating the Scriptures. Often only one missionary couple is allotted to a district of from 1,000 to 9,000 square miles in extent. The missionary must build his home, service his automobile, visit the villages of his vast parish, care for the sick, and somehow find time to learn a language and translate Scripture portions and hymns.

The hope of such districts is for more teacher-evangelists, or catechists, to shepherd the village churches. These catechists receive a mere stipend from the Mission and must partly support themselves by working their own farms.

Reports from French West Africa for 1948 listed 27 mission stations and 401 outstations; 113 full-time native workers; 6,327 baptized church members and 8,870 inquirers; 131 organized and 356 unorganized church groups, of which 79 were fully self-supporting. The churches of the Sangha district of the Soudan, and most of those in the Ivory Coast were self-supporting, while the majority of churches in other parts of the Soudan gave 50 per cent of their support, and the Guinea churches, 15 per cent or more. The offerings at Telekoro showed an increase of 27 per cent over the preceding year. The work in Guinea is smaller numerically, being affected by the strong Moslem influence in many regions.

French West Africa is wide open to the gospel now but who can tell how long the door may remain open? While other lands are in the throes of civil wars and revolutions against existing governments, threatened by Communist advances, French West Africa's open doors present an unparalleled opportunity to spread the gospel throughout the length and breadth of a land more than half the size of the United States. The present staff of a total of some 300 missionaries of all Protestant societies working in the country is a mere handful. A number of the staff are always on furlough, leaving stations vacant with no one to fill up the gaps. A leader from Nigeria visiting French West Africa said that a thousand missionaries would not be too many for so vast a territory. Districts covering thousands of square miles each, and with populations of from 100,000 to over 300,000 each are entirely unoccupied. The author of *The Soul of French West Africa* challenges us with the question,

"Watchman, what of the night? Watchman, what of the night? The morning cometh, and also the night." Will it be for Africa the red dawn of communism and atheism? Will the coming generation be Moslem? Catholic? Or will it be enlightened by the Word of God?

CONGO

The principal part of the great colony of Belgian Congo is in the interior of south Central Africa. It has only a short coast line on the South Atlantic at the mouth of the Congo River. To the north and west of it lies French Equatorial Africa, and on the northeast it touches the Anglo-Egyptian Sudan. On the southwest is Angola (Portuguese), beyond which and to the east is Northern Rhodesia; also to the east are Uganda and Tanganyika, which are parts of British East Africa.

Area and Population

Belgian Congo, whose area is variously given as from 902,000 to over 904,000 square miles, is more than three times the size of Texas. The population (1946), composed chiefly of Bantu Negroes, with some Nilotics and Pygmies, was 10,702,859. Ruanda and Urundi, with an area of 20,535 square miles and an estimated population of 3,767,000, are united administratively with the Belgian Congo. They were formerly a part of German East Africa.

The Alliance field in the Belgian Congo covers a comparatively small area near the mouth of the Congo River. The principal portion of our work is in a section called the Mayombe, north of Boma, but one district lies across a river in the northern part of the Portuguese enclave of Cabinda. Cabinda, with two ports on the Atlantic Ocean, lies between Middle Congo (French), and Belgian Congo, and although separated from Angola, is really a part of that colony. Cabinda's area is approximately 7,000 square miles, with a population of about 25,000.

History

Most of the early explorers of the Lower Congo were there to devastate, and Boma long had the reputation of being the "slave pen of the West Coast." This reputation was not helped when King Leopold II of Belgium entered the scene. The Congo Free State had its origin when he, roused by Stanley's discoveries, realized the economic possibilities of the vast Congo basin. King Leopold founded and largely financed the International Association of the Congo which sent Stanley back there in 1879. By 1885 the territory was founded as a free state, under the recognized sovereignty of King Leopold. It was formally ceded to Belgium by treaty in 1908, and has since been known as the Belgian Congo. Under King Leopold's regime, tales of massacres and senseless torture of the natives continued to reach the outside world. Europe became aroused and sent an investigating committee in 1904. The charges were found to be all too true, but the committee's report brought about reforms and gradually the nefarious slave trade was abolished. Years later under the wise administration of the late King Albert, changes were introduced which really benefited the country, and the old days of ruthless exploitation were replaced by a policy of commercial development. Today it is safe to travel the Congo forest paths.

Government

The central government is at Brussels, Belgium. The Congo is administered by the Minister of the Colonies at Brussels, and a Colonial Council of 14 members. The Governor-General at Leopoldville, capital of the Congo, is assisted by a Government Council of nominated members. The weakness is that apparently there has been no aim of ultimately making Congo self-governing. Development of the country is for the benefit of stockholders in Belgium and the home government. Although Belgium has attempted to maintain the old native form of government by restoring village and district chiefs and native institutions, it has been said that the chiefs are merely civil servants of the ruling power.

Climate

The climate is hot and moist. The average mean temperature is 80.6 degrees Fahrenheit, and the average rainfall is 43.27 inches.

Physical Features

The surface of the Congo is a depressed plateau basin, tilted westward. It is unbroken by mountains except in the western part near the Atlantic, where it rises on its borders to elevations of 6,000 feet or more. Less than half of the area is covered by forests. The remainder is composed of savannas and arable land.

The mighty Congo River offers what appears to be an inviting gateway to the inland plateau of rich possibilities. Nine miles wide at its mouth, the river pours fourth a million tons of water every minute, and discolors the ocean for two hundred miles by its waters. The inviting gateway, however, is beset with traps—first, swamps entangled with the roots of mangrove trees, and then cataracts and dangerous rocks. Today these obstacles have been overcome. The first 95 miles of the river is navigable to Matadi. The rapids beyond have been overcome by a railroad to Stanley Pool (Leopoldville). Above the Pool are 1,000 miles of navigable water to Stanley Falls, and tributaries furnish further waterways for nearly 600 miles more.

For years scientific study has been going on in a tract of land set apart for the preservation and study of animal and plant life. The tract was enlarged in 1935 to include one of the most ideal sections in the world for this purpose. In the heart of the tropics, with a great range of elevations, it offers for study an unusually large number of varieties of plant and animal life.

Resources

Vast sunless and well-nigh impenetrable tropical forests fill the upper reaches of the Congo River, covering about 25,000 square miles. Among the principal products of the country are palm-oil, cotton, palm kernels, coffee, cocoa, rubber, sugar and ivory. Congo's greatest riches are her minerals. The diamond fields produce more than six million carats a year, making Congo the world's largest producer of industrial diamonds. The uranium ore from the Katanga district furnishes 90% of the world's supply of radium. The Congo's 1945 production of uranium ore was estimated at 10,000 tons. Congo ranks high among copper producing countries, with the Katanga copper belt 250 miles long and 25 to 50 miles wide.

Progress

Today there are a thousand or more boats on the Congo where in 1885 there were half a dozen. In 1911 a pipeline was constructed for transporting crude oil from Matadi to Leopoldville. This line, 246 miles long, provides oil for operating the river steamers. About 14,000 miles of inland waterways have been made navigable. The three trading companies in Congo in 1885 have multiplied to nearly three hundred. In 1944 the United States exported to Belgian Congo less than twenty million dollars worth of merchandise, but in 1947 Congo received from the United States alone nearly fifty million dollars worth of goods.

Nearly 3,000 miles of railway and 44,000 miles of roads have been built. One motor road connects Stanleyville with Rejaf, the Nile terminus of navigation from Khartoum. A coast to coast railroad more than 2,000 miles long connects Lobito Bay on the west coast with Beira Port on the Indian Ocean. Insignificant in comparison, but of great value to our Mission is the ninety-mile railroad north from Boma, which eliminates days of weary walking for the missionaries traveling from Boma to Kinkonzi. The Mission has built a road connecting Kinkonzi with this railroad terminus six miles distant. The government and some of the plantation owners have built motor roads in recent years, so that now most of the main church centers are accessible by car. However travel to most of the villages throughout our part of the Congo field is still along narrow foot-trails. In all of this district, the only post office is at Boma.

Leopoldville, the capital of the colony, has a population of 120,000 natives and over 6,000 Europeans. The most thriving city, however, is Elizabethville, where there are more white people than in any other place in tropical Africa. Away from the cities, the mode of living is still most primitive. Homes are mere huts built of reeds or the ribs of palm branches, roofed with a thatch of leaves. There are no real farms. Crops are grown in small fields, and animals of the forest often destroy much of the crops before they can be harvested. The government is seeking to improve the crude agricultural methods used.

Currency

The unit of currency in the Belgian monetary area is the Congo franc, worth two cents in U. S. currency. In Portuguese Cabinda, angolares are used. The present value of the angolare is between three and four cents U. S., having approximately the same value as the Portuguese escudo—28.75 escudos to one U. S. dollar.

Languages

The Kikongo language, which includes various dialects, is used in the Alliance area, and is sometimes also called Kifioti. Kiswahili is the language of natives who have been under Arab influence. Bangala is the commercial language on the Upper Congo. Fioti is used near the coast and Erhiluba in the southern part. Alliance missionaries and native workers use the Kikongo, and French or Portuguese languages, in the various districts of the field.

Religions

The native religion is gross fetishism, or animism. There is no religious community as in the highly developed religions of the Orient, but each village or group of villages has its religious leaders, generally witch doctors. (See *Religions, Africa.*) The Roman Catholic Church is making every possible effort to turn the people of Congo to the Church of Rome. Since 1935 they have increased the number of foreign priests in Congo from 805 to 1,569 (1948), not including the religious brothers and nuns. (See under *Missionary Occupation.*)

Missionary Occupation

In the work-span of a single life Christianity has come to the Congo. During the years 1878-1879, the first little band of devoted men and women missionary pioneers struggled for a foothold on the very fringe of the deadly western

coast that hid the equatorial empire then beginning to be known as the conventional basin of the Congo.

The records list six missionaries at the beginning; by 1930 there were 1,000, with 180 mission stations and one-half million adherents. The missions began by occupying about 200 square miles of territory, and are now spread over at least a million and a half square miles.

The Congo Protestant Council reports for 1947 as follows:

Number of missions	44	Sunday schools	4,302
Mission stations	249	Sunday school scholars .	145,714
Missionaries in Congo ..	1,162	Rural schools	13,295
Missionaries on furlough	354	Station schools	265
Church members	416,612	Normal schools, semi-	
Inquirers	238,618	naries, etc.	97
Baptisms	38,598	Trade schools	26
African Personnel:		Students:	
Unordained pastors ..	923	Primary schools	348,500
Ordained pastors	256	Elementary grades ...	3,952
Evangelists and Moni-		Normal schools, semi-	
tors	19,775	naries, etc.	4,169
Medical workers and		Trade schools	633
others	2,347		

The World Christian Handbook, published in 1949, reports a total of 1,551 Protestant missionaries, and 433,161 communicants or full church members in Belgian Congo.

The Society for the Propagation of the Faith gives the following statistics of Roman Catholic missions in the Belgian Congo, including Ruanda and Urundi, for the year 1948: Foreign priests, religious brothers, nuns, total 3,955; native priests, brothers, nuns, 1,161 including novices; catechists, 24,545; mission stations, 454; native Catholics, 3,247,597; foreign Catholics, 33,922. Adult baptisms numbered 102,313; infant baptisms, 132,824. There were 2,023 Seminarians, and 882,928 pupils enrolled in other Catholic schools.

The Apostolic Delegate speaking at Leopoldville some years ago said: "The Catholic Church is not Belgian, nor French, English, Italian or American, it is Catholic; Belgian in Belgium, French in France, Italian in Italy. . . . In the Congo it must be Congolese: in the construction of sacred edifices, in the manufacture of objects for use in liturgical functions, . . . all the elements of Congolese art must be scrupulously observed. . . . When the natives are in church they must not feel that they are in a strange house."

The Christian and Missionary Alliance

The field of The Christian and Missionary Alliance in Belgian Congo and Cabinda is a territory north of the mouth of the Congo River, with a population of between 400,000 and 500,000. The Congo was the first Alliance field to which a band of missionaries was sent. In the fall of 1884, several years before the Alliance was organized, a group of young men sailed for the Congo, members of the first class of the New York Missionary Training Institute. (In 1897 the Institute was transferred to Nyack, N. Y.)

The Annual Report of the International Missionary Alliance, October, 1892, states that the Alliance Congo Mission had been founded five years previously with headquarters at Ngangila, and that in the year 1892 there were 28 missionaries on that field. The early years were arduous ones for the missionaries, the deadly climate taking a toll of thirty-one lives. The news of these tragedies drove friends at home to more earnest prayer, and God heard. There was a lessening of the number of lives laid down. Before the end of the first thirty years, there was one period of seven years in which no death occurred among our Congo missionaries.

Despite all the hardships and losses, the work went on; reinforcements were sent out; and the records show that during almost the entire period of the Alliance work in Congo, this field has had a larger number of missionaries in propor-

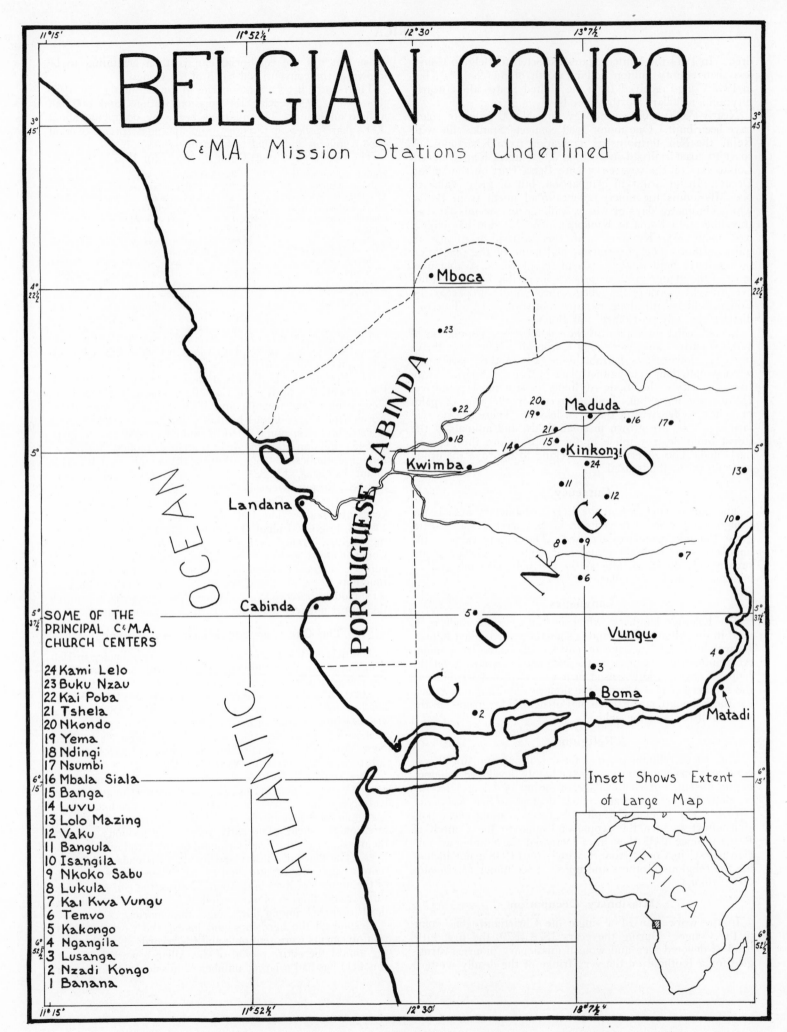

BELGIAN CONGO

C&M.A. Mission Stations Underlined

• Mboca

•23

• 22
•18
Landana •
14 •
15
Kwimba •

20
19
21
Maduda
•16   17•
Kinkonzi
•24
•11
•12
13•

PORTUGUESE CABINDA

OCEAN

ATLANTIC

Cabinda •

SOME OF THE
PRINCIPAL C&M.A.
CHURCH CENTERS

24 Kami Lelo
23 Buku Nzau
22 Kai Poba
21 Tshela
20 Nkondo
19 Yema
18 Ndingi
17 Nsumbi
16 Mbala Siala
15 Banga
14 Luvu
13 Lolo Mazing
12 Vaku
11 Bangula
10 Isangila
9 Nkoko Sabu
8 Lukula
7 Kai Kwa Vungu
6 Temvo
5 Kakongo
4 Ngangila
3 Lusanga
2 Nzadi Kongo
1 Banana

C O N G O

•8 •9
•6
•7
10•

5 •

Vungu •

•3
Boma
•2

4•
Matadi

Inset Shows Extent
of Large Map

AFRICA

34

tion to the population for which we are responsible than in any other field. The field records would seem to justify this policy of adequate occupation, for there are more national Christians in the Congo field than in any other Alliance field.

In the first twenty years of our work in the Congo the results were discouraging. A number of the native workers had backslidden, and the little church was practically disbanded. During the Missionary Conference that year, one of the missionaries ventured the remark that perhaps they should not expect the same results of the Gospel in the lives of Africans, as were being seen among educated Indians or Chinese. Whereupon a young man, one of the younger missionaries, arose and with great earnestness said, "Brother, I refuse to believe that the grace of God or the Spirit of God can do less in the heart of any man in Africa than in the heart of a man in India or China." The missionaries took up the challenge, returned to their stations with new faith, and soon an awakening came. In the villages of the Maduda district and later in the Yema district, hundreds of Africans turned to the Lord in the next few years.

The most rapid growth of the work came after thirty years of faithful ministries on the part of missionaries and the loyal aid of a number of devoted native evangelists. During these years a solid foundation was laid. A report printed at the end of this period told of a gracious revival when the Holy Spirit quickened both the missionary staff and the native church, and there followed a number of remarkable cases of divine healing.

Many fields, opened after the Congo, had had several visits by deputations from the Board in New York, but Congo had been passed by. No such visit was made until 1924—forty years after the opening of the field. In that year the Foreign Secretary was privileged to visit the Congo field, and another member of the Board of Managers made visits in 1931 and 1946. These visits resulted in more rapid progress in the development of the native church as a self-governing body, and in the enlargement of the plans and work of the Bible Training School, and other school work throughout the field.

From the following six mission stations the missionaries minister throughout the ten church districts of the field.

Kinkonzi Opened in 1895, Kinkonzi has become the central station for the Alliance work in Congo. It is located nine miles east of Tshela, the government seat for the Mayombe territory, and the terminus of the railroad from Boma.

The Kinkonzi staff of workers is usually larger than on any other station of the field. One missionary couple is in charge of the Bible Institute. A lady missionary is in charge of the Women's Department of the Bible Institute and of the two-year Bible School, while another supervises the primary school on the station as well as in the nineteen church centers of this district. Except for the Advanced Bible School, most of the teaching is done by Africans, all products of our own mission.

There is a large, well built, brick church at Kinkonzi, with a main auditorium seating 600, and a wing that may be used for classes and conferences. The native churches have built houses for their Bible school students on land secured for them by the Mission.

Boma The work at Boma, a port on the Lower Congo, began in 1896. Here the Receiving Home accommodates missionaries who arrive or leave by steamer, or who come from inland stations on business. The financial affairs of the Mission are carried on through the Boma office. Routine duties of the Boma staff include everything from representation to the government in legal matters, and the en-

tertaining of transient missionaries, to the purchasing and forwarding of groceries and notions to missionaries on the inland stations.

A lady missionary is stationed at Boma to supervise the five-grade station school, as well as the primary schools of the district. The missionaries at Boma are responsible for the oversight of seven church centers including the hitherto unresponsive Banana area along the Atlantic coast. There, native workers from the Mayombe district have labored long, but have seen little fruit. Some years ago a deputational visitor said concerning a meeting of the evangelists of the Banana district:

I had a profitable time with them and gleaned something of the difficulties attending the preaching of the Gospel in this section. Fetishism, witchcraft, and the poison test abound here. In addition to the necessity of breaking down the old superstitions, there is a ceaseless fight against our workers by the Roman Catholics. It would seem that the principal objective of the Roman Catholics is not to change the hearts and habits of the heathen, but merely to keep them from accepting the Word of God as preached by the Christians of the Mission.

Now after the breaking of much fallow ground, and much seed sowing, there appears to be a budding that predicts a certain harvest.

At Boma, frequent visits to the hospital, the jail and the military camp bring help to hungry hearts. The church, built in the early twenties, with a seating capacity of nearly 300, has become too small. A new edifice, with three times the floor space of the first church, has been erected on a high hill adjoining the native section of the town, where there is a population of 113,000. The church, seating about 1,500, has been dedicated.

Vungu Vungu, opened about 1892, was the second station in our Congo field. Ngangila, now a part of the Vungu district, was the first station opened. Lolo, a former station area, is now divided and under the supervision of Vungu and Maduda. These early stations are marked by many missionary graves: five at Ngangila, two at Kiama, four at Lolo and six at Vungu. Most of the stone markers bear dates in the nineties, silent reminders of the high cost of missionary pioneering.

The Vungu district extends almost to the town of Matadi, a thriving port on the Congo River. The industrial opportunities in the lumber camps and plantations there have lured the youth of the Vungu district to seek high wages. Employment is available for every able-bodied man, until at present the Vungu district is being depopulated, and tribal foundations are being undermined. Caught in the meshes of these changes, the church shows a lack of stability, but efforts to evangelize the labor camps are well organized, and for the most part the messengers are eagerly received.

Four pastors shepherd the 1,345 members of the eight church centers of this district. The two-year Bible school serves both the Boma and Vungu districts. A class of twenty-two Christian workers have just completed the first year's course.

Maduda In the early history of Alliance work in the Congo, Maduda (1893) and Yema (1894) were both important mission stations. Later, as the churches developed and native pastors were ordained, these districts were supervised from Kinkonzi. However, it was decided in 1933 to reopen Maduda station for the purpose of establishing a normal school, in order that native workers throughout the field might be more adequately trained for the important work of teaching mission primary schools, a few of which have now attained the maximum fifth-year standard. The Normal School at Maduda and the Bible Institute at Kinkonzi, both of eighth grade standard, supplement each other, for frequently students are graduated from both schools, and are thus better equipped for a varied ministry.

Maduda missionaries, with native aid, also carry on the standard two-year Bible school and a five-year primary school on the station, besides supervising the primary schools of lower grades in the district church centers, of which there are 21 in the Maduda area, with seven ordained pastors. An imposing church built in memory of Rev. and Mrs. Gabriel MacGuire, early Congo missionaries, was completed at Maduda in 1948.

Kwimba Because of the growth of the work in this district, the Kwimba station was opened in 1925. In addition to an itinerant ministry in twelve church centers, the missionaries on this station conduct the standard two-year Bible school and a five-grade primary school for children.

As in other districts, Workers' Institutes or Bible conferences are held annually for two full weeks. All official workers and those who are interested in becoming workers, attend throughout the entire session. An annual Sunday school convention with delegates from all the churches has grown to be an especially interesting feature in the Kwimba district.

M'Boca This station in the Portuguese enclave of Cabinda was opened in 1907. The Alliance field is in the northern portion of Cabinda, while another Protestant society has work in the southern portion, with their headquarters in the town of Cabinda, which is the government seat.

The Portuguese government requires all native workers to pass a government examination before granting them permission to teach. On the whole these examinations have been fair enough. Students who satisfactorily pass the standard mission two-year Bible course, together with reading and writing in Portuguese, are usually able to obtain government permits. All teaching must be done in the Portuguese language and only Portuguese nationals may direct school work. Schools must be confined to the station or the work may be closed by the government.

Many of the people of this district are slaves, their parents having been brought over from the French and Belgian Congo generations ago. There is an instability of character which retards the work, but generally, the people are favorable to gospel work. From every direction towns are calling for teacher-evangelists. Although Catholic persecution is often severe, souls are being saved. There are two native pastors in this area and a church membership of 1,000.

Translation and Publication Work

A new edition of the entire Bible in Kifioti was printed by the British and Foreign Bible Society about 1933. Baptist, Swedish and Alliance missionaries, all using the same translation, had made the revision. For seventeen years the Alliance Sunday school committee has edited the Sunday school lesson notes in Kifioti, appearing in a monthly magazine published by a Swedish mission. The magazine has a wide circulation among four mission societies, and nearly 2,000 subscribers in the Alliance. Published by our missionaries, and available in Kifioti, are: the Congo youth magazine, *Mbangi*, with a circulation of about 800; Dr. Simpson's books on Romans, The Fourfold Gospel, and Christ in the Tabernacle; Pilgrim's Progress, Bible stories, a Topical Textbook, and helps for Christian workers. Planned for the near future, among others, are a concordance, a book on Christian doctrine, and Bible types.

Schools and Literacy Campaigns

The report of Alliance school work in Congo for the year 1948 gives the following information. There were 595 bush schools with a total enrollment of 9,236. These bush schools provide a place for Christians to learn how to read. One of the requirements for church membership in Congo is to be able to read, although an exception is made for the aged. The teacher-evangelists hold regular services and also conduct the bush schools.

The seven five-grade primary schools of the Mission had an enrollment of over 4,000. The Bible is taught along with the three R's, and no pupil can pass to the next grade if he fails in Bible study. In the primary schools which are conducted on mission stations, the Mission provides the buildings, the pupils helping in the construction of the dormitories. In the station schools the Mission also pays the teachers, but in the primary schools in native church centers, the Mission pays only about half of the salaries of the teachers, and the buildings are erected without mission aid.

The Normal School, located at Maduda, had an enrollment, in 1948, of over 60, and the Bible Institute, located at Kinkonzi, had 35 men students, besides the wives of students, for whom separate classes are conducted. The Mission conducts four girls' schools and three women's schools in various parts of the field. The Bible Institute (eighth grade standard) is for advanced students and covers three years of study. The objective of self-support is maintained in the Institute, and the students are regular evangelists, chosen by the church and partially supported by it. The balance of support must be secured by the individual students. In addition to the Bible Institute, a two-year Bible school for Christian workers is conducted on all stations except Boma. Workers' Institutes are also held annually for two weeks, and are attended by all official workers and by those who desire to enter Christian service. Five such institutes were held in 1948 with a total attendance of 768. Three short term Bible schools were also held, average duration nine months, with a total enrollment of 77.

The aim of our educational program is: first, to have a Bible-reading constituency; second, a well trained ministry; third, to provide schools with a Protestant Christian environment for the children of believers.

The Church and the Challenge

By the end of the first thirty years of the Alliance work in the Congo, there were less than 800 church members and only 70 native evangelists. Then came a gracious working of the Holy Spirit, and subsequent growth has been so rapid that now during each year there are more converts baptized than the total number of Christians at the end of the first thirty years of the work. The yearly report for 1948 showed a church membership of 20,760, and 6,706 inquirers. The number baptized during the year was 1,606.

The 83 organized churches are entirely self-supporting; of the 783 native workers, 32 are ordained pastors, and 625 are wholly supported by the native church, although in many cases they have to supplement their meager income by other work. The church offerings for the year totaled the equivalent of $14,492.10, an increase of more than 35 per cent over the total of the previous year. The 30 church centers and 52 outstations are grouped into ten church districts. Quarterly meetings are held in each of the church centers under the direction of the ordained native pastors. The 639 Sunday schools present an unusual challenge, with an enrollment throughout the field of 27,345.

The work of the churches is supervised by a native Board of Elders, who are elected by the annual conference of delegates representing all the churches. From the native church conferences have come the rules which govern the Congo church. The deciding factor in formulating these rules has not been, "What is the white man's custom?" but "What does the Word of God say about these things?"

The Congo church is facing tremendous problems in relation to the government and to Roman Catholicism, which exercises great influence in the government educational system. The colonial government conducts no regular grade schools though it does have a few professional schools. The government subsidizes mission schools which meet its requirements. For years only Catholic schools were subsidized, and the Roman Catholic Church has made a tremendous drive to compel the younger generation to enroll in these so-called government schools. Our Mission and Foreign Department are carefully studying the matter of government subsidies for certain of our schools but no decision has yet been made.

The Belgian government now offers subsidized coöperation to Protestant schools also, but the conditions attached are difficult. All non-Belgian missionary teachers, doctors and nurses who wish to do state-subsidized educational and medical work, must spend at least twelve months in Belgium, where they must take a colonial course with a final examination. Teachers will be required to take some work in a Belgian normal school, and medical workers must take the course in tropical medicine at Antwerp.

The government has refused to recognize the self-governing, independent status of the native church in Congo. This increases the burdens of the church leaders, and necessitates the continuance of missionary service, both for a spiritual ministry to the churches, and to aid the church in relations with the government.

GABON

Colony of French Equatorial Africa

The Gabon is situated on the west coast of Africa straddling the equator. It is bounded on the west by the Atlantic, on the south and east by Middle Congo, one of its three sister colonies of French Equatorial Africa, and on the north by French Cameroun and Spanish Guinea. French acquisition began in 1841, through exploration and settlement, its limits being defined in a series of international conventions.

Area and Population

The Gabon is a part of what was formerly known as French Congo. In 1910 the French Congo was renamed French Equatorial Africa. It is divided into four colonies, as follows:

(World Almanac, 1949)

Colony	Square Miles	Population (1946)
Gabon	93,218	383,715
Middle Congo	166,069	655,497
Ubangi-Shari	238,767	1,062,300
Chad	461,202	1,902,221
	959,256	4,003,733

The European population numbers over 8,300.

People and History

The Pygmies, thought to be the aboriginals of Gabon, were destroyed in large numbers by tribes which descended into Gabon from the northeast. The Pygmies who remained were taken as slaves. Today there is left only a small remnant, found in scattered villages or hidden deep in the jungle. The Bantu-speaking Negroes are now in the majority.

French sovereignty was first established by the treaty of 1839 under the King of Gabon, who was on friendly terms with French missionaries and traders. He ceded his territory to France and effective occupation took place in 1844. In 1848, Libreville, the capital, was founded by settling freed slaves there. The territory was explored in several expeditions by Paul du Chaillu, and from 1862 onwards, French control was extended until it reached the Ogooué River. In 1880 Count de Brazza reached Stanley Pool, where today stands Brazzaville, the capital of French Equatorial Africa.

Government

The Gabon has its own capital, Libreville, and Governor, who is responsible to a local assembly appointed by the Minister of Foreign Affairs. Since 1947, when the nationals were granted citizenship, they have been enjoying the rights and protection of their new status. Each district has its own national representative in the Governor's cabinet. There is a growing desire on the part of French officials and nationals to unite small scattered villages into larger towns in order to gain the resulting benefits of education and sanitation.

The Gabon and its three sister colonies compose French Equatorial Africa, which is under a single administrative unit with a Governor-General located at Brazzaville, the capital of all French Equatorial Africa.

Climate

The heaviest rainfall occurs between October and December when the equatorial rain-belt is moving southwards. From the latter part of December to the early part of February there is a considerable decrease. As the sun moves northward, there is a second rainy season from the middle of February until June. Then follows the dry season, during which the rainfall is reduced to a minimum. The temperature is high and humid throughout the rainy season. A decrease of from 10 to 15 degrees is noticeable during the dry season. The upland districts in the interior are cooler the year round. Official reports, available for two districts only of the Alliance field in Gabon, give the average annual rainfall at Mouila as 94 inches, and in the Echira region, as 69 inches.

Physical Features

The topography of South Gabon is varied. Vast areas of rolling, grass-covered plains are dotted here and there by stretches of marsh. The Du Chaillu and Crystal mountain ranges reach a height of 2,000 feet. Rare tree ferns grow majestically amid the luxuriant vegetation bordering the swift, clear, mountain streams which are often interrupted by waterfalls and rapids. The rivers, some of which are tributaries of the great Ogooué River of North Gabon, are unnavigable for the most part.

Resources

The resources of Gabon are now being developed. Commerce is chiefly with France. The main exports are palm-oil and gold. Coffee, cocoa, peanuts, cotton and rubber are produced. Some ivory is exported. Copper, zinc and lead have been found. Port Gentil is the greatest lumber port in all Africa, and there ships are continually loading logs which have been floated down the Ogooué River.

Progress

Miles of trails have been cut through the jungle by the French, many of which are now being made into automobile roads. A splendid network of roads will soon make all parts of the Gabon easily accessible for missionary occupation. The largest river, the Ogooué, is found to the north of our field of labor. It is navigable for small river boats for about 200 miles. Motor transport companies are rapidly taking over the bulk of the transportation business, as the river transportation is slow and dangerous due to sand banks and rapids. The chief river of South Gabon is the N'Gounie, which is only partially navigable.

Currency

As in all French colonies in Africa, the official currency is French, the franc being the unit. However, French Equatorial Africa issues its own currency in bank notes of the usual denominations from five francs up. The value of the franc in this colony is a little more than one-half cent in U. S. money, or about 175 francs to one American dollar.

Languages and Tribes

There are thirty tribes in Gabon, as follows:

Bandjavi	Bavoumi	Shékés
Bapounou	Bawandji	Shamailles
Massango	Badouma	Batumbidi
Echira	Bavili	Boumoueli
Mitsogo	Bakiela	Batchangui
Bavoumbou	Batéké	Bassimba
Bangomo	Bakouta	Bapindji
Bavarama	Babamba	Bavuvi
Baloumbou	Bandassas	Babongo (Pygmy)
Bavoungou	Bassissions	Barimba (Pygmy)

All of the above tribes can be reached through one of the four major languages: those spoken by the Bandjavi, Bapounou, Massango-Echira, and Mitsogo tribes.

In some of the tribes the name of the language spoken by the people is slightly different from the name of the tribe. For example, the language of the Bapounou people is called Yipounou.

Religions

Gabon lies beyond the full range of Moslem influence, but Moslems are now coming in. The people are animists, worshiping fetishes and practicing witchcraft. (See *Animism*, under Africa, Religions.) The human leopard society is secretly active in parts of the country. Dressed in a leopard skin, with iron claws, one of the society may carry off a human victim, but the natives firmly believe that a man who had transformed himself into a real leopard did the deed. The witch doctors are now beginning to feel that the coming of the Gospel is making them lose their hold on the people. Their newest tactic is to claim revelation from *Nsambi*, God. This new teaching is a more deadly enemy than the old, simple fetishism.

The Roman Catholic Mission is working throughout this territory and has put forth every effort to hinder the Protestant missionaries from reaching the people with the gospel message.

Missionary Occupation

The Paris Evangelical Mission took over the work of the Presbyterian Mission in northern Gabon in 1892. Their work is located on the north side of the Ogooué River, and their responsibility extends north and northeast to the border of Spanish Guinea and includes some territory in French Cameroun. The Paris Evangelical Mission (1948 report) has 7 stations, 49 European missionaries, 324 African pastors, evangelists and catechists, and 63 African teachers. They have 12,874 communicants and 9,656 inquirers. Pupils in their mission schools number 3,288.

When Alliance missionaries first became burdened for the evangelization of the unreached tribes in French Gabon to the north of our Belgian Congo field, our Foreign Secretary wrote to France to the Paris Evangelical Mission, which was working in North Gabon, and inquired if they were planning to extend their work into South Gabon. A little later the Paris society secretary was in New York and called at Alli-

ance headquarters to confer with the Foreign Secretary about the matter. This occurred at the time when the Alliance was just beginning to expand its work in French West Africa. The secretary of the Paris Mission stated that since the Alliance had such a great field in French West Africa for advance, their society would be glad if we would refrain for a few years from entering South Gabon in order to give them the opportunity to extend their work in that area. However, some years later the Paris Evangelical Mission reported to the Alliance that they were unable to increase their work sufficiently to meet the need in South Gabon. Arrangements were then made for the Alliance to enter and we opened work there in 1934. The Paris Mission desires that we assume the responsibility for nearly all the country south of the Ogooué River, reserving only a small strip along the southern shore for themselves. This gives the Alliance an area in South Gabon and part of North Gabon of about 60,000 square miles, with a population of between 200,000 and 250,000 people who had never before heard the gospel.

The Christian and Missionary Alliance

The Christian and Missionary Alliance opened work in South Gabon as a result of the vision and sacrifice of our Belgian Congo Mission, which provided two missionary couples for the task and sent them off with a love offering. Because of the distances involved and the necessity of dealing with a different government, the Gabon was recognized as a new and separate African field. During the first years, Bongolo, the only station, was synonomous with the Gabon work as a whole. For a number of years the work was supervised by a field superintendent appointed by the Board in New York, but a field conference was organized in 1946.

The missionary staff is responsible for seven stations, which are the ultimate goal of this field. God is enabling them to expand in order to meet the full responsibility. Five years ago there were just two mission stations. The field conference of 1949 voted for the establishment of a seventh station and appointed a missionary couple to that work. The Bongolo, Ileka and Mouyanama stations are already well established. As yet motor roads in the interior of Gabon are few, but the missionaries have nevertheless made a civilized world in the heart of the jungle. Waterfalls have provided the power for electric equipment at Bongolo. Where water power is lacking, gasoline motors have gone in to run the saw and planer to provide lumber for building. Brick kilns are turning out quantities of brick daily. Gradually mud and bark houses and churches are being replaced by permanent buildings of burnt brick which the heavy rains cannot wash away.

Bongolo The busy heart of gospel activities in the Gabon field is the Bongolo station, set upon a connected chain of hilltops, and offering a panoramic view of jungle-covered mountains. The beautiful Bongolo waterfall tumbles over a rocky precipice into the wide Louetsi River below, dividing the spacious grounds of this, the first, mission station. After preliminary arrangements had been made on the station site by the two missionary men who had gone to spy out the land, the first missionary family arrived there in February, 1935. They had reached this primitive spot by following watercourses for 250 miles inland from the coast.

Today, in place of the first bark and clay buildings, there are at Bongolo four permanent missionary residences which can accommodate three families and two single ladies. Building materials are being prepared for the erection of the first permanent church, Bible school buildings, an adequate dispensary, and a girls' dormitory. Residing at Bongolo are the missionary pastor of the large surrounding church dis-

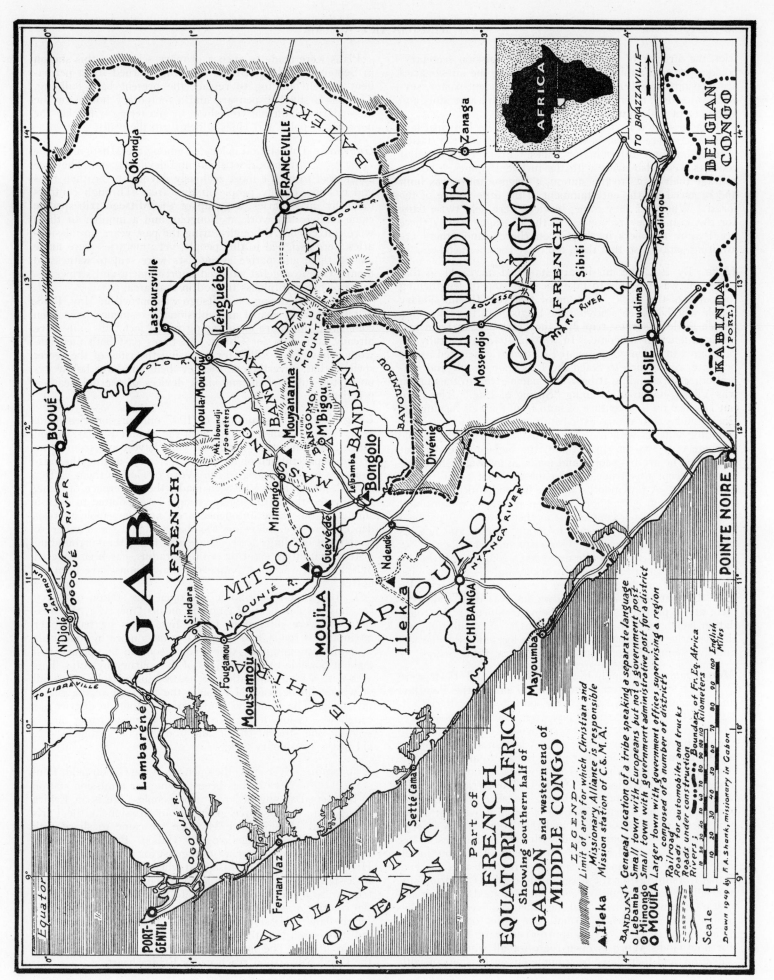

Part of
FRENCH
EQUATORIAL AFRICA
Showing southern half of
GABON and western end of
MIDDLE CONGO

LEGEND—

BANDJAVI General location of a tribe speaking a separate language
Lebamba Small town with Europeans but not a government post.
Mimongo Small town with government administrative post for a district
MOUÏLA Larger town with government offices, supervising a region
composed of a number of districts
▲Ileka Missionary Alliance is responsible
Mission station of C.&M.A.

Railroad
Roads for automobiles and trucks
Roads under construction
Rivers;   Boundary of Fr. Eq. Africa

Scale 0 10 20 30 40 50 60 70 80 90 100 English Miles
       0 10 20 30 40 50 60 70 80 90 100 110 Kilometers

Drawn 1949 by F.A.Shank, missionary in Gabon

39

trict, the director of the Bible school, the mission secretary-bookkeeper, and a missionary nurse. Aiding the missionaries are mission-trained nationals including a student-pastor, several evangelists, a school teacher, a multigraph operator, and a competent male nurse.

Bongolo station is strategically located. The principal language used there is that of the Bandjavi tribe, but the station borders on three other major tribes. From Bongolo, first contacts were also made with the furtive Pygmies. To encourage their visits to the station, a Pygmy house was built and reserved for the entertainment of the little people of the forest. Whenever they came, services were held twice daily for them, and they responded to the message. Today there are Pygmy members in the Gabon church, and others are awaiting baptism so that they, too, may become members.

Ileka By 1942 the missionary staff had increased so that it was possible to take the first step in lengthening the cords of the work. In June of that year the missionary couple who had been studying the language of the Bapounou people made a survey trip into the heart of that tribe and received a warm welcome. In March, 1943, a centrally located area in a densely populated district was selected as the best site from which to reach the Bapounou people and several other surrounding tribes. The name given to the station was Yileka yiMonyu, meaning "Spring of Life." The Lord put His seal on this venture of faith from the very beginning. Each Sunday four evangelistic bands reached some thirty surrounding villages with the Gospel. After hearing the simple message only two or three times, the highest chief of that area stood before his people and made an avowal of his decision to accept this true light no matter what others might decide to do. A few months later he lay on his deathbed, and again he denounced the old life of sin and fetish worship and urged his people to accept Christ as their Savior. A national trader also made his decision to follow Christ, and left his trading in order to carry the Gospel to another tribe.

During the absence of the missionary couple on furlough, Paul N'Doba, a gifted national worker, and his faithful wife, Lois, carried on the work alone for almost two years. By 1947 the first permanent brick dwelling was built and occupied, and a primary school was being conducted; the foundation had been laid for a brick church; nine full-time national workers and one lay worker were located in the district; and five young men had gone to the central Bible School.

Mouyanama Although by 1946 Bongolo and Ileka were well established centers among the Bandjavi and Bapounou tribes, respectively, only a few scattered villages of the Massango tribe had been reached. Those were Massango villages located near Bongolo. The Massango to the north were largely unreached. A station site was chosen among them from which four paths radiate to all parts of the Massango district. This site is the highest of any of our stations, with an elevation of 2,000 feet. The terrain is heavily wooded and mountainous, with an abundance of crystal-clear streams, one of which falls over a seventy-five foot rocky precipice on the mission site, and then continues in a series of rapids between banks lined with rare and majestic tree ferns. The waterfall is called Mouyanama, the name meaning "Wide Open" and the spot was revered as a place of fetish worship. After the Mission chose this as a station site, the village elders came with offerings of food for their ancestors, the water spirits, and they then removed the fetishes which they had hidden in a small cave at the foot of the falls. *Wide Open Falls* is still an appropriate name for the place, for now God's Word is open there for all who would seek salvation, and there have been numerous professions of faith.

Plans were made to open a primary school on this station in September, 1948. Bricks are being burned for a permanent church building to replace the present bark building. There is a small dispensary and a temporary house for the missionaries, built native-fashion by plastering with clay the network of poles and vines which form the walls.

Guévédé This station is located among the Mitsogo, a tribe of fanatical fetishists and devil dancers. They are considered to be the most zealously devoted to heathen rites and customs of any people in this area. Through contacts made by missionaries, a group of the Mitsogo tribespeople came to live and work at Bongolo, and a number of them were converted. Although during the past years no missionaries were assigned to this people, yet itineraries were made among them and native evangelists were sent to witness to them. One evangelist suffered imprisonment and stripes because of his faithfulness to God in that area.

This station among the Mitsogo was opened in May, 1948. A tamped-earth chapel and missionary residence have been completed, but more encouraging is the fact that souls have already been won for Christ. In times past both men and women have been killed for exposing the rites of the secret societies but, nevertheless, the new believers have boldly exposed the ruses, sham and dark devices of the old heathen practices.

Lénguébé In the summer of 1947 our missionaries made the first contact with the distant Koula-Moutou area. Since that time persistent calls have come from some of the important nationals of the territory, urging the missionaries to come and give the Word of God to them. After several survey trips had been made, the conference of June, 1948, voted that a missionary couple be appointed to open a station in this large untouched area, and they took up residence there the following October. Already a number of temporary buildings have been erected and the surrounding district, within an eight or ten-mile radius, has been covered by evangelistic bands. Numerous conversions have been reported.

To reach their new home and open this station of mercy for those in darkness (Lénguébé means "mercy"), the missionaries were obliged to travel five hours by truck over mountainous roads, and four or five days more by foot-trails over more mountains. A new road, soon to be opened, will make it possible to do two days of the journey by auto. This area with a total population of 100,000 includes 15 tribes, all of whom can be reached through the language of the Bandjavi tribe. The Bandjavi church of the Bongolo district has caught the vision of the need of this virgin territory and is sending one student-pastor and four teacher-evangelists to aid in the missionary task.

Mousamou Ever since the opening of the Gabon field, Paul N'Doba has been praying for a mission station to be opened among his own tribespeople. He is an Echira young man, one of three given to our Mission by the Paris Evangelical Mission in 1934 when we came to share with them the task of evangelizing the Gabon. Paul N'Doba has been an outstanding teacher-evangelist for a number of years. His prayers began to be answered when, in 1947, it was voted to assign a missionary couple to the Echira work. Survey trips were made and a station site near a road leading into the interior was chosen and official request has been made for the land. Missionary furloughs have delayed occupation but it is hoped that this station will have a resident missionary by 1950. The name Mousamou means "news." May the Good News soon reach every Echira heart.

Mouila The field conference of 1949 voted to open a seventh station near the main government post of Mouila, among the Bapounou people. A missionary couple has been appointed to this new post, which involves new problems and methods of work. Most of the other stations in Gabon are located at some distance from so-called civilization, but at Mouila are a hospital, government school, and motor roads giving access to a large number of villages. Huge crowds visit the local market weekly; the hospital offers possibilities for visitation; and native children in the government school offer definite opportunities for evangelistic effort.

Translation and Publication Work

The Scripture portions in permanent form are the Gospel of John and the book of Acts, in the Yipounou language, printed by the American Bible Society. The Bible Society lists these translations as being useful to 100,000 people. Also available in Yipounou, in multigraphed or mimeographed form, are Matthew, Mark, James, and brief portions of some Old Testament Scriptures.

Matthew, Luke and John are available in Yissango; Mark, Acts, James, and a summary of Paul's life are available in Yindjavi; Luke and the first epistle of John are translated in Getsogo. The goal of the next few years is to have a complete translation of the New Testament in Yipounou and Yindjavi.

Schools and Literacy Campaigns

A Bible school is conducted at Bongolo with 23 students in attendance (1948). Farming and vocational training are also given to these candidates for future Christian service. The statistical report for 1948 listed three primary schools on the field, with a total enrollment of 248, and three literacy schools with an enrollment of 130. One hundred attended the two short-term Bible schools. School work is being carried on in four languages: Yindjavi, Yipounou, Yissango and Getsogo. Bible study is a part of the daily school program.

The Church and the Challenge

There are no unoccupied areas in the Gabon field so long as the missionary staff remains large enough to carry out the present program. There are 27 church centers and 120 out-stations (1948 report). There are 40 full-time national workers, and four associate pastors were appointed by the 1948 conference with a view to ordaining them within a year or so.

Besides evangelism the task includes the translation of the Scriptures into the major languages, through which the many small tribes can be reached also. Illiterate Christians must be taught to read and must be built up in the faith. The Gabon churches, of which there were three organized and two unorganized in 1948, must be guided into a program of self-government in order that they may be able to face wisely the political situation of this postwar era when nationals, newly given the right of citizenship, are looking forward to political independence. With 600 baptized church members and 722 inquirers, the Gabon church, national and missionary, is pressing forward and trusting God to enable them to fulfill their entire responsibility to more than 200,000 souls.

(Photo by courtesy of American Bible Society)

Reading the Life-giving Word in Africa

INDO-CHINA

In the cockpit of Southeast Asia lie the Federation of Indo-China (French Indo-China) and the country of Siam. They occupy the greater part of a vast peninsula hanging on the southeastern tip of the continent. Indo-China is south of China and east of Burma and Siam. Siam occupies the central portion of the Indo-Chinese peninsula and a considerable portion of the Malay peninsula. Tonkin, Annam, Cochin-China, Laos and Cambodia, the five Associated States of Indo-China, represent four distinct mission fields: namely, Viet-Nam, Laos, Cambodia and the Tribes. Siam is an entirely separate field.

The name Indo-China is a geographical term. The country is neither India nor China but it has been influenced by both of them. On the north, Indo-China touches the three Chinese provinces of Yunnan, Kwangsi and Kwantung; on the east and south it borders the Gulf of Tonkin, the South China Sea and the Gulf of Siam; Siam and Burma bound it on the west.

Area and Population

Indo-China's area of 280,849 square miles is only a little larger than the State of Texas in the U. S. A. or the province of Alberta in Canada, yet Indo-China's population is more than twice that of all of Canada. The population includes about 43,000 Europeans, mostly French, and about 300,000 Chinese, including those of mixed blood. The Annamese, or Vietnamese, who predominate throughout Viet-Nam, make up about two-thirds of the total population of Indo-China. The following shows the area and population of the five Associated States comprising the Federation of Indo-China in the French Union:

State		Area		Population
Tonkin		40,530 sq. mi.		9,851,200
Annam	Viet-Nam .	56,973 " "		7,183,500
Cochin-China		26,476 " "		5,579,000
Cambodia		67,550 " "		3,527,000
Laos		89,320 " "		1,189,000
		280,849		27,329,700

People and History

As early as 2537 B. C. Chinese annals make mention of the "Giao-Chi," a name signifying "separated big toe." Some historians believe that the Annamese descended from this Mongolian tribe, which came from southern China and occupied the territory now known as Tonkin. For twenty centuries they were governed under the suzerainty of China. About 200 B. C. a Chinese emperor, coveting the rich province of Annam, sent a force of half a million men to conquer the country, which was thereafter ruled by Chinese governors until about 900 A. D., when the Annamese began to shake off the yoke. Annam did not win complete independence, however, until the 15th century. The Annamese, who either took their name from or gave it to the State of Annam, are not Chinese but they do show Chinese influence. They eat with chopsticks; both men and women wear trousers; they are ancestor-worshipers; their system of writing was based on Chinese characters.

The kingdom of another tribe, the Cham people, was strong and independent and occupied the territory between Hué in Annam and Saigon in Cochin-China. The Cham race is a cross between the Cambodian and the Malay. Imposing Cham towers still standing in various parts of Annam testify to their architectural ability. For centuries there was a struggle between the Chams and the Annamese, but the Chams were conquered completely by about the 17th century A. D. From that time on the Chams disappear from history except for a few isolated groups found here and there through the country. It is estimated that there are between 20,000 and 30,000 Chams still living near Nhatrang, and about 40,000 more scattered throughout Cambodia.

The history of the Cambodians goes back to the Mon-Khmer race. The Mon-Khmer people, as they are technically classified by ethnologists, migrated eastward from India, subduing all the more primitive peoples of Southeast Asia, and establishing a vast empire which endured for centuries. The ancient Khmer Empire once included not only what is today Cambodia but also the whole of Cochin-China and large areas in southern, central and eastern Siam. It was called the Kingdom of Cambochea and embraced a population of upwards of 60 million people. The capital city of Angkor, judging by the area included within the great wall surrounding it, could easily have contained a million inhabitants. All their early kings, inspired with the genius of Brahman culture, assumed distinctly Hindu names upon their ascension to the throne. King Bravavarman is credited with having built some of the most wonderful of the world-renowned temples and palaces of Angkor. In the twelfth and thirteenth centuries the once powerful Cambodian Empire began to suffer reverses as a result of the twin migration of the Thai (Siamese) and Annamese peoples. Caught by this pincer movement, the Cambodians lost territory and were gradually driven back. But for the timely arrival of the French, who took them under their protection, their once mighty nation would have been completely assimilated by their assailants. Since the decline of Cambodia, the people have lost much of their ancient skill and initiative. This is largely due to the deadening effects of six or seven centuries of Buddhism, to which religion the Cambodians have long been strongly attached. Of a total of four and one-half million Cambodians, today only about three and one-half million actually live in Cambodia; the others are to be found still living in Cochin-China and Siam. At Angkor in Cambodia, with its ruins of massive temples "grander than anything left to us by Greece or Rome," one sees the relic of an ancient and great civilization.

While the more powerful races were extending their conquests throughout Indo-China, vast numbers of aboriginal tribespeople were gradually being driven back into the mountains and jungles. The Annamese, the dominant race of Tonkin, Annam and Cochin-China, as well as the Cambodians, and the Thai people of Siam and Laos took possession of the great coastal plains, the deltas of the large rivers, and the fertile valleys farther inland. Back into the higher altitudes, into the more remote jungles, were crowded the aboriginal tribes. These primitive groups speak more than a hundred languages and dialects in which there is no system of writing. Little is known of their origin. Some of them are believed to be of the same stock as the aborigines of the South Seas and Borneo, but the northern tribes are of either Mongol or Thai origin.

In 1760 the great revolution broke out in Annam. One of the princes sought refuge in Bangkok, Siam, where he appealed to the Catholic Bishop to obtain the aid of France in helping to establish him in his kingdom. This was the beginning of French ascendancy throughout all of what is now Indo-China. Cambodia sought the help of France against Siam in 1863, and became a French protectorate. In 1894 Siam recognized French sovereignty over eastern Laos.

Among the Annamese, the nationalist movement known as the Viet Minh began in 1941 and gained impetus during World War II. The most active element in this movement was the Indo-Chinese Communist party. When the Japanese invaded the country the nationalists stood with them, and when the Nipponese were defeated and obliged to leave Indo-China, they strongly urged the Annamese to continue their struggle for independence from European control. Fierce fighting and much bloodshed continued between the Annamese and the French in the three States of Tonkin, Annam and Cochin-China, which are almost entirely occupied by the Annamese, or Vietnamese, as they now prefer to be called. The Vietnamese fought for the union and independence of the three states above mentioned, that they might form the Republic of Viet-Nam, which was the ancient name of their country. France recognized the Viet-Nam Republic on March 7, 1946, as a "free state within the Indo-Chinese Federation and French Union." On February 4, 1947, Cochin-China was proclaimed a free republican state, giving it a status different from that of Tonkin and Annam.

After many political vicissitudes, there was set up on June 4, 1949, a new Provisional Government of the Republic of Viet-Nam. On June 23rd, the Provisional Government of Cochin-China ceased to exist, thus confirming the union of Cochin-China with the State of Viet-Nam under the new regime. The members of the present Vietnamese Government include His Majesty Bao Dai, formerly King of Annam, as Chief of State and President of the Government; and General Nguyen Van Xuan as Vice-President and the Minister of National Defense. On July 2nd from his residence at Dalat, the Emperor Bao Dai announced the formation of his Government and in the course of his proclamation said: "As soon as the people can freely express its will, the March 8th (1949) Agreements, signed in Paris, will be subjected to the constitutional processes and the people shall freely determine the political statute of the State."

The tribespeople have not been involved in the political turmoil and conditions are peaceful in their areas. Conditions are quiet in Laos also. Peace was restored in Cambodia when the French government reached an amicable agreement with the King. However, an Independence Movement known as the Issarak Party has been gaining in influence, bringing considerable unrest and insecurity to the border provinces in both the west and the east.

Government

The Federation of Indo-China within the French Union is composed of the five Associated States of Tonkin, Annam, Cochin-China, Cambodia and Laos. There is a French High Commissioner (*Haut-Commissaire*) for the entire country, and French Commissioners for Cambodia and Laos respectively. Tonkin, Annam and Cochin-China, the three states composing the Republic of Viet-Nam, now have a new all-Vietnamese Cabinet, and practically all the administrative posts of the republic are now handled by the Vietnamese themselves, with the French acting more in the capacity of advisors. If Viet-Nam decides to adopt the principles laid down in the Agreements signed in Paris by Emperor Bao Dai on March 8, 1949, then "the Vietnamese people, after all the necessary preparations on a pacified and organized territory, will choose, by their sovereign will, their constitutional regime, political institutions and government." Meanwhile the Bao Dai Government will be responsible for drafting the text of the "Organic Charter," which will serve as the provisional constitution of the country.

Laos was recognized in 1948 as an independent state with His Majesty SiSavang Vong as titular head of all eight prov-inces. Thus Laos became an Associated State in the French Union, having its own cabinet working with the French Commissioner and his group of technical advisors.

The independence of Cambodia, long a French Protectorate, was recognized in 1948, and now this nation also is an Associate Member of the French Union with French technicians as advisors. Since the war the young King Siahnouk Monivong has given his people a democratic constitution. While clearly stating that Buddhism is the state religion of Cambodia, this constitution grants religious liberty and freedom of speech and press. Hitherto a royal edict had forbidden Christians to proselytize among Cambodians. The government has now given authorization to evangelize, to build churches and to establish Bible schools throughout the land.

Climate

Lying within the tropics, most of Indo-China, especially along the seashore and in the valleys, has a hot, damp climate so enervating that it is important for the missionaries to spend a brief time each year, if possible, at some hill station like Dalat. Here, as in other mountain regions, the weather is invigorating. In Tonkin the rainy season comes during June, July and August. In Annam it comes during October, November and December. In Cochin-China and Cambodia the rains come from June to October, and the climate is more equable than in the other provinces, the temperature averaging 80 degrees the year round.

Physical Features

Most of Tonkin consists of forest-covered mountain regions inhabited principally by various aboriginal tribes. One-sixth of the area is a delta formed by the branches of the Red River and the Thai-binh. Here and in Cochin-China, with its low-lying lands, watered by the many mouths of the Mekong River, are the rich delta lands which are among the best rice producing regions in the world. In these fertile regions and along the coast of Annam live the Vietnamese, formerly called Annamese. The western boundary of Annam is a chain of mountains and plateaus, the home of many primitive tribes. Laos is made up mostly of mountainous areas with vast forests and torrential rivers. The Mekong River, which rises far to the north in western China, forms the western boundary of Laos and flows south through Cambodia and Cochin-China, a total distance of 2,600 miles before it empties into the South China Sea. Cambodia for the most part is a level, well-watered country. In the northern part of Cambodia are the ruins of Angkor, a mecca for tourists from many parts of the world. In the wilder mountainous regions of Indo-China, elephants, tigers and other wild animals are numerous. About two-fifths of the total area of Indo-China is forested.

Resources

The chief exports are rice, rubber, fish, coal, lumber, pepper, cattle and hides, corn, zinc and tin. The chief product is rice, which is grown on irrigated lands which must be flooded during most of the growing season. Ingenious contrivances, some mechanical, others hand-operated, lift the water from streams and canals and empty it into the rice fields, which are surrounded by dykes.

The chief minerals are iron, tungsten and manganese, but also include phosphates, chrome, graphite and lead, besides those mentioned among the exports above. The forests supply rare hard woods, including teak; also dye-woods, bamboo, rubber, coconuts and medicinal plants. Sugar, tea, cotton, spices, maize, coffee, tobacco, vegetables and fruits are grown. Silk is produced in some Annamese homes through its entire process from the feeding of the silk worms to the weaving of the cloth. However, much of the cotton and silk cloth is imported, as are also metal articles, kerosene and automobiles.

Progress

Under French influence an excellent school system, from primary schools to colleges, has been established principally among the Vietnamese, whose language has been Romanized, the Latin alphabet displacing the old system of phonetics which was based on Chinese characters. In 1944 there were almost one million pupils in school, representing about 35 per cent of the population of school age. The number of school books published by the Board of Education in native languages is over 10 million.

The French government has built an excellent system of colonial highways, besides local or secondary roads, opening up a large part of the country to auto travel. One may travel on good motor roads from Haiphong, a seaport in Tonkin, south through Annam, and across Cochin-China and Cambodia, a distance of about 1,500 miles. Autobuses operate throughout the country on all suitable roads. Over 1,800 miles of railways have been in use since 1936. Hanoi, Haiphong, Tourane and Saigon are the principal terminals. More than 1,100 post offices have been established; telephone and telegraph lines connect most sections of the country. In the principal cities where French officials reside there are good hospitals, electric lighting and ice plants. Saigon, the Paris of the east and the capital of Cochin-China, has a population of close to one million.

At the beginning of World War II weekly air service for passengers and mail was being carried on between Indo-China and France from the airports of Saigon, Hanoi and Vientiane. Dutch, English and Eurasian air companies also called at Indo-China and provided connections with Singapore, Indonesia, China and other parts of the Orient. At the present time (1949) Air France maintains regular, direct service between France and Indo-China. Air France and the Siamese Air Lines alternate in weekly service between Bangkok, Pnom Penh and Saigon. Air France also maintains regular, scheduled air service between the principal cities of Indo-China and also to Hongkong. The cities of Haiphong and Saigon are principal ports of call for several steamship lines, especially French, and coastwise steamers also ply between Saigon, Tourane, Haiphong and other ports.

Currency

In 1930 the piaster was legally established on a gold basis, 10 francs (French) equalling one piaster. Today (1949) one piaster is worth five cents in U. S. currency.

Languages and Tribes

The Vietnamese (Annamese) language is the native tongue of from 16 to 20 million people in Tonkin, Annam and Cochin-China. Cambodian is spoken by about three and a half million people in Cambodia alone. The Lao dialect of the Thai language, spoken in Laos, is next in importance, although two distinct languages, Cambodian and Laotian are both of Sanskrit origin. French is used throughout the country by the educated people in business and in government offices.

In addition to the three principal language groups there are many tribal languages. In fact one survey claims that there are 160 languages and dialects in Indo-China, but no one knows exactly how many tribal people there are, nor how many languages they speak. Some of the tribes have similarities of language and customs, yet show enough difference to be listed as separate tribes. There may be two million tribespeople in Indo-China. The more primitive groups of the jungle, sometimes referred to as the loin-cloth tribesmen, number a million or more, and are scattered through the vast interior of Indo-China, mostly in the mountains and high plateau regions. In northern Indo-China are the more civilized tribes of Mongol or Thai origin, among them the Black Thai, Meo, Tho, Muong, Man and others who number approximately another million. No accurate survey has been made in the north. A few of the tribes in Laos are advanced in art. The Cham tribe, with a language of Sanskrit origin, is one of the most civilized. The Vietnamese call all the primitive peoples "Moi," meaning "savage." The Laotians call them all "Kha." The tangle of life and languages among the tribes has baffled both ethnologists and linguists. The following languages were being used to present the gospel in 1949. It is expected that several more of the primitive dialects will shortly be employed.

Used by Missionaries	Additional Languages Used Only by National Workers	
French	Chinese	
Vietnamese (Annamese)	Cham	
Laotian		
Cambodian	*Primitive Dialects*	
Thai	Tho	Khamoo
	Katu	Mnong Preh
Primitive Dialects	Krung	Mnong Gar
Raday	Bahnar	
Jarai	Hdrung	
Pnong	KhaMhu	
Chil	Sre	
Koho	Mnong Budang	

Religions

A vertical line drawn down the map of Indo-China from northwest to southeast will divide the country into two great zones which show decided differences from cultural and religious standpoints. The eastern zone is made up chiefly of the Vietnamese. They are wide-awake, enthusiastic, quick to respond to foreign ideas and to the gospel. The western zone, which includes Laos and Cambodia, although it comprises races with different languages, still has some unifying factors, of which Buddhism is chief. Here the response to the gospel has been much slower. The imaginary line dividing these two zones runs through the mountain regions where the tribespeople dwell. They are distinct. Animists as were their ancestors, they have remained largely unmoved either by Buddhism or by the Chinese and European influences that have left their mark on the Vietnamese.

The Vietnamese are to some extent nominally Buddhist but are actually not religiously inclined. The temples are not kept up; the people give little attention to religion except during festivals and then it is a matter of feasting rather than of worship. All the Vietnamese have one cult in common— ancestor-worship. This is a result of Confucianism imported from China in ancient days. (See *Confucianism*, under China, *Religions*.) The Vietnamese are animists also to an extent. They believe that all affliction comes because they have displeased the evil spirits or the spirits of the dead, and sacrifices are made to appease them.

The "Nam Giao" religion is perhaps the most purely native of any in Indo-China. Its origin is too ancient to be traced but it is similar to the ceremony which the ancient emperors of China used to perform at Pekin. Once every three years the King of Annam makes a burnt offering of bullocks to the God of Heaven, whom they recognize as the Supreme Being. Only the emperor may approach Him and he makes the sacrifice as the representative of his people. Missionaries have sometimes been able to explain the gospel to the people by starting with "Nam Giao" and pointing the way to the true God whom the Vietnamese acknowledge but do not know.

Within the last twenty years a new religion has appeared and gained more than a million followers. A French-trained Annamese (Vietnamese) introduced it, and called it "Cao-Dai-ism," or the religion of the Most High. Its distinguishing symbol is an eye, placed above an altar and watching over images of other religions, placed on the altar. Not only images of the heathen religions are there, but an image of the Virgin Mary, and one of Jesus Christ. Cao-Dai-ism teaches that all other religions are stepping-stones leading to the worship of the Most High God. It is made easy for anyone to follow this cult no matter what his previous affiliations may have been. The idea is stressed that this is no imported religion but one that is purely Vietnamese. Strongly nationalistic, the cult seems to be more of a political movement than a religion.

The Cambodians are bigoted Buddhists and the Laotians are even more so. By teaching that desire is sin, Buddhism has to a great extent brought its followers "to the place where they do not want to have anything, to be anything, to know anything, or to get anywhere." In the countries blanketed for centuries by this deadening religion, the people of various regions may show greater or less indifference to the gospel, but there are times when their indifference approaches the absolute. The King of Cambodia is the High Priest of Buddhism for his country. The education of the people is largely committed to the Buddhist priests. At least one son from every Buddhist family becomes a priest. (See *Buddhism*, under India, *Religions*.)

The animist tribespeople make much of blood sacrifices to appease the spirits. Sorcerers are called in to reveal which kind of animal the spirits are demanding on a certain occasion. The animals which may be sacrificed vary in the different tribes. Some tribes sacrifice any domestic animal except cats, dogs, horses and elephants. The Hdrung tribe will sacrifice horses, and the Radays may sacrifice dogs. Once a year they make a village sacrifice to the "Grandfather of the Skies," to his wife and to the devil. To them God is simply one more spirit, and not necessarily all-powerful. They give little thought to a future life. After death a female spirit is believed to nourish the soul for a time, and then after a final sacrifice has been made, they believe that the grave is abandoned and no one knows what happens after that. Superstitions abound to enthrall the people, and countless taboos hamper their every act. Fetish worship, as the animists in Africa practice it, is little known among these tribes. Some of them have a small fetish stone which is thought to be inhabited by a spirit. A block of wood may be placed under a tree which is said to be inhabited by a spirit, and the spirit of the tree may be honored in minor ways, but no sacrifices are offered to it. (See *Animism*, under Africa, *Religions*.)

Jesuit missionaries reached Annam as early as the 17th century, and the emperor and many of his subjects were counted among the converts to Catholicism. Later rulers were not so favorable to the new religion but the Roman Catholic Church is strong today throughout Viet-Nam.

The International Review of Missions, January, 1949, issue, gives the following information on Indo-China: "There are two million Roman Catholics and under 10,000 Protestants, these latter served almost entirely by The Christian and Missionary Alliance, which has a valiant record of work covering the last 25 years."

However, reports direct from the field list 14,000 active members in the national churches of the Alliance at the close of 1948.

Missionary Occupation

There are French Protestant churches in a few of the larger cities of Indo-China. The Roman Catholics have several hundred foreign priests and nuns throughout the country besides many national priests. The Christian and Missionary Alliance is the only evangelical missionary agency primarily responsible for the evangelization of all Indo-China, with the exception of southern Laos, where the Swiss Brethren Mission has been working since 1902, with three stations in the region of Savannaket. They have made preaching trips and done colportage work in the northern part of the colony, but their work has been chiefly confined to the south, where they have a group of several hundred Christians scattered through the country. The Swiss missionaries have translated the Bible into the Lao language, the New Testament having been printed in 1926 and the entire Bible in 1932.

Early workers of the North Siam Mission of the Presbyterian Church made trips through the kingdom of Luang Prabang with such good results that there are now several hundred believers among the Kha people of Laos. Several years ago, however, the Presbyterian Mission in Siam turned over to the Christian and Missionary Alliance this large field in northern Laos, as they had no main station there, only one national pastor. The Siamese Church, however, continues to have some ministry among the Khas.

Seventh Day Adventists entered parts of Indo-China and were proselytizing among the Christians before the recent war. After the war, through their reconstruction work, they gained a foothold near Dalat, on a plantation where there was a Christian chapel. The Adventists are also in Saigon and Tourane.

The Christian and Missionary Alliance

As early as 1887 Dr. A. B. Simpson wrote: "The southeastern peninsula of Asia has been much neglected. The great kingdom of Annam should be occupied for Christ." In 1893 Rev. David Lelacheur, who was closely associated with Dr. Simpson in the beginning of the Alliance work, visited Saigon and reported to Dr. Simpson later that the door was open in Annam, as all of Indo-China was then called. In his report of 1895-96, Dr. Simpson said, in speaking of the work in Kwangsi, South China: "Mr. and Mrs. R. have recently made a trip up the entire length of the West River, and have succeeded in crossing over into the province of Tonkin, part of Annam, and plans are now under consideration for opening, in connection with our South China Mission, a work in that great adjacent empire of Annam where there is not a single Protestant missionary among all its 22,000,000."

Alliance missionaries in South China continued to feel the call of God to open work in French Indo-China. In 1905 when the station of Lung Chow was opened in South China, it was hoped that this might be the gateway from which the Gospel could be carried across the border into Tonkin. But it was impracticable. The French were naturally more suspicious of such a back-door entrance, and it proved to be wiser to enter by one of the large port cities of Indo-China.

Three missionaries from South China entered the port of Tourane in 1911, and purchased our present mission property there. The property was owned by a Frenchman, an agent of the British and Foreign Bible Society. Our missionaries succeeded the Bible Society agent, fell heir to the good will he had won for the gospel in Tourane, and were able to open that year the first Protestant mission station in the Annamese section of French Indo-China.

In 1915 our missionaries entered two new stations: Faifoo near Tourane, and Haiphong, the principal seaport of Tonkin. It was planned also to enter Hanoi, the capital of Tonkin,

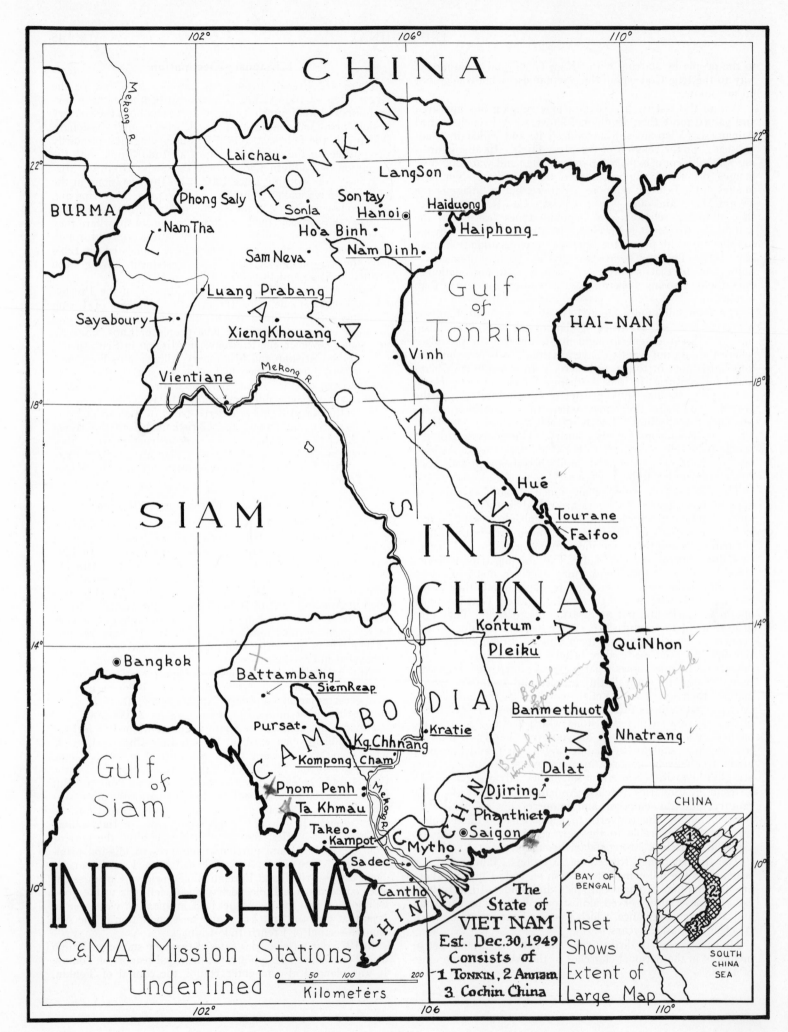

CHINA

Mekong R.

BURMA

Laichau.

TONKIN

LangSon.

Phong Saly

Son la

Son tay

Haiduong

NamTha

Hanoi

Haiphong

Hoa Binh

Sam Neva

Nam Dinh.

Gulf of Tonkin

Luang Prabang

HAI-NAN

Sayaboury

XiengKhouang

Vientiane

Mekong R.

Vinh

SIAM

Hué

Tourane

Faifoo

INDO

CHINA

Kontum

Bangkok

Pleiku

QuiNhon

Battambang

SiemReap

Banmethuot

CAMBODIA

Pursat

Kratie

Nhatrang

Kg.Chhnang

Kompong Cham

Dalat

Gulf of Siam

Pnom Penh

Djiring

Ta Khmau

Phanthiet

Takeo.

Kampot

Mytho

Saigon

Sadec

Cantho

INDO-CHINA

C&MA Mission Stations
Underlined

50 100 200
Kilometers

The
State of
VIET NAM
Est. Dec.30, 1949
Consists of
1 Tonkin, 2 Annam
3. Cochin China

Inset
Shows
Extent of
Large Map

CHINA

BAY OF
BENGAL

SOUTH
CHINA
SEA

46

and of all Indo-China, but the first World War was on and all foreigners were being closely watched. The French government became jittery and in 1915 issued a decree prohibiting any further work among the natives. Five out of our force of nine missionaries were permitted to remain and live in Tourane, Haiphong and Hanoi, but they were not allowed to do any active missionary work.

In 1916, Rev. R. A. Jaffray again visited Indo-China, had an interview with the Governor-General and much of the misunderstanding regarding missionaries was cleared up. Official authorization was obtained for our Mission to work in the parts of the country that were considered French colonies. That included the cities of Haiphong, Hanoi, Tourane, and the state of Cochin-China and southern Laos. In the fall of 1916 a missionary couple opened work in Hanoi; a printing press was purchased for that station, and the task of translating and printing the Scriptures in the Romanized Annamese script went steadily on. The British and Foreign Bible Society appointed a sub-agent for Indo-China and promised hearty coöperation in publishing and circulating the Scriptures. In January, 1917, Indo-China reports told of eighteen baptisms, bringing the native church membership up to twenty-five. From that time on the work has continued to grow, and new stations have been opened in each of the five states of Indo-China and also in eastern Siam. For many years, however, the states of Tonkin and Annam, which were Protectorates and not French Colonies, were closed to missionary residence except for the cities of Hanoi, Haiphong and Tourane, which were considered to be French possessions. In 1923 Faifoo was reopened, but not until late in 1927 were missionaries permitted to labor in any other cities of those two great states. From 1927 on, increasing freedom was granted to work in many more provinces of Tonkin and Annam. The state of Cochin-China was a French Colony and therefore the government could grant more freedom there. After the Mission entered the city of Saigon in 1918, the government granted permission to reside and minister in many of the provinces of Cochin-China.

The promising work of the entire field had a severe blow with the coming of World War II, and the invasion and occupation of Indo-China by the Japanese. Some of the missionaries were evacuated, others were interned, not to be released until after Japan was defeated. Most of the released internees then returned to America to recuperate. For ten months one lone missionary in the country carried on as the sole administrator for the society, and the only missionary counsellor for the distressed national church.

As soon as possible after the close of the war, missionaries began to return to the field. They found scenes of desolation and ruin throughout Viet-Nam especially. Although not one piece of mission property was actually destroyed, nearly all had been looted and every building required extensive repairs. The damage to property was nothing in comparison with what the national church had suffered. Some pastors and many Christians were martyred. Of those who were spared many were left destitute, sick and afraid. Travel was unsafe through Viet-Nam except by airplane or convoy, and even convoys were sometimes attacked and destroyed. Nevertheless, in spite of the continued guerrilla warfare, missionaries had been able to reoccupy many of the pre-war stations in the three Viet-Nam states. Missionaries to the tribespeople in South-Central Annam were able to fly in to occupy their posts. Missionaries have also resumed work in the more peaceful countries of Cambodia and Laos. Gradually the great task of rehabilitation is being carried out. Shipments of clothing have been sent from America to help the destitute Christians. Slowly the scenes of desolation are changing for the better and thousands of evacuees are returning to the cities.

The Christian and Missionary Alliance today has more missionaries working in French territories in Africa and Indo-China than any other one Protestant missionary society. We are responsible for four distinct mission fields in Indo-China: namely, Viet-Nam, Cambodia, Laos, and the Tribes fields. Over the work there is a Field Chairman and six regional sub-chairmen. Our missionaries call Indo-China six fields in one, and truly the three states comprising Viet-Nam —Tonkin, Annam, Cochin-China, and the other three sections—Cambodia, Laos and the Tribes in Southern Annam— each form a mission field of great responsibility and promising opportunities.

VIET-NAM

Annam

Annam has a total population of 7,183,500. The first station opened by the Alliance in Indo-China was in Annam, which is the largest of the three Viet-Nam States. The blessing of God on the work was manifest, but government restrictions hindered the missionaries from opening any other stations in this state. Annamese evangelists, however, went into many parts of Annam but endured persecution. Annam had its Philippian jail, for sometimes the Christians were arrested on false charges, or for preaching without government permission. The adverse interpretation of an old treaty forbade gospel work in many sections. In 1929 the tide turned. Instead of bitter antagonism to the gospel on the part of officials, and in the place of strong edicts prohibiting Protestant propaganda in various places, official authorizations were granted giving the missionaries freedom to reside and labor in many different parts of Annam.

Tourane Alliance missionaries entered Tourane in 1911. A tiny thatched chapel was built in 1913 and two years later a living church was organized. By the end of 1934 there were 34 church groups throughout Annam, including 16 organized churches, of which 12 were self-supporting and self-governing. The gospel spread to many other towns, and although the work in the Tourane district passed through much persecution especially prior to 1930, yet this district has furnished a large number of the preachers in the Annamese work.

In 1921 a great step forward was taken when the Annamese Bible School was established in Tourane for the training of Annamese Christians from Tonkin, Annam and Cochin-China. From 1930 to the outbreak of World War II, the school enrollment averaged approximately 100. When Indo-China was occupied by the Japanese, and while the missionaries were interned, Christian leaders kept the Tourane property in excellent condition. However, in December, 1946, the national Christians, too, were forced to evacuate, everything was looted, and the property was occupied by troops.

When the missionaries were finally able to return to Tourane, they were heartily welcomed by the Vietnamese Christians. However, war, hunger, fear, had left its mark upon them. Some were in rags and their emaciated bodies were covered with sores. Nearly all were suffering from malaria. Now most of the Christians have returned to the city from their involuntary exile and are gradually getting back to normal living. The homes of many had been burned. Temporary housing was provided for them in the Tourane Bible School dormitories. Church services, Sunday school and young people's services were resumed with excellent attendance. Evening services were not permitted but evangelistic services were held Sunday afternoons, with souls saved at each service. In 1948 in spite of political turmoil and exorbitant living costs, the Bible School was reopened with 35 students. In September, 1949, the new term began with about 50 students in attendance. There are serious difficulties in the work, one being the great scarcity of rice and its excessively high price. In May, 1949, 100 kilograms of rice cost 400 piasters. By the time school reopened, in September, the price had tripled to 1,200 piasters.

Hué This ancient city, long the seat of the Annamese Empire, is still a royal city. It was the residence of the King of Annam, Bao-Dai, until he abdicated in 1945, bowing to the wishes of the Viet-Nam Republic. Missionaries were not permitted to labor there until 1930. From then on until World War II, a missionary couple was in charge of the station and district. Not only the common people, but many in the royal court heard the gospel and were saved. The missionary had an audience with the young King Bao-Dai and left with him copies of the Scriptures in Annamese and French. After long search, the Mission learned late in 1949 of a house that could be secured for missionary residence and thus Hué will again become a center of missionary service.

Nhatrang Opened first as an outstation with an Annamese evangelist in charge, Nhatrang was occupied by a missionary couple in 1929. Intense opposition soon developed and the Annamese preacher was imprisoned for several months. The work in the district prospered and two vigorous self-supporting churches and four outstations were developed. Work was begun among the ancient Cham race, and some converts were won. This station also has been reopened since the war.

Dalat This hill station in southern Annam is about 4,500 feet above sea level. It was opened as a mission station in 1929, when a home and school for missionaries' children was established. There is now a strong, self-supporting Vietnamese church.

Dalat is the residence of the Field Chairman, the center where the Indo-China missionary conferences are held, and it also provides a rest home where missionaries may have an annual vacation with change of climate. Even in these days of internal warfare, Dalat is one of the most peaceful centers in the country. New missionaries are located here for language study before being sent to mission stations throughout the field. The school for missionaries' children has been reopened, accommodating not only the children of Indo-China, but those from Siam and some from Indonesia as well. The printing plant is being established at Dalat and the great work of publication will be carried on once more. Even before the printing presses could be put in operation, 60,000 sheets of mimeographed material were sent out monthly. These contain, in the Vietnamese language, translations of Dr. Simpson's writings and other valuable helps for Sunday school and church work, and for Christian instruction.

Tonkin

Tonkin, with a total population of 9,851,200, has within its boundaries over 30 provinces. In addition to the Vietnamese population, numbering about nine million, there are at least seven major tribes with populations of from 9,000 to over 300,000 each, among them the Black Thai, Meo, Tho, Nung, Man and Muong tribes. Smaller tribes bring the number of diverse peoples up to twenty. The major tribes are scattered through more than 20 provinces, in three of which, at Sonla, Hoabinh and Langson, the Alliance has had mission stations for work among the tribes.

Sonla Sonla, center for work among the Black Thai, will be reopened (D.V.) by the missionaries formerly working there, as soon as peace is restored to that section of Tonkin in a measure sufficient to permit missionary occupation and ministry.

Although most of the people of Tonkin are Vietnamese, their speech differs somewhat from that of the people of Annam and Cochin-China. Undoubtedly their characteristics and language are influenced by their proximity to China.

Tonkin was entered by Alliance missionaries in 1915, and the first station was opened in 1916. Many provinces in Tonkin are still unreached, but the Mission and the Vietnamese Evangelical Church of Indo-China are pressing forward into the unoccupied provinces as rapidly as government permission can be obtained and postwar conditions permit. At the close of 1948, there were unoccupied areas in Tonkin which included over 400,000 tribespeople and over 200,000 Vietnamese.

Hanoi This capital city and important commercial center was entered in 1916 as a mission station. For years the work grew slowly, for the government permitted no work outside the city in the surrounding areas. In 1924 more freedom was granted, permitting work to be begun in Tu-Nhien as an outstation. Succeeding years saw the work spread to many districts and to several provinces. One missionary, with the help of national workers, opened five street chapels in Hanoi, held regular Bible classes, and saw the work grow until thirty weekly services were being held in various parts of the city. A mission station was established at Sontay and outstations at Bac-Ninh, Hung-Yen, and Ha-Dong. The mission property, well located in the city of Hanoi, provided a missionary residence and a well equipped printing plant. From this plant all Indo-China was supplied with Bibles, tracts, religious books, magazines, hymnals and Sunday school literature, written or translated by our missionaries in various languages in which they were working. Near the mission property is the large church building and a house for the Annamese pastor. The Hanoi Church, though suffering greatly through the war and revolution, and with only thirty per cent of its regular members back from their enforced evacuation, is now fully self-supporting. The members made all necessary repairs at their own expense and are looking forward to opening at least one street chapel within the next few months.

The war disrupted the publication work completely. It is being re-established at Dalat, Annam, and a press, purchased in England, has reached the field. During most of 1949, three missionary couples have resided in Hanoi, one man being the Sub-Chairman for Tonkin. Two of the couples, new missionaries, have devoted themselves to language study.

Haiphong This important seaport and gateway to northern Indo-China has a population of over 65,000. Missionaries resided here for language study for a short time prior to 1916, but it was opened as a station in October, 1916, when the first meetings were held in a rented chapel. From 1917 to 1921 work there was carried on from Hanoi, but in 1921 missionaries again resided there and it continued as a regular mission station. From Haiphong the work spread to the towns of Kien-An, Ninh-Giang, Quang-Yen and Haiduong, which became outstations, some of them with organized churches. Since the war, a missionary couple has reopened Haiphong. The Vietnamese church and parsonage are being rebuilt, and a fruitful work is being carried on among both Vietnamese and Chinese. A missionary couple from South China is expected to reach Haiphong in January, 1950, for ministry among the Chinese in Haiphong and Hanoi.

Nam Dinh This city of some 50,000 in the southeastern part of Tonkin near the border of Annam, became a mission station in 1929. However, for several years before that time, the gospel had been preached by an Annamese evangelist and an earnest group of Christians was won for the Lord. Besides two organized churches, one at Nam Dinh and one at Ninh-Binh, there were outstations at Thai-Binh and Phy-Ly. A missionary couple is again occupying Nam Dinh since the close of the war.

Langson In earlier years Langson in the far northeast of Tonkin was an important and fruitful mission center first entered in December, 1929. However, because of the war raging between the Viet Minh and the French it has not yet been possible to reopen this important city as a mission station. It is hoped, however, that the many Christians of the Tho and Man tribes who were won to Christ before the war are continuing to faithfully serve Him and to witness to others of His saving and keeping power.

Sontay This city was occupied by a missionary couple before the war and the Mission hopes that soon it may be reopened to missionary residence and service. This is a strategic center in an area with a population of 280,000. There are over 100 Christians in this section. As soon as property for residence and chapel can be repaired the other new missionary couple from Hanoi will enter Sontay.

Haiduong This city and the province of the same name offer a vast opportunity for missionary service in a parish of 820,000 souls. Property has been secured for a mission residence and a chapel. The location is excellent and the living quarters will be probably the coolest in Tonkin as the house faces the river and the distant rice fields beyond. The Chef de Province (Vietnamese) has promised every necessary help to the new missionary couple from Hanoi assigned to Haiduong. A Vietnamese preacher arrested by the French and later released, then taken by the Viet Minh, is now able to return to his work in Haiduong to aid in the ministries in this field.

Cochin-China

The state of Cochin-China, with a population of 5,579,000, is the most highly developed and prosperous section of the entire country. Because Cochin-China was a Colony of France rather than a Protectorate, the government could grant more freedom to the missionaries living there. As a result this state was more widely evangelized at an earlier date than any other part of Indo-China. Some gospel witness has been given in each of the twenty provinces, and in many of them strong, self-supporting churches are the result. The work began in Saigon in 1919. Within a few years stations were opened in the principal cities of several provinces, hundreds of converts were won, and churches were established. After the work had grown sufficiently, it was possible to transfer some of the missionaries to needier sections in Annam and Tonkin, as rapidly as government permission was granted for the opening of new districts in those states. From 1922 to 1932 eight centers in Cochin-China were opened: Sadec, Chaudoc, Mytho, Vinhlong, Bienhoa, Long-Xuyen, Bac-lieu, and Thudaumot. In all of these places self-supporting churches were established with the exception of Chaudoc, which became an outstation of the Binh-Long church. By 1934 there were in Cochin-China 43 self-supporting churches with a total membership of over 4,900, and four other unorganized groups. The work of the missionaries in Cochin-China today is a spiritual ministry to the self-governing churches, giving them counsel and also aiding in the development of the work in sections not so well occupied.

4

Saigon This seaport city, capital of Cochin-China, is the seat of many departments of the French government. Multitudes of Vietnamese, and also many foreigners, chiefly French, make up its population of close to a million. Adjoining Saigon are the large Chinese city of Cholon, and the suburb of Gia-Dinh, inhabited chiefly by Vietnamese.

Soon after Saigon was opened as a mission station (1919) the Alliance secured a good property to serve as a residence and Missionary Receiving Home. Today the Home is taxed as never before to accommodate incoming missionaries. Another property was purchased in September, 1949, to serve as missionary residence and regional headquarters for Cochin-China.

Early in the work chapels were opened in Saigon and nearby cities. A room was rented in a large building on a principal street near the railway station. Services were conducted there daily by a national evangelist with the coöperation of the missionary, and within a few months hundreds had accepted the Lord. Thousands heard the gospel there, many of them visitors in the city from distant parts of Cochin-China and Annam, from sections which were without any witness of the gospel. A large church building was dedicated in 1940 and was the center of fruitful ministry and soul-winning throughout the war years. The blessing of God continues in this Vietnamese work and also in the growing church among the Chinese in Cholon.

Cantho This was one of the first three provinces of Cochin-China to be entered (March, 1922). There were three baptized by the end of the first year and six more by the following Easter. From these nine believers, two deacons, a secretary and a treasurer were elected for the newly organized church. They served as the Executive Committee, with the pastor, a student from the Vietnamese Bible School, as Chairman. In 1923 an outstation was opened at Cairang. Membership in Cantho increased to 115 by the end of 1924. A neighboring province was opened to the gospel and a third outstation opened at Long-Xuyen in 1925. By the end of that year the church membership numbered 267. Offerings continued to increase yearly, and in October, 1925, Cantho became a fully self-supporting church. In 1926 the church called the man of their choice, ordained him and made him their pastor. Thus Cantho became a self-governing church and missionaries residing there since have acted only in an advisory capacity. By the end of 1926 there were 398 members. Light went out from the Cantho church to provinces all around. Individual believers converted in Cantho witnessed in other provinces and were the means of starting a number of churches. A brick church which for years was the most imposing of all the churches in Cochin-China was built at Cantho, planned and constructed by the Christians themselves. The Christians of other towns in the district which had been opened to the gospel began to build their own chapels also. Fifteen men and seven women went from Cantho to the Tourane Bible School. Six of the men graduated and one of them became Chairman of the General Assembly; another became a member of the Cochin-China Executive Committee.

Dark days were ahead for the happy church. The missionary family went on furlough in 1942, and then followed the internment at Mytho of the missionaries left on the field. That was the signal for twin wolves to attack the flock: the flesh and false doctrine. Strong differences of opinion arose between the native pastor and some of the members, with disastrous results. The flesh had crept in. Seventh Day Adventists were on hand to entice and the pastor decided to throw in his lot with them. He drew away a large part of the flock with him although they did not agree with the new doctrine. The wolves had gotten in. There followed a dispute between the two factions over the ownership of the church. A lawsuit decided that the Adventist pastor must leave the building, but it was a hollow victory, for the bitterness and disillusionment were so great that few cared to come to church. The scattered Christians felt that they were indeed forsaken as they saw their church home occupied in turn by Japanese, Viet Minh and French soldiers; saw it stripped of most of its furniture and finally turned into a government school.

For months no services at all were held. The spiritual life was at a low ebb. Then came a Vietnamese pastor who knew the meaning of sacrifice. He rented a small room and served without remuneration. There in the little room with an earthen floor the Christians were meeting when missionaries finally returned in October, 1947. The coming of the missionaries gave a new lift to the church. Faith sprang up. A written request to the government resulted in the restoration of the church property to the believers. The building was in a sorry condition and the special offerings taken were insufficient to make the needed repairs. Again God performed a miracle. A wealthy but backslidden member who had refused to attend the services was arrested on the charge of being an active Viet Minh. (The Viet Minh is the party that is trying to promote Vietnamese independence and overthrow French control.) The missionary went to the authorities to plead for the man, and as a result he was spared a possible beating or a term in jail. He came to thank the missionary, whereupon the missionary seized the opportunity to exhort the man to close his store on Sundays and to return to the church. Chastened and humbled, the man appeared in church, and it was he who contributed funds which made possible full repairs on the church. On a Sunday the people said good-bye to the earthen-floor chapel, picked up benches and pulpit and deposited them in a sampan to be transported to the old, now new church. On December 7, 1947, the church was filled. About nine-tenths of those who had followed the Adventist pastor were safely back in the fold of the Eglise Evangélique. After five years of wandering the sheep were home.

Cambodia

No Protestant Mission was permitted to work in Cambodia until 1922. In that year the Alliance began work in that country, and today we are still the only Protestant Mission there. The Cambodians, descendants of the ancient Khmer race from India, are not so aggressive as their Vietnamese neighbors. When the French government officials gave permission to undertake missionary work in Cambodia, they declared it was useless for the Alliance to think of winning any converts among the Buddhists. Our missionaries entered Pnom Penh in February, 1923, in humble dependence upon God, to point souls to the Lamb of God that taketh away the sin of the world. During the early years the government restricted the work to a very few areas. The King of Cambodia wanted Buddhism to remain supreme in the land. In 1933 the Government sent to all the local Governors throughout the country, copies of a proclamation restricting missionary work to those counties and villages only where work had been established prior to December 31, 1932. This proclamation of the King of Cambodia apparently closed most of the land to gospel ministry, but in reality the work continued to progress through the ministry of the missionaries and the Cambodian Christians.

Pnom Penh The most important city in Cambodia is Pnom Penh, with a population of 124,000 according to official statistics, but with a reputed population of about 200,000. Located on the Mekong River, navigable for river steamers, it has the advantage of having trade routes both by water and by excellent automobile roads. It is the capital of Cambodia and the residence of the French Commissioner and the King of Cambodia, His Majesty King Siahnouk Monivong.

As soon as Alliance missionaries took up residence here they began to study the Cambodian language. Later, services were conducted in both Annamese and Cambodian, and five Annamese and two Cambodian converts were baptized before the end of the first year. As the missionaries became more proficient in the language they began translating the Scriptures. In addition to their ministries at Pnom Penh, the missionaries had for many years the responsibility for the carrying on of work throughout all of southern Cambodia, and the oversight of Cambodian churches across the border in Cochin-China. One round trip to the outstations south of Pnom Penh required more than 250 miles of travel by automobile.

Church services are conducted in Pnom Penh in three languages—Cambodian, Vietnamese and Chinese. Each of these groups is an organized church with a pastor. These churches and the Mission are planning to erect, as soon as funds are available, a church building large enough to meet the needs of the three congregations. Cambodia is a strongly Buddhist country and it has been the custom that travelers from one part of the country to another should be permitted to live on the Buddhist temple compounds during the few days of their stay. In order to meet this situation on behalf of our Cambodian Christians and inquirers, it is hoped that sufficient land can be secured in Pnom Penh not only for the necessary church property but also to provide a simple hostel for Christian travelers visiting Pnom Penh from their homes in outlying districts.

A couple from South China has been transferred to Pnom Penh for service among the many Chinese in that great capital city.

Battambang One hundred and eighty miles northwest of Pnom Penh is the large center of Battambang, which was also entered in the year 1923 by a missionary couple. Souls began to turn to God from the very beginning and the Cambodian Bible School was opened here in 1925. The school continued in this city until it was moved to Ta Khmau in 1949. Eleven men were enrolled in the second year the school was in operation. Siem Reap, a town near the ancient temple of Angkor Vat, was one of several outstations established throughout a large area. By the end of 1934 the Battambang district had seven organized churches.

In September, 1948, the first gospel church to be built in Cambodia was dedicated here. Souls are being won regularly and recently a mother and daughter who had resisted the witness of relatives for twenty years were wonderfully saved. A Malay who has studied in Moslem schools and who has been coming a long time for talks with the preacher has now come out openly for Christ. A convert such as he could have a ministry among the 80,000 Moslem Malay and Cham people of Cambodia.

Kampot This district was opened in 1931 with missionaries residing in the town of Kompong Trach, 20 miles from the city of Kampot. The district had not been reopened for missionary residence until 1949, but Cambodian and Vietnamese evangelists have continued to carry on the work. There is a thriving church in the city of Kampot comprised mostly of Vietnamese and Chinese, with a few Cambodian believers. A Vietnamese evangelist is in charge of the church. There are many Vietnamese and Chinese, as well as Cambodians, in this section. Kampot with the two neighboring Provinces of Takeo and Chaudoc (Cochin-China), formerly ministered to from this station, have a total population of about three quarters of a million.

Kompong Cham A station was opened in 1939 in this the third largest city in Cambodia. Situated on the Mekong River, it is the center of a province of the same name with a population of about 400,000. The town takes its name from the Cham people, of whom there are about 40,000 living along the river to a point as far north as the Province of Kratie. A motor houseboat is now operating along the banks of the Mekong and its tributaries. There is a small but growing church of Cambodians in this city, with an ordained Cambodian pastor in charge. There are several groups of Christians widely separated throughout the province. The adjacent Provinces of Kompong Thom, Kratie and Stung Treng are largely untouched with the gospel.

Kratie A missionary couple resided here for a short time some years ago. A new missionary couple has now been appointed to enter Kratie and property has been secured for their residence. The four provinces above-mentioned have a combined population of between 800,000 and 900,000. In addition to the 40,000 Chams, there are 11,000 Stiengs and Pnongs in the Province of Kratie, and 20,000 Khas in the Province of Stung Treng to the north.

Siem Reap Originally operated as an outstation of Battambang, this city was occupied by missionaries in 1939. Owing to disturbed conditions in this frontier area, no regular missionary work has been carried on among the scattered groups of believers in this province since the war. However, a number of Christians have been able to attend the annual conferences held in the city of Pnom Penh. After eight years of interruption caused by the war and subsequent unrest, missionaries were appointed in 1949 to reopen this district as soon as possible. The population of Siem Reap Province alone approaches 300,000, but the people are scattered over a large and difficult terrain.

Ta Khmau This station near Pnom Penh is now the home of the Cambodian Bible School. The students form evangelistic bands and, between Bible School sessions, go out to work in Pnom Penh and throughout the whole of Cambodia. Four students graduated in 1947, while the school was still located in Battambang, the first students to receive diplomas from this school. They and others already in the work bring the number of Cambodian preachers up to about twenty.

Kompong Chhnang This city in the midst of a populous district was chosen as a center for missionary residence and labor by the Mission Conference in June, 1949, but it could not be entered until after property was secured for missionary residence late in 1949.

Laos

Laos is the largest in area of the five states of Indo-China, but its population is the smallest, 1,189,000. In 1893 Laos became a French Protectorate. Access and travel are difficult because it is so mountainous, and it is the only state not bordering on the sea. It is inhabited by the Lao people, also called Laotians, a branch of the ancient and now widespread Thai race.

The Thai people were driven out of their home in China many centuries before Christ. Some went to the mountains of southwestern China, others to Burma, Siam, Laos and northern Tonkin. In addition to the Lao, there are thousands of tribespeople of varied origin; in the one province of Luang Prabang, out of a total population of over 200,000, at least 70,000 are tribespeople.

Luang Prabang This, the first station of any Mission to be opened in northern Laos, was opened in February, 1929. It is the royal city of the kingdom of Luang Prabang, a province of the country. Situated 1,200 miles from the mouth of the Mekong River, Luang Prabang is the center of a mountainous district accessible, for many years, only by difficult, slow and tiring horse trails, or by dangerous travel over the rapids of the many rivers which afford entrance into almost all parts of the region. There will probably never be motor roads that will reach the hundreds of small villages, but travel is speeded up where motor-powered boats are available. Since the war, sections hitherto almost inaccessible are now accessible by airplanes using military landing fields. However, the real work of reaching the people in their villages must be done by long itinerations during the dry season, the missionary taking with him a complete camping outfit for travel over remote trails. Itinerations have been made, and converts have been won, with the greater results being among the tribal peoples of this province. Following World War II, the Bible School was transferred from Vientiane to Luang Prabang, where it was reopened in 1948. The complete Bible is available in Laotian, the work of Swiss missionaries of the Brethren Mission of southern Laos. The revision of the New Testament is a current project of the North Laos missionaries.

Vientiane This second Alliance station in Laos, opened in 1931, is 250 miles downstream from Luang Prabang, and is the seat of the French and Laotian Administration for Laos. The immediate territory is a fairly large plain with mountains in the distance. Travel here is of a different nature and many villages can be reached by auto, but others must be evangelized by river travel. Early in the work an Annamese preacher was brought in to give the gospel to the thousands of Annamese in the city, and a number were converted and baptized. Up to the time the missionaries were interned, the Annamese Church was making satisfactory progress. However, in the interim between internment and the reoccupation of Vientiane, this body of believers had scattered to other areas of Indo-China and Siam. The response among the Laotians is moderate.

Xieng Khouang Geographically this station is the third point of a triangle, with Luang Prabang and Vientiane constituting the other two points. It is approximately 320 miles east of Luang Prabang and about the same distance northeast of Vientiane. It is located on a plateau surrounded by high mountains where a minimum number of villages can be reached by automobile. To reach the majority in this province, one must go by horse or on foot. Fifty per cent of the population of this province are tribal people. Xieng Khouang was opened in 1939 as a mission station.

These three stations have been reoccupied since the war and are the centers of aggressive work. A small French plane was purchased in the fall of 1949 for use by the Mission in Laos so that the missionaries might spend less time in tedious travel and more time in effective ministry. The cost of the plane was little more than a moderate priced automobile. Under the blessing of God it should prove to be a great help in the carrying on of the work in this land. Among the tribes north of Luang Prabang the Alliance is profiting from the ministry of Presbyterian missionaries and national workers from Northern Siam who came across the border in earlier years to bear witness for Christ among a number of tribes. Several scores of Christians are now serving the Lord as a result of these ministries and thus are aiding in the evangelization of these areas.

The Tribes

In the late 1920's missionaries in widely separated areas became interested in the tribespeople of their districts. At Dalat in southern Annam missionary work among the primitive peoples began in 1929 and by 1933 the first church was organized. A year later the language had been reduced to writing, a small grammar prepared, and the Gospel of Mark translated. Because of the other activities in Dalat, the work among the tribes is included in the general description in the Annam section of the Vietnamese division of the field, and thus is not being repeated here under the tribes.

In 1930 the missionaries occupying Kratie, Cambodia, discovered that they were on the border of territory inhabited by the Pnongs. It was unsafe to visit their village at first, but a survey was made which later revealed the stupendous fact that literally scores and scores of unreached primitive tribes still lay in darkness in the vast interior of Indo-China.

The Muong tribe of Tonkin was first reached by the opening of a station at Hoabinh in 1932. Thus a small beginning was made in an endeavor to take the gospel to these other lost sheep.

Banmethuot In March, 1934, the missionary couple at Kratie was transferred from Cambodia to open the station of Banmethuot, the center of a large tribal district in the plateau country of South-Central Annam. The Raday language was the first to be studied, enabling them to reach about 200,000 people. Other tribes, far and near, were reached either through the Raday language or through interpreters. The gospel has now been preached among 15 tribes and dialect-groups of that section of the country. Converts were won, a Bible school was started, and students trained in the school have gone out to preach to others. Outstations in strategic centers have been opened, with longhouse chapels as centers of evangelization in charge of tribes' workers.

After the close of World War II, the missionaries returned to the field with an airplane, and in October, 1947, authorization was received to operate the mission plane between Dalat, Saigon and Banmethuot. The flight across the mountains to Banmethuot takes only 35 minutes, and instead of the wearisome and dangerous trip by convoy to Saigon, the trip is made by plane in one and a half hours. From Banmethuot, however, the missionaries must change from plane to elephant back in order to visit some of the villages of their district. We regret to report that the plane was so damaged during a forced landing in August, 1949, that it could not be repaired at reasonable cost and thus it can no longer be used.

Since the reopening of this station souls are being continually won to Christ. In one district a national evangelist reported that 340 have prayed and accepted the Lord. Throughout the district more than 600 prayed and professed acceptance of Christ during 1948. In the same year over 300 believers were baptized. The Bible School was reopened in 1947. In 1948 a new missionary couple began the study of the Raday language in preparation for the work in the Bible School and district.

Pleiku Ten years ago the province of Pleiku, about 125 miles north of Banmethuot, was opened with an Annamese worker in charge. Translation of the four Gospels, the Acts, and other literature has been done for the Jarai, Hdrung and Bahnar tribes, and has established the work on a firm basis. The Bible School at Pleiku, begun in

1938, was reopened in 1947. In 1948 a new missionary couple took up residence on this station and began the study of the Jarai language.

The Mission has now received permission to build a chapel and open work at Three Frontiers (where Annam, Cambodia and Cochin-China meet), a vast region inhabited by several tribes who are among the most savage in Indo-China, and who have been subdued only in recent years. In this region are the Mnong Preh, Mnong Prang, Mnong Tih Bri and Mnong Biat tribes. These last named are the same as the Pnongs of Cambodia. Throughout this new region there are no roads except the main highway which cuts through their territory. The villages can be reached only over winding trails in tiger-infested country.

Dalat The first attempt, in the Dalat and Djiring districts, to reach the mountain tribes of the Langbian and Haut Donnai provinces was made by employing these primitive people to clear the jungle on property that had been secured for the building of the home and school for missionaries' children at Dalat. Each noon and again at night the missionary sought to present the gospel in its simplicity through an interpreter as the workmen sat around their fires.

The reducing of the language of these forest folk to writing was of prime importance. It was necessary at times to coin words to express religious terms which had no equivalent in the uncivilized man's vocabulary. The translation of certain scripture portions followed, and with the first interested inquirers a Bible class was organized.

The peoples of this region are spoken of as the Koho, a Cham word meaning barbarian. In reality there are six different tribes in this group: namely, the Sray, Riong, Lat, Chil, Ma and Roh; and a person knowing one of their dialects can be understood by all. This greatly facilitated the missionary's approach to the inhabitants of these mountain ranges.

The gospel is indeed the power of God unto salvation and it was not long before a number of divinely called men desired to study the Word of God. A Bible School was organized at Dalat with regular classes for all. The school is conducted in the Koho language but the students represent many different tribes. Urged by the Holy Spirit, these men returned to their heathen villages, where they witnessed with much boldness. Formerly held by the fear of demons, to whom they sacrificed their cattle and pigs, goodly numbers of the people, oftentimes almost entire villages, have turned to the Lord.

In December, 1949, the Board of Managers approved the seeking of funds for the purchase of a property in Dalat which is especially needed as a center for work among the tribes. This will provide a residence for the missionaries and a location for the Bible School for the training of workers from the many tribes in the Dalat and Djiring areas.

In 1933 the first Mois church was organized with the first Moi convert as the pastor. Jungle folk from various Moi tribes who come to Dalat to trade, congregate at the shelter built for them on mission property and hear the Word preached to them. Through these services and also through trips made by Moi workers and missionaries into the jungle, tribespeople representing fourteen different groups have heard the gospel. During Christmas week of 1948 a special Conference was held at Dalat attended by about 700 Christian tribespeople. Some of them had walked six days to attend this Conference.

Under the blessing of God the gospel has been heard along many jungle trails, but many villages are still without the Light and Life which only Christ can give. We must press on until all have heard.

Djiring Eighty kilometers south of Dalat at Djiring a mission station was opened recently (1949) in the heart of a great tribal area. Valuable contacts have been made and encouraging signs are evident.

It is planned that two new missionary couples, after several months of language study in France, shall enter Budop for work among the Stieng tribe and Cheo Reo for work among the Jarai. It is hoped that within a year or two after these centers have been occupied in the south, one or more new mission stations may be established in the area north of Pleiku.

In December, 1949, the Board of Managers approved the establishing of a small leper colony in the Banmethuot area for work among the many lepers in the various tribes. One or two missionary nurses who have volunteered for work among lepers will comprise the mission staff with the help and under the supervision of the missionary in charge of the work throughout the district. Buildings of modest design and cost will house people in the colony and those able to work will care for garden and farm crops to help provide food. The work will be supported in this way and through special gifts designated for work among the lepers.

Translation and Publication Work

The Alliance missionaries in Indo-China have had the responsibility and joy of translating the entire Bible in Annamese (Vietnamese), which is spoken by about 20 million people; also in Cambodian, the mother tongue of three and a half million people of Cambodia. Gospels and other portions have been translated and printed in the tribal dialects, Raday, Jarai and Koho. The missionaries of the Swiss Brethren Mission in southern Laos translated the entire Bible in Laotian.

The first printing press was purchased and established in Hanoi in 1918. Later other presses and equipment were added and gospel literature was printed in Annamese, Cambodian, Laotian, and several tribal dialects. Publications in French and English were also printed. In the year 1933 over 25 million pages were printed, as against over three million pages in 1922. Five thousand copies of the New Testament in Annamese were printed in 1923. Translations of *Pilgrim's Progress,* Dr. A. B. Simpson's *Wholly Sanctified,* and other religious books were published. The press began to issue Christian literature in the Cambodian language in 1925, including 5,000 copies of the Gospel of Luke. In 1926 the entire Bible in Annamese was printed, making the Word of God available for the first time to one of the largest language groups then remaining in the world without the Scriptures in their own tongue. The New Testament in Cambodian was printed in 1928. The entire Bible has now been translated in Cambodian and the manuscripts are being revised. The New Testament is also undergoing revision and the goal is to have the entire Bible revised and printed within the next two or three years.

Although the war disrupted the work of the press, yet during their internment the missionaries continued to translate Christian literature, even the monumental work of a Bible dictionary and a systematic theology, both in the Vietnamese language.

Since the war, societies in England and also many individuals and groups in America are again giving invaluable assistance in printing and distributing literature. The British and Foreign Bible Society printed, in Shanghai, by the offset method, a new edition of the Vietnamese Bible. With the help of a mimeograph on the field, literature is being prepared and sent out to scores of Christian groups. This literature includes translations of portions of the valuable writings of Dr. A. B. Simpson, Sunday school helps, Bible studies, Bible magazines, tracts and missionary biographies. *Christ in the Tabernacle,* by Dr. Simpson, is now ready for printing. A Vietnamese committee of four under the leadership of a missionary is revising the Vietnamese hymnbook with a view to publishing as soon as possible by the photo-offset process in the United States an edition of 10,000 copies with music, 450 pages of hymns and 50 pages of responsive reading. A word edition of 5,000 will also be published. A Pastor's Handbook is also being prepared.

One Vietnamese pastor asked for twelve copies of Dr. Simpson's book on Hebrews, as well as for other literature. He explained, "So Christians can study at home when they dare not go to church. So many have either been killed or imprisoned that no one dares to go to church any more."

The translation and publication work of Indo-China cannot be dissociated from the names of the late Rev. and Mrs. W. C. Cadman, who devoted their lives to the preparation and printing of Christian literature for all Indo-China. Mrs. Cadman passed away soon after the close of the war. Mr. Cadman was enthusiastically beginning the re-establishment of the press at Dalat when he also was suddenly called home in the year 1948. As other hands take up the task may the important work of the press go forward with increasing blessing.

Bible Schools

Six Bible Schools are now operating in Indo-China. For the Vietnamese people there is the Bible School at Tourane, Annam. The Laotian Bible School is located at Luang Prabang. The new home of the Cambodian Bible School is Ta Khmau, near the city of Pnom Penh. For the Tribes there are the following Bible Schools: in the Raday language at Banmethuot, in the Jarai language at Pleiku, and in the Koho language at Dalat.

In Cambodia the children of Christians who attend the government schools at Battambang, Pnom Penh, and Kompong Cham are given a home on the mission compounds of those cities. Sixty boys and girls attending the Battambang school are all children of Christian parents who live in the country, where the only schools are Buddhist temple schools; hence the necessity imposed upon the missionaries of providing some means of education for these children. The missionaries are endeavoring to make the hostels self-supporting as far as possible. The parents contribute rice and money for the children they send, but, of course, some of the children who are half-orphans or of poor parents need help. For this small investment of time and money, the missionaries are given the inestimable opportunity of regularly teaching the children in the hostels the things of God.

Christian education pays high dividends. During the war years a graduate of the Vietnamese Bible School was in charge of the tribes' work at Pleiku. This man speaks French and Annamese, reads English, and at Pleiku applied himself to learn the Jarai language, then translated portions of Scripture. During the war he spent much of his time fleeing through the jungle and his health was impaired by the hardships endured. When he was free to go back to Pleiku, instead of retiring, he stayed at his post, doing the work of two or three men. Services were conducted every night in the chapel; a Bible School was conducted during the day for prospective native preachers; in his spare time he translated Scripture portions, fearful lest he die before his task was completed.

The Church and the Challenge

In 1911 our missionaries first gained an entrance into Annam. Thirty years later there were 14,000 church members in about 200 organized churches. In what is now called Viet-Nam, including Tonkin, Annam and Cochin-China, the churches were grouped into three conferences, distinct and separate from the Mission. In 1927 the Indo-China field adopted a plan which recognizes the national church as a separate body from the Mission. Each has the responsibility of directing its own affairs under the guidance of the Holy Spirit, yet at the same time provision is made to ensure fellowship and harmonious working together in matters which affect both the Church and the Mission. An Executive Committee of five Vietnamese is elected by the Vietnamese Church Conference. The Executive Committee of the Church and that of the Mission meet together for transacting business requiring joint action. In 1928 the Church Constitution, drawn up by the Joint Executive Committee, was adopted by the conference of the Annamese Evangelical Church. In addition to the general conference of the churches, to which both pastors and lay delegates are sent, there are annual conferences held in each district.

The total responsibility of The Christian and Missionary Alliance in Indo-China includes a population of approximately 21,500,000 in Viet-Nam, three and one-half million in Cambodia, and over one million in Laos. Between one and two million of the population constitute the challenge of the tribespeople. In the fall of 1949 we had in Indo-China 19 mission stations, 122 church centers and 93 outstations. Of the 113 Sunday schools, more than 100 were in Viet-nam. There were 244 national workers, and 145 students enrolled in the six central Bible Schools. Baptized church members numbered more than 14,000, of whom 1,505 were baptized during the year, and inquirers numbered 950. However, the unsettled condition of the country has made it impossible to get complete reports from all areas.

Viet-Nam During World War II when the missionaries were interned and foreign funds were cut off, services and schools were carried on by the national Christians, and new churches were built. While there was some dislocation of the work and suffering among the Christians during World War II the major tribulations and losses have come since the war ended and the Japanese left the country.

The war between the Viet Minh, who are striving for national independence, and the French, who have sought to hold Indo-China in colonial status, has caused and is still causing very heavy loss of life and property and tragic suffering among the people, including the Christians. During the war between the Viet Minh and French, disaster has come to many Christian homes and death to not a few of the pastors. They wandered in the mountains and when they returned, in rags, they found all their possessions gone. The church has gone through fire and blood, and some have grown cold, for suffering and want do not always result in increased faith and devotion. As in other lands in this postwar era, carelessness has crept in and a light view of sin is noticeable in some. A great number of believers were without spiritual teaching for months, with their churches closed, burned or occupied by the military. Some Christians have faltered but others have come through purified and perfected. A preacher from one of the country churches in Cochin-China recently came to the home of the missionary, wearing a borrowed suit. He told this story. Armed soldiers had invaded his home, looted it, and taken his clothing. Not believing the preacher's claim that he had no money, they forced him to his knees and placed the points of their bayonets against his throat while two others tried to strangle his wife, all the while demanding where his money was hidden. This is a sample of what many undershepherds are facing in their isolated posts during these days of guerrilla warfare.

The Rev. Le Van Thai, President of the Viet-Nam Alliance Churches, wrote:

Praise the Lord, most of His servants are still among the flocks He has committed to their care. . . . When they have not clothes enough, they coil up on a heap of straw. One of them has only a coat and a Bible left, but keeps on living with his little flock, for he cannot leave them.

In the three states of Viet-Nam in the fall of 1949 nine mission stations and 104 church centers were occupied.

Cambodia Cambodia's fourteen provinces with a total pop-
and Laos ulation of three and one-half million, have (1949) four mission stations, six church centers and 23 outstations; there are 27 national workers and over 400 church members. The Mission is planning to open four new stations as soon as residence can be secured for the missionaries. Buddhism has 60,000 priests in the land, one for every 58 persons.

In our Laos field are three mission stations; four student workers, and over 360 baptized Christians.

The power of Buddhism in both Laos and Cambodia has made the preaching of the gospel a difficult task. It is said that "for every Buddhist who has turned to Christ, there have been five converts from primitive paganism." Nevertheless, even among Buddhists the gospel is gaining an entrance in both of these countries. Laos is seeing a moving among the tribespeople also. A former national worker walked over 30 miles to tell the missionary of the increasing number of tribal believers in Luang Prabang Province.

The Tribes

In the Banmethuot-Pleiku districts there are two mission stations, five outstations and 30 national workers. There are seven churches and one thousand inquirers, and over 300 were baptized in these two districts during the year 1948.

In the Dalat district, besides the mission station at Dalat, and the new station at Djiring, there are 12 church centers and 23 outstations; 17 national workers and over 400 baptized church members. Baptisms numbered 133 during the year 1948. The first conference among the tribes was held at Dalat, in June, 1939, when the missionaries engaged in this work realized that a mighty effort would have to be made in order to adequately reach the scores of unreached tribes and dialect-groups in the south and central part of Indo-China. During the Christmas season services in 1948 at Dalat, more than 700 tribespeople came from their distant villages to worship God together and be instructed in His Word.

The actual number of tribes and dialect-groups is unknown, but at least a hundred have been located in the vast interior of this land, and their names listed. While several Vietnamese evangelists are helping the missionaries in this great task, the work is mainly being done by the tribes' evangelists who are being trained in three Bible Schools: namely, at Dalat, Banmethuot and Pleiku. It is expected that soon there will be one hundred national workers among the tribes, and plans are being made to open two stations in great unreached areas among the Steing and Jarai tribes on the arrival of two new missionary couples.

"The challenge of the tribes of Indo-China," wrote one of our missionaries, "is indisputably the greatest remaining single challenge to pioneer endeavor in all our world-wide work . . . and they represent 80 per cent of the known tribes of our global mission fields. . . . Some day some lost tribe is going to be the last tribe."

SIAM

Siam, in Southeast Asia, occupies a good portion of the central part of the Indo-Chinese Peninsula. Circling west around the northern shores of the Gulf of Siam (a part of the China Sea), it also occupies the neck of the Malay Peninsula as far as the Federation of Malaya. Siam has a total coastline of about 1,300 miles. It is bounded on the north and northwest by Burma; on the northeast, east and southeast by Indo-China; on the south by the Gulf of Siam, and on the southwest, in the Malay Peninsula, by the Federation of Malaya and the Bay of Bengal.

Area and Population

Siam is over 1,000 miles long from north to south, and about 480 miles wide at its widest part. It is about the size of France, having a total area of 200,148 square miles, and a population of 17,256,325 (1947 census). The capital, Bangkok, is a modern city with over 900,000 inhabitants.

The Chinese constitute the largest minority group in Siam, and are important in the economic life of the country. The 1937 census, which took into consideration only immigrant Chinese, gave their number as about 524,000. Semi-official Chinese estimates run higher than two million, but include persons of mixed blood born in Siam. About one and a half million people in Siam consider themselves to be Chinese. The Malay population is about 325,000; Europeans number nearly 100,000, and of them British subjects are in the majority.

The population of Eastern Siam, which is the missionary responsibility of The Christian and Missionary Alliance, is 6,617,026 (1947 census). This responsibility covers 19 of Siam's 70 provinces, as follows:

Province	Population
Ubon	850,526
Korat	723,257
Khonkaen	590,664
Roi Et	535,662
Srisaket	451,576
Surin	435,382
Mahasarakam	390,294
Udorn	382,564
Buriram	339,496
Kalasin	307,795
Nakorn Panom	307,173
Jayabhum	293,753
Sakon Nakorn	273,262
Prachinburi	217,395
Nongkhai	144,201
Loey	134,202
Chantaburi	110,808
Rayong	84,197
Trat	44,819
Total of the 19 provinces	6,617,026

People and History

The origin of the Thai (Siamese) race is still in doubt, though recent discoveries have thrown considerable light on the subject. As of about 2000 B. C. the Thai race is mentioned in Chinese annals as living in the Yangtze River Valley, where they migrated under Chinese pressure westward from Kwangsi and Kwangtung. They eventually established the first Thai capital, Nan-Chao in Yunnan. The Thai race is now to be found not only in Siam, but in Burma, Indo-China, and over a large part of southern China. The language spoken by all of them is still essentially one, but the Thai in Siam very early developed a distinctive alphabet.

Until 1932 Siam was one of the last of the absolute monarchies, but in June of that year a well planned, bloodless revolution succeeded in causing the government to sign a new constitution declaring a limited monarchy with full franchise for the people and an elected parliament. During the years following, there have been two successful coups d'état, the last one occurring on November 9, 1947. In 1946 King Ananda signed a new constitution providing for a Senate and a House of Representatives elected by the people. It opened on June first of that year, the first wholly elected parliament in Siam. King Ananda was killed later in the same year and was succeeded by his brother. Another revolution resulted in the adoption, on November 9, 1947, of a provisional constitution creating a Supreme Council of State to act for the king. The Siamese Cabinet invited the present King Phumibol Aduldet to be crowned following his 21st birthday, December 5, 1948, but as late as August 1, 1949, the coronation had not yet taken place.

Siam has been experiencing the birth pangs of democracy. This last coup d'état, the creation of a Supreme Council of State, was a backward step in democratic government, but a timely one. A major obstacle of unlimited democratic processes in Siam lies in the fact that the people are almost wholly lacking in parliamentary traditions. The present set-up will give the people further opportunity to be educated in the intelligent use of democratic processes.

Government

At present Siam's government is a constitutional, semi-parliamentary monarchy with a Supreme Council of State acting for the king. The Premier is Field Marshal Luang Pibul Song-gram, head of the military junta. The country maintains a small navy and air force. Able-bodied men between the ages of 18 and 30 are liable to military service.

Climate

Siam lies between five and twenty-one degrees north of the equator. It has a periodically dry and rainy tropical climate. There are three seasons: the rainy season, entirely under the influence of the southwest monsoon, which begins about the first of May and continues to about the middle of November; the so-called cool season, which begins at the end of the rainy season and lasts until about the middle of February; lastly, the hot season, extending from the middle of February to the end of April.

Statistics running over a twenty-year period show the average duration of the rainy season to be about 200 days. The average yearly rainfall is 63 inches, but the variation is great in the different areas. On the Korat plateau, which includes a large part of the Alliance field, the average yearly rainfall is 50 inches, but the average for some of the southern coastal provinces is 130 inches. The maximum extremes of the air temperature in the shade are 55 degrees and 107 degrees.

Physical Features

The surface of the country is characterized by flat, alluvial plains which become inundated during each rainy season and which are intersected by winding rivers and streams; by mountains covered with dense tropical forests; and also by a certain amount of rolling country.

Eastern Siam consists of a saucer-shaped plateau tilted to the southeast, and a narrow strip of swampy country to the north. The Mekong River separates it on the north and east from Laos, in Indo-China. The plateau is bounded on the west by the Petchabun range of mountains, and the massive flat-topped peaks of the Dong Phya Yen range; on the south by the Sankampeng range and the Don Rak Scarp. The plateau proper is guarded on the north and east from the Mekong River by a line of hills varying in height up to 2,000 feet. It is drained entirely by the Nam Moon river system, which empties into the Mekong at the southeast corner of Siam. The western and northern sides of the plateau vary in elevation from 400 to 700 feet above sea level. At Ubon the elevation is only about 200 feet.

Resources

The chief product of Siam is rice. About seven and one-half million acres are devoted to its cultivation. The annual yield is approximately five million tons, of which there is an average exportable surplus of one and a half million tons. Teakwood is an important export from the forest areas. Other principal exports are tin, para-rubber, stick-lac (from which shellac is made), charcoal, copra, hides, leather and— elephants, monkeys and reptiles. Coconuts, tobacco, pepper and cotton are produced; iron, manganese, tungsten, antimony and mercury are among Siam's extensive mineral resources.

Progress

Siam has nearly 2,000 miles of railways. There are rather extensive networks of roads throughout the country, making the use of automobiles practical. These roads connect the main cities, while countless villages are reached only by roads which are impossible for auto travel in the rainy season. These latter so-called roads through the forests are a risk at any season because of ditches, broken bridges and fallen trees.

Primary education is compulsory and free in local public and municipal schools.

Currency

The official currency is the baht (also called the tical). The exchange value varies greatly on the open market. The official rate of exchange is one baht for ten cents U. S., but on the open market the baht is worth only about five cents.

Languages and Tribes

Siam is peopled in the main by different branches of the Thai race, with tribespeople in the north. Eastern Siam, however, is inhabited by people who, though now being brought under the influence of their sister language, Thai, by means of government schools, still own the Lao language as their mother tongue. This is due to the fact that, following a period when the Siamese more or less ruled a large part of Laos, they enticed or coerced great numbers of the Lao to cross the Mekong River, which forms the Lao-Siamese boundary for hundreds of miles, and settled them in Eastern Siam as nationals of Siam. There are also in Eastern Siam about 500,000 people listed as Siamese in the census, but whose mother tongue is Cambodian. The races and tribes known to exist today in Siam include Negritos, Austronesians, Tibeto-Burmans, Khmers or Cambodians and many branches of the Mon-Khmers. Of the various groups of the Lao people who predominate in northeastern Siam, the Lao-Kao and Lao-Wiengchan are the most numerous branches.

Today compulsory education in the Thai language, general conscription and modern means of communication have all helped to reduce the lines of distinction between the languages and customs of the various races living in Siam. Thai is the only official language of the country. The government's policy is to suppress the use of all other indigenous languages and dialects. This policy of long standing has been fairly successful, for the younger generation is fluent in the

use of the Thai language even though in general usage it takes second place to the mother tongues. Consequently, throughout most of northeastern Siam the language one hears commonly is a mixture of Thai and Lao-Kao or Thai and Lao-Wiengchan. The only written language generally used is Thai. A few of the older people can read the Laotian script or the Cambodian script, but in most cases the same persons can read the Thai script as well.

The following languages are being used to preach the gospel in the section of Siam where the Alliance is working:

Used by Missionaries	Additional Languages Used Only by National Workers
Thai	Chinese-Mandarin
	Chinese-Swatownese
	Dialects
	Lao-Kao
	Lao-Wiengchan
	Lao-Yaw
	Lao-Putai

Some of our missionaries have picked up a sufficient vocabulary in the local dialects of Lao-Kao and Lao-Wiengchan to preach the gospel intelligibly to the most primitive of the people, the older generation now retiring over the horizon. Most of the national workers speak fluently both Thai and the dialects which are their mother tongues.

Religions

Buddhism prevails in Siam. In 1939 the Buddhists had 18,416 temples and 140,774 priests in the land. As the State religion, supported by the State, Buddhism is taught in all public schools, and is interwoven in all the institutions of the country. According to the constitution the king must profess the Buddhist religion. Theoretically religious freedom is granted to all others, but in reality, official pressure is exerted in behalf of Buddhism to the extent that it is unusual and most difficult for Christians to be government employees. It can be stated, however, that there is no public, official opposition to Christianity. (See *Buddhism*, under India, *Religions*.)

Missionary Occupation

The first Protestant missionaries to go to Siam were Carl Gutzlaff (German) and Jacob Tomlin (English) in 1828. Gutzlaff saw the opportunities and appealed to American church missionary societies. The American Baptists were the first to respond. They sent missionaries who worked among the Chinese in Siam more or less continuously from 1833 until shortly before World War II. The Congregational Church also sent missionaries about the same time as the Baptists, but the Congregationalists withdrew fifteen years later. In 1840 the American Presbyterian Mission began their work in Siam, which has continued up to the present time. They have specialized in institutional work, making outstanding contributions in the fields of medicine and education. They maintain some of the finest schools and hospitals in the land.

In 1854 a Mormon missionary arrived in Bangkok. He soon withdrew, for he found that the Siamese needed no incitement to polygamy.

In 1903 the Churches of Christ in Great Britain sent their first missionaries to Siam. They have one station located at Nakon Pathom. They maintain a hospital, a girls' school, a boys' school, and a thriving church composed of Siamese, Chinese and Mons.

The Seventh Day Adventists came to Siam in 1918, and ultimately opened four stations, one of which is now abandoned. They have specialized in medical work and the profuse distribution of literature in which their false doctrines are usually subtly hidden. Most of their converts have been among the Chinese. The only work they maintain in Eastern Siam was opened at Ubon about a year after The Christian and Missionary Alliance became established in that strategic city.

The Christian and Missionary Alliance entered Siam in 1929, assuming the responsibility, under God, for the propagation of the Gospel in 15 eastern provinces, to which four more adjacent provinces have since been added. The Alliance has specialized in pioneer evangelism and in the training of national workers and leaders in the only Bible School of its kind in Siam.

In 1947 two new missionary societies opened work in Siam. The first to arrive were three Pentecostal missionaries from Finland. They have not observed mission comity, for they are establishing themselves and are proselytizing in an area occupied by the American Presbyterian Mission.

The World-wide Evangelization Crusade sent four missionaries to Siam in 1947, and they are establishing work in a pioneer area released to them by the American Presbyterian Mission.

Roman Catholics in Siam number 35,000. Protestants number as follows:

American Presbyterians	....	10,000
Baptists	......................(estimated)	500
Christian and Missionary Alliance	.....(nearly)	250
Churches of Christ	....	300
Seventh Day Adventists	....	100
Other Societies	.........................no statistics	
Total	....	11,100

The Christian and Missionary Alliance

A number of the missionaries in French Indo-China, especially those in Cambodia, early caught the vision of the great need in the unreached parts of Siam, north of the Cambodian section of the field. This was made known to the Foreign Secretary during a visit to the Indo-China field in 1927. He carried the appeal of this new territory to the Board at home, with the result that The Christian and Missionary Alliance entered Eastern Siam in 1929. American Bible Society colporteurs had been there prior to that time, and the Secretary of the Bible Society had urged the Alliance to undertake the evangelization of that great area. The American Presbyterian Mission had work in only one center there, Korat. They stated that they had no expectation of reaching the rest of that vast territory, and were glad to have the Alliance accept the responsibility for it. Only Korat and its surrounding district were reserved by the Presbyterians as an outpost for the National Church of Siam (the native church of the Presbyterians), a church with 10,000 members in western, northern and southern Siam. In 1934 this National Church decided to withdraw from Korat, and they joined with the Presbyterian Mission in urging The Christian and Missionary Alliance to assume the responsibility for all fifteen of the provinces of Eastern Siam. Four more adjacent provinces have recently been added, giving the Alliance a total responsibility for 19 out of Siam's 70 provinces.

The first years in this difficult Buddhist land yielded little fruit. From 1929 to 1941 there was a total of only 85 baptized believers. Since the war there has been a change. In 1947, 107 were baptized and 389 others prayed, confessing Christ as their Savior. In 1948, 76 were baptized, bringing the total of baptized believers up to 248. There are now more than 20 centers where the Gospel is being preached regularly, double the number of centers open in 1946. Six

stations have resident missionaries, and there are 16 outstations, four of which were opened in 1948.

The task is barely begun in the 19 provinces, with a total population of over 6,600,000. These 19 provinces are among the most densely populated provinces in all Siam, comprising over 38 per cent of Siam's total population.

Ubon The first Alliance mission station in Eastern Siam was established in the city of Ubon when a missionary couple was transferred from Cambodia and opened this station in January, 1929. A railway and motor road connect Ubon with Bangkok, the capital. The first year of missionary occupation was spent principally in language study. During the second year witness in the native tongue began and a street chapel was opened. The first convert was baptized in 1931. Later a humble church building was built and paid for by the native Christians and in 1934 a small church was organized, the members being converts won through open-air preaching and chapel work.

The general attitude of the people in these parts of Siam was one of spiritual apathy and indifference, the typical attitude in Buddhist lands. The difficulty of the task was increased by the presence and methods of the Seventh Day Adventist missionaries with their dangerous, false teachings. God has blessed the evangelistic efforts in spite of the opposition, until now there are more baptized church members in Ubon who are receiving no financial aid from the Mission or missionaries than at any other station in Siam. After the war, the station was reopened (1946), and the crude bamboo and thatch chapel has been exchanged for rented, better quarters. In 1948, the world-wide Alliance Day of Prayer, observed at Ubon, resulted in the salvation of six souls and the return of two backsliders.

This strategic city is now connected with Bangkok by the Siamese Airways as well as by daily train service. The Ubon province has a population of over 850,000, the immediate parish of *one* missionary family.

Khonkaen This city was opened as a mission station in 1930, closed during the war, reopened in 1946. It is the center of a district of nearly 600,000 people. Khonkaen is connected with Bangkok, Korat, Udorn and Ubon by regular airplane or railway service. Greatly improved auto roads enable the missionary to reach more villages than previously. Two years after the station was opened there were four baptized believers. A small church was established in 1934. By the end of 1936 hundreds had prayed and the Gospel witness was spreading from village to village through the testimony of the new converts. To date there has been a more favorable response to the Gospel in the Khonkaen district than elsewhere in the field. The first Alliance churches to be organized and the first simple village church buildings to be constructed are in this area.

The Bible School, which was begun at Korat in 1936, was moved to Khonkaen one year later. It has been carried on there ever since, except during the war years (1942-46). God's blessing continues to rest upon the school and the extensive practical work assignments filled by the students. In 1947 the Toledo Gospel Tabernacle in America gave $10,000 for the purchase of a choice plot of ground and buildings. This magnanimous gift provided for the greatest material need of the Mission, for this property now accommodates our growing Bible School and dormitories. The buildings on the property are also temporarily accommodating two missionary couples engaged in language study. Temporary church accommodations are also available, and a splendid site is there for a permanent church building.

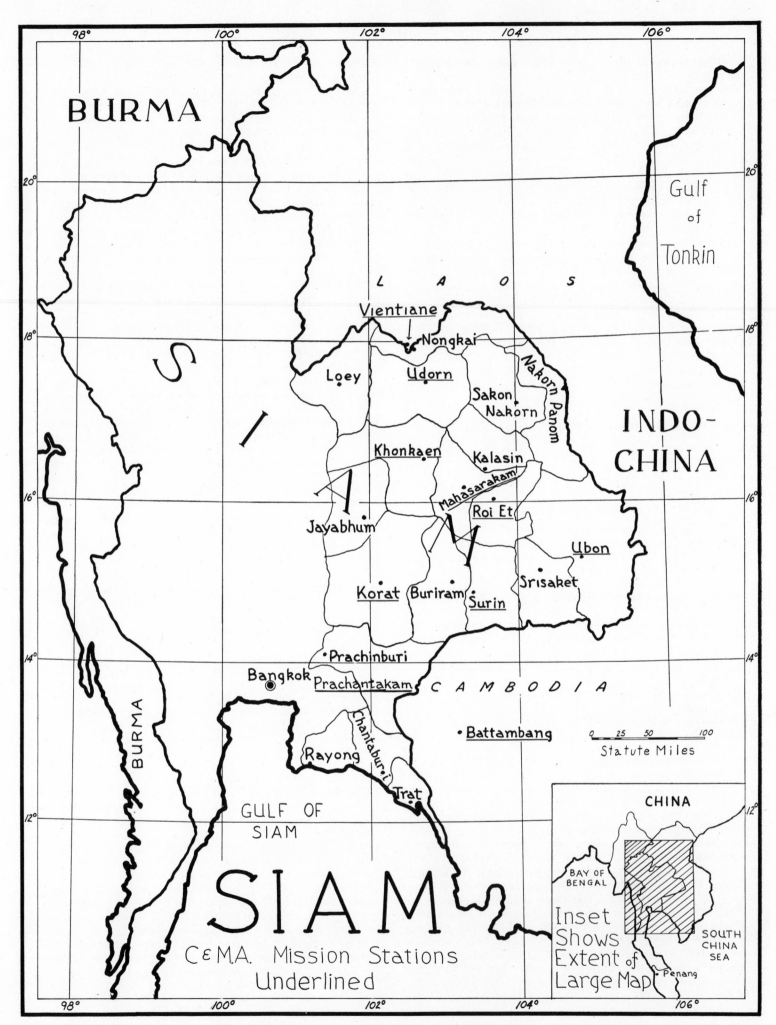

BURMA

Gulf
of
Tonkin

L A O S

Vientiane
• Nongkai
Loey
• Udorn
Sakon
Nakorn
Nakorn Panom

INDO-
CHINA

Khonkaen
Kalasin
Mahasarakam
Roi Et

Jayabhum

Ubon

Korat
Buriram
Surin
Srisaket

• Prachinburi

Bangkok ⊚ Prachantakam

C A M B O D I A

• Battambang

0 25 50   100
Statute Miles

Rayong

Chantaburi

Trat

GULF OF
SIAM

BURMA

SIAM

C&M.A. Mission Stations
Underlined

CHINA

BAY OF
BENGAL

SOUTH
CHINA
SEA

Inset
Shows
Extent of
Large Map

• Penang

Korat (Nakorn Rajsima) Korat was originally occupied in 1929 by a Siamese worker of the American Presbyterian Mission and its churches in Siam. These groups requested The Christian and Missionary Alliance to take over the work, and our missionaries occupied Korat in June, 1934. The district was found to be largely unevangelized and the work truly pioneer. With the coming of World War II the station was necessarily closed.

When the station was reopened in 1948, the Mission, unable to rent anything satisfactory, purchased a house, which serves as a residence and headquarters office. This is one of the only two pieces of real estate owned by the Alliance in Siam. A new building in a good location in the city was found and the Mission expected to rent it for a chapel. The owner went back on her word and made every effort to rent it to someone else. The building stood vacant for over three months. Then the repentant owner came and confessed her wrongs and requested the Mission to rent the building.

Korat is an important commercial center and a communications hub. All of the northeastern provinces are served and reached via Korat. Here are located the government's administrative headquarters for all of northeastern Siam. From Korat, Bangkok the capital, and every Alliance mission station is within one day's travel by train and bus. Surin, the nearest mission station, can be reached from Korat in five hours; Ubon, the farthest, can be reached in about ten hours. The population of Korat and its province is over 723,000. The missionaries who make up the headquarters personnel are the only ones available to minister in this province, to say nothing of the needy adjacent provinces. The Gospel is being presented in the city each week in Siamese, Chinese and English. In addition to the regular attendants at the services, contacts are being made with many new people.

Mahasarakam This station was opened in 1947. The city and province have a combined population of over 390,000, and the adjoining province of Kalasin brings the responsibility up to 700,000 souls. There are four Christian groups in this area and souls are being won continually among the Siamese. A street chapel at reasonable cost has been secured in a fine location in the city. It is the property of a Chinese merchant who failed in business. He is now a Christian and with his Christian wife desires that his shop become a street chapel.

Udorn Udorn, with an immediate population of over 380,000, was opened in 1939 and work was carried on there for two years before the war brought a break in activities. The station has been reopened since 1947. Two provinces adjoin Udorn which are considered a part of the Udorn district, and which add a population of 417,000 to the responsibility here. Intensive and extensive evangelistic work has barely begun but the early response is encouraging.

Roi Et This station was opened in 1939 also. Just two years later, early in 1941, it had to be closed because health conditions made it necessary for the missionaries to go on furlough. At the close of the war when the Mission tried to reopen Roi Et as a station, no housing was available for the missionaries. Late in 1948 it was found that the owner of a house, which was once remodeled by the Mission and occupied briefly by missionaries, is now eager to rent the property once more to the Mission, as soon as he can get possession of another of his houses for his own use.

God wonderfully blessed the first efforts at Roi Et, a hitherto untouched area with an immediate population in the city and its province of over 535,000 souls, besides the many neglected people in adjacent provinces. From the very beginning there was interest in the Gospel and souls were saved. At the close of the second year a church had been organized in the city of Roi Et with 16 charter members, and the first village chapel had been built by the Christians. This church has produced several Bible school students. Roi Et was reoccupied as a mission station in July, 1949.

Surin Five months after the opening of the station in 1940 the missionaries had to withdraw because of political and military conditions brought about by border incidents between Siam and Indo-China. During the five months that the station was open, a street chapel was secured and services were conducted regularly to capacity audiences. In the month of October of that year, 900 visitors came to the missionary's home, and in November 1,150 came. Frequently the entire day would be spent in witnessing to the steady stream of visitors. Tracts were given out profusely and Gospel portions were sold.

Surin was reopened early in 1949. A ten-year lease was obtained on a house built on the ashes of the house which had been occupied by the missionaries who opened the station in 1940.

Surin has an immediate population (city and province) of more than 435,000, and is the center of an untouched area with a total population of over 1,200,000. The Surin area is the largest untouched area in this Alliance field. Its population is largely made up of people of Cambodian descent. It is highly desirable that the missionaries working this field acquire a knowledge of Cambodian after they have become proficient in Thai. An advisable method would be to seek to win converts from among the bilingual people; train them in our Thai Bible School and send them back for service in this Surin area.

The communications throughout this region are exceedingly poor. Motor roads are still largely in the blueprint stage. Apart from the railway line which passes through Buriram, Surin, and Srisaket, the roads are little more than trails or ox-cart roads. Here is a pioneer field of vast and rugged proportions.

Prachantakam This city in the Province of Prachinburi was opened as a mission station when a missionary couple took up residence there on September 9, 1949.

The Alliance has no station in Bangkok, the capital city, but one of our Siam missionary couples is at present loaned to the American Bible Society as their Siam Agency Secretary. The missionary here serves also as our unofficial business agent, thereby reducing greatly the number of trips required to be made to Bangkok by the Chairman of the field. The missionary and his wife have placed their home in Bangkok at the disposal of our missionaries as their Receiving Home.

Translation and Publication Work

As a result of the war all stocks of mission publications were either confiscated and destroyed or secretly distributed. Nothing remained when the missionaries returned in 1946. During 1947 our Publication Committee accomplished the following task: 135,000 of six tracts were reprinted; 1,000 copies were printed of the first Siamese edition of *Hymns of the Christian Life,* containing over 150 selections from the English edition.

There has been an unprecedented sale for gospel portions and other Christian literature. At least 100,000 of the publications were sold during 1947, about two-thirds of them on trains and along the railway lines. A number of people responded to the invitation, printed on the literature, to contact the missionaries for further information, and several have been saved by this means. The American Bible Society reported that sales for the year 1947, in one section of the Alliance field, undoubtedly surpassed all previous sales records. In the year 1948 this Bible Society sold 200,000 New Testaments and Scripture portions in Siam. The complete Bible in Siamese, of which stocks were exhausted during the war, is still unobtainable.

The Alliance has produced and published a distinctive type of Christian literature in the Siamese language. The pamphlets entitled, *Way to Heaven, Heart of Man, Gospel Summary,* and *From Death to Life,* have gone through several reprintings and have a sale to members of other missions also. A new booklet, *The Only Way,* is proving to be very popular. Presumably, we are the first in Siam to publish gospel literature in the popular poetical form. A Buddhist scholar and professor, recently converted, a member of Rev. Boon Mark Gittisarn's church in Bangkok, rewrote three of our Siamese booklets in poetical form. The Alliance published, in 1948, 500 copies of the first edition of a Bible magazine, called in Thai by a title meaning "Bible Light."

American Bible Society workers have translated the entire Bible in the Thai language. Besides printing the New Testament in a separate edition, each of the books of the Bible is available as a separate portion. Two of our missionaries are serving on the American Bible Society's Bible Revision Committee. The Alliance has produced translations for Scripture Gift Mission publications in Siamese, and it has published hundreds of thousands of tracts and booklets written by missionaries or national Christians of other missions, as well as by our own workers.

Bible Schools

It has been the policy of the Mission to conduct annual Short Term Bible Schools in each district as far as possible. The minimum term is one month. Three such schools were conducted last year.

The Alliance maintains at Khonkaen the only Bible school in Siam. It has previously operated on a schedule of six months of training per year. Generally speaking, it has been the policy to keep the students out in the districts to gain practical experience as colporteurs and evangelists for one and one-half years between each six months of training in school. Since the war a stepped-up program has been in operation. In the past the small missionary staff did not make it possible to teach more than one class of students at a time, but within the next two years it is hoped that three classes of students can be taught simultaneously. Thirty-two students were in the Bible school in 1948.

To date there are 22 men and 20 women who have had some Bible school training and are either employed by the Mission or are currently in Bible school. At the beginning of 1949 only one class had been graduated, composed of four Siamese and one Chinese. The Chinese student came from the Baptist Church and has become the pastor of the oldest Protestant Chinese Church in Asia—the large Baptist Church in Bangkok. Of the four Siamese graduates, two are serving effectively; one has been ordained and is a teacher in the Bible school.

The Church and the Challenge

The automobile, ox-cart, horse, bicycle, raft and boat have all been employed to get the Gospel to the people of Siam. Street chapel evangelism, preaching in the markets, colportage work, Bible conferences, visitation work and Sunday Schools have all had a part, to say nothing of the translation and publication of Christian literature. Today there are nearly 250 baptized believers and a larger number of inquirers. Ten Sunday schools with a total enrollment of 511 were reported for 1948. Today there are 26 missionaries and 25 full-time national workers (one of them ordained) ministering in a territory where our responsibility is to take the Gospel to over 6,600,000 souls. Eastern Siam's population is the third largest of all Alliance fields, and is exceeded only by South China and Indo-China.

Although eleven new missionaries reached Siam during 1949, including six transferred from West China, the Mission appeals for many additional couples in order that the multitudes living in each of the 19 provinces for which we are responsible, should have an opportunity to hear the gospel. Assigning the present staff to as wide an area as possible, the following provinces will still be unoccupied:

Srisaket	451,576
Buriram	339,496
Kalasin	307,795
Nakorn Panom	307,173
Jayabhum	293,753
Sakon Nakorn	273,262
Nongkhai	144,201
Loey	134,202
Chantaburi	110,808
Trat	44,819
Rayong	84,197
Total	2,491,282

In the meeting of the Board of Managers December, 1949, it was voted to approve the Foreign Department recommendation that we endeavor to send out twelve new couples to Siam during the next three years so that within four years at least one couple could begin witnessing in each of the provinces named above. This is a true pioneer venture and these are people who have never heard the gospel. May God grant that not only in Siam but in every one of our fields a true advance shall be made in obedience of the Great Commission.

Bible Training School, Khonkaen, Siam

LATIN AMERICA

The expression "Latin America" has various meanings. Primarily the name indicates those countries whose language is of Latin derivation (Spanish, Portuguese, French); geographically speaking, it comprises usually all territories, continental and insular, in the Western Hemisphere from the southern border of the United States to Cape Horn; in a political sense, and the one most commonly implied, the term is used to define the twenty republics south of the Rio Grande: namely, Mexico; six in Central America; ten in South America; and the island republics of Cuba, Haiti and Santo Domingo. The ten republics of the South American continent are: Venezuela, Colombia, Ecuador, Peru, Chile, Brazil, Bolivia, Paraguay, Uruguay and Argentina. In South America, besides the republics, are the Guianas, three colonies belonging respectively to Great Britain, France and the Netherlands.

Since the announcement of the Good Neighbor policy by President Roosevelt in 1933, six international conferences of the American nations have been held. The project of the Pan-American Highway will be another link uniting South American republics. When completed it will reach from the Mexican border, down the western coast to Chile, where it will cross the Andes and extend to Buenos Aires in Argentina.

Following the Inter-American Conference at Bogota, Colombia, in March, 1948, the Pan-American Union was superseded by the Organization of the American States. However, the Pan-American Union was retained as the permanent central organ and general secretariat of the new Organization. The Bogota Conference approved a treaty of hemispheric economic coöperation, and adopted a resolution, sponsored by the United States, calling for united resistance to the threat of international Communism to democracy.

Latin America is watching Mexico. It remains to be seen to what extent the forces that caused Mexico's upheaval will influence other Latin American countries. Forces of change are especially active in Peru and Brazil. The revolutionary Apra party, which is Pan-Hispanic and socialistic, has been outlawed in Peru, but it still has great strength. Moreover, it envisages a program for all of Latin America, not just Peru. Its name in full is *Alianza Popular Revolucionaria Americana,* and the members of the party are called Apristas. They propose separation of church and state, division of large estates, national ownership of public utilities, and better conditions for the Indians. Their program for all of Latin America includes opposition to American imperialism, and internationalization of the Panama Canal.

SOUTH AMERICA

The area of the South American continent, from Panama to Patagonia, is about 6,800,000 square miles. That is not much less than the area of North America (9,000,000 square miles), but maps drawn of Mercator's projection make South America appear much smaller. The total population of the continent is nearly 102 millions. (The total population of all Latin America is variously estimated at from 125,000,000 to 150,000,000.) The following table gives the approximate area and population of South America's various countries:

Country	Area Sq. Mi.	Population
Argentina	1,678,270	16,100,000 (census 1947)
Bolivia	416,040 (estimated)	3,854,000 (estimated 1947)
Brazil	3,286,170	47,550,000 " "
Chile	286,322	5,100,000 (census 1940)
Colombia	439,830	10,545,000 (estimated 1947)
Ecuador	175,830 (estimated)	3,400,000 " "
Paraguay	150,515	1,225,000 " "
Peru	482,460	7,719,000 " 1945)
Uruguay	72,172	2,300,000 " 1947)
Venezuela	352,150	4,398,000 " "
British Guiana	83,000	381,320 " "
French Guiana	34,740	36,975 (census 1936)
Netherlands Guiana (or, Surinam)	55,143	189,484

People and History

The mainland of South America was first sighted by Columbus in 1498. Spanish conquest began in the western part of the continent with the subjugation of Peru by Pizarro accomplished in 1535. The story is an ugly one—eight million proud Incas were reduced to about one million serfs when the conquest was completed. The Inca and Aymara Indians had given to Ecuador, Peru and Bolivia, even in their earliest days, a fairly well advanced civilization. Now their empire was gone, their civilization destroyed. The Indian civilization of the other South American countries was very much inferior to that of the Incas.

Of the South American countries, Brazil only was conquered by Portugal. Independence was secured for the Spanish colonies by the year 1822 through the efforts of leaders like Bolivar and San Martin. In that same year, also, Brazil declared her independence from Portugal and proclaimed the regent, Dom Pedro I, as Emperor of Brazil. Brazil became a republic in 1889.

Physical Features

South America bears a marked physical resemblance to the continent of North America. It is roughly triangular in shape, with the base of the triangle in the north and the apex at the south. In the eastern part of Brazil it has older, worn-down mountains (the Serra do Mar, Serra da Mantiqueira, etc.) that correspond to our Appalachian system; and in the extreme western part of the continent it has the younger, rugged Andean Cordilleras that match our Western Cordilleras, the Rockies. We speak of a mountain chain; the Spanish speak of a string or rope of mountains, for *cordillera* in old Spanish meant a little rope.

The Andes are 4,400 miles in length with three parallel ranges in Colombia; they spread to a width of more than 300 miles in Bolivia; they are most narrow in Patagonia in the extreme south. From north to south the principal mountain peaks range from the Sierra de Santa Marta in Colombia (16,640 feet) to Aconcagua in Argentina (23,080 feet). This latter peak is usually associated with Chile, but it actually lies within the territorial limits of Argentina. It is second only to Mt. Everest in height. While the majority of the peaks of our Rocky Mountains are between 14,000 and 15,000 feet in height, and the highest 20,300 feet, yet in the Andes, 21 of the peaks are more than 20,000 feet in altitude, and nine of them are more than 22,000 feet high.

Between the eastern and western mountain systems, South America has a vast interior plains area, corresponding to our Mississippi region. The interior of South America, however, is drained by three major river systems instead of one. The mighty Amazon and its numerous tributaries form the largest river system in the world. The main stream is navigable from Para on the Atlantic seaboard to Huallaga, Peru, in the lee of the Andes, a distance of more than 3,000 miles. The La Plata system, uniting the Paraguay, Parana and

Uruguay Rivers, empties into the Plata River estuary, thus forming one of the greatest trading harbors in the world. The Orinoco River rises in the headlands between Venezuela and Brazil, and flows in a west and northerly direction before turning eastward toward the Atlantic. Together these three river systems drain more than one-half the area of the entire continent.

The bulk of North America is in temperate and sub-arctic zones; whereas the larger portion of South America lies in the tropics with unfavorable, enervating climatic conditions. This region is largely tropical jungle or unwieldy savanna, and but a fraction of the area of South America is open woods and prairie land, such as abound in our Middle West. However, the countries of Colombia, Ecuador, Peru and Bolivia, although in tropical latitudes, have a decidedly temperate climate due to their altitude, and in the case of the coastal countries, due to the Peru Current (formerly called the Humboldt Current).

In North America three-fourths of the inhabitants live on the plains (under an elevation of 1,000 feet), but in South America only one-third of the people live in similar regions, and the great majority of these latter are found in the temperate regions to the south.

Languages and Tribes

The people of nine of the republics of South America speak Spanish; those of Brazil speak Portuguese. The vast majority of the Indians, numbering, according to some authorities, about 15 million, can be reached only through their tribal languages. Ecuador, Peru and Bolivia are the home of the majority of the South American Indians. Of the total Indian population, more than one-half are to be found in Peru. Kenneth Grubb conservatively estimates that there are about 6,230,000 Indians on the continent. Probably his estimate is the more nearly correct, but no accurate figures are available, and as Mr. Grubb says, such calculations belong to an extreme order of vagueness. The estimated population includes 5,775,000 Indians of the mountains, in Colombia, Ecuador, Peru and Bolivia. They live under the civil government of their respective countries and are nominally Roman Catholics. The remaining 455,000 Indians are found in the Amazon and Orinoco River basins, the Gran Chaco and southern Chile. These are savage or semi-savage pagans. In Tierra del Fuego are the Onas, the Alikuluf and the Yahgan tribes.

Religions

The Indians of the far interior forest regions are pagans—animists who fear the human dead, and imagine that inanimate objects, such as trees and stones, are the dwelling places of spirits. They believe that the work of the medicine man, the masked dances, and all manner of witchcraft, are necessary in order to placate the evil spirits who would harm them. Most of the pagan Indians have no definite idea of a Supreme Being, a single deity. (See *Animism,* under *Africa.*)

Roman Catholicism prevails in all parts of South America except among the Indians mentioned above. Though religious liberty is a constitutional guarantee in most of the South American countries, Roman Catholicism still is the state religion in some of them. Introduced as it was by the Spaniards and Portuguese centuries ago, it maintains even today a very intolerant position, and in many instances manifests a fanatical spirit.

Many will argue that Latin America does not need missionaries, that she has the Roman Catholic Church and is therefore not a heathen land. But Rome has failed in the task. Her priesthood is corrupt, and one of her own Arch-

bishops in Quito, himself asserted that after 400 years of trying to make the Indians good Catholics, the aborigines were in a worse moral condition than before the coming of the white man. He added that the Catholic religion among the Indians was mere idolatry. Not only among the Indians is Catholicism idolatry. The devout ladies of European descent pray to the various saints for specific blessings. When their prayers are not answered, the image of the saint whom they invoked is stood on his head, or put in a shoe, as punishment. A certain saint did not give his devotee success in the lottery, and so the lady concerned turned his image with its face to the wall.

Roman Catholicism alleges that the New Testament has no authority over the Church because Christ established the Church first, before the New Testament was written. They believe that the Roman Church is the one true Church and declare that it never changes. Since the Church is older than the written New Testament, one would expect to find in the New Testament references to the practices of the so-called unchangeable Catholic Church, if it be indeed the Church that Christ founded. Yet in the New Testament not a word does one find about popes and papal infallibility, about cardinals and monks—only apostles, bishops, deacons and elders are mentioned. One finds nothing regarding candles, altars, crucifixes and rosaries. Masses, the Confessional, Mariolatry, purgatory, prayers to the saints, and holy water are taught nowhere in the New Testament. Nor were all these things existent in the Roman Church from the beginning, as they allege. Its doctrines were not formulated until the fifteenth century. The fabrication of holy water began about the year 1000; the rosary was invented in 1090; the doctrine of transubstantiation was adopted in 1215; auricular confession to the priests was instituted in 1225; Roman Catholic traditions and the apocryphal books were declared to have equal authority with the Holy Scriptures by the Council of Trent in the sixteeth century; the doctrine that Mary was born without sin was invented in 1854; and the infallibility of the Pope was accepted as a doctrine in 1870. In 1587 the Pope approved the title, "Mary, the Mother of the Creator." She is also called the "Queen and Gate of Heaven." Prayers to and worship of Mary were a matter of contention for centuries but the doctrine was finally adopted in 1854. The Catholic Church represents Christ as the stern Judge from whom leniency can more easily be obtained by praying to His gentle mother. As early as the close of the sixth century, the practice began of invoking angels and saints, who "by their own merits can obtain blessings for us."

The Roman Catholic Church says that the priests stand between God and the sinner. They hold that the office sanctifies, and that the priests, even if they are living in sin, can still exercise their function of forgiving sins.

At death a good Catholic can look forward only to the fires of purgatory; a bad Catholic to the fires of hell. The word purgatory is not found in any version of the Bible, not even in the Douay Version which the Catholics use. The doctrine of purgatory did not become a dogma of the Church until the fifteenth century. The Catholic Church teaches that the great majority of souls descend into purgatory after death, and that the number of those who go direct to heaven is so small that they can be counted, that they are, namely, the canonized saints. Masses and alms are believed to shorten the sufferings of those in purgatory, and of course the hope held out involves the payment of money to the church for the masses and prayers.

Wherever Roman Catholicism wields its power, there is ignorance, superstition and deceit. The newness of life spoken of in 2 Corinthians 5:17 is not manifest in converts to Catholicism. Rome's efforts in Latin America have left the ignorant Indians in chains of superstition and idolatry; they have left the intellectuals without any religion, although the agnostics may still contribute to the church. Viscount Bryce made the following observation of religion in South America: "Both the intellectual life and ethical standards of conduct of these countries seem to be entirely divorced from religion. The women are almost universally 'practicing Catholics,' and so are the peasantry. . . . But the men of the upper or educated class appear wholly indifferent to theology and Christian worship." These intellectuals, left in the bonds of materialism and indifference, present the gravest peril in South America today.

Missionary Occupation

Protestant missionary efforts in South America began first in 1555 when a company of French Huguenots went to Brazil with the hope of founding a colony for persecuted Protestants. This attempt failed, and the survivors perished within a few years. Another attempt was made by the Dutch after their capture of Bahia in 1624, but this also came to an untimely end. With the opening of work by the Moravians in British Guiana in 1735 and in Dutch Guiana in 1738, the modern era of evangelical ministry in South America may be said to have begun.

Early in the nineteenth century a project began in England for schools for children with the Bible as the main textbook, and in 1820 a British Society and the British and Foreign Bible Society united in sending Mr. James Thompson to South America to carry on similar school work. Within six years many schools were opened in Argentina, Uruguay, Chile and Peru, and Bibles were sold in large numbers. Soon, however, the influence of the priests caused a strong reaction and the efforts of Mr. Thompson and his coworkers were abandoned.

Captain Allen Gardiner, a British naval officer, and a Christian with a passion for the souls of men, became a witness for Christ in the southern portion of South America, principally among the Patagonians. In 1844 he was instrumental in the formation of the South America Missionary Society. He died in 1851 of cold and starvation, while awaiting the ship of supplies that was too late in arriving.

The Methodist Episcopal Church sent the first missionary from the United States, in 1836, to Brazil. The Presbyterian Mission was founded in Brazil in 1859. Work began in Chile in 1845, and in Colombia in 1856. In the latter half of the nineteenth century the American Bible Society began effective colportage work through colporteurs and missionaries. It is estimated that over two million copies of the Word have been distributed in South America during the past fifty years.

A recent census states that today there are three million Protestant Church members throughout Latin America, which is a very small per cent of the total population.

An authority on missionary work in Latin America said: "In Mexico is a more violent anti-religious movement than in any part of the world except Soviet Russia; yet a leading official of the Mexican government wrote with the approval of the government, 'If Mexican children are to be Christians, let them learn Christian doctrine from the fountain head as found in the Gospels of Jesus Christ.'" Not only in Mexico but throughout all Latin America many of the leading men, who have nothing but contempt for the presentation of Jesus Christ as given by the Roman Catholic Church in Latin America, have expressed their longing for a true understanding of Christ and His way so that He will become a reality to those who profess His name, and they, in the Spirit of Christ, will be interested in the welfare of their fellowmen.

The speaker told of prominent business men and officials in Argentina who acknowledged the supremacy of Jesus Christ as revealed in the Gospels. This leader went on to say that among Latin Americans the personality of a leader, religious or otherwise, has more influence than the precepts he presents. The increasing demand is for witnesses whose lives show forth the compassion and holiness of Christ Jesus. The people of Roman Catholic lands are tired of sham.

COLOMBIA

Colombia, in the extreme northwest of the South American continent, is the first country south of Panama. Its land frontiers touch Panama, Venezuela, Brazil, Peru and Ecuador. Colombia is the only South American country touching both the Pacific and Atlantic Oceans. Its northern coast is 600 miles nearer to New York than is San Francisco.

Area and Population

The area of Colombia is 444,270 square miles, equal to that of the Atlantic seacoast states from Maine to Florida, with the addition of Ohio and West Virginia. The population (estimated 1947) is 10,545,000, which figure is exceeded in South America only by Brazil and Argentina. The majority of the inhabitants are of mixed blood. Only about seven per cent (105,800) are pure-blooded Indians; five per cent are Negro; twenty per cent are white; and the remaining sixty-eight per cent are of mixed blood.

People and History

Before the Spaniards invaded Colombia it was peopled mainly by the Chibcha and Quimbaya Indians. They did not come under the influence of the powerful Incas to the south, nor did they attain their high standards of civilization. They worshiped the powers of nature and offered human sacrifices.

The honor of the discovery of Colombia belongs to Alfonso de Ojeda, who arrived at the harbor of Cartagena in 1509, but no permanent achievement was accomplished. Exploration and colonization of the country were begun in 1536 by Gonzalo Jimenez de Quesada, who founded the city of Bogota in 1538, and named the country New Granada. From 1740 on it was a viceroyalty of the Spanish Crown until independence was secured by the decisive victory of Boyaca, August 7, 1819. The revolutionary leader, Simon Bolivar, became the first president of Great Colombia. This unwieldy country broke up in 1830 into the republics of Venezuela, Ecuador and New Granada (later called Colombia).

In 1861 Mosquera, leading the liberals, suppressed the religious communities, expelled the Jesuits who had entered the country, and confiscated much church property, fanatically persecuting the clerical body. After many years of strife, which was a constant drain on the resources and manhood of the country, the conservative, or church party, triumphed in 1885. After the Civil War, which lasted from 1900 to 1903, the Conservative Party, in connection with the Church, ruled the land until the year 1930. With the election of Dr. Olaya Herrera in 1930 the Liberal (anti-clerical) Party was in control for the first time since 1885. As their influence increased such important subjects as the Concordat between the Church and State, as well as the old Constitution, were studied with the intention of modifying them. The regime was also marked by much progress in road building, new schools, primary education, and general economic and industrial conditions. However, a Conservative, Mariano Ospina Perez, was elected President on May 5, 1946, and the effect of a less tolerant regime was soon felt regarding the entrance into Colombia of missionary personnel, Scriptures and evangelical literature.

Government

Colombia is a republic with a President elected by direct vote for four years, and ineligible for re-election the following term. The Congress consists of a Senate of 57 members, elected for a term of four years, and a House of Representatives of 119 members, elected directly by the people every two years. Women are barred from voting and holding elective office. Military service is compulsory.

Climate

Although Colombia lies in the Torrid Zone, it possesses every climate in the world. There, it is simply a matter of altitude. Many of the more populated sections have a temperate climate due to their altitude. From sea level to the heights of the Andes, one encounters every degree of temperature from summer heat to perpetual winter. Due to Colombia's proximity to the equator, the changes of season are only from the dry to the rainy, the former called summer and the latter called winter. Change of seasons occurs about every three months but not uniformly throughout the country, as each region is affected by its geographical position and vegetation. In general the dry seasons occur from December to February, and from June to August; and the rainy seasons from March to May, and from September to November. The amount of rainfall varies considerably. In the Choco district there is a heavier reported rainfall than in any other part of the continent. At Buenaventura, farther south, the average rainfall is 281 inches.

Physical Features

Three great ranges of the Andes spread fan-like from the southwest corner of Colombia north and northeast across the country. The Western or Choco Cordillera, with a maximum altitude of less than 12,000 feet, runs parallel to and not far from the Pacific Coast, which is a strip of damp, rather unhealthful land. The fertile valley of the Cauca River separates the Western Cordillera from the Central or Quindio Cordillera, whose highest peak of Tolima attains a height of 18,430 feet. The third range is the Eastern or Sumapaz Cordillera. These three mountain ranges cover approximately one-third of Colombia's total area, yet within these mountain areas dwells almost the entire population of Colombia. The population centers especially around Bogota, the capital, situated in the Eastern Cordillera at an altitude of 8,660 feet. The famous Tequendama Falls, near the city, are an attraction to tourists.

The plains, called llanos, and the forests to the east occupy the other two-thirds of Colombia's area. Beginning where the mountains end, the llanos cover that part of the immense eastern territory which is watered by the tributaries of the Orinoco River. The forests, called selvas, lie south of the plains and cover the regions watered by the tributaries of the Amazon River. The rivers in these forests are not suited to travel because of cataracts. This great interior region of llanos and selvas covers nearly 290,000 square miles of territory.

Of the navigable rivers, the Magdalena is the most important, and is the principal highway of the country. It flows north between the Central and Eastern Cordillera for more than 1,000 miles and empties into the Caribbean Sea near Barranquilla. It is navigable for more than 800 miles, and even for 500-ton steamers for a distance of 560 miles, from Barranquilla to El Dorado. There are over 100 steamers on the Magdalena River, with a total capacity of 22,000 tons. The Sinu River is navigable for 100 miles and is an important waterway for the transportation of cattle raised on the pasture land in its basin. Also navigable are the Caqueta, Putumayo, San Juan and lower Cauca Rivers.

Resources

Colombia is the second largest coffee-producing nation in the world (Brazil is first). Sugar cane and bananas are also among the principal products, and like the coffee, go in large measure to the United States. Cotton, rice, cocoa, tobacco, wheat, maize and tagua (vegetable ivory) are also produced in large quantities. There is extensive cattle raising, with meat and dairy products for local consumption, and hides and skins for export. Dyewoods are important commercially; rubber, tolu balsam and copaiba trees are being exploited. Colombia has long been noted for its mineral wealth. Seventy-five miles from Bogota are the Muzo emerald mines, which have been in operation for four centuries. The Chivor emerald mines are near Somondoco. Colombia is the principal source of platinum, and there are also large exports of gold, silver, emeralds, and petroleum. Coal, iron, asphalt, copper, lead, mercury and manganese are found also.

Progress

Colombia has 7,700 miles of automobile highways and 35,000 miles of secondary roads. There are 2,087 miles of railways, of which 1,380 miles are owned by the National Government. Future plans call for three main lines, but at present they are scattered lines, built with a view to getting an outlet to the Magdalena River. The nearest semblance to a network of the railways is the junction of the Pacific, Antioquia and Caldas railways, totalling only about 700 miles.

Telegraphic communications are maintained throughout the republic; there is telephone service in the larger cities, and long distance service from certain cities to the United States and Europe. There is tri-weekly airplane service to the United States.

The public schools are supported by the civil government, but are largely under the administration of the Roman Catholic Church. Due to the shortage of rural schools, the majority of the children are illiterate. Not including children under seven years of age, 46.8 per cent of the population is illiterate. Education is free but not compulsory. Since the public schools are largely under the direction of the Roman Catholics, pupils are compelled to attend services in the church, and this makes the problem of educating the children of believers a difficult one.

In Bogota is the National University, founded in 1572. There are four other universities, one in Medellin, one in Popayan and the other two in other Departments of the republic.

Currency

The monetary unit is the gold peso worth fifty-three cents in U. S. money. Recently the gold peso has become of lower value following the devaluation of many currencies and the gold value in banking exchange often varies from month to month.

Languages and Tribes

The language of the country is Spanish, except among a small minority of the Indian tribes. The Indian peoples of mixed blood make up the bulk of the population, and they have intermarried with both the Spaniards and the Negroes. The Indians who inhabit the three main divisions of the Andes highlands are mostly semi-civilized. They speak their own particular dialect but many of them also speak Spanish. The same is true of the Indians of the lowlands.

The many jungle tribes are the minority who speak little else than their own dialects. They seldom come in contact with the white man although there are trading posts and government representatives along some of the rivers.

The Alliance is working among the following tribes which have their own dialects—languages that have not yet been reduced to writing: the Paez and the Guambiano Indians who are to be found in the Western and Central Cordilleras; the Cholo on the steaming Pacific Coast; and the Huitoto in the Amazon Basin which covers a large portion of Eastern Colombia. Contacts have also been made with other tribes in the Amazon sector.

Religions

Roman Catholicism is recognized as the religion of the country. Relations between the government and the Vatican are regulated by the Concordat of 1892. Its terms declare that "the public education and instruction shall be organized and directed in conformity with the dogmas and morals of the Catholic religion." The Concordat has given control to Rome over the *Intendencias* and *Comisarias,* that is, over districts that have not attained the status of a *Department.* Certain parts of the Departments of Nariño, Cauca, and others, also come under the Concordat, and are considered "missionary areas," but after more than 100 years, the Catholic orders and missionaries have failed to do anything constructive in those areas.

In spite of the terms of the Concordat, there is a limited tolerance which, according to Article 40 of the Constitution, provides that "the exercise of all forms of worship, which are not contrary to Christian morals nor to the laws, is permitted." The degree of tolerance varies with the political party in power at the time, and with the attitude of the local authorities.

Missionary Occupation

The Rev. James Thompson, agent of the British and Foreign Bible Society, arrived at Bogota from Ecuador in 1825. He founded a National Bible Society among the Roman Catholic priests, and the society's first meeting was held in a convent, with a monk as one of the secretaries. From Colombia, Thompson returned to England, and was never able to return to South America where such wonderful openings had been made. There was a reaction on the part of the Roman clergy and the results of the work were lost.

A permanent Protestant work was begun in 1856 when Rev. H. B. Pratt of the Presbyterian Church, U. S. A., opened the first mission station in Colombia, at Bogota. Among other achievements, Mr. Pratt made a well-known translation of the Bible into Spanish. The first church was organized in Bogota in 1861, but its six members were all foreigners. The first Colombians were received into the church in 1885, revealing the fact that only after twenty-nine years of ministry did any nationals become members of the church. The Presbyterian Mission has done effective work in church ministries, evangelization, and in educational work in the northern and eastern parts of the republic.

The Gospel Missionary Union entered Cali and Palmira in the western part of Colombia in 1912. The Mission has been active in evangelization; churches have been organized in many places; the native church is largely self-supporting. In Palmira this Society has a Bible Institute and a medical clinic which serve the evangelical cause throughout this area.

The Cumberland Presbyterian Church of the U. S. A. maintains a church and school in Cali, founded in 1926, and the Mission also has a number of preaching points in the Department of Caldas. The Brethren Mission entered Pasto

in 1935 and has several rural preaching points near there and also in the district of Putumayo. In 1933 the World-wide Evangelization Crusade established work in the Departments around Bogota, with headquarters in that city. Their work has grown, with a good ministry through the printed Word, and they also have a printing establishment for publishing gospel literature. They maintain a Bible Institute for training national workers.

The British and Foreign Bible Society has centers in Bogota and in Barranquilla, offering a sufficient supply of Scriptures for the many new Missions that have entered Colombia within the last few years.

The Christian and Missionary Alliance

With the exception of Peru, Colombia is our youngest field in South America. Alliance missionaries from Ecuador made several trips over the border into Southern Colombia, and through these visits some contacts and friendships were formed. From the beginning, there was strong opposition from the Roman Catholic Church. However, in 1923, missionaries located in Ipiales in the Department of Nariño, an area containing nearly half a million souls. Although it is one of the most fanatical countries on the continent, Colombia is proving to be one of the most encouraging of our five fields in South America. Our responsibility in Colombia, in six Departments and in the Intendencia de Amazonas, is for 1,675,000 souls. We have 12 mission stations and 18 church centers.

Department of Nariño

Ipiales is the land port of Colombia, the entrance from Ecuador. During a season of earthquakes in 1923, God gave an open door in this city. In 1924 missionaries crossed the border and a center was established, the first Alliance mission station in Colombia, yet today Ipiales is closed due to a shortage of workers. When the station was first opened, the response of the people was encouraging, but the Roman Church continued unremittingly its efforts to get rid of the Protestants. People in Protestant countries can hardly understand the lengths to which a fanatical priest of Rome will go to vent his deep-seated hatred on a Protestant. The law may be on the side of the Protestant, but that which is written on the books and seldom read is too far away to be of much help. That which is burning in the heart of a fanatical priest brings the desired action more quickly. The effect on the missionary is deadly. Long before the storm breaks, the atmosphere is oppressive with hatred and depressing because of the degradation. Such was the experience of the missionaries who opened Ipiales. In 1926 an organized mob besieged the home of the missionaries. Stone, bricks and heavy poles were hurled at the building; doors and windows were broken. The mayor and the police begged the missionaries to cross the border and escape into Ecuador, promising that they would be responsible for the house and goods left behind. There was a promise that the missionaries might return when things quieted down but the real purpose was to rid the land permanently of the Protestants. God overruled and within two weeks the missionaries were back in Ipiales, but under a guard of soldiers for over a month. Twelve years later the work in Ipiales was still showing the effects of those first terrible days. Progress was slow, but in the outlying regions groups of believers were growing and churches were organized. The town of *La Union* was opened, and the work there is going on under a national worker. Until 1935 this section of Colombia was supervised by our Mission in Ecuador, but it was then taken over as a part of the Colombian field. A review of the history of this

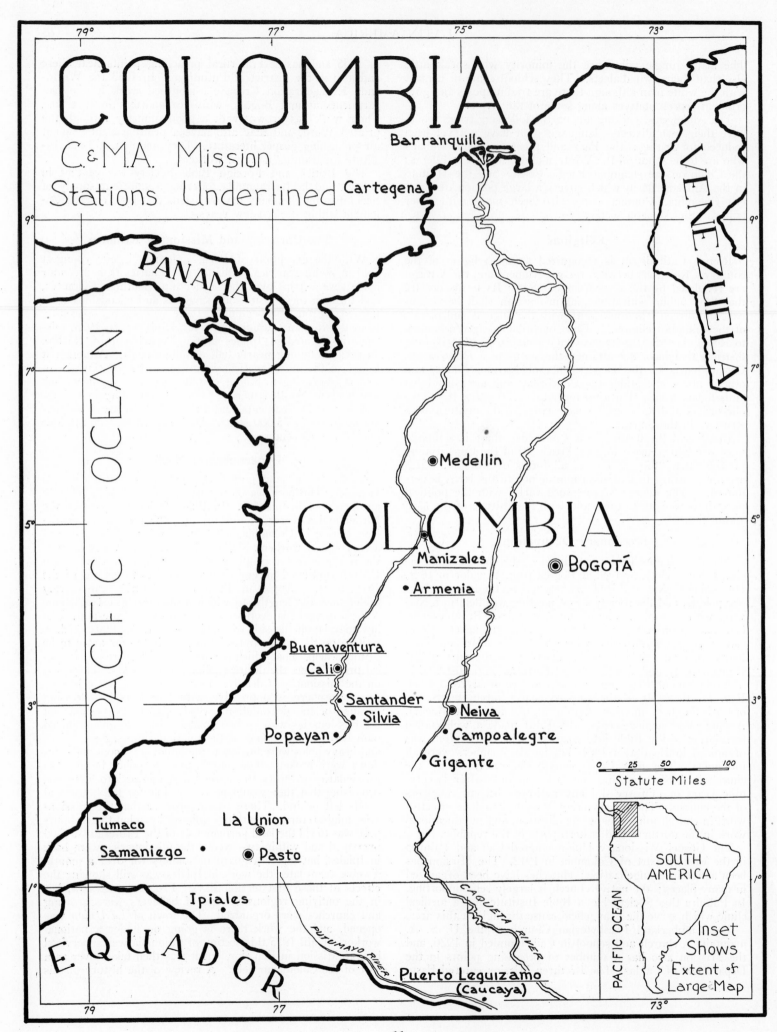

COLOMBIA

C.&M.A. Mission
Stations Underlined

VENEZUELA

Barranquilla

Cartegena

PANAMA

PACIFIC OCEAN

COLOMBIA

Medellin

Manizales

●Armenia

◉BOGOTÁ

Buenaventura

Cali●

●Santander

●Silvia

Popayan●

●Neiva

●Campoalegre

●Gigante

0   25   50   100
Statute Miles

Tumaco

La Union

Samaniego   ◉Pasto

Ipiales

SOUTH
AMERICA

PACIFIC OCEAN

Inset
Shows
Extent of
Large Map

EQUADOR

PUTUMAYO RIVER

CAQUETA RIVER

Puerto Leguizamo
(Caucaya)

station cannot but stir us to pray that the battle may yet be won there.

Tumaco This important port south of Buenaventura has shown much interest in the Gospel, and for years was ministered to by a lay worker. Since 1945 a missionary couple has resided there, and they have found an abundant ministry opened to them. The population of 35,000 is composed largely of Negroes. There are many Indians to be reached in the country districts and in the highlands of this area.

Pasto Just over the international border, the two Cordilleras passing through Ecuador form a knot known as the Nudo de Pasto, whence they branch out into the three Cordilleras which cross Colombia. Pasto is the capital of the Department of Nariño. It was entered by Alliance missionaries in 1946 with a view to reaching the people throughout the Department as well as the 50,000 inhabitants of the capital itself. National workers are in charge of *Sion*, a country section reached through Pasto. A school is maintained there and the church contributes toward the support of the pastor.

Samaniego Two lady missionaries opened this station in October, 1946. On the night of their arrival they found a group ready to stone them. The stones were not thrown—perhaps the sight of merely two women and a small child either disconcerted them or softened their hearts. Within six weeks of the time when the station was opened, friendly contacts had been established and some interest shown. Among the Bibles sold, one went to the Director of the school, who used it in teaching literature classes. A Sunday school was started and the attendance gradually increased. Late in March, 1949, fanatical Roman Catholics attacked the missionaries and threatened their lives. By the fall of that year the opposition was so fierce that the Mission decided it was better for the two ladies to leave, at least temporarily, until after the coming election. In spite of many encouragements, and the opening of a few hearts to the gospel, the missionaries have experienced fierce opposition and real danger almost continually since the opening of Samaniego.

Department of Cauca

Popayan Work in the northern part of our field was begun in 1926 at Popayan, the capital of the Department, which has an area of 10,384 square miles and a population of 356,000. Popayan is also the seat of academic and ecclesiastical activity. One of the older South American universities is located here. Our workers were the first evangelical missionaries to reside in this place and they met much opposition. Only by prayer and perseverance were advances made. The first evangelical baptismal service was held in Popayan in October, 1931, when five were baptized. Two of the five were later in service for the Lord. The country around Popayan is so mountainous that most of the itinerating has had to be done on horseback. Many of the people live in the mountains, especially the Indians, who compose 32 per cent of the population of the Department. The contacts made with the Indians of the Western and Central Andes resulted in a flourishing work, and the Indian Christians have taken an interest in evangelizing their own people. There are six organized churches in the Department, with many outstations that reach two distinct tribes.

Santander This town was first opened in 1927 as an outstation of Popayan. In 1930 a missionary took up residence here and the work has grown, extending into the outlying districts. Many of the mountain Indians who come into town on market day have been reached with the Gospel, and also the Word has reached the Negro population of that area.

Silvia This station was opened in 1941 in order to serve the vast Indian population of that area. The town is the center for reaching about 50,000 Paez and 20,000 Guambiano Indians. While the district was being visited, the village priest was trying to get rid of the missionaries. When the missionaries had won enough friends to begin holding services, the opposition of the priest increased. Only about three families remained faithful through the persecution that followed, but the prospects are more hopeful now.

Many of the Guambiano Indians have responded and there is an organized church among them. Groups of the Christian Indians go from farm to farm on Sunday afternoons, witnessing for the Lord. In 1949, with an initial enrollment of 15 students, a Bible Institute was opened for the training of Indian workers in this region. Work among the Paez Indians has been less encouraging than among the Guambianos.

The town of *Toribio* was opened in 1945 by a national worker and reaches a district with a population largely Indian. *Belalcazar* and its district was occupied and is being evangelized by a national worker. It is a fanatical center in the hinterland which is known as Tierra Adentro, a territory under the Concordat.

Department of Huila

Neiva As a result of a long itinerating trip the Department of Huila, representing 10,394 square miles and a population of 216,700, was entered by the Alliance in 1930. The missionaries who settled in Neiva found a few families interested in the Gospel and meetings were begun. There is a faithful group of believers in Neiva today.

Gigante was next opened, in '1935. On market day the town is a place of intense activity, and the national pastor begins the day with a very early gospel service.

Campoalegre For many years this town was an outstation of Neiva. A missionary took up residence there in 1944. Most of the church members live in the country but they have in the town a chapel on which they have almost completed the payments. The vast upper Caqueta region can be reached from this center, and the people there are showing an interest in the Gospel.

From Neiva the work has been enlarged to include the southern part of the Department of Tolima. Through the missionaries and a faithful layman the work has prospered until, in the country district of *Campohermoso,* there is now found our largest church, with a membership of 300. A church building has been erected and a self-supporting school is being conducted. Through the personal witnessing of the zealous believers of Campohermoso, there are three or four new congregations in the outlying districts and a work among the Indians has been started.

In *Chaparral,* which was opened in 1944, the national pastor has suffered much opposition, but now the congregation is increasing and the people are taking steps to erect a chapel.

Department of Caldas

Armenia This city has a population of about 60,000 and the Department a population of 800,000. Armenia is doubly important, for it is in one of the principal coffee districts of Colombia, and is also on the main route from the Pacific to the capital city of Bogota. The work here was opened in 1932 and many groups of believers have been formed. This is also the home of the Bible Institute.

The capital of the Department of Caldas is *Manizales,*

where a national pastor is stationed. The work in this city of 86,000 inhabitants was begun in 1934. A good church has been established in spite of fanatical opposition.

Another city, *Salamina*, with a population of 3,000, is occupied by a national worker who is tactfully endeavoring to get a foothold in this, one more fanatical center of vast importance. The believers in Armenia are largely responsible for the work opened in *Genova, Salento, Circasia* and *Mectezuma*.

Department of Valle

Cali This is the most important city of Western Colombia, with a population of more than 100,000. The headquarters of The Christian and Missionary Alliance is located here, as it enables the Chairman to better look after the business interests of the Mission, and to serve the entire territory under his care. A privately owned bookstore, "La Aurora," was opened here in 1940 by one of our missionaries, for the distribution and publication of Christian literature. The field Conference has voted to recognize the Aurora Book Room as the official bookstore for our Colombian field.

Buenaventura This port city on the Pacific Coast has a population of about 30,000. It is a place of great activity both for imports and the exporting of coffee. The majority of the population is Negro. Missionaries and national workers had made occasional visits here, and a real beginning was made about 1937. A missionary couple is located here; a new chapel was recently dedicated; and the church is making strides toward self-support.

Intendencia de Amazonas

Puerto Leguizamo This jungle station was opened in the year 1943 under the name of Caucaya. The government has since changed the name of the town in honor of a soldier who was killed there while defending his country against the Peruvians. The missionaries began a primary school here but, due to pressure from the Roman Catholic Church, it had to be closed, as this district is one of those covered by the Concordat. Our evangelical program has won the support of the people and meets their need. The priests, seeing that they were losing ground, appealed to the government to bring legal action to bear on the Protestant missionaries, for they cannot compete with the evangelical program and have to resort to the government for support. The Concordat will expire in 1954. Now is the time to begin praying that a change will be made. Under the present government there is not much hope. Many children of believers are denied an education because of the Concordat, which requires them to go to a Catholic school. The Concordat has been established for 50 years, but it was never put into effect until we had such good success in the jungle work at the station of Leguizamo. When the school there had to be discontinued, one was opened just across the border in Ecuador at La Esperanza. A national couple was placed in charge there and the work gave much promise. When the missionary at Leguizamo found himself too burdened with work to oversee the work at La Esperanza any longer, it was turned over, at least for the time being, to an independent missionary.

In spite of opposition, the work in Leguizamo has made progress and contacts have been made with several Indian tribes. Prior to 1943 the Gospel had never been preached there. By 1948 there was a splendid chapel and a flourishing church group. Some Huitoto Indians are among the baptized believers there and are outstanding Christians.

Early in 1949 a fire wiped out the village including our two mission properties and all the personal possessions of the missionaries, but the missionaries stayed on, continuing to witness to the white, brown and black races found there. A property of brick and tile is being purchased which will give the believers a fine little chapel, and the missionaries a comfortable home with no further fire worries. A 1500 watt electric light plant has been donated and an outboard motor has been promised for travel on the river.

Translation and Publication Work

From the beginning of the work, our missionaries have coöperated with the Bible Societies in the distribution of the Scriptures. For a time one of our missionaries acted as agent for the British and Foreign Bible Society. Many of the present-day churches are the fruit of early colportage work. *La Aurora* bookstore in Popayan has grown in usefulness until now, not only our own Society, but every Society working in Colombia patronizes it, especially to procure the Spanish edition of "Hymns of the Christian Life." This bookstore distributes Alliance publications and others to more than ten countries in North and South America. The main store is in Cali, with branch depots in the Bible Institute at Armenia, and in Betania and Santander in the Department of Cauca. The Colombian manager of the Cali store, a full-time colporteur, and the agents in the branch depots are all under the direction of the missionary owner of the bookstore.

In our Colombia field, translation work has been limited to small tracts, with the exception of the translation, by Rev. E. A. Prentice, of *Divine Healing*, by Dr. A. B. Simpson. A revolving book fund has been made possible, through the voluntary contributions of churches and individuals in the United States and Canada, for the purpose of publishing needed gospel literature. This fund has made it possible to publish in Spanish: *Introductory Bible Studies*, by Dr. Latham; *Advice to New Church Members* and *Commentary on Galatians*, by Dr. Lund; and various books for children. The fund made it possible to publish a new edition of Dr. Simpson's commentaries on *Genesis* and *Exodus*, first published in Spanish by our Alliance Press in Chile, our main publishing plant for Spanish America.

Schools

Five Short Term Bible Schools were held (1948), with an attendance of 77, the schools running usually for about two weeks at a time. One Workers' Institute was held with an enrollment of 24. The 27 primary schools (Standards 1 to 6) had an enrollment of 590. About 10 per cent of the pupils in primary schools later enter Bible School. Thirty Daily Vacation Bible Schools were held with a total enrollment of 827. Many of these schools, conducted high up in the Andes, could be reached only after hours on horseback, riding over steep, slippery trails. Adults and young people were enrolled, as well as children.

The Bible Institute of Armenia is in session eight and one-half months of the year, and offers a two-year preparatory course followed by a four-year Bible course. In 1948 there was an enrollment of 53, the proportion of men and women students being about equal. The majority of the students are supported without foreign help.

The Bible Institute was begun in 1933 in a single classroom, with a crowded dormitory. The dusty, crowded city quarters have now been replaced by property owned by the Mission in quiet surroundings. Two large cement buildings provide classrooms, also dormitory accommodations for the single students. A smaller building houses the married students.

The Church and the Challenge

After twenty-five years of work in Colombia, the Alliance churches there have a total membership of 1,231 baptized believers. In 1948, there were 83 baptisms, and the church offerings totaled about $9,000 in U. S. money. There are 21 organized and 59 unorganized churches, of which 28 are entirely self-supporting. There are 136 outstations, and a total of 47 national workers. These workers include 12 pastors and 27 school teachers. The national churches wholly support 26 of the workers and partially support 14 others. The churches conducted 64 Sunday schools with a total enrollment of 2,000 pupils.

ECUADOR

"El Ecuador" is the Spanish name for "the Equator," and the country is crossed by that imaginary line. Ecuador is wedge-shaped like a piece of pie cut between Colombia on the north and Peru on the south. At the eastern point of the wedge, the boundaries of Colombia and Peru meet, and on the west Ecuador is bathed by the waters of the Pacific. The republic extends 100 miles north of the equator and 400 miles south of it, and is the smallest of the South American countries excepting Uruguay and Paraguay.

Area and Population

Estimates of the area of Ecuador vary as much as from 175,830 square miles to 279,224 square miles. For a hundred years there was a boundary dispute between Ecuador and Peru, and although it was settled in 1944, there is still no definite figure for the area of the country. The vast frontier east of the Andes in the drainage basin of the upper Amazon is unsurveyed, and various geographers disagree greatly in their calculations. The Oriente, as the territory east of the Andes is called, extending to the Amazon flats, is not all within the limits of Ecuador. Roughly speaking, the upper reaches of the rivers are in Ecuador, the navigable parts within Peru. Included in the area of Ecuador is the Archipelago of Colon (Galapagos Islands), 500 miles from the continent, with an area of some 3,000 square miles.

The population of Ecuador (estimated 1947) is 3,400,000. It is estimated that 40 per cent of the population is pure Indian. Much of the unexplored area in the east is sparsely populated, for about 60 per cent of the total population lives in the inter-Andean region. Beginning at the northern end of the inter-Andean valley, the principal centers of population are Quito, the capital, Ambato, Latacunga and Riobamba. Cuenca and Loja are the important towns in the southern part of the Sierra. Guayaquil is the most important city on the coast, but included in the coastal region are the smaller cities of Bahia, Manta, Portoviejo and Jipijapa.

People and History

Two events stand out in the history of Ecuador—the conquest by the Incas, and the coming of the Spaniards. Little is known of the country or its civilization before the Inca conquest. It was occupied chiefly by Indian tribes who probably came from Central America. Of these, the Caras established a kingdom known as the kingdom of the Shiris, or Cara-shiris. In the 15th century A. D. the Incas of Peru determined to conquer them, and the Emperor Tupac Yupanqui, the eleventh Inca, and his son Huaina Capac, finally accomplished the conquest. The son spent most of his later years in Ecuador, and towards the end of his life the first word came of the arrival of the white man at Panama. Atahualpa, the son of Huaina Capac, was the third and last Inca to govern Ecuador. Quito was his northern capital.

The Incas imposed the Quichua language on the tribes whom they conquered in Ecuador, but they never conquered the Indians of the Oriente except those of the upper Napo River region.

In 1532, Francisco Pizarro, Spanish captain and conqueror of Peru, with his associate, Diego de Almagro, explored Ecuador. A few years before, the Spanish pilot, Bartolome Ruiz, had visited the coasts of Ecuador but Pizarro was the first to lead an expedition into the interior. He beheaded Atahualpa, the Inca emperor, and then, after many daring adventures and difficulties, Pizarro finally turned over much of the conquest of the country to Sebastian Benalcazar, one of his commanding officers, and to Almagro. In 1534 they conquered the Indians and founded the first Ecuadorian city, Santiago de Quito, which is now known as Riobamba. In 1535, Benalcazar also founded Guayaquil, which was twice destroyed before it was rebuilt in 1537.

The movement for independence from Spain began in 1809, but it was not until May 24, 1822, that the royalist troops were finally defeated at the battle of Pichincha, by Bolivar's famous General Sucre. At that time Ecuador was a part of the Great Colombia, under Simon Bolivar as President. It separated, and from 1830 on, became a self-governing state. Garcia Moreno was the next great figure in the country's history. He was President from 1861-1865 and again from 1869-1875. Both periods under this man of great activity and strong personality experienced a degree of peace. However, in 1861 he delivered the republic to the Papacy by a Concordat, which placed all education in the hands of the Catholic clergy, and the influence of that move is still felt in the country. Weak presidents followed Moreno until 1897, when Eloy Alfaro became the first liberal president of Ecuador. He instituted civil marriage and freedom of worship.

Government

Ecuador is a constitutional republic, composed of 17 provinces. Under the Constitution (promulgated March 6, 1945), the President is elected for four years directly by the people. The National Congress is bicameral, consisting of senators and representatives. Every Ecuadorian becomes a citizen at the age of 21, provided he is literate.

Climate

The climate varies with the altitude, ranging from tropical to sub-arctic. In the city of Quito, almost on the equator but with an altitude of 9,250 feet, the temperature in the shade averages from 58 to 60 degrees Fahrenheit. There the direct rays of the sun are always hot, but inside the houses it is almost too cold for comfort. The Peru Current (formerly called the Humboldt Current) makes the temperature of the Pacific littoral moderately cool. The city of Guayaquil, although in the heart of the tropics, has an average temperature of 78 degrees. In the eastern Amazonian plains, amid the forests and jungles, the climate is warm and humid. Ecuador has two major seasons, the dry, from June to December, and the rainy, from January through May. For the tropics, the climate on the whole is healthful.

Physical Features

Two parallel cordilleras of the Andes cross Ecuador from north to south. Of the dozen peaks which are more than 16,000 feet above sea level, Chimborazo (21,424 feet) and Cotopaxi (19,550 feet) are the highest. Both these volcanoes are far above the line of perpetual snow which begins at about 15,750 feet. The symmetrical crater of Cotopaxi rivals the Japanese Fujiyama and exceeds it in altitude by 7,000 feet. In fact Cotopaxi is the highest active volcano in the world, and 14,000 feet higher than Vesuvius. Cotopaxi is relatively quiet at present, but in the 18th century it was active continuously for 26 years and desolated an entire province. On August 5, 1949, an earthquake affected the three central provinces of Chimborazo, Tungurahua and Cotopaxi. Several towns were completely destroyed and many others were greatly damaged. It is estimated that from 4,000 to 6,000 lives were lost.

Ecuador has three distinct divisions: the Coast, the Sierra (the Andean highlands), and the Oriente (the forested region of Amazonia). Between the two cordilleras which cross the country is a narrow valley crossed by transversal ridges which average 8,500 feet in elevation and make several elevated plateaus in the valley. In this zone between the cordilleras, and on their slopes, dwells the bulk of Ecuador's population. The valleys are well adapted to agriculture.

The Coast section is about 100 miles wide with some swampy areas but with quite a large area of forested land also.

The Oriente begins on the eastern slopes of the Andes and extends down into the lowland plains watered by tributaries of the Amazon. The upper reaches of the rivers in the mountains lead down through precipitous gorges, but farther east the rivers are navigable, the Napo being the longest and most navigable of the rivers. This region of dense forests is sparsely populated and largely unexplored.

Resources

Ecuador is rich in undeveloped minerals: rich silver ore, copper, iron, lead, coal and sulphur. The petroleum output is increasing. The agricultural products are: cacao, rice, cereals, fruits, coffee, tobacco, cotton and tagua (vegetable ivory). Most of the supply of balsa wood comes from Ecuador. It is only half as heavy as cork, yet so strong that it is useful in aircraft and marine construction. The so-called Panama hat is a product of Ecuador; the finest of these, the Montecristi, is made in the Province of Manabi.

There is a great reserve of unharnassed power in the numerous falls and cataracts of the rivers, capable of producing millions of kilowatts of light, heat and power. The flora and fauna of Ecuador are rich and display some rare specimens.

Progress

Of the 687 miles of railroads in the country, the principal line is the Guayaquil and Quito Railway, completed in 1908. Automobile and bus service are possible in different sections of the republic. There is telegraphic and telephone service in some of the centers. Radio and airplane service have been greatly increased both internally as well as with the outside world. There are radio broadcasting stations operating in the larger cities. Thousands of receivers are now installed in private homes and the radio audience is growing rapidly. The Shell Oil Company maintains airplanes for transporting their personnel into the eastern jungles. A missionary aviation program has been inaugurated to serve jungle stations, while several airlines give service to the principal cities of the country.

Primary education is compulsory and government schools are carried on throughout the republic, but the training of the youth still lies to a great extent in the hands of the Roman Catholic Church. There are four universities located respectively in Quito, Guayaquil, Cuenca and Loja.

Currency

The monetary unit is the "sucre," named after Bolivar's famous General Sucre of Independence fame. At present the sucre is worth 6.7 cents in U. S. currency.

Languages and Tribes

There are three main classes of people in Ecuador, the Spanish, the Indians and the mixed or *mestizo* class. Spanish is the official language of the country but not the only one in use as about 40 per cent of the population is pure Indian.

The Indians of the Sierra speak Quichua (also spelled Quechua), the language imposed on them by the conquering Incas. Although more civilized than the jungle Indians, the Sierra Indians are apathetic toward spiritual matters and are materialistic, for their souls have been warped by four centuries of a debased form of Roman Catholicism.

The Indians of the northern jungles of the Oriente in the Archidona-Tena-Napo region also speak the Quichua language. In the central part of the Oriente are the jungle tribes of the Canelas region, the savage Aucas who are hostile to the entrance of the white man and to missionary effort. They are so unapproachable that they will kill a white man on sight. In the last 15 years they are reported to have made 13 raids and killed at least 50 persons. To the east and north of Tena on the border between Ecuador and Colombia are the Cofanes, who are more civilized and approachable.

In the southern Oriente jungles are head-hunting Jivaros, who have the gruesome custom of preserving the heads of their enemies as trophies, shrinking them by a secret process to the size of an orange. Blood feuds among the Jivaros are handed down from father to son. The killings are nearly always done from ambush with old muzzle-loading shotguns and lances. Blowguns and poisoned darts are used only to kill game and never against an enemy. A missionary who has worked for years among them says of the Jivaros: "They are unclean physically and morally. They are cruel and implacable—an enemy is never forgiven; he must be killed." The Jivaros have their own language as they were never conquered by the Incas and so were not compelled to learn Quichua.

Forest Indians are also found in the coastal province of Esmeraldas, which is one of the most sparsely settled provinces in the country. They are the Cayapas, numbering only about 1,500, yet speaking their own language.

Alliance missionaries are working in the Spanish, Quichua and Jivaro languages.

Religions

Liberty of conscience and freedom of worship are guaranteed by the Constitution of Ecuador and the government takes a fair attitude toward evangelical missions. However, fanatical Roman Catholicism prevails in the Sierra, and religious indifference is characteristic of the coastal provinces. Ever since the Spaniards came, the Indians of Ecuador have been catechized by priests and most of them are considered to be Catholics. However, Rome has never succeeded in converting the Jivaros from their head-hunting. They are animists and believe in a devil but not in a Supreme Being. The savage Aucas of the central part of the Oriente are also animists.

Missionary Occupation

James Thompson landed in Guayaquil in 1824, and sold over 700 Bibles there. In Quito he sold 25 copies to a convent, for the friars. Three years after he moved on to Colombia (see *Missionary Occupation,* under *Latin America*), Louis Matthews, also an agent of the British and Foreign Bible Society, visited Guayaquil, but from then on until the Methodists arrived in 1877, no Protestant missionary set foot in Ecuador. Penzotti of the American Bible Society took a cargo of Bibles into Guayaquil in 1888. They were returned to the ship with the statement: "The Bible will not enter Ecuador as long as Chimborazo stands." In 1896, missionaries of the Gospel Missionary Union entered the country. The year before they entered, a band of young men in the United States had spent a night in prayer for the opening of the doors of Ecuador. They did not know that at that very time, the liberal General Eloy Alfaro was marching on Quito, and that soon a liberal government would be in power. Of the two men who entered Ecuador under the Gospel Missionary Union, one later went to Colombia. The other worked independently in Ecuador for many years, making wholesome contacts for the gospel while he taught in the leading college of the city of Guayaquil. In 1922 he and his wife joined The Christian and Missionary Alliance. Alliance missionaries had first entered Ecuador in 1897.

Since 1896 there has been continuous missionary effort in Ecuador, but progress has been slow. The Sierra has been less responsive than the Coast. The work of the gospel has been greatly furthered through the excellent work done by the British and Foreign Bible Society and the American Bible Society, now amalgamated and known as the United Bible Societies, and operating throughout the republic through their colporteurs. Protestant Missions in Ecuador today include the following:

	Number of Missionaries on the Field September, 1949
Brethren Mission	4
Christian and Missionary Alliance	40
Christian Missions in Many Lands (Brethren)	4
Evangelical Covenant Mission	10
Gospel Missionary Union	29
Missionary Church Association	8
Radio Station HCJB	33
United Andean Indian Mission	4
United Bible Societies	2
	134

Unfortunately, the Seventh Day Adventists and Jehovah's Witnesses both have representatives in different parts of the country.

Since 1931 the gospel has been going out over the air in Ecuador. In that year the Voice of the Andes, Radio Station HCJB, began its work. There were at that time only six receiving sets in all Ecuador; today there are some 50,000. The six transmitters belonging to the Voice of the Andes are operated on both long and short wave, reaching all of South America and circling the globe. Programs are broadcast daily, except Monday, in 13 different languages. Educational programs are also broadcast over HCJB, but there is a preponderance of gospel programs, more than 10,000 a year.

The Missionary Aviation Fellowship recently sent a four-place Stinson Voyager to the jungle region of Ecuador to be used in coöperative transportation of the personnel of three evangelical missionary groups. Its service will be available to the two jungle fields of the Alliance. When fully established this service will eliminate days of travel over arduous trails on foot and muleback, and will insure supplies being sent to the jungle stations with greater ease and less damage to the goods en route.

The Christian and Missionary Alliance

The first missionaries of the Alliance went to Ecuador in 1897, entering first the cities of Quito and Montecristi. There was much persecution and opposition from the Catholics. Because of the fanatical mobs on the streets of Quito, the government at times had to call out either the police or army to afford protection. The high altitude made it necessary for those early missionaries to retire from the field before their first term of service had expired. The Coast region was always much more liberal and open to the missionaries than the Sierra region. For many years the work showed few results. Not many of the people were open-minded and courageous enough to listen to the gospel message, but in spite of prejudice and fear a few converts were won even in those first hard years. Because of the opposition of the Catholics, it was found that more effective work could be done by circulating the Scriptures and tracts, and by personal work, than by holding public services. The next advance was to hold meetings in homes. There are believers in the churches of Ecuador today who were converted during those difficult years.

Two deputations from the Home Board visited Ecuador between the years 1921 and 1924. After those visits the work of the Society began to show progress. Gradually it spread to include the Indians. Of the three stations among the mountain Indians, the oldest is at Agato. The second, the Indian work at Colta, is under national leadership. More recently a third station in the mountains has been opened among the Salasaca Indians near Ambato, and excellent beginnings have been made. Cuenca in the south is the post-office for the jungle station of Chupientsa, the base for work among the Jivaros in the southern Oriente. Three stations for Indian work are open in the northern Oriente, of which the first was at Tena, opened in 1926.

A Bible Institute was opened in Guayaquil in 1928, and several primary schools for Indian children are being conducted. The work in Ecuador may be best understood by dividing the field into its natural divisions, diverse regions whose people and their response to the gospel are distinct one from the other: namely, the Coast, the Sierra, and the Oriente.

The Coast

Guayaquil In this region there is an apathy to spiritual things but little opposition. The city (population, 216,863) is the chief seaport and commercial center of Ecuador. Situated on the banks of the Guayas River, about 30 miles from its mouth, it is the center of Protestant activities for the Guayas province (population, 500,000). Missionary work was begun here in 1897 by the Gospel Missionary Union. The Christian and Missionary Alliance began work here in 1920. The late Rev. W. E. Reed had established a church here before he joined the Alliance in 1922, and this church has proved to be the hub of Alliance work throughout the country. However, the work did not develop rapidly in Guayaquil. As late as 1919 there were only fifteen members in the church, and Mr. Reed wrote in 1925 or 1926: "About five years ago something new took place. The public in Guayaquil began to understand what our message was, and real converts began to appear. . . . Perhaps the greatest single impulse to the spread of the gospel in this section of the country came through the conversion of a woman, a daughter of the most notorious procuress in the city. . . . She made her testimony known as widely as the fame of her former life had been."

Today the large church, supported by nationals, carries on, with national pastors and lay workers, extensive activities in the city and province. Over forty meetings a week are held—Sunday schools, Child Evangelism, youth meetings, Bible classes, Teacher Training classes, literacy campaigns, evangelistic and open-air services, besides the regular church services. Through this church 520,000 tracts were given out last year. A primary day school, with over 200 enrolled, is maintained in order to give the children of the Christians the best kind of secular education under Christian leadership. The large floating population of Guayaquil has

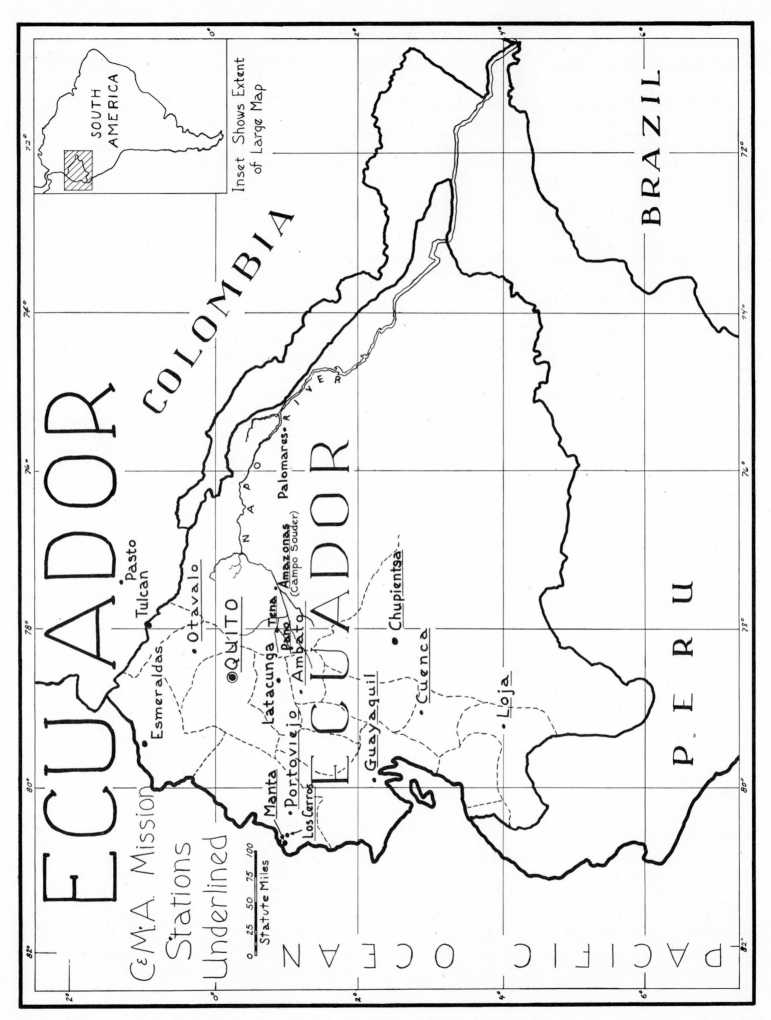

ECUADOR

C&M.A. Mission
Stations
Underlined

0 25 50 75 100
Statute Miles

COLOMBIA

BRAZIL

PERU

ECUADOR

PACIFIC OCEAN

SOUTH AMERICA

Inset Shows Extent
of Large Map

Pasto
Tulcan
Esmeraldas
Otavalo
QUITO
Latacunga
Manta
Portoviejo
Los Cerros
Ambato
Pano
Tena
Amazonas
(Campo Souder)
Palomares
NAPO RIVER
Chupientsa
Guayaquil
Cuenca
Loja

made it possible to win converts who have carried the witness back into the highlands, to fanatical places where it would have been hard to reach the people directly. At one time it was estimated that 60 per cent of our church members in other parts of the country were either converted in Guayaquil, or first became interested in the gospel while there.

Four former outstations of the Guayaquil Church, namely, *Ancon, La Libertad, Milagro* and *Duran,* are now organized churches under the National Christian and Missionary Alliance, while *Bucay* and several other centers are being evangelized from Guayaquil. The odd name of Bucay was given to the railroad town near the foot of the Andes, by the American engineers who built the railroad. They called it Buckeye in honor of their native Ohio, hence the name Bucay.

Los Cerros This is the name given to the farm located a few miles from the seaport of Manta, which has been the home of the Bible Institute since 1947. As the months have gone by, real enthusiasm has been aroused regarding this new location away from a city, and a marked change for the better is seen in the students.

The town of *Manta* (population, 16,325) is an important port of the province of Manabi. Although Manta is listed in the Prayer Manual as a mission station, the missionaries actually live in Los Cerros and Portoviejo, but the post office address is Manta. Several successful Youth for Christ campaigns have recently been held in Manta. The pastor is a graduate of the Bible Institute. A national layman is in charge of the work at *Montecristi,* another town near the Bible Institute, and the birthplace of the first liberal president of Ecuador, General Eloy Alfaro.

Portoviejo This city, with a population of 15,271, is the capital of the province. Missionaries reside here, also the national worker. The near-by towns of *Sucre, Jipijapa* and *Santa Ana* are reached from this city.

Bahia, the center for the northern section of this province, is in charge of a national worker, as is also *Vinces* in the province of Los Rios. There is no regular pastor in the province of El Oro but services are held regularly in *Machala, Porto Bolivar, Portovelo* and *La Bocana.*

The Sierra

The Sierra is the Andean highlands, with a narrow valley and transversal ridges. Its cities lie at an elevation of from eight to ten thousand feet above sea level. The Roman clergy holds the reins of power, the people are fanatical, the Indians are dull and obstinate, but the last 25 years have shown an advance in the progress of the Gospel.

Quito Quito, capital of Ecuador (population, 210,679), is situated at the base of the volcano Pichincha in a picturesque valley. This city was the ancient capital of the Shiri Indians, and later of the conquering Incas. Rainfall is abundant, with an average of 40 inches throughout the year, but occurring chiefly from October to May. The average temperature is 60 degrees Fahrenheit. Quito is so near the equator that the days and nights are of equal length and darkness falls regularly about 6:00 p.m. The city is connected with Guayaquil, to the south, and with Otavalo and Ibarra, to the north, by railroad; and by motor roads to Riobamba and southern Colombia. Quito is the seat of the Roman Catholic archbishopric and is noted for its many convents and churches.

Alliance missionaries first entered this city in 1898. Today the Quito Church is independent of the Mission inasmuch as it is one of the National Christian and Missionary Alliance Churches which calls its own pastor and is entirely self-supporting. Besides the activities of the church in the province, a work is being carried on at the penitentiary under the leadership of one of the church elders. The headquarters of the Alliance in Ecuador are here; the school for missionaries' children is on the outskirts of the city; the bookstore, *Realidades,* is operated from this center, and most of the gospel literature is printed either here or in Guayaquil.

A single center, *El Centro Biblico,* houses the offices of The Christian and Missionary Alliance, the Covenant Mission, Radio Station HCJB, the United Bible Societies, the English Fellowship, and the book store, *Realidades.* About two miles north of the city, on the way to the Pan-American airport, in a property adjacent to the Alliance Home and School for missionaries' children, are the broadcasting studios and homes of the staff of the Voice of the Andes, Station HCJB.

Otavalo (Agato) Otavalo is the post office for the Indian station at Agato. Located among the Quichua Indians, this is our oldest mountain Indian station. The region was surveyed by one of our early missionaries at Quito in 1918. Building operations were begun on the new station in 1919. In those early days the only means of travel to Quito was on horseback. Now there are both a motor road and a railroad. There are no less than 40,000 Indians in the immediate vicinity. A national pastor is located at Otavalo. The missionaries give themselves to the Indian work at Agato, where a primary school has been carried on for several years, with government recognition. Late in 1935 there came a marked increase in spiritual blessing, and there is now a fine, though small group of baptized believers. The Indian Christians are beginning to show initiative in witnessing to others. They have made visits to other Indian centers in the mountains to help establish new gospel centers. The Agato Christians also send delegates to the National Conference.

This work is in the province of Imbabura. In 1948 our Conference turned over to the Covenant Mission the section from Ibarra (capital of the province of Imbabura) northward, embracing the province of Carchi and part of Imbabura. The Covenant Mission has stationed missionaries in Ibarra.

Ambato Ninety miles south of Quito on the Guayaquil and Quito Railway is Ambato (population, 34,000, before the earthquake of 1949). The climate is temperate and this is a rich fruit center. Alliance work began here in 1922, and for some time the Bible Institute was located here. The presence of the Shell Oil Company here has been responsible for a marked growth in population in recent years. Ambato has been the center of an important itinerating program among both Spanish and Indian peoples, and the base for the work among the Salasaca Indians, who number about 10,000. Ground has now been secured among these Indians, permission has been granted for a school, and a modest house has been erected in the country district among them about ten miles from Ambato.

In August, 1949, a severe earthquake had a devastating effect upon the city of Ambato and a large area round about. Towns and villages were destroyed or severely damaged and many lives were lost and farmlands seriously affected. The Alliance Mission and others undertook prompt relief work to supplement that done by the government. There was no loss of life among our church members, and the missionaries were unharmed. The rented houses which they occupied were not seriously damaged. The mission building in a near-by center among the Salasaca Indians also withstood the tremors, though many homes of the Indians were demolished. The work of reconstruction is under way.

Latacunga is an outstation 25 miles north of Ambato. It is the capital of the province of Cotopaxi, a city with a population of 21,000. *Colta,* another outstation in this central region of the Sierra, is the second of our highland centers for Indian work. Situated by a beautiful lake of the same name, Colta, at an elevation of over 11,000 feet, is under the shadow of the mighty volcanic peak, Chimborazo. Work was opened here by missionaries in 1934, and a national worker now has charge of the church and school for Indian boys. The near-by town of *Cajabamba* is worked from Colta.

Cuenca This is the capital of the province of Azuay and the third largest city in Ecuador (population, 56,271). It is in the southern part of the Sierra, 190 miles south of Quito. Cuenca boasts a university and a normal school. It is not connected by railroad with the rest of the country and therefore has less of a cosmopolitan aspect than some of the other cities. It was first occupied by Alliance missionaries in 1930. The first years saw little fruit but some friends were made among people of the better social class. Because of an inadequate staff, Cuenca was unoccupied for some years. Now it is again the center of an aggressive local and itinerating program, and is also the base for work among the Jivaro Indians.

Loja This station is on the southern border of Ecuador, just north of Peru. Loja (population, 22,365) is the capital of the province of the same name. It has a university, and the reputation for speaking the purest Spanish of any place in the country. There are few Negroes and few foreigners here. The city, founded in 1545, has an altitude of over 7,000 feet, and is in good farming country, but the only industry is a match factory. In its isolated situation, Loja has clung to old and unusual customs. Crepe is hung not only on the door of a house visited by death, but on the doors of the houses of near relatives of the deceased, as well. The custom has given Loja the name of the "city of eternal mourning." This is the most Catholic province in Ecuador and the adoration of the Virgin holds first place.

There are about 6,000 Quichua Indians in the province, located chiefly in Zaraguro. Many of them are literate and they seem to be more prosperous than Indians of other sections. Both missionaries and national workers have done much itinerating and visitation in this area.

The Oriente

Chupientsa The work of this station in the southern jungle is devoted to the Jivaro Indians. Alliance missionaries first entered this section in 1926. After a journey of four days on horseback and four on foot, they reached Sucua, a station of the Gospel Missionary Union, which Society began work among the Jivaros in 1903. Our missionaries remained at Sucua studying the Jivaro language until 1929, and then moved to Chupientsa, about 20 miles to the south, on the Upano River, where the new station was to be located. For months Indians had been clearing the jungle and planting crops for the missionaries. Three Ecuadorians had been sawing by hand the lumber for the house. Construction was begun under the menaces of a witch doctor, who threatened to kill the missionaries, and internal strife and killings among the Indians were frequent. The Jivaros are not a numerous tribe but, because they live in isolated huts, they are scattered over such an immense territory that the missionary task calls for more workers than would be necessary if the Jivaros were concentrated in villages. Visiting them is difficult as all itinerating must be done in the dry season, on foot-trails, for the rivers are neither bridged nor navigable. Traveling southeast from Chupientsa, the nearest

mission station is at Iquitos, Peru, a journey of nearly a month.

Fruit has come slowly. The first convert in Alliance work was a Jivaro woman won after 12 years of labor. In 1941 a boarding school was opened for Indian boys and it has proved to be effective in reaching both the children and their parents. Among these children are sons of killers who should be mortal enemies according to Jivaro custom. Instead, they have become friends learning together the gospel that breaks down all barriers.

Tena, Dos Rios Tena, in the northern part of the Oriente along the upper reaches of the Napo River, is a strategic center for reaching seven Indian tribes, among them the Napos, Panos, Tenas and Archidonas. The station, called Dos Rios (Two Rivers), near the town of Tena, was entered by Alliance missionaries in 1926. Thousands of Indians have visited the station, some coming from a distance of six or seven days' journey. Two primary schools to which the government gives encouragement and backing, are conducted, one for Indian boys and one for girls. A trading center is maintained which gives contact with the Indians and helps to provide food for the workers and pupils. A small clinic is carried on and in times of epidemics the missionaries and workers are busy day and night helping to alleviate suffering. In 1948 there were twenty baptized believers in this sector, most of them Indians.

Pano, Sumac Hogar The station here is located also in the northern jungle, five days by mule-trail from Quito. It was first opened in 1943 for the Alliance by a missionary of the Plymouth Brethren. It is now manned by our own workers. Quichua-speaking Indians of this region live in huts scattered through the jungle. A boarding school for boys is the heart of the work. A trained national teacher and an Indian helper conduct the school. The missionaries have ample opportunities for a spiritual ministry to the pupils and others in the morning devotional services and regular services held four times a week. Outside interest and attendance is encouraging. Several believers outside the school show evidence of the new birth. Many of the schoolboys have been converted and three of them were recently baptized.

Campo Souder, Amazonas This is the newest station in the northern jungle. A site on the Napo River was secured only recently and a missionary couple is in residence there. A primary school for Indian boys has been opened.

Translation and Publication Work

For many years the Spanish Bible has been in circulation throughout the country. Most of the Indians, however, are illiterate, and those who can read, naturally understand their own language better. The Gospels of Luke and John have been translated into the Quichua language. The translation was done chiefly by a missionary of the Gospel Missionary Union, although some help has been given by a Quichua Committee with representatives from the Alliance and other Missions. The Gospel of Luke, in Jivaro, was also translated by a missionary of the Gospel Missionary Union. Mark and Acts are now being translated into Quichua by a missionary of the Brethren Society, working in conjunction with the missionary translator of the Gospel Missionary Union. Also assisting in this work is Aldelmo Rodriguez, a normal school graduate and a teacher in The Christian and Missionary Alliance school at Dos Rios.

Reed and Reed of Guayaquil publish many useful school books, and they have recently published a Spanish translation of *The Preacher and Prayer,* by Bounds. The magazine *Salud y Vida,* Hymns of the Christian Life, Sunday school helps and leaflets are all available from the Alliance Press in Chile. (See *Translation and Publication Work,* under *Chile.*) *Realidades,* the field magazine in Spanish, was published for a number of years but has been succeeded by a monthly paper called *El Evangelista Ecuatoriano,* and published by the national church, which also publishes tracts weekly. Radio Station HCJB gives a book review of evangelical books twice a week over the air, announcing that the books reviewed can be secured at the *Libreria Realidades.* There is a ready sale for evangelical books and literature. One missionary in a single year gave out over 100,000 tracts in a most fanatical province, and sold many Bibles and hundreds of Scripture portions. Many are clamoring for the Scriptures. We must be on the alert, for Seventh Day Adventists, Jehovah's Witnesses, and other false cults are taking advantage of this hunger for knowledge and are flooding Ecuador with their literature. It does little good in South America to confine the gospel message to within the four walls of a hall or chapel. Two of the principal means of evangelization are itineration and the distribution of the printed page. As one missionary said, "The tract is the missionary's best weapon."

Schools and Literacy Campaigns

The Bible Institute of Ecuador is the outgrowth of group meetings of young Christians who met regularly in the Guayaquil Church to be taught by the missionary. As the interest increased it was evident that a more formal type of school would be necessary to train satisfactorily those who were to become the future leaders of the Church in Ecuador. In 1928 the Bible Institute was opened in Guayaquil; in 1932 it was moved to Ambato, and for seven years the students were trained in that city. The Institute was moved back to Guayaquil in 1940 and remained there until it was established in the present location at Los Cerros in 1947. The new location is in the coastal province of Manabi, only a few miles from the seaport of Manta. The faculty consists of five missionaries and two national teachers. The 1948 enrollment was 19, and most of the students are partially self-supporting through their work in the Farm School. Progress has been made in the academic status of the school. The Institute insists on a thorough Bible training, and strives to instill in each student a Spirit-inspired missionary zeal. A large number of Bible Institute graduates are serving as national pastors, and the first President of the National Confederation of Churches in Ecuador is a graduate of this Bible Institute.

The total number of Alliance primary schools in Ecuador in 1948 was nine, with a total enrollment of 380. Six grades are covered in the William E. Reed Primary School in Guayaquil; the eight Indian schools vary in the number of grades covered, but all have government recognition and most of the teachers are normal school graduates. The majority of the schools still have to be subsidized to some extent by the Mission.

More Indians were baptized in 1948 than in any other year of Indian work, and most of the ones baptized are the result of our primary schools for Indian children of the jungle. In 1948 the enrollment in the Dos Rios school was 81, of which 15 were girls, and to get Indian girls into school is a great victory. Two Indian boys have entered the Bible Institute at Los Cerros, the first Indian students to be enrolled there. Catholic priests are boasting that they will yet rid the northern jungle of our missionaries. They are more hostile since the new station was opened on the Napo River, and they have threatened to build one of their schools in close proximity to each school we try to open there.

Five Short Term Bible Schools were held in 1948 in our Ecuadorian field with a total enrollment of 96, and an average duration of three weeks each. Child Evangelism classes enrolled 195, and Daily Vacation Bible Schools numbered 36, with a total enrollment of 1,292. Fifty-six Sunday schools had a total enrollment of 2,415.

The Church and the Challenge

A National Assembly meets annually as the final legislative body of the national church in Ecuador. Regional conventions are held in different parts of the field. The National Assembly is composed of nationals who come from all sections of the field, as well as official delegates sent to represent their local churches or groups. Only the official delegates take part in the business matters and decisions made. They elect their own governing committee of five members. This committee has the final word on all matters pertaining to the National Confederation of Churches, but the committee works in close harmony with our Missionary Field Executive Committee. The National Confederation of Churches is composed entirely of Alliance churches.

The Alliance has (1948 report) 29 national workers, of whom nine are fully supported by the national church. Eight of the workers are women. Throughout the field there are 21 organized and 17 unorganized churches. Ten of the churches are fully self-supporting. Baptized believers number 889, of whom 98 were baptized during the year. Inquirers number 370. The offerings of the national churches totaled the equivalent of $9,220 in U. S. money. There are 12 mission stations, 21 church centers, and 42 outstations.

In the year 1948, tent services were held for the first time in Quito and on the Coast. The response was good, with attentive crowds packing the tent. Youth for Christ meetings have become a regular feature with much benefit. Although economic conditions are serious, church offerings have increased.

The spiritual condition of the Indian population of Ecuador is a challenge to more effective intercession. In all the Alliance work among the various Indian tribes, less than 100 persons have made open confession of Christ. It is difficult, however, to judge actual results, for some of the children in our schools are interested but have not dared to come out openly because they are minors.

The Alliance is concentrating on and reaching more jungle Indians than Indians of the Sierra, but more recently encouragement has come in the Sierra among the Salasacas near Ambato. By visitation and ministering to the sick, the missionaries witnessed in that district for more than 10 years before even a small parcel of ground could be purchased on which to build a mission house. The Salasacas have been known as the only really hostile group among the Sierra Indians. The miracle was finally accomplished when one friendly family, in spite of persecution for the move, sold a portion of their land to the Mission. Outward results would still indicate that little advance has been made but those who are familiar with the past years of struggle praise God for this foothold. Most of the Indians of that region are now friendly and a school for their children has been opened.

After more than 20 years of labor among the Jivaros, our missionaries could report only two baptized believers, but in the summer of this year (1949), six young men expressed their desire to take the step.

No missionaries are working among the Aucas or the Cofanes, although interested ones are reconnoitering and praying. The Cofanes and other unreached tribes to the north toward Colombia are more approachable, but to the south, only two days' journey from our mission station at Dos Rios, is the fringe of the territory of the Aucas, who have resisted to the death all attempts to set foot on their land. Although the population of the Cofane and other tribes in these areas average only a few hundred to each tribe, yet they must be given the gospel that they too may have opportunity of life eternal.

PERU

The name Peru, originally spelled "Piru," was given to the country by the Spaniards, and is of uncertain origin, but to the conquistadors, the land of the Incas meant the fabled source of inexhaustible riches.

Peru lies on the west coast of South America. Its coast-line along the Pacific Ocean is 1,400 miles long, or as great as the distance from New York City to Cuba. Its maximum width from west to east is 800 miles. Peru is bounded on the north by Ecuador, on its extreme northeast by Colombia, on the east by Brazil, on the southeast by Bolivia, and at its southernmost tip is Chile.

Area and Population

Peru is the largest of the west coast South American countries, with an area greater than that of France, Germany and Italy combined. A long-standing boundary dispute between Peru and Ecuador over an area of some 100,000 square miles, was settled by the advisory action of other South American powers, sponsored by President Roosevelt, who had undertaken to deal with the matter by an agreement made in 1934. Peru's area is 482,460 square miles.

Official figures place the total population of the country at 7,719,000. The Indians are in the majority, comprising 60 per cent of the population; 10 per cent of the population is white, chiefly of Spanish descent; the remainder, the mestizos, are chiefly of mixed Indian and Spanish blood. There are several thousand Asiatics and Negroes—the descendants of Asiatic coolies imported in the 19th century to work in the guano deposits, and the descendants of Negro slaves imported from Africa. The bulk of the population lives in the Andean highlands, the region known as the Sierra. About one-fourth of the population lives in the coastal region, and only about ten per cent in the forest regions east of the Andes.

People and History

Culturally, Peru is the oldest of the South American countries. For centuries it was the leading political power on the continent, first as the center of the Inca Empire and later as the foremost viceroyalty of Spain in the Western Hemisphere.

The ancient Incas, sedentary Indians, made their homes centuries ago in the well irrigated upland valleys of Peru. Their empire embraced all of Peru, Bolivia and Ecuador, about one-third of Chile and a portion of the northwest section of Argentina, with the center of the empire in southern Peru, at Cuzco. They had an advanced civilization, and sections of their military roads may still be seen in the mountains of Peru. Their crafts included textile weaving, the making of pottery, and work in metals.

Francisco Pizarro and Diego Almagro were among the first Spaniards to be attracted to the land by the lure of gold. Pizarro and his men quickly overran the country and conquered the Incas. Pizarro founded the city of Lima in 1535, and it became the seat of the Spanish viceroys. Peru, the center of the Spanish colonial régime, was the last of the South American countries to throw off the yoke of Spain. The final battle for liberation was fought in December, 1824, by General Sucre, at Ayacucho.

After the war of Liberation, Peru entered the "Guano Era," which lasted from 1846 to the middle 1880's. The guano was secured on the desert islands along the southern coast and found a ready market in Europe and in the United States. During the boom years it supplied three-fourths of the revenues of Peru, and furnished capital for irrigation, railroad and highway projects. The result was that Peru was 50 years ahead of the other South American countries. Difficulties with Chile brought on the Nitrate War (1879-1884), with disastrous results for Peru. The nitrate regions were lost, the foreign debt was increased, and the guano trade almost ceased to exist. Peru was at a standstill until 1905, but since then much progress has been made. The Tacna-Arica boundary settlement with Chile was achieved in 1929; the frontier question with Colombia had been adjusted in 1924; and the boundary dispute with Ecuador was settled only recently.

Government

By provision of the new Constitution, promulgated April 9, 1933, the President of the Republic and two Vice-Presidents are elected by direct suffrage for a five-year term, and are not eligible for re-election until one term has elapsed. Only literate citizens can vote. Voting is compulsory for literate men between the ages of 21 and 60. Adult women can vote in municipal elections.

Congress consists of a Senate and a House of Deputies. The senators serve for six-year terms, and the members of the House of Deputies are elected for five-year terms. The Supreme Court sits at Lima, and there are 12 judicial districts with minor tribunals. There are 24 departments, divided into 134 provinces.

Climate

There are three climatic zones, thanks to the Peru Current, the Andes Mountains and the country's situation in the tropics. The narrow coastal belt is relatively arid, but the air is damp, and high temperatures are moderated by the Peru Current offshore. The Sierra region is cold or freezing according to the altitude. The line of perpetual snow begins between 15,000 and 16,000 feet above sea level. Rainfall in the Sierra ranges from 10 to 50 inches per year, mostly between October and March. Scorching heat and great humidity are the rule the year round in the Montaña, the tropical eastern lowlands lying in the Amazon Basin.

Lima, the capital, has an equable sub-tropical climate. There is never any smoke in the air, for the homes have no cellars nor furnaces. Summer heat is not severe, but in winter the city is enshrouded in gloom from the low-lying cloud, and it is very chilly and raw from June to September. The winter temperature shows an average low of 61 degrees in August, and the summer temperature an average high of 75 degrees in February.

Physical Features

Like Ecuador, Peru is traversed from north to south by the Andean Cordilleras. There are two well defined ranges, the Eastern and Western Cordilleras, running parallel but broken by cross ranges and spurs which form *nudos* or knots. One of these is near Cerro de Pasco; and the one near Lake Titaca in the southeast is the Nudo de Vilcanota, from which point one range enters Chile, and another, Bolivia. There are seven peaks in Peru which tower above 19,000 feet; three or four others in the south reach an elevation of over 21,000 feet; and the famous Huascaran peak in the Department of Ancash tops them all with an elevation of over 22,000 feet.

The coast of Peru is a strip only 30 miles wide, is practically rainless, and is barren except for the valleys which are irrigated by the 58 short rivers coming down from the mountains. The Sierra is extremely rugged country, much of it 12,000 feet above sea level, and with no pass that is under 7,000 feet elevation. East of the Andes is a vast tropical jungle which begins at the foothills of the mountains and sweeps across the Amazon flats, ending only within sight of the Atlantic Coast at the other side of Brazil. In these tropical lowlands of the Amazon Basin there is much wild rubber and the land is fertile. The country is sparsely populated in spite of its fertility.

The major rivers of Peru rise in the Sierra, break through the mountains in magnificent gorges known as *pongos,* and are not navigable until they reach the Amazon flats. The Amazon itself rises in Peru in the Department of Huanuco, not more than 110 miles from the Pacific Coast. It breaks through the mountains about 500 miles above Iquitos, the capital of the district, and from this point is navigable to its mouth, a distance of nearly 3,000 miles.

Resources

The mineral wealth of Peru is its chief economic asset. Some of the mines still being worked date back to the days of the Incas. Peru ranks fourth in world production of silver; it is the principal source of vanadium, supplying 80 per cent of the world demand. It produces copper, gold, lead, zinc, and coal. These minerals are now overshadowed in importance by petroleum, often called black gold, which is found in large quantities at sea level along the northern coast.

Agricultural and pastoral products comprise 40 per cent of the exports, but 85 per cent of the population is dependent on them, directly or indirectly. Corn is native to Peru and is a staple food for much of the Indian population. It is thought that the potato was first cultivated in Peru. The total arable area of the country is over 29 million acres, yet only 12 per cent of that area is under cultivation. Cotton is the leading agricultural export, with a considerable export of wool also, especially that of the alpaca. Some forest products are exported from the Montaña, such as wild rubber, balata, tagua and medicinal plants, which include quinine and copaiba.

Progress

The Central Railway of Peru is the highest standard gauge road in the world, reaching a maximum altitude of 15,693 feet above sea level. It requires the use of 65 tunnels and 67 bridges, with numerous switchbacks. Peru has 2,581 miles of railroads, built under staggering difficulties. Callao, the chief seaport, is connected with Lima by one railroad and three highways. Peru has completed her portion of the Pan-American highway. Much of its length has been asphalted, and branch highways have been pushed over the Andes. The first of the trans-Andean highways to penetrate the Amazon Basin of Peru was completed in 1943. It extends north from Lima and crosses the Andes via Oroya, Cerro de Pasco and Tingo Maria to Pucallpa, a river port on the navigable Ucayali River. This road, 500 miles long, opens up a vast, hitherto undeveloped region to settlement and progress. Gradually the isolation between the centers of population, caused by the lofty Andes, is being overcome. Automobile roads are replacing the old mule-trails in many departments. It is easier and much less costly to build motor roads than railroads. Railroad construction over the mountains demands skilled labor. The cheap Indian labor available in Peru makes it simpler to build motor roads.

Good air transportation is maintained north and south through the country, and to Iquitos and the Brazilian frontier on the Amazon River. The service of two international air lines brings New York to within a day and a night of travel from Peru.

Manufacturing has been slow to develop but is now expanding rapidly. There is a considerable industry in textiles, leather goods and tires. An attempt is currently being made to establish a steel industry. In February, 1921, the government made education compulsory and free between the ages of seven and fourteen. There are four universities in Peru, one of which, the University of San Marcos at Lima, was founded in May, 1551, and is the oldest university in the Western Hemisphere.

Currency

The basis of Peruvian currency is the sol, worth normally 15 cents, but at present only 5.35 cents in U. S. currency. Nickel and copper coins include the sol, the half-sol, and centavos. There are 100 centavos in a sol.

Languages and Tribes

Spanish is the language of the country. Many of the highland Indians speak Quechua or Aymara, and those of the Montaña have their own tribal languages.

The chief Indian peoples are the Quechua and the Aymara. The highland Indians, called either Incas or Quichuas, compose the bulk of the population. Once free subjects of the magnificent Inca Empire, they are now peons, oppressed by landowners and frequently unprotected by the authorities. Most of them are rural people, living in small villages or scattered over the mountains in adobe houses and thatched huts. Those who work for landowners are virtually their slaves; as to those who cultivate their own land, the local priest usually becomes rich at their expense.

The jungle Indians to the east of the mountains are primitive pagans, more or less savage, with no history of any civilization. They include, among others, the Campas, the Cashibos (cannibals), and the Amueshas. There is little community life among them, for they live in isolated homes hidden in the forest or on the river banks. Kenneth Grubb estimates that there are 80,000 to 90,000 of these forest Indians.

Our missionaries in Peru use only the Spanish language. Many of the national workers speak Quechua also.

Religions

Religious liberty is guaranteed by the Constitution but the word tolerance would better express the true situation, even today, than the word liberty. As to the past, not until 1868 could a non-Catholic be buried in a cemetery. Not until 1897 was civil marriage granted to non-Catholics. Tolerance of religions other than the Roman Catholic was granted on November 11, 1915. Roman Catholicism is the State religion, and churches and converts are under government protection. Lima is the seat of the archbishopric, and there are 13 bishoprics. The Romanist hierarchy has shown considerable intolerance toward any liberalization of the laws regarding religious worship, as is evidenced by the decree of 1929 which prohibited non-Catholic schools, and that of January, 1945, which prohibited all religious activity outside of recognized places of worship, except for Roman Catholics. This latter decree was aimed particularly against open-air meetings and has been enforced with varying rigor in different parts of the country, according to the degree of influence exerted by the clergy over the local authorities.

The jungle Indians are animists. The highland Indians used to worship the sun—now they kiss the crucifix. The Catholic Church has converted them to idolatry and brutalized them through alcohol. Some persons try to maintain that the religious practices of the Roman Church have not encouraged the drunkenness of the Indian. The religious *fiestas* tell a different story. Long before the day for the Catholic *fiesta*, the Indians lay in a store of liquor and begin to get drunk the evening before the feast-day. The next morning they go to the temple, already in a drunken condition, and there the priest, often also drunk, officiates at mass. This is the program during all the days of the *fiesta*.

Missionary Occupation

So far as is known, James Thompson, who arrived in Peru in 1822, was the first evangelical missionary there. He soon secured the coöperation of many priests in the founding of schools and in the distribution of the Scriptures. As a result of the eagerness with which the New Testaments were received in Peru and other South American republics, the British and Foreign Bible Society issued its first complete Spanish Bible.

Between the years 1825 and 1833, a Presbyterian minister and a representative of the American Bible Society visited Peru, but both of them reported discouragingly regarding the possibility of missionary work in that field. In 1877 Bishop William Taylor of the Methodist Episcopal Church founded the William Taylor self-supporting missions, but the work was discontinued later.

The real beginning of the evangelization of Peru was the ministry of Francisco G. Penzotti, agent of the American Bible Society, who arrived in Callao in 1888. He sold Scriptures extensively and built up a large congregation. In 1890 he was imprisoned in southern Peru but was later set at liberty. In the same year he was again imprisoned, this time in Callao. At his trial the Roman Catholic priests took a firm stand against him. The authorities tried to persuade him to escape from the country and so save them from the embarrassment of the trial, but he refused and the trial became a matter of interest throughout the civilized world. Not until March, 1891, was this hero of the Gospel set free, and the first great battle for religious liberty in Peru won.

In 1891 the first resident missionary of the Methodist Episcopal Church began work in Callao. In 1893 three English missionaries arrived. At first the progress was slow, but gradually both the interest of the people and the number of missionaries in the country increased. In 1948, according to the report of the National Evangelical Council, five British Societies and nine United States Societies are doing missionary work in Peru. Both the British and Foreign Bible Society and the American Bible Society have worked aggressively in the country and are now combined to form what is known as the *Sociedades Biblicas Unidas,* with headquarters in Lima.

There are two national Christian organizations—the *Concilio Nacional Evangelico del Peru* (National Evangelical Council of Peru), and the *Iglesia Evangelica Peruana* (Peruvian Evangelical Church). The object of the first named is to "promote fraternal relations and coöperation between the various evangelical groups in Peru." The *Iglesia Evangelica Peruana* has as its object "the evangelization of Peru." Concerning this work the Directory of Foreign Missions states: "The income is partly provided by subsidies from the Evangelical Union of South America; from London, England; and from The Christian and Missionary Alliance, New York. The balance is subscribed by the members of the churches." To date the *Iglesia Evangelica Peruana* is organized only in Central and Southern Peru. There are over 200 organized congregations and groups in fellowship with it.

The Bible Crusade, which has had phenomenal success in Mexico, is being greatly used of God in Peru also. Alliance missionaries have taken a leading part in this strategic work, and Christians of all evangelical denominations are uniting with a view to reaching every home in their respective countries with the Word of God. The plan is to visit every home and to attempt to read a portion of the Word and have prayer in the homes. Literally thousands of homes have been visited, and as a result believers have been quickened and converts have been won.

The Christian and Missionary Alliance

The Christian and Missionary Alliance entered Peru in the year 1925 when a party of three was sent out with a view to opening a station among the Campa Indians of Eastern Peru. Besides language study, much hazardous exploration was necessary before deciding on the best point for the establishment of a base, and it was not until August, 1926, that the party actually started work among those uncivilized sun-worshipers of the jungles.

During the year of preliminary exploration it became obvious that there were wide areas in the mountains which were unoccupied by any missionary society. Further exploration resulted in opening work in Huanuco in March, 1926. This town of 15,000 inhabitants is of strategic importance as a base for work in the whole region among the Quechua-speaking Indians of the northern part of Central Peru.

A missionary of a British society had for many years carried on a fruitful ministry among some of the Indians of the central mountain region, and a promising indigenous work was begun. Later this missionary arranged that a considerable portion of the field, where this excellent work was begun, should be turned over to the Alliance. The work is growing in spiritual power and numbers. The spirit of loyalty to Christ is strong among these Indian Christians.

It was not until January, 1930, that the Alliance opened work on the Coast, in Lima, the capital of the republic. Not only does Lima and the surrounding area with a population of some 450,000 souls, offer a fruitful field of evangelization, but it has become increasingly necessary to have representation in the capital.

Thus it came about that the Alliance was working in all three sections of the country: the Coast, the Sierra, and the Eastern Jungle. The plan of the Society in undertaking work in Cahuapanas in the jungle, had been to establish a base in the river town of Iquitos, from which to work among various tribes of Indians. However, through an arrangement of mission comity, the Inland South America Missionary Union entered Iquitos and within a few years it seemed to the two Missions that it was advisable for the Cahuapanas station and the work among the Campa Indians to be transferred to the Inland South America Missionary Union. This was done in 1934. One of the missionary couples formerly working among the Campas was then on furlough, and with the approval of the Board of the Christian and Missionary Alliance they became missionaries of the other Society and returned to their work in the jungle.

Huanuco Huanuco, situated at 6,000 feet elevation, with a population of about 15,000 is a strong Catholic center. It is the see of a bishop, the seat of a Franciscan monastery, a convent and a seminary, and the home of a large number of priests. The town is not essentially an Indian center, but it is the capital of the Department and a center whose occupation is necessary in order to successfully evangelize the Indian territory around and beyond it. Huanuco was opened in 1926, but not until 1929 did the work extend into the provinces among the shepherd Indians of

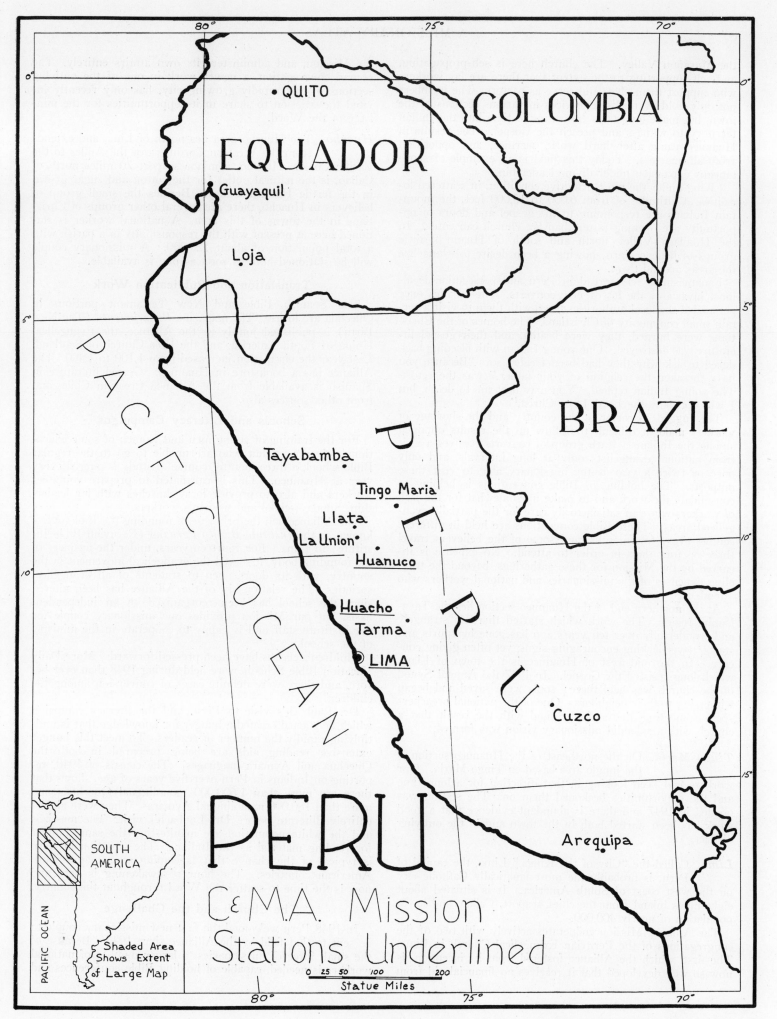

80° 75° 70°

QUITO

COLOMBIA

EQUADOR

Guayaquil

Loja

PACIFIC OCEAN

BRAZIL

P E R U

Tayabamba

Tingo Maria

Llata

La Union

Huanuco

Huacho

Tarma

LIMA

Cuzco

Arequipa

PERU

C&M.A. Mission
Stations Underlined

SOUTH
AMERICA

PACIFIC OCEAN

Shaded Area
Shows Extent
of Large Map

0 25 50 100 200
Statue Miles

the Marañon Valley. The church here is self-propagating, and self-supporting to the extent that there are lay workers who support themselves and serve as pastors. The members not only hold evangelistic services in various sections of the town, but make long trips from time to time into the Indian territory to witness and preach the Gospel. The results in Huanuco came after hard work, sacrifice, and opposition from all quarters. Today this field is an example of spontaneous expansion under divine leadership.

Living under the most primitive condition, in scattered localities at altitudes of from 6,000 to 15,000 feet, the mountain Indians are responding to the gospel and doors of opportunity are opening faster than the church can enter. In the Huallaga Valley north and south of Huanuco, little groups of believers are showing a keen desire to evangelize the areas around them.

Fanaticism is widespread in Peru and persecution is almost invariably the lot of new converts. The fanatics once persuaded the local authorities to go with them to visit a certain small community of Christians. The homes of the Christians were burned, they were beaten, and their gospel literature was destroyed. One young Indian with bleeding back dared to ask why they had been treated so. "Because you have forsaken the religion of your father," was the retort. The young Indian replied, "You may beat me to death, but I will not deny the Lord Jesus Christ."

The rugged character of the country and the shortage of workers make it difficult to follow up the results obtained among the Indians. Each group of converts receives a visit from national evangelists only at long intervals, and only once or twice a year is the missionary able to visit these outposts. The holding of Bible conventions is helping to consolidate the work and to make up somewhat for the lack of workers who can satisfactorily care for the partially evangelized areas. These Bible conventions are held in different centers every few months, and some of the believers travel three or four days in order to attend. No expense is incurred by the Mission for these gatherings, beyond the traveling expenses of the missionaries and national workers who attend.

At the northern end of the Huanuco section lies the Tayabamba region. The work which started there so strangely and wonderfully over ten years ago has gone by spurts and starts, never lacking encouraging signs, yet often giving concern. In the mid-west of Huanuco is the town of Llata, which long resisted the Gospel. In 1947 the Annual Synod of the church was held there; souls were saved and began witnessing to their neighbors. One of the national preachers spent some time there after Synod with the result that a church with a splendid missionary vision was formed.

Tingo Maria   On the northeast of the Huanuco section is the jungle area based on Tingo Maria. Our workers had been looking in that direction for a long time and the opportunities beckoned them on. The station was opened in 1947 and there is abundant evidence that a good work has been started both in the town and in the outlying district.

Lima   Called the "City of the Kings," Lima, the capital of Peru, is probably the most fanatically Catholic city on the west coast of South America. It is situated about eight miles inland from the chief seaport, Callao, and has a population of nearly 400,000.

The Alliance Mission coöperates actively with two of the congregations of the Peruvian Evangelical Church in Lima. The first, which the Alliance fostered from its inception, is now so well developed that it receives no financial aid from the Mission, and administers its own affairs entirely. The second congregation, a newer work in one of the outlying sections of this rapidly growing city, has only recently invited the Mission to share in its opportunities for the ministry of the Word.

Huacho   The Huacho area lies north of Lima and extends from the Western Cordillera of the Andes to the Pacific Coast. Huacho, a minor seaport 70 miles north of Callao, is the natural outlet for the cotton and sugar grown in the fertile Huaura Valley. Besides the small group of believers in Huacho, there are several other groups of Christians in the towns of this area. A national worker is stationed here at present with the responsibility of a parish with a total population of about 120,000. A missionary couple will be stationed here as soon as one is available.

Translation and Publication Work

The Spanish Bible and New Testament portions in Quechua are in use. The magazine *Renacimiento* (The New Birth) is published jointly by the Alliance, the Evangelical Union of South America, and the Free Church of Scotland. Last year the circulation increased from 1,100 to 1,400. The Alliance has a bookstore in Huanuco. Gospel literature in Spanish is available from the Alliance Press in Chile, and from other sources also.

Schools and Literacy Campaigns

For the training of young men and women of some educational advantages, but who are unable to go to the regular Bible school, a three-months' course of study is offered every year at Huanuco. This is calculated to prepare volunteer workers and also to provide local churches with lay leadership, Sunday school and women's workers.

The Alliance had the privilege of founding the Bible school known as the *Instituto Biblico Peruano* (Peruvian Bible Institute) in Lima. For fourteen years, under the auspices of the founding body, it served the evangelical movement in the country, with its doors open to students of all evangelical societies. The relationship of the Alliance has been altered since the school has been reorganized on an independent basis, but our Mission provides one missionary couple for the Institute staff and is happy to coöperate in the ministry of the school.

Children's classes have been pressed forward. More Daily Vacation Bible Schools were held during 1948 than ever before, and there were definite cases of conversion among the children.

Dr. Laubach's visit to Peru, and the literacy campaign which he started created a hunger for knowledge that is multiplying rapidly the number of readers. To meet this hunger extensive reading aids are being prepared in both the Quechua and Aymara languages. The census of 1940, reporting on Indians in Peru over five years of age, shows that there are more than 1,600,000 monolingual Quechuas and more than 180,000 monolingual Aymaras. They were almost entirely illiterate before Dr. Laubach's visit. The mestizos and the white population are manifesting the same hunger for reading material as the Indians. The situation in Peru is typical of the change that is coming over many South American countries. The hour of awakening is here and now is the time to scatter the Word throughout the country.

The Church and the Challenge

In 1948 Peru welcomed the first new missionary couple to be sent to that field by the Alliance since 1945. Because of the small force of missionaries, a larger number of national workers is needed, capable of holding Bible conferences and

Short Term Bible Schools among the believers in the various sections of the field. To this end the work of the Bible Institute is proving both necessary and productive.

Few mission fields have a more hopeful outlook for the development of truly indigenous and spiritual churches than the Alliance field in Peru. The goal of all missionary enterprise—the development of a self-supporting, self-governing and self-propagating national church—seems definitely near today. More and more the Mission is assuming the position of counsellor rather than that of overseer. Unfortunately the material upon which the church can draw for leadership is not of the best, as most of the converts have come from the poorest classes.

In the Lima area the relationship of the Mission to the national church is well advanced. The Huaquilla congregation in Lima, organized by the direct work of the missionaries, is now practically independent of the Mission and works as a unit in the Peruvian Evangelical Church. The missionaries take no regular active part in the administration of the church, but their spiritual ministry is welcome. However, the task of the missionary has not been lightened. He has more to do than ever, answering calls to minister in three infant churches now found in and near Lima as a result of the expansive effort of the older churches.

CHILE

Chile, "the shoestring republic," lies on the west coast of South America, occupying the narrow strip of land between the Andes and the South Pacific. It extends from 20 degrees to 55 degrees south of the equator, a length comparable to the distance from Labrador to the West Indies. Chile is bounded on the north by Peru and Bolivia; on the east by Argentina, from which it is separated by the Andes. The Pacific Ocean lies to the west, and in the extreme south Chile stretches to the Antarctic Ocean. Chile's port city of Valparaiso, although on the Pacific, lies farther east than the city of New York.

Area and Population

Seventh in size among the republics of South America, Chile ranks fifth in population and third in per capita wealth. It is one of the most prosperous nations in Latin America. It extends for an extreme length of 2,620 miles from north to south with a coast line of 2,900 miles. At no point is the eastern boundary along the crest of the Andes; and at no point is the country wider than 221 miles. Its area of 286,322 square miles is greater than that of Texas.

The census of 1940 showed a population of 5,100,000, an increase of about 800,000 in ten years. Estimates of the number of full-blooded Indians vary from 30,000 to 100,000 for the Araucanians, and an indeterminate number (not large) of nomadic Fuegians in the far south. In all, about five per cent of the population is Indian. From 20 to 30 per cent of the people are of white ancestry; the majority is mestizo of superior stock. The Spaniards who effected the conquest and settlement of Chile came largely from the more energetic elements of northern Spain, and the Araucanian Indians with whom they intermarried were inferior to none on the continent. The upper class of Chile is of Spanish descent, with intrusions of British, Irish, German and other European stocks.

People and History

The oldest inhabitants of Chile left no history, only the remains of their primitive civilization, which seem to indicate that they lived by the sea, were fishermen, and knew

nothing of the use of fire. They used stone weapons and had few tools. Some of their descendants are found in the north, where they are known as *Changos*. Their descendants found near the Straits of Magellan are the Fuegians. The Indians inhabiting the country when the Spaniards arrived evidently reached Chile long after the aborigines, and historical records show that they came from Brazil and Argentina. The Araucanians are descendants of the more intelligent of those tribes.

After the initial exploration of Chile by Diego Almagro in 1535, colonization was undertaken the next year by Pedro de Valdivia. The Spaniards found the Araucanians of Middle Chile to be a highly developed, homogenous people who offered fierce resistance to the advance of the white man. Spain spent more men and money in the conquest of Chile than in any other part of the world. After the middle of the 19th century the Indians were subjugated and driven beyond the Bio-Bio River.

Independence from Spain was secured (1810-1818) through the efforts of leaders like Bernardo O'Higgins and Admiral Cochrane. After the Indian Wars, the attention of the Chileans was turned to agricultural development and the nitrate trade. After her victory over Peru and Bolivia in the Nitrate War (1879-1883), Chile prospered through her greatly expanded mineral production. There was a period of strained relations with the United States on account of the "Baltimore Incident," the conduct of Minister Egan, and the seizure of the contraband vessel "Itata" in Chilean waters, but relations improved after the turn of the century. By arbitration of King Edward VII, the boundary with Argentina was settled in 1902. The boundary with Peru was adjusted in 1929. Early in 1948 the Chile government laid official claim to a large section of the Antarctic Continent, basing the claim chiefly on Chile's geographical proximity to the polar regions.

Government

Due to the traditions of creole aristocracy, the Chilean Constitution of 1833 provided for a highly centralized form of republican government; but through the years this Constitution has been gradually liberalized. In 1925 a new Constitution, drafted by President Arturo Alessandri, was adopted. The President of the republic is elected for a six-year term by direct vote of the electorate, and he appoints the nine Cabinet members. All legislation is initiated by the Chamber of Deputies (143 in number); and the function of the Senate (45 members) is revisionary. The Deputies are elected for a term of four years, and the Senators for eight years. All literate males, 21 years of age and over, can vote.

Climate

Upper Chile is a desert, "a land from which everything has been removed except space." In some regions there is no record of rainfall for more than 200 years. Middle Chile enjoys a "Mediterranean" climate—rigorous winters with frequent rains and long sunny summers. Lower Chile has abundant rainfall, is cloudy, cold and stormy, and is known to sailors as the "Roaring Forties." There the summer temperature averages 51 degrees and the winter, 35 degrees Fahrenheit.

Physical Features

Chile is prosperous and progressive in spite of its topography. With 70 per cent of its terrain mountainous, 40 per cent parched desert, and 30 per cent too cloudy and cold for agriculture and human comfort, only 10 per cent of the territory, largely in Middle Chile, fosters a marked agricultural

6

development. There are three physiographic regions: namely, Upper Chile, the arid region north of the 30th parallel; Middle Chile, between 30 and 42 degrees south latitude; and Lower or South Chile, from 42 degrees south to bleak Tierra del Fuego.

In Upper Chile the coastal escarpment rises abruptly out of the sea to a height of 3,000 feet in some places, and as a result there are no good harbors. Fifty to seventy miles inland lie the broad nitrate pampas, desolate except where human industry extracts wealth from the desert. To the east rise the lofty Andes. Until it became commercially profitable to extract nitrate from the atmosphere, 95 per cent of the world's supply of sodium nitrate came from two provinces of Upper Chile. Synthetic nitrates can now be produced more cheaply than the natural, and so was ended the Chilean nitrates monopoly.

Middle Chile, between Osorno and Puerto Montt has been called the Switzerland of Chile. Traveling south from Coquimbo, the country has beauties that can hardly be surpassed anywhere. The mountains come down to the sea in Middle Chile also, but there are several good harbors, among them Valparaiso and Puerto Montt. Inland in the Central Valley, where rainfall is augmented by irrigation, the arable land is abundant and very productive. Four-fifths of Chile's inhabitants live in Middle Chile. Eastward rise the Andes, with the highest peak in the Americas found here, but it is over the border within the limits of Argentina. In Chile are the peak of Corcoputi (22,162 feet) and El Muerto (21,227 feet). The Upsallata Pass, crossed by the Trans-Andean Railway to Buenos Aires, lies at an altitude of 12,780 feet above sea level. Near the railroad, on the frontier, and facing northward, stands the "Christ of the Andes" to commemorate the settlement of boundary with Argentina. The statue is made of Chilean and Argentine cannon, molten together, a symbol of lasting peace between the two nations. As neither would concede the honor of having the statue face the other's country, the face and raised hand of the Saviour are turned to the north, perhaps a symbol that He is expecting His blessing to reach these lands from His people of North America.

Lower or South Chile is rugged, heavily wooded, with many rapid rivers, some lakes, and numerous islands offshore. Population decreases toward the south, and sheep raising is the principal industry.

Easter Island, 2,000 miles west of Chile with its hundreds of stone figures, and also the two Juan Fernandez Islands less than 500 miles west, are national parks of the Chilean government. Chile boasts the southernmost city in the world —Punta Arenas (population, 30,000) in the Straits of Magellan. Ushuaia, the capital of the Argentine Territory of Tierra del Fuego, is farther south, but has a population of only 1,100. The Tierra del Fuego Archipelago belongs partly to Chile and partly to Argentina.

Resources

The principal wealth of Chile lies in its minerals. Of these, nitrates from Upper Chile have predominated until recently There are 152 nitrate works, but only about 25 are in actual operation. The industry has been demoralized by competition of synthetic nitrogen fertilizers developed largely in the United States and Germany. Iodine is produced as a by-product of the nitrate industry and Chile furnishes 90 per cent of the world's supply. Chile ranks second in world production of copper, and is a large exporter of iron from the provinces of Aracama and Coquimbo. The coal reserves (mostly inferior grades) are estimated at two billion tons. Agricultural exports include fruits and wine. Chile is quite self-sufficient, with grains and vegetables, and has large quantities of live stock. There is considerable export of wool.

Progress

All Chile faces the sea, and *Chilenos* are world-famous sailors. Most of the transportation of the country is seaborne. There are, however, over 6,000 miles of railroads, the longest line being the Longitudinal (2,862 miles, and with spurs, 3,133 miles). Another important rail link was opened in 1948 between Argentina and Chile, called the Trans-Andean of the North, stretching over 500 miles between Salta in Argentina to Antofagasta in Chile. At one point this railroad reaches an altitude of 14,282 feet.

Within the last fifteen years the impact of the industrial age has struck Chile, and the old simple life is being replaced with a new and more complex mode of living. Chile has nearly 29,000 miles of motor roads, of which 5,000 miles are improved. Modern airports serve the 2,308 miles of airlines. There are 30 commercial radio stations; cable, telegraph and telephone service; and Santiago and Valparaiso are linked by wireless telephone with the United States and Europe.

Since the Corporation for the Promotion of Production was created in 1939, with a capital of 40 million dollars, there has been a great increase in the production of agriculture and manufactures.

Education is free, supported by the State, and (since 1920) compulsory. A National Library, the University of Chile and a Catholic University are in Santiago. The State University has about 4,000 students; the Catholic one-fourth as many. There is also a university in Concepcion, and a technical university in Valparaiso. The quality and methods of education are constantly under scrutiny for improvements. Educational experts from the United States have been brought in to help effect certain changes.

Currency

The unit of Chilean currency is the peso. In 1935 the gold peso was stabilized at a par value of 5.19 cents U. S. money. However, recently its value is now 2.45 cents in U. S. currency.

Languages and Tribes

The official language, Spanish, is spoken by practically all the inhabitants except the aboriginal Fuegians in the extreme south. German is spoken by a considerable number of the people of German descent. When the Spaniards arrived, most of the Indians in Chile called themselves Mapuches, which means "people of the land." Other tribes were the Aiaguitas and the Calchaquies, who settled in the north. The great majority of the Indians had come over from Argentina some 1,500 years ago. The more hardy and intelligent tribes settled in what is now called Araucania, and the Indians of today are principally Araucanian. Many of the Indians live on reservations established by the government.

Religions

Until the new Constitution in 1925, Roman Catholicism was the State religion and it is still the dominant one, but there is now complete freedom of worship. The power of the Roman Catholic Church in Chile today is largely social and political. In 1947 the Senate approved a bill giving the Roman Catholic Church the exclusive right to give religious instruction in any of the public schools. The House of Deputies had not yet acted upon this bill early in 1949.

The Mapuche Indians have hardly been touched by the Catholics. Their religious ideas are few and vague, although they live in dread of the invisible powers. They believe there are two spirits, one good and one evil. They have some idea of a Supreme Being, but believe He is inaccessible to the ordinary mortal. The spirit of evil is considered responsible for physical calamity and personal disasters. The Mapuche "medicine woman," called "machi," is a power among her people, filling the various offices of prophet, priest and physician.

Missionary Occupation

As in other South American countries, James Thompson was the pioneer of evangelical missions in Chile. The government invited him to come and the Chapel of the University of Santiago was used for his first school. Before he left for Peru, in 1822, he was made a citizen of Chile. For 20 years after Thompson's departure no one attempted to preach the Gospel in public. From 1845 on evangelical missions were represented in Chile.

Today three British Societies are working in the country: the British and Foreign Bible Society, the Salvation Army, and the South America Missionary Society. Seven U. S. A. Societies are working in Chile, with about 50 missionaries of the various Societies. The oldest Missions are the Methodist and the Presbyterian. The Presbyterians, until quite recently, had limited their activities to the north and central portions of the country. Their work extends from the nitrate fields in the north to as far south as Concepcion. The one Salvation Army couple now in Concepcion will soon be retired. The Methodists have some churches established in the section where the Alliance is working. The Southern Baptists, in addition to their work along evangelistic lines, have a splendid school in Temuco. Other American Societies, besides those mentioned above, and The Christian and Missionary Alliance, are the Y. M. C. A., the Y. W. C. A., and the Seventh Day Adventists. Some years ago a Pentecostal church was established under the name, *The Methodist Pentecostal Church*. In Santiago, theirs is the largest evangelical church in the country, and all their churches are completely self-supporting. In Southern Chile, with headquarters in Temuco, are: The South America Missionary Society; nine missionaries working exclusively among Indians; the Southern Baptists, eight missionaries; Soldiers' and Sailors' Gospel Mission, 19 missionaries.

The Christian and Missionary Alliance

In the year 1896 the late Rev. Henry L. Weiss and his wife applied to our Society as candidates for missionary work in Chile. The Society, then in its infancy, had no missionary work in South America, and delayed in considering Mr. Weiss' appeal. Feeling the urgency of the call, the Weisses decided to set forth with what funds were at their disposal, and they, with a like-minded missionary, Albert E. Dawson, arrived in Chile early in April, 1897. A little later, Mr. Weiss left his first home in Concepcion to live and minister among the Christian German colonists who had waited upon him, begging him to settle among them in the town of Victoria. In this place Mr. Weiss began, through interpreters, to work among the Chileans also. In 1898, he undertook the publishing of hymns and Christian literature. About the middle of the year 1898, the Alliance Board in New York, hearing of the activities of Weiss and Dawson, decided to offer their support. Thus encouraged, the missionaries began to lengthen their cords and made difficult journeys still farther to the south.

To the work being done in Victoria, the first Alliance mission station in Chile, they added evangelistic efforts in Valdivia, accompanied by attacks from the Roman clergy.

On one occasion the local priest offered a barrel of wine to all who would promise to stone the meeting hall while a service was in progress. Months passed before anyone in Valdivia dared to accept Christ, but finally a break came and souls were won. It was here that the first national pastor began his work; and here also that, at the close of 1900, the first Alliance chapel in Chile was dedicated. This caused a fresh outbreak of opposition and every window in the building was broken. However, the continued ministries of the missionaries and Chilean workers bore fruit and today the church in Valdivia, with a membership of 108, is entirely under national church government.

The turn of the century saw new advances in Chile. A missionary and a Chilean helper made an evangelistic trip to the Island of Chiloe, which for years afterward remained the southernmost border of our Chilean work. Only within the last few years have we advanced beyond this point.

In 1901, the first annual conference was held, and several new missionaries were sent to the field between the years 1902 and 1905. In the year 1910, Dr. Simpson visited Chile and was greatly impressed by the progress and possibilities of the work there. A Bible Institute was opened in 1923, and fifteen missionaries went to the field between 1920 and 1927. The Foreign Secretary brought new inspiration to the field in his visit of 1937, at which time important steps were taken. The field was then divided into two districts for the conduct of business matters, and the Bible Institute, which had been closed for several years, was reopened.

There are three mission stations: Temuco, Ancud and Concepcion. Work among the Mapuche Indians is being done in and near the towns of Pua (near Victoria) and Traiguen, where primary schools for the Indians are conducted.

Temuco Work was begun here in 1898 and a chapel was built in 1907. In 1908 the chapel burned down but was speedily rebuilt, and the work has grown steadily. In 1933 it was necessary to enlarge the building in order to accommodate the hungry souls who attended the services. In 1940 the municipality expropriated the lot occupied by this church, and for a number of years services were held in a building owned by the English community. In April, 1946, a new brick and concrete church and parsonage were dedicated to the Lord.

Temuco is the headquarters of The Christian and Missionary Alliance in Chile, and also of the work among German colonists. The Bible Institute is located here in its own three-story building with adequate space for dormitories, class and dining rooms. Also at Temuco is located the Alliance Mission Press for the publishing of Christian literature in Spanish.

Ancud This town is the center for work in the exceptionally hard field of the Island of Chiloe. The Roman Church resists every attempt to reach the people in this their last citadel in Chile, yet the doors there are now open to the gospel as never before. A missionary couple and a graduate of the Bible Institute stationed here were so used of God that the chapel was enlarged to accommodate the many who were interested. The activities of the missionaries and two national workers now located here extend to many sections of this large island and also to the archipelago of the region. A new motor launch is greatly needed to reach points otherwise inaccessible.

Concepcion A few years ago migrant members of the Alliance became an organized church in this the third largest city of Chile. Opened as a mission station in February, 1948, it is our newest field of labor in this land.

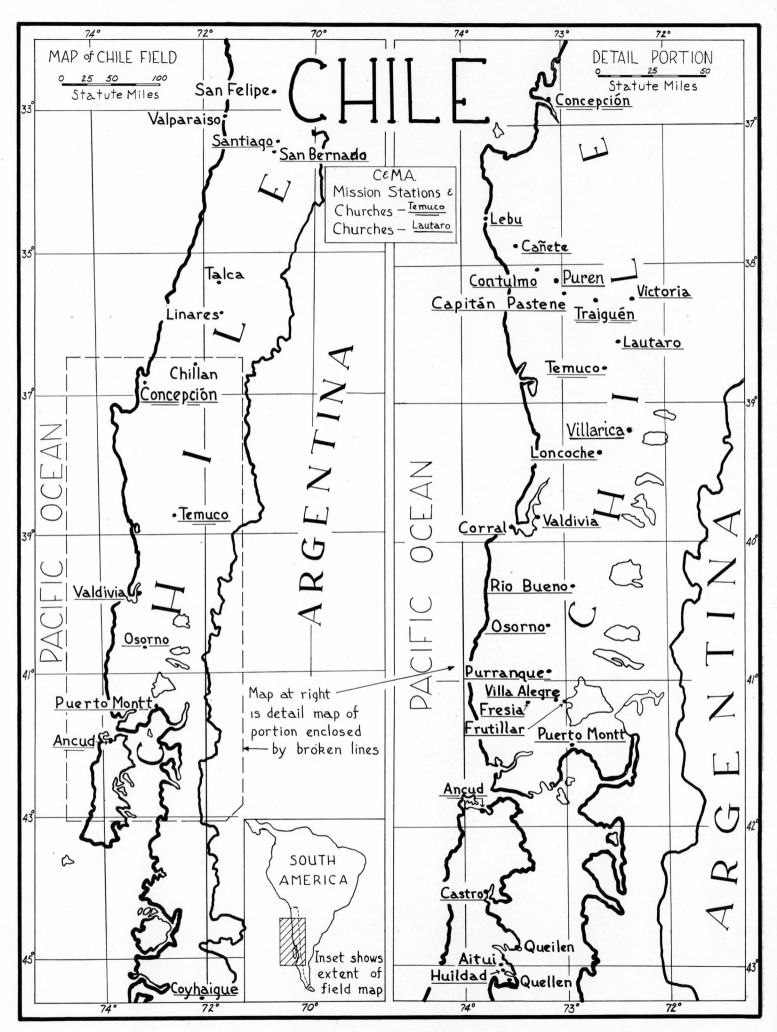

MAP of CHILE FIELD

0 25 50 100
Statute Miles

CHILE

DETAIL PORTION

0 25 50
Statute Miles

C&M.A.
Mission Stations &
Churches – Temuco
Churches – Lautaro

San Felipe•
Valparaiso•
Santiago
•San Bernado

Talca•

Linares•

Chillan•
•Concepción

•Temuco

Valdivia•

Osorno•

Puerto Montt•

Ancud•

PACIFIC OCEAN

CHILE

ARGENTINA

Map at right
is detail map of
portion enclosed
← by broken lines

SOUTH
AMERICA

Inset shows
extent of
field map

Coyhaique

Concepción

•Lebu
•Cañete
Contulmo• •Puren
Capitán Pastene •Victoria
Traiguén
•Lautaro
Temuco•

Villarica•
Loncoche•

Corral• •Valdivia

Rio Bueno•
Osorno•

Purranque•
Villa Alegre
Fresia•
Frutillar Puerto Montt

Ancud

Castro•

•Queilen
Aitui•
Huildad Quellen

PACIFIC OCEAN

CHILE

ARGENTINA

84

The city is an important center of coal, textile, ceramic and glass industries, and a section where Communism is making rapid headway. A valued colporteur has joined the missionary family in residence here and notable progress is being made. When the fine, well-situated building which the Alliance is now occupying was put up for sale, generous gifts from friends in the United States made it possible for us to acquire it.

Canete As soon as a missionary couple returns from furlough early in 1950 it is planned that they will locate in Canete in an area where there are many colonies of Indians who need the message of Christ. Missionaries living in Canete can work as far as Quidico, where not only Indians but Chileans are without the gospel.

Translation and Publication Work

The founder of the Chilean Alliance, the late Rev. Henry L. Weiss, began to print evangelical literature in 1898, the year following his arrival in Chile. He paid for type out of his meager income and with his own hands made a small press on which he was able to print the words of some 100 hymns. Toward the end of that same year, Mr. Weiss began publishing a weekly six-page paper entitled *La Alianza*. Throughout the years the press, now located at Temuco, has played an important part in the evangelization of Chile. In spite of inadequate equipment it has been possible to publish about six million pages of literature each year (1948 output, 6,568,580 pages). The official magazine of the Chilean Alliance, *Salud y Vida* (Salvation and Life), was first published in 1913 and was the successor of similar publications under different titles. For the last 13 years the magazine has had an average paid circulation of 4,200 copies per month, with a total of 56,100 copies printed during the year. (This and following figures are from the field report for the year 1948.)

Since 1939 Sunday school literature has also been printed in the Spanish language and made available for other South American countries as well as Chile. Our Spanish Sunday school literature includes a Teacher's Quarterly (present circulation, 3,000, output for the year, 11,400); a leaflet for adults with a circulation of 7,000 copies weekly; a leaflet for children, circulation, 5,000 copies weekly; total number of leaflets printed, 676,900.

The Alliance Press published 1,443 religious books, and printed 228,000 tracts, of which nearly 180,000 were distributed. It also distributed 481 Bibles, 856 New Testaments and 5,339 Scripture portions. A number of Dr. Simpson's books have been translated in the Spanish language and are much in demand. The most recent among them, *Christ in Isaiah,* has recently been printed by a press in Buenos Aires, Argentina. With new equipment our press in Chile could do all our own printing. All type still has to be set by hand. The urgent need is for a press and a linotype.

Schools

The Bible Institute in Temuco was first opened in 1923. Closed for several years, the school was reopened after the visit of the Foreign Secretary in 1937. The present building houses the Bible Institute, the second branch of the Alliance Church, the pastor's apartment, the superintendent's office, the book store and the publication department. In 1948 the enrollment in the school was eleven, with six students graduating. A Teacher Training Institute for women was held during the year with an enrollment of fifty. Primary schools among the Mapuche Indians are conducted in Pua and Traiguen.

It has been truly said that the Bible Institute has been the greatest contributor, through the years, to the efficiency of the work on this field. The present President of the Chilean Convention was a member of the first graduating class of the school, in 1924, and his gift for Bible exposition is bringing blessing to many hearts. All except one of the Chilean pastors now in active service are either graduates of or students in the Bible Institute.

The Church and the Challenge

The Christian German colonists among whom the work of The Christian and Missionary Alliance in Chile began, have, through the years, given substantial backing to evangelistic efforts both among the Chileans and the Indians. In 1938 they brought a worker from Switzerland to minister to them. They have purchased property in Temuco for a headquarters, with a hall for services and a hostel for school children. Two German evangelical magazines are printed monthly, the one for youth finding its way to German colonists in other South American countries also.

Since January, 1928, much of the work has been under the direction of Chilean brethren. The Chilean Alliance, incorporated with the government, now has an Executive Committee composed of four national pastors, two laymen, and the missionary Superintendent representing the Board at home. Until 1941 administration of the work was centered in one Executive Committee. Since 1942 the field has been divided into two districts, each with its own committee. In the Chilean Alliance (1948 report) are 19 full-time national workers, of whom seven are entirely supported by the national church. The baptized church members number 1,881, of whom 125 were baptized during the year. Church offerings for the year totaled the equivalent of $14,848 in U. S. currency at the official rate of exchange. There are 36 organized and 108 unorganized churches, of which 75 are entirely self-supporting. The 48 Sunday schools have an enrollment of 2,814.

A weekly radio program over a long-wave Temuco station has been maintained for 10 years. Occasionally other missions coöperate financially and in the planning of programs. By using the "Gospel Recordings" from California, we are able to broadcast from a distant station also. An annual camp for young people has brought gratifying results. More recently a camp for smaller children was held and a number accepted Christ. Tent evangelism was begun a few years ago and the effort has been successful beyond all expectations. One converted through this medium referred in a testimony to "that blessed tent."

Church centers and outstations include the following places:

Santiago. At the time of Dr. Simpson's visit to the field in 1910, he recommended that work be opened in the nation's capital. Accordingly a property was purchased, the printing press installed, and meetings were held. Adverse circumstances brought the effort to an end in 1915 and the property was later sold. For reasons of health a missionary couple took up residence in Santiago for brief periods between 1939 and 1941, and while there organized 28 Alliance members into a church. Again there was a gap in occupation, but early in 1946 one of the younger Chilean pastors, with his family, was transferred to Santiago for health reasons, and a church and parsonage, no longer used by the Presbyterians, were purchased. Our present church there has 65 members, is self-supporting, and has a large circle of friends in this city of great opportunity where lives one-fifth of the total population of Chile.

As an immediate result of the effort in Santiago, a group of brethren opened a preaching point in *San Bernardo,* about 10 miles south of the capital. A modest property has been purchased and a pastor installed.

Castro, with its fine, protected harbor, is the commercial center of the large island of Chiloe in the southern archipelago. A national worker has resided here for some years, and a cement-block chapel is being constructed. Farther south at *Huildad* is a splendid congregation of about 70 members, and another organized church is near by at *Aitue.*

From Temuco to Puerto Montt, a full day's journey southward by train, there is no resident missionary. On the mainland, two days' journey south from Castro by steamer, is the growing city of Puerto Aysen. It is the outlet on the Pacific for the large sheep-raising industry of the interior and presents a great opportunity. The expenditure of time and money necessary to reach this southern sector of our field makes visitation very difficult.

In all the world there is no Alliance church so near the South Pole as the one at *Coyhaique,* 46 degrees south of the equator. It is literally the "uttermost parts." In 1944 a group of brethren at this frontier post asked to be visited by a pastor. A number of believers there have been baptized and steps are being taken to purchase a property in this fast-growing frontier settlement.

We desire to penetrate still farther south beyond this last outpost and to see work opened in the world's southernmost city, Punta Arenas, which with the surrounding territory in the Straits of Magellan offers a challenge of 150,000 souls.

ARGENTINA

Almost 7,000 miles southward from New York lies Argentina, considered by many to be the most progressive of all Latin American republics. It is bounded on the north by Bolivia; on the northeast by Paraguay; on the east by Brazil, Uruguay and the South Atlantic Ocean; and on the west by Chile. In the extreme south, Argentina's Territory of Tierra del Fuego touches the Antarctic Ocean. Ushuaia, capital of the Territory, is the southernmost location of organized government in the world. It is the site of a penal colony to which political prisoners are exiled.

Area and Population

Argentina is the second largest country in South America (area, 1,678,270 square miles), and third largest among all American republics. From north to south it extends for 2,300 miles from Bolivia to Cape Horn; from east to west its greatest breadth is 930 miles.

The Argentinians believe their land to be capable of supporting one hundred million people. Its present population is over 16 million. It is a cosmopolitan nation and there is no such thing as an Argentine race. The population is chiefly of European origin, with about one million of the people of Italian extraction. Spanish blood dominates the population. About 80 per cent of the people are Argentine by birth; about three per cent of them show a mixture with Indian blood; the remaining 17 per cent are foreign-born. The wave of immigration that began at the turn of the century reached its height by 1918, and has practically been cut off during the last 25 years. Now it is being stimulated anew by the present administration, for immigration has made for political stability in the country. The influx of immigrants has contributed to the rapid economic success of the republic by increasing the manpower of the nation and by introducing habits of thrift and industry.

People and History

Little is known of the Indians who were the earliest inhabitants of Argentina. They have been driven back, destroyed by military expeditions, or assimilated by inter-marriage until only about 40,000 pure-blooded Indians are left within the entire republic. There are said to be several tribes living in the northern and western provinces, especially in the Chaco and Formosa.

Argentina was first discovered by Spanish navigators. In 1508 Juan Diaz de Solis and Vicente Yañez Pinzon sailed right past the mouth of the Plata River thinking it was a gulf. In 1516 Solis returned and explored the northern seacoast, taking possession of it in the name of Spain. Fierce Indians attacked the party which had landed on their shores and killed many of them, including Solis, the leader. The rest, discouraged, returned to Spain. In 1535 Don Pedro de Mendoza laid the foundations of the port, which he named "Buenos Aires." The new town was soon razed by the hostile Indians, and those of the people who escaped death were carried into captivity. In 1573 the town was rebuilt on the same site.

The first Spanish settlers soon intermarried with the Indian population and became the progenitors of the wandering, romantic race called the *Gauchos,* celebrated in song and story for their fearless deeds. Gauchos today are the cowboys of Argentina.

From 1810 to 1816 the George Washington of Latin America, Jose San Martin, led the growing colonies through their War of Independence. Years of turmoil and chaos followed until 1853, when they adopted a Constitution modeled after that of the United States. The development of the country since that time has been one of the marvels of Western history. The events of recent years, as in other nations, show currents of unusual unrest. President Juan Domingo Peron was elected in 1946, receiving 304 out of 376 electoral votes, more than any other presidential candidate of the country ever received. A five-year plan of economic and social development has begun under Peron's administration. It affects industries, transportation, public works and natural resources. In August, 1948, the Chamber of Deputies voted to reform the Constitution. The present tendency is toward the creation of a corporate state, with government ownership of all public utilities, and participation in the large industries. The nation's entire banking system, including private deposits, was placed under government control by decree in 1946. All foreign-owned railways were purchased and taken over by the government during 1947 and 1948. A law was recently passed requiring every foreigner to either become an Argentine citizen within two years or leave the country. Later this law was modified to provide that any foreigner who resided continuously in Argentina for two years after the law was passed would automatically become a citizen of Argentina unless he took the proper action to refuse such citizenship.

Government

The Constitution, adopted in 1853, vests the executive power in a president, elected for a term of six years. He must be a Roman Catholic and an Argentine by birth. The Congress consists of a Senate of 30 members, and a Chamber of Deputies, numbering 158. The Senate members are elected for nine years, and the Deputies for four years by universal suffrage. Voting is compulsory, and women have the right to vote in presidential and congressional elections. There are 14 provinces, which elect their own governors and legislatures, and 10 territories, administered by governors appointed by the President.

Climate

Argentina has as varied a climate as the United States. It also is in the Temperate Zone, but the season and areas are the reverse of ours, for "it is bounded on the north by groves of palms and on the south by eternal snows." The products of the sub-tropical area of northern Argentina are similar to those of our Gulf States. The bleak, semi-arid sheep lands of Patagonia in the south may be compared to our state of Montana. Between these extremes lie the vast grassy pampas, comparable to our western prairies, and bare of trees except for those planted by man. This is the heart of Argentina, with a climate so benign that the cattle can graze out all winter, and never need a stable. Rainfall is heaviest in the northeast and slightest in the central west and south. Although snow rarely falls except in the south, the rainy winters in houses with no heating plants are trying to North Americans. The ideal tourist months, in the capital, Buenos Aires, are June, July and August. From January through March the summer heat is oppressive there.

Physical Features

At Buenos Aires, although it is 120 miles from the ocean, the Rio de la Plata is 28 miles wide. Called the "River of Silver" by early explorers, the Plata is really not a river but the estuary of the Parana River, which with its tributaries drains a larger area than the Mississippi. It extends north from Buenos Aires through Paraguay and forms the highway for transportation of products for all that section—the hardwoods, citrus fruits, rice, cotton and tobacco. Of the five river systems of Argentina, the Parana is the only one of great importance. Ocean-going vessels can ascend it for 400 miles to Rosario, the second city of importance in the country. On the boundary between Argentina and Brazil are the Iguazu Falls, which dwarf Niagara, and are higher than any other falls in the world.

The highest peak of the Andes, and the highest of the Americas, is in Argentina, the famous Aconcagua, with an elevation of 23,080 feet. In the southern part of the Andes are beautiful lake districts, glaciers, forests and skiing grounds. Still farther south in Tierra del Fuego are fjords which rival those of Norway.

In the northwest are the Serrano Provinces in the hills west of the pampas, and in the lower mountains reaching up to the massive wall of the Andes. Here are large cities with populations varying from 50,000 to 320,000. Salta, Jujuy and La Rioja are arid regions of oil wells and mines. The great city of Cordoba is the gateway to the vast northwest area.

The Gran Chaco is the section near the boundary of Paraguay, a rolling country of forests interspersed with grasslands. From this region come pine and quebracho, also maté, or Paraguay tea, which is just as necessary to the people of this land as tea is to the British.

By far the most important region is that of the pampas, extending from the lower Parana River and the Atlantic Coast, westward and northward for hundreds of miles. Here are abundant rainfall, black, alluvial soil, and a climate without extremes. Consequently, here are some of the greater cities, most of the population, and immense farms and ranches.

Patagonia, the great, sparsely populated region to the south, extending to Cape Horn, is arid and the climate is austere. Most of the land is leased by the government to sheep-raisers.

Resources

Buenos Aires has the largest refrigerating plant in the world. Corned beef and butter from Argentina are sold the world over. The ranches of the pampas region produce a great wealth of cattle, sheep, swine and goats. Packing houses have been established on a large scale and meat refrigeration is the chief industry.

Wheat, maize, linseed and oats rank first among the agricultural products. Sugar, wine, cotton and fruit are progressing. Alfalfa is raised in huge quantities. Flour milling is the second industry of the country. The black, alluvial soil of the pampas is so fertile that corn is planted thickly, and often is untouched by plough or cultivator from seed-sowing to harvest. No fertilizer is needed. Corn is grown in greater quantities than in our own land and only one nation competes with Argentina in the raising of flax.

Although the pampas were almost treeless—due to the fact that the plains were once covered by a sea—fast-growing trees have been planted in some sections: the eucalyptus, the casuarina, the acacia and the willow. Of the indigenous trees, the gigantic *ombu* is the most noteworthy, yet botanists say that the *ombu* is not a tree, but the earth's greatest herb, for its trunk is only pulp.

Of the hardwoods from the Parana River Basin, the quebracho (axe-breaker) is the most important. Quebracho extract has been exported the world around wherever tanneries are found. There has been little exploitation of the mineral wealth of the country, except in the petroleum fields.

Progress

As in other countries of rapidly developing industries, Argentina also is suffering from over-congestion in the cities. In the poorer sections of Buenos Aires as many as twelve people often live in one room. The poor people from the provinces can afford to live in the city only if they are willing to be herded together like cattle in a corral. However, Buenos Aires presents to the tourist's view a city of wide avenues and modern subways, a place of beauty with 157 parks and plazas. This New York of the Southern Hemisphere, founded in 1536, has a population of over three million (Greater Buenos Aires, four million).

Industrially Argentina lags far behind the United States, but it is the wealthiest nation of South America, with no foreign debt. Inflation threatens the country at the present time. There are 26,710 miles of railways. In February, 1948, the new link was opened between Chile and Argentina, the Trans-Andean of the North. The older and longer railway connecting with Chile extends from Buenos Aires to Valparaiso. Modern trains make this trip of 900 miles in 36 hours, over the Andes and through a two-mile tunnel.

Civil aviation has developed rapidly in recent years. Visitors are often amazed at the excellence of the newspapers and the phenomenal amount of cabled news published. Eighty-six per cent of the Argentine citizens are literate. Free, secular education is compulsory between the ages of six and 14, but the percentage of illiteracy is still high in some rural districts. There are six national univerisities: in Cordoba (founded in 1613), Buenos Aires, La Plata, Tucuman, Rosario and Mendoza.

Currency

The money in current use in Argentina is the paper peso, with coins for small change. The gold peso is worth about 44 cents, and the paper peso 11.25 cents in U. S. currency.

Languages

The language generally spoken is Spanish. Here it is beginning to show slight changes due to the influence of the large Italian population. Colonies of considerable numbers still speak the language of their European parentage. Many English-speaking people live in Argentina.

Religion

It is required that the President be a Roman Catholic, and the government supports that church in part. Other religions are tolerated but do not enjoy full liberty of action.

Until almost the end of the 19th century no provision was made for the marriage of non-Catholics. Neither was there any respectable burial place for them. After long persistent controversy these rights were finally conceded.

Only 100,000 of the people are Protestants, nominally or otherwise, out of a total population of over 16 million. Actually there are many atheists. The Thirty-second Eucharistic Congress, held in Buenos Aires in 1934, strengthened the bonds of Romanism there and made the work of evangelical missions more difficult. Through a recent political maneuver on the part of the Catholic clergy, compulsory religious education has been introduced by federal law into the public schools. This religious instruction is Catholic and pupils can be excused from it only if the parents present a written petition to the school authorities. This does not always eliminate the persecution of non-conforming children.

Missionary Occupation

The forerunner of evangelical missions in Argentina was James Thompson, representative of the Lancastrian School Association, and agent of the British and Foreign Bible Society. Thompson founded hundreds of schools in which the Bible was the textbook used to teach the children to read. Bibles were distributed freely and sermons preached with the hearty support of the authorities. After three years Thompson pressed on into Chile. He left behind well organized schools which should have become ever widening circles of blessing, but the Christian Church did not see its opportunities and follow-up workers were not sent out. "Had prepared, consecrated men and women been sent out in sufficient numbers to carry on the work begun by Thompson, the religious history of the region, and of all of South America, during the past century, would have been a very different one."

The Methodist Church began work in Argentina in 1836. As early as 1877 the Stundists of Russia organized meetings in their farming communities, later to become part of the vigorous work of the Southern Baptists. Seventh Day Adventists, Mormons, and Jehovah's Witnesses have entered the country with their pernicious literature and audacious workers.

A number of Mission Boards with a limited force of missionaries are working within the Argentine Republic. They include: Methodists, Baptists, Disciples of Christ, United Lutherans, various groups of the Brethren, Mennonites, Nazarenes, Pentecostal, the Salvation Army, the Evangelical Union of South America, the Conservative Baptists, and The Christian and Missionary Alliance. At present the Alliance is legally responsible for the Conservative Baptists in Argentina. There are a few other independent Protestant groups. In the face of the greatness of the task, the total forces are inadequate.

The Christian and Missionary Alliance

In 1897 the Christian and Missionary Alliance began work in Argentina in sections entirely unoccupied by any other Society. This same policy has been followed through the years, save in the case of great cities like Buenos Aires and Cordoba. Some of our missionaries from Brazil were transferred to Argentina, and in 1903 the first church was erected in the city of La Plata, the capital of the province of Buenos Aires. The work of this station was later transferred to the Baptist Society. Another work, begun in Entre Rios

Province, was also transferred to the Baptists. Later, other sections were ceded to the Mennonites. All this was due to the financial crisis that affected our work profoundly at that time.

A review of the first period of our work in Argentina reveals a noble, but reduced number of missionaries laboring under great difficulties. The second period reached its peak of activity in 1925, with 18 missionaries on the field, a Bible Institute opened for training national workers, and a large tent in use in aggressive evangelism in the provinces of Buenos Aires and the Central Pampa. The third period began when the Alliance as well as a great number of other evangelical Mission Boards were studying and adopting the policy of the development of a self-supporting, self-propagating native church. The adoption of the policy was due in part to the scriptural basis for such action, but also to the rising tide of nationalism that began springing up in the churches of many lands. The result in the Alliance work in Argentina was that some of the missionaries were transferred to other fields, some came home, and an irreducible minimum of missionaries and subsidy was left for the work of the field. The great depression in the United States followed, but in spite of reduced forces and a severe reduction in the missionary budget, the work continued to expand. Our responsibility at that time was listed at 300,000 souls. Now our borders have been extended more than 100 per cent and our responsibility is one million souls. Much of our original goal has been reached for there is an indigenous church manned by national pastors and guided by a national committee. The missionaries give much time to traveling in the districts and ministering in the churches besides teaching in the Bible Institute.

Buenos Aires The headquarters of the Alliance are located at this our only mission station on this field. This is also the home of the Bible Institute. Greater Buenos Aires with a total population of four million presents a great missionary opportunity. For 300 years after it was founded no gospel work was carried on here and even at present there are relatively few churches in the city. There are still sections with a population of more than 100,000 without a single evangelical mission or church. Within the last five years the Alliance has established church centers, with resident national pastors, in two such sections within the city. One, *Liniers,* now has an organized church of more than 60 members, and the second, *Boedo,* in the center of the city, also has an organized church and gives liberally to the work. *Villa Lynch* is an outstation of Buenos Aires.

The economic situation has been one of the serious hindrances to the establishment of strong churches in Argentina. Few of the provincial towns and cities have local industries, as these are located in the great urban centers. Apart from farming and cattle raising, few trades are open to the youth of the provinces. Our district churches are constantly being decimated by migrations to the cities. For these reasons we have felt impelled to take the Gospel to the neglected sections of the great cities, where the people live in great poverty and unsanitary congestion, and where sin, sickness and hopelessness abound.

Translation and Publication Work

The Alliance, and other Societies also, maintain a bookstore where Bibles and Christian literature in Spanish may be obtained. Sunday School supplies and a varied selection of books are available from the Alliance Mission Press in Chile. Many of Dr. Simpson's books, especially his *Christ in the Bible* series, are already published or are in the process of being translated.

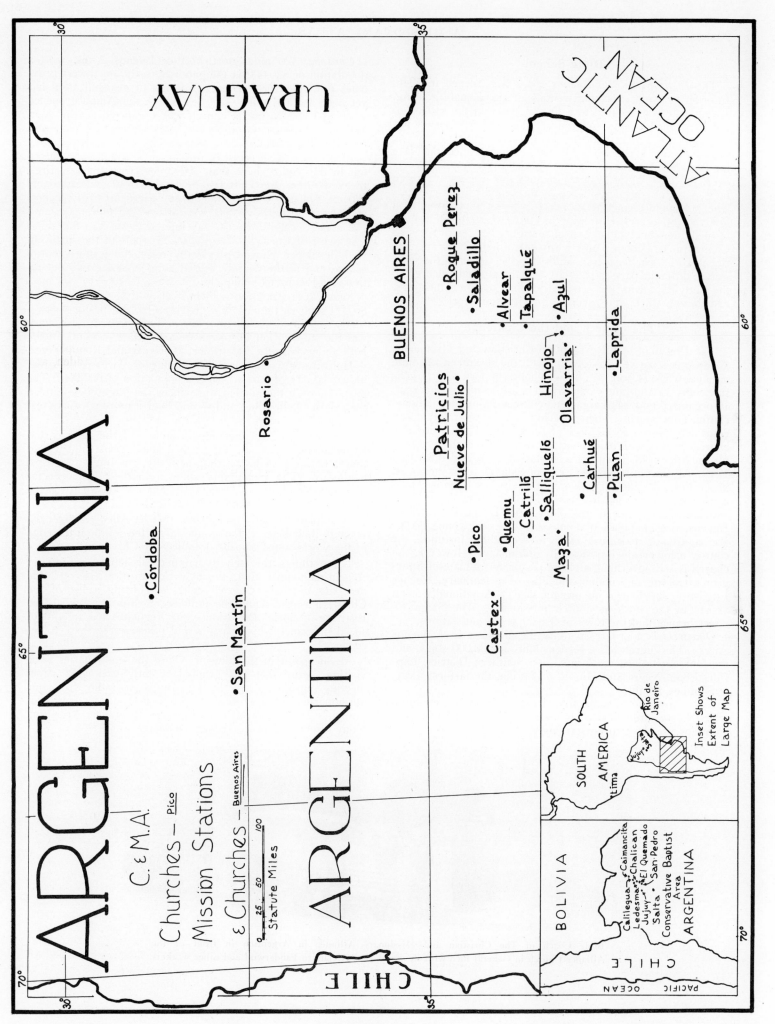

ARGENTINA

C.E.M.A.
Churches — •Pico
Mission Stations — •San Martín
Churches — Buenos Aires

0 25 50 100
Statute Miles

ARGENTINA

BOLIVIA

Calilegua • Caimancita
Ledesma • Chalican
Jujuy • El Quemado
Salta • San Pedro
Conservative Baptist
Area
ARGENTINA

CHILE

PACIFIC OCEAN

SOUTH AMERICA

Rio de Janeiro

Inset Shows
Extent of
Large Map

URUGUAY

BUENOS AIRES

•Córdoba

•San Martín

Rosario •

Patricios
Nueve de Julio •

Castex •

•Pico

•Quemu
•Catriló
•Salliquelo
Maza •

•Carhué

•Puan

•Roque Perez
•Saladillo

•Alvear
•Tapalqué
•Azul

Hinojo
Olavarria •

•Laprida

ARGENTINA

CHILE

ATLANTIC OCEAN

Bible School

The *Instituto Biblico Buenos Aires* was opened in 1946. In order to avoid exorbitant rentals and inadequate housing, a clear title was secured to a fine property in the section of the city called *Barrio Belgrano*. This property serves not only for the Bible Institute, but as headquarters of The Christian and Missionary Alliance, and as a meeting place for the annual conventions and special conferences. Moreover, the laws of the country require that we, as a foreign body, have our legal residence in the capital of the country. The indebtedness on the property is being slowly met at a low rate of interest. In March, 1949, when the new term opened, the school had a staff of seven teachers, with the field Chairman as Director and with both missionaries and national workers as teachers. Halls have been opened for services in different parts of the city and the students also go to the outlying towns for service, holding open-air meetings, distributing tracts and carrying on visitation work.

The Church and the Challenge

The President of the Argentine Christian and Missionary Alliance is a native of Argentina. Of the seventeen full-time national workers, four are being wholly supported by Argentine churches and nine of the workers are women. There are 10 organized and 40 unorganized churches, all under national church government. Their offerings for the year totaled an equivalent of over $9,700 in U. S. currency. There were nine church centers and 16 outstations listed in the above report for the year 1948. Two more outstations were added early in 1949. All the church centers except Saladillo own their own properties. Besides the two in the city of Buenos Aires, church centers are located in the following places:

Azul. This is one of the older cities in the Province of Buenos Aires, population about 60,000. As the young people are continuing to move away to seek their fortunes, the church membership is practically stationary. However, the church is self-governing, and the pastor, a graduate of Spurgeon's College in London and also of a seminary, teaches English to supplement his meager salary. A national woman assists in the work as church missionary. The Santa Fe street branch and the town of Tapalque are outstations.

Olavarria is a progressive city 25 miles south of Buenos Aires. The church has a responsibility for 80,000 souls, and the four outstations are located at: Southern District, Laprida, Loma Negra and Hinojo. Laprida, the farthest away, is 57 miles distant.

Nueve de Julio. In this fine city there is an active church which has a large field of ministry. Western District and Patricios are the two outstations.

Cordoba, 420 miles northwest of Buenos Aires, with a population of 320,000 is the gateway to the northwest provinces for which no adequate program of evangelization has yet been worked out. Two years ago the Alliance opened work in Cordoba and a church was organized a year later. We now also have an outstation at San Vicente, a section of the city of Cordoba.

Pico offers the greatest of missionary challenges. Situated out in the pampa more than 300 miles from Buenos Aires, the self-supporting church of Pico has four outstations at Castex, Quemu, Catrilo and Maza; the nearest of the outstations is 30 miles distant, the farthest, 85 miles.

Carhue, located on a railway line, is more than 300 miles southwest of Buenos Aires. The Christians of the small but well developed church practically meet the pastor's entire salary, and in the densely settled rural area are two outstations, at Puan and Salliquelo.

Saladillo is a mission field in itself with a parish of about 80,000 souls in the city and district. Until a pastor was recently appointed to Saladillo, one national woman missionary was the only worker in this entire area. The two outstations, both about 30 miles distant, are at Elvear and Roque Perez.

Halfway between Cordoba and Buenos Aires is the great industrial city of Rosario with a population of 600,000. The people here in the northern provinces are more open-minded than those of the south and should have a more adequate testimony.

The people of the Serrano provinces of the pampas and western mountains are impoverished and priest-ridden, and there, entire provinces are practically without any gospel testimony. The inhabitants show a marked strain of indigenous blood and the Sierra Indians are known to be the most fanatical of all Roman Catholics.

To expiate the guilt of a church that let Allen Gardiner die through their neglect, Patagonia, far to the south on the edge of the world, must also be occupied for Christ.

Three things threaten to hamper missionary activity in Argentina today: first, the new Constitution; second, the necessity of registering all cults, submitting a list of the Christian workers and the number of churches; third, the Institute of Social Prevision which regulates the amount of social insurance which pastors and other workers are to receive.

At one point in the interior where the missionaries were visiting, permission was granted recently to hold a street meeting outside the city limits. But as to radio work, our missionaries have been told, "There is no room for your programs." In spite of all that threatens to hinder, Argentina today offers a great missionary challenge.

Bible Coach of The Christian and Missionary Alliance in Argentina in front of the Alliance Church in General Pico with Rev. and Mrs. Alejandro Fanderwud and other workers

CHINA

China, called Cathay by Europeans in the Middle Ages, has a history that goes back more than 2,000 years before the Christian Era. It was the home of a highly civilized race when Europeans were still primitive barbarians. The Republic of China occupies a territory in Eastern Asia about one-third larger than continental United States. To the north lies Outer Mongolia and Siberia; to the west Russian Turkestan; to the southwest and south the barrier of the Himalayas forms the Tibetan-Indian frontier; Burma and Indo-China are on the south; on the east the China Sea and the Yellow Sea separate it from the Philippines, Japan and Korea.

Area and Population

At the close of World War II all the territories which Japan had seized from China were restored, including the island of Taiwan (Formosa). By the Sino-Soviet Treaty signed in Moscow August 15, 1945, the Chinese Government agreed to grant independence to Outer Mongolia, and it is now a Republic. Revised data has also been provided on the area and population of the northeastern provinces, so that at present China's northernmost point is Usuri on the Amur River east of Taheiho. The easternmost point is the confluence of the Amur and Usuri Rivers, longitude 135 degrees east. The southernmost and westernmost boundaries are still unsettled, for mountains in the extreme west, the Pamirs, constitute an undemarcated area between China, the U.S. S.R., Pakistan and India. The boundary between China and Burma is also unsettled in the northern section.

According to revised data from the Ministry of the Interior, the Republic of China, since the withdrawal of Mongolia and the addition of Taiwan, included an area of 3,970,410 square miles. The population was estimated at 469,140,533. However, no complete census of the entire population has ever been taken and the estimates vary greatly. The Republic of China included 35 provinces; the Territory of Tibet; several special municipalities such as Nanking, Shanghai, Peiping, Tientsin and others; and the special administrative districts of Weihaiwei and Harbin. The areas of the various sections are as follows:

China Proper (the 18 provinces south of the Great Wall)	1,434,997 sq. mi.
17 other provinces (Kansu, provinces of Manchuria, Inner Mongolia, etc.)	2,059,029 " "
Territory of Tibet	474,887 " "
Special municipalities and districts ...	1,497 " "
Total area	3,970,410 " "

In the eight provinces where The Christian and Missionary Alliance has missionary work the following estimates of area and population (1944-45) are given:

Provinces	Area	Population
Anhwei	54,952 sq. mi.	21,978,667
Hunan	80,303 " "	28,165,981
Hupeh	72,793 " "	24,658,988
Kansu	152,922 " "	6,528,726
Kiangsu (Shanghai)	42,546 " "	36,469,321
Kwangsi	86.448 " "	14,927,438
Kweichow	68,933 " "	10,770,014
Szechwan	146,686 " "	46,184,777

Every fifth person in the world is Chinese. The country is large enough to accommodate its immense population but there is congestion in the coastal areas and along the rivers. About 350 millions of the population live in one-third of the land area. China Proper occupies the fertile southeastern part of the country, and here the population has an estimated density of 174 to the square mile. Shanghai, China's commercial capital, with a present estimated population of 6,000,000, has the most strategic position economically of all cities in China. The province of Kiangsu, in which it is situated, is the most densely populated political unit in the world. Nanking, formerly the capital of the Republic, has a population of over one million.

There was a tremendous shift of population during World War II, as the people fled westward before the invading Japanese. The overall estimate of that shift of population is as high as 60 millions. In May, 1946, the Office of Repatriation estimated that 29 million displaced persons were still awaiting repatriation over great distances from one region to another.

People and History

China's culture can be traced in a fairly unbroken line back to the Stone Age. The Chinese race probably entered from Western Asia and settled in the northwestern part of China. The traditional history of the country begins with 2500 B.C. when three emperors brought the people out of barbarism and tribal rule to a comparatively high state of civilization. The authentic history begins with 722 B.C. and by that time there existed such a high state of civilization as to corroborate the Chinese claims to a great antiquity. By the sixth century B.C. Chinese influence had spread through the Yellow River valley and beyond the Yangtze River.

In 2205 B.C. the Hsia, first of a long succession of dynasties, was founded by Yu. The Chou dynasty, the longest (1122-245 B.C.), produced the three great philosophers, Confucius, Mencius and Lao-tse. This was the feudal period of China's history, and between 481 and 221 B.C. the period of the "Fighting States" intervened, with four states most prominent. The era of contending states ended in 221 B.C. when Chin Shih Huang Ti established a centralized empire. During this Chin dynasty the Great Wall was started (214 B.C.) as a measure of defense against the invading Huns. China remained an empire for 2,000 years. During that period architecture, art and literature flourished, and the empire was extended until at one time the frontiers reached to the Persian Gulf and the Caspian Sea.

In the seventh century A.D. the southern provinces of China were included in the Empire. Dynasties rose and fell; there were internal strife and external wars with Tartars and Mongols. The great Mongol warrior, Genghis Khan, conquered empires stretching from the Black Sea to the Pacific Ocean. In 1260 A.D. after more than a hundred years of struggle, the Mongol dynasty was established in China under Kublai Khan, grandson of Genghis, but after three centuries all returned to China's rule under the Ming dynasty.

Once again aliens acquired the land when the Manchus, a Tartar tribe, established their rule and maintained the Tsing dynasty for over two centuries. The Manchus furnished the most intellectual succession of emperors that ever ruled continuously over China. The Taiping rebellion (1850-1864 A.D.) was an attempt to overthrow the Tsing dynasty and establish a native Chinese dynasty to be called Tai-ping (Great Peace). The American soldier of fortune, General F. T. Ward, and the noted English General, then Major C. G. Gordon, "Chinese Gordon," led the Imperial forces in crushing the rebellion. Manchu rule continued until the establishment of the Republic in 1911.

As the Chinese became acquainted with more liberal forms

of government through their intercourse with Europeans and Americans, they became dissatisfied with the absolute monarchy which, under various dynasties, had ruled their country for more than 3,000 years. The first attack upon the monarchial system was led by Sun Yat-sen in 1895 at Canton. The Manchu Emperor, in 1908, promised that a parliamentary form of government would be established within nine years. That was too long to wait, and on October 10, 1911, a revolt broke out with fighting in Central and South China. The liberal faction, called the Kuo Min Tang (National Party) held a Provisional Assembly in Nanking and, on December 29, 1911, elected Dr. Sun Yat-sen as its President. After six weeks Dr. Sun gave way to General Yuan Shih-kai, the Commander-in-Chief of the old Imperial Army, and he ruled until his death in 1916. The Chinese have always been distinguished for their industry, courtesy and filial piety. Dr. Sun Yat-sen taught the Chinese to add to their filial piety, or clan loyalty, a new virtue—national patriotism. He also worked for popular government, social welfare and economic reform. After Dr. Sun's death in 1925 the Kuomintang was guided by General Chiang Kai-shek, who was first in power from 1928 to 1931.

The Japanese annexed Manchuria in 1931-32. They had been extending their power over China for 50 years, beginning with the Sino-Japanese War of 1894. In 1935 they came through the Great Wall north of Peiping into the province of Chahar. The principal Chinese officials in Peiping and Tientsin, and in Hopei and Chahar provinces were replaced by new men acceptable to the Japanese leaders. In 1937 Japan set up a so-called independent government in Peiping. Japan's aggression brought on war (July 7, 1937), which was the beginning of World War II for the Chinese. The National Government moved its capital from Nanking to the interior city of Chungking, and the Japanese, in 1938, established a puppet regime in Nanking, calling it "The New Reformed Government of the Republic of China." After the defeat of Japan, all the territories which she had seized were returned to China and the Chinese once more established their capital in Nanking.

On October 10, 1943, Generalissimo Chiang Kai-shek succeeded to the office of President of the National Government for a term of three years, on the death of Lin Sen. He retained his practically dictatorial powers under the coalition government formed in 1947 by the Kuomintang, the Young China Party, the Democratic Socialists and a group of non-partisans. The two largest minority parties, the Communists and the Democratic League, did not participate. A new constitution was adopted by the National Assembly and President Chiang became China's first President under the new Constitution when he was re-elected on April 19, 1948. He was vested with power to govern by decree for the duration of the present civil war emergency. In December, 1948, President Chiang announced that he was retiring, and Vice-President Li Tsung-jen became Acting President in his stead. The retirement of Chiang did not bring about the desired effect of improved relations with Mao Tse-tung, leader of the Communists, and the Nationalist government retreated successively to temporary capitals in Canton, Chungking, Chengtu and Formosa.

Communism was brought into China soon after World War I. Sun Yat-sen, although working for democratic principles, did not distinguish those principles from Communism. In 1923 he enlisted advice from Russia, and Soviet leaders sent him a corps of Russian advisors under Michael Borodin. Later when Chiang Kai-shek came into power, he severed diplomatic relations with Russia, Borodin was banished, and the Kuomintang fought the growing influence of the Communists in China for 10 years. Finally, in 1937, the Kuo-

mintang and the Communists agreed to set aside their differences and put up a united front against the Japanese invasion. After more than eight years of war with Japan (July 7, 1937-August 5, 1945) serious threats of civil strife arose, principally between the Kuomintang and the Communist Party. In May, 1945, the Nationalist Party promulgated a resolution, which reads in part as follows: "In September, 1937, the Chinese Communist Party announced its four pledges to support the National Government . . . (but) it has persisted in armed insubordination. . . . However, our Party has maintained a policy of forbearance and has spared no efforts to preserve unity." Such a statement bears out the affirmation that the "Chinese have a genius for compromise." They even have a proverb for it: "A tall man should bend at the waist; a short man should stand on tiptoe—then they will meet." But compromise with the Communists has proved to mean Nationalist surrender of one province after another until the entire Chinese mainland has come under Communist domination.

Government

China has long had a strong system of local self-government, for according to the ancient Chinese idea, a man should be governed and punished by those who know him best—his family or the people of his village—rather than by a government whose center may be hundreds of miles distant. The idea of a united nation, governed by the people, was comparatively new to China, and manifested itself in the revolution of 1911.

The Kuomintang (National Party) established the Republic of China in 1912, and in 1931 the central government at Nanking called a People's National Convention. The 450 delegates adopted a provisional constitution which declared all Chinese equal before the law, and guaranteed free speech and a free press.

The National Government was a committee form of government composed of a National State Council, who with a chairman known as President of the National Government, and with five Yuan (Councils). The five Yuan were: Executive, Legislative, Judicial, Examination, and Control Supervisory. The Executive Yuan was the most important and resembled a responsible cabinet. The National Assembly was the supreme organ of the people, with members elected on the basis of territorial and professional representation, and serving for six-year terms. The Assembly elected the President and Vice-President for six-year terms, and it also had the power to amend the Constitution. On December 25, 1946, it adopted a new Constitution, which became effective on December 25, 1947, and which included many features of the American form of government.

Climate

There is a wide variety in the climate of China since it extends from the colder temperate regions of the north to the semi-tropical southland, and from the Pacific Coast to the high mountain areas in portions of the interior, especially in the west.

Physical Features

About 30 per cent of the total area of China is mountainous; 43 per cent consists of hills and plateaus; and about 26 per cent is made up of plains and basins. China's rolling topography rises to high elevations in the north in the Khingan Mountains which separate Manchuria and Mongolia; in the Khangai Mountains in Mongolia; and in the Himalayan and Kunlun Mountains in Tibet to the southwest. In western Kansu is a series of parallel ranges belonging to the Nan-Shan Mountains, a branch of the Kunlun. As the mountains advance toward the east in Kansu their outline is hidden under a thick covering of loess, which is the distinctive feature of that section of the country.

China Proper is one of the best watered countries of the world. The three great rivers, descending from the western mountains to the Pacific Ocean, drain four-fifths of the country. The northern river is the Hwang Ho or Yellow River, and its valley is the most ancient home of Chinese culture, the area first definitely settled by the Chinese people as we know them today. South of the Yellow River is the Yangtze Kiang, which is bigger than the Mississippi and is the most heavily populated river valley in the world. The southernmost is the Sikiang, or West River, which is called the Pearl River from Canton to the sea.

The Yellow River basin has an area of about 600,000 square miles and includes six of the eighteen provinces of China proper: namely, Kansu, Shensi, Shansi, Hopei, Honan and Shantung. The Yellow and the Yangtze Rivers divide China culturally as well as geographically. The Yellow River valley may be taken as characteristic of North China. There the climate, the food and the character of the inhabitants differ from those obtaining in the south.

The Yellow River rises in the far west in the plain of Odontala at an altitude of 14,000 or 15,000 feet above sea level. As it leaves Chinghai and enters Kansu it flows through a valley where in the course of 150 miles it descends from an elevation of 8,000 feet to 5,200 feet at Lanchow. The river flows about 2,500 miles to its mouth in the Gulf of Chihli. It is not navigable to any great extent, it has changed its shallow, turbulent course many times, and its annual floods which cause so much devastation have given it the name "China's Sorrow." In its great basin live about 100 million people.

The Yangtze Kiang is the largest river in China. Its basin forms a second great division in the country. The headwaters of the Yangtze, in the confused Central Asian mountains, are fully 16,000 feet above sea level even at 200 miles from its source. For the first 400 miles of its course the river does not fall more than 200 feet; it then descends from the Tibetan plateau to the lower Szechwan level, a drop of 6,800 feet in 150 miles. Just before its junction with the Min River the Yangtze forms the boundary between Szechwan and Yunnan.

The Yangtze is 3,200 miles long and its entire basin covers 756,500 square miles. It opens up to foreign trade the greater part of China Proper, for it is the main artery of trade and communication with Central China. The 180 million people of the Yangtze basin absorb no less than 60 per cent of the foreign trade of the whole country. The Yangtze basin is not only larger than any other in China, but it is also richer where it flows through China Proper. The great treaty ports of Shanghai, Wuhu, Hankow and Changsha are open to foreign trade (or have been, under the Republic of China); and the river is navigable for small boats nearly 2,000 miles, while ocean-going vessels can go as far as Hankow, 600 miles from its mouth; and river steamers can travel almost 400 miles farther.

The West River or Sikiang basin includes four provinces with an area of about 390,000 square miles and a population of 60 millions. The West River rises in the northeastern part of Yunnan Province and flows through Yunnan and along the frontier between Kweichow and Kwangsi. It then flows across Kwangsi Province to the city of Wuchow, 900 miles from its source, and thence into the Province of Kwangtung. The river has a total length of 1,118 miles, of which 387 miles are in the Province of Kwangsi. It is navigable for steamers for more than 200 miles, and for small craft, 100 miles more. It flows for the most part through tropical and semi-tropical regions. A continuous line of mountains, with only two passes of any importance, separates the West River basin from its northern neighbor in Central China.

Resources

China is essentially agricultural. In some sections the Chinese have maintained the fertility of the soil for 4,000 years. Vast areas have in the past suffered from erosion, but on experimental farms methods have been developed to overcome this. As in colonial days in America, 90 per cent of the people were engaged in farming in order to ward off starvation, so in China, because of a lack of modern machinery and methods, over 378 million, or fourth-fifths of the population, are required to raise the necessary food.

China produces annually nearly 53 million tons of rice, which is grown in all but three of her provinces. More than 34 million tons of wheat and barley are produced; over seven and one-half million tons of soybeans; and 22 million tons of sweet potatoes (1936 statistics). Tea, cotton, sugar and indigo are also important products.

The silk industry has flourished for 4,000 years. Cotton is produced mostly in the Yangtze and Yellow River valleys. Modern cotton manufacturing began in 1895 and the country now ranks as one of the great cotton fabric producers of the world.

Excluding the northeastern provinces, over one and one-half million tons of iron, and over 15 million tons of coal are produced, besides large quantities of antimony. There are coal reserves estimated at over 243 billion tons. The oldest iron industry in the world is in Shansi. China is rich also in tungsten, bismuth, tin, manganese and mercury. She has large deposits of lead, zinc and oil.

The chief exports are silk, minerals and metals, piece goods, oils, wax and tallow, tea, cereals, wools, hides, skins and furs, seeds, chemicals, cotton, beans and peas.

Progress

China gave to the world not only the mulberry, persimmons and soybeans, but also oranges and walnuts—the variety commonly called, in the United States, the English walnut. China was the first to use printing and the mariner's compass; the first to produce gunpowder, silk, porcelain, paper, ink, lacquer, kites, and a cotton gin. Tea was first used as a beverage in South China about 270 A. D.; the longest wall was started in China in 214 B. C.; the oldest and longest canal (started in 540 B. C.) had a total length of 1,687 miles, and China's canal mileage today is greater than that of any other country of the world. China had books as early as 800 B. C. and put out the first printed book in 868 A. D.

In spite of the lack of an alphabet and in spite of an ancient system of education, China had begun the fight against illiteracy before the Japanese attacked in 1937. Christian missionaries had set the pattern for the modern schools in China. Dr. James Yen worked out a simplification of the language, and Dr. Hu Shih, at one time Ambassador to the United States, initiated a renascence of Chinese literature and thus the project of mass education in interior towns and villages was speeded up. There are now some excellent secondary schools in China. At the time of the Japanese invasion about 50,000 students were enrolled in 114 colleges and universities. Many of these were closed or moved inland to the far west during the war years. In 1944 the Chinese Government provided for the establishment of one public school for every 100 to 150 households in the country. Education is free, and in 1946 there were 269,937 primary schools with 21,831,898 pupils; and 4,530 secondary schools with 1,394,844 pupils. Universities, colleges and technical schools totaled 185, with

129,336 students. China's new constitution provided that 15 per cent of the total budget of the Central Government, and no less than 30 per cent of the provincial district and municipal budgets shall be appropriated for schools. Twenty years ago about one-tenth of the population could read. Since 1936 it is reported that 10 million Chinese have learned to write the minimum vocabulary of 1,200 characters. During the war middle school students in the city of Kweilin taught the people while they were crowded in cave shelters during aerial bombardments. At present about 135 million Chinese can read simple books and millions more are being added each year to the number of literates.

The first railway in China, a short line running from Shanghai to Woosung, was opened in 1876, constructed by foreign enterprise, but later purchased by China. At the time of the revolution, Dr. Sun Yat-sen made a breath-taking proposal for the construction of 100,000 miles of railways and one million miles of hard-surfaced highways. He envisioned swift communications with Russia, Europe, India and the Near East. Up to the time of the Manchurian "Incident" in 1931, the railways of China had a total mileage of less than 10,000 miles, and were chiefly in North China and the northeastern provinces. Work was progressing on new lines, but after seven and a half years of war with Japan, only a little over ten per cent of the old railways in the coastal provinces or in North China still remained in Chinese hands. Up to the end of 1944 only 887 miles of all lines constructed before the war were in operation in Free China. The construction of several new railways was undertaken during the war, many miles of them through difficult terrain in Central and South China.

In July, 1937, there was a total of about 72,300 miles of highways, of which over 25,000 miles were surfaced. During the war about 8,300 miles of highways were completed, and about 56,000 miles of road were reconditioned. By the end of the conflict more than half the roads had to be either repaired or completely reconstructed.

When China's great port cities fell to the Japanese, 90 per cent of China's modern industry located in these cities was dismantled or destroyed. It was reported that 120,000 tons of modern machinery were taken from the coastal regions and set up again in Chungking, and there operated during the war.

In China traditionally the scholar, not the successful business man, was honored. However today both scholars and technicians have devoted their utmost efforts toward the reconstruction of their war-impoverished country. The CNRRA (Chinese National Relief and Rehabilitation Administration), the corresponding administration of the United Nations, and Missions Boards have coöperated in the distribution of food, clothing and medical supplies to the suffering people of China.

Currency

During the early years of Protestant Missions in China the only coinage was a round copper cash with a square hole, one thousand of which was called a "string." Larger financial transactions used lumps of silver called "shoes." The unit of value was an ounce of silver called a "tael." Silver dollars from Spain and Mexico were first introduced by foreign traders. Late in the last century the Manchus imitated these with "dragon dollars" and all the resultant currency was called "Mexican."

About the same time the foreign banks in Hongkong and Shanghai began to print large denomination "Mex" banknotes, which soon found wide favor. After about fifteen years of the Republic, the Chinese government banks issued paper money, which replaced silver except in the remote interior, where the people still demanded "hard" money.

Chinese government banknotes held up well until the Sino-Japanese war, which produced fabulous inflation. By July, 1948, an ordinary foreign meal in Shanghai cost one million dollars national currency, the cheapest bus fare was $60,000, and soft coal cost $140,000,000 per ton. By August, 1948, one dollar U. S. bought from eight to twelve million Chinese national currency.

As a result of this frenzied finance, silver dollars came out of hiding everywhere and soon were worth more than U. S. banknotes. The government then issued a new currency called "gold yuan," which presumably had some gold or silver backing and was fixed at four to the U. S. dollar. Despite stringent regulations for exchange control, this new currency soon became as deflated as the old, and eventually depreciated even more rapidly.

Communist occupation has everywhere brought its own paper money to displace all other currency. Its local purchasing power seems to be fairly well maintained, but its foreign exchange value is still to be proved.

Languages and Races

The Chinese spoken language is literally musical and employs a number of different tones ranging from four in the north to eight in the south. The same sound given in the different tones may have disastrously different meanings. To the foreigner this makes the language most difficult, but the natives use the correct Chinese tones as instinctively as we do the correct pronunciation of English.

The Chinese written language consists of thousands of ideographs, which we generally call characters. These are pronounced differently in different provinces but mean practically the same whether in Mandarin, Cantonese or local dialects. Chinese characters are not letters but conventionalized pictures. The nearest they come to having an alphabet is found in 214 radicals, that component part of the character which gives a clue to the meaning and forms an index for the Chinese dictionary. The remaining portion of the character is called a phonetic and gives a clue to the pronunciation. There are about 900 phonetics. The combinations of radicals and phonetics produce between 40,000 and 50,000 ideographs, but if the missionary learns 5,000 of them he is doing well.

In order to simplify the tremendous task of acquiring such a language, Romanized writing was introduced and became popular in some coastal provinces. A system of phonetic symbols was also developed and used by the Missions, but did not meet with universal Chinese approval. Several Chinese leaders evolved systems of several hundred selected characters to teach the illiterate multitudes to read, specially literature limited to the selected characters.

Besides the National language (formerly called Mandarin), in its local variations, there are also the Cantonese tongue and many different tribal languages spoken by the aborigines back in the mountainous interior. The speech of some tribes has been reduced to writing by the missionaries. In a word, China is the present-day Babel, and one of the greatest tasks of the missionary has been to give the Gospel to "every man in his own tongue wherein he was born."

The Tibetan alphabet is a variation of Sanskrit and only consonantal, the vowels having to be supplied by certain marks. It also has an elaborate tone system.

The Chinese refer to themselves as "The Five Peoples": namely, (1) Han, the sons of the Han dynasty; (2) Man, the former ruling Manchu class; (3) Mung, the Mongolians; (4) Hwei, the Moslems who are distinct by race as well as by religion; (5) Ti, the Tibetans. Besides these five groups there are about 10 million aboriginal tribespeople. They comprise half the population of Yunnan and Kweichow, and there are large numbers of them in other sections of Southwest China.

Religions

Religion plays an important part in the life of the Chinese. The principal religions are Confucianism, Taoism and Buddhism, and most Chinese profess all three. Besides the temples erected to many gods, every pagan home has its idols and shrines. Ancestor-worship has the prominent place in nearly every home for it is the great national duty, and the cult about which all the later religions are built. Although ancestor-worship is primarily Confucian, yet even among the Taoists and Buddhists the ancestral spirits are faithfully worshiped.

The ancient inhabitants of China deified and worshiped the important phenomena of nature. There were gods of Rain, Wind and Rivers, lords of Thunder and Lightning, and even the god of the Kitchen. The people made no clear differentiation between the human and the divine; the dead became gods—hence ancestor-worship.

Confucianism is not strictly a religion, but really a system of political and social ethics based on the teachings of Confucius (551-479 B. C.). The sacrifices made to the founder are customs drawn from the ancestor-worship of the Chinese rather than from the teachings of Confucius himself. His teachings are contained in the Four Books and Five Classics. There is insistence on the five constant virtues: benevolence, righteousness, propriety, wisdom, sincerity. The duties of the five relationships are: the relationship of prince and minister, of husband and wife, of father and son, of brother and brother, and of friend and friend. To the Chinese Confucius was "a great sage whose teachings promote peace and good order in society and encourage moral living by the individual."

Taoism began as a philosophy and is traced back to Lao Tse (604 B. C.), born about fifty years before Confucius. His doctrine ruled out the formation of a religion, but 700 years after his death, his teachings had degenerated into a superstitious ritual. Animism in China finds its manifestation in Taoism. In theory Taoism teaches that, to attain true happiness, one must conform to the *Tao* or order of the universe. Actually Taoism includes polytheism, demonology and witchcraft. The religion has priests, temples and rituals, and the sacred book is Lao Tse's *Book of Way and Virtue*, full of teachings far removed from the true Way in the Word of God.

Buddhism was introduced from India by the Emperor Ming Ti in 67 A. D. when he sent emissaries to the west to inquire for the true religion. Buddhist missionaries from India were quick to seize the opportunity of the open door in China. However, the Buddhism of China has little resemblance to the original teachings of Buddha himself. A number of legends and rites and many of the deities of Taoism have been added which give it a strong Chinese flavor. There are now more than 267,000 Buddhist temples and 738,000 monks and nuns in China. It is difficult to estimate the total number of adherents.

Lamaism is the form of Buddhism followed in Tibet and Mongolia. It is a mixture of Buddhism and the ancient practices of Shamanism, which include witchcraft. Reincarnation in a higher state is the goal of those in Lamaism. A "Living Buddha" is believed to be an incarnation of some Buddhist saint and therefore to possess the powers of a savior. When a Living Buddha dies his spirit is believed to enter a boy born at the time of his death. Special methods are used to find the one in whom the spirit of the Buddha has chosen to be reincarnated, and the boy selected becomes the new Living Buddha. The Dalai or Grand Lama is the spiritual head of Buddhism in Tibet. There are Living Buddhas in other Buddhist centers of China also. (See *Buddhism*, under *Religions, India*.)

Islam entered China in 651 A. D. and now claims 48 million followers there, although some authorities place the number at from 10 to 15 million. (See *Islam*, under *Religions, India*.)

In the days of the empire, Confucianism was the state religion of China, and the emperor officiated at the annual sacrifices made to Heaven and Earth. Buddhism and Taoism were also under imperial control and the State recognized Islam. In 1939 the National Government, in response to a petition by a Moslem federation, made the study of Islamic culture a regular feature in Chinese universities. Religious freedom was extended to Christianity in the various foreign treaties from 1842 to 1903. In 1914 the Republic of China adopted Confucianism as the state religion, but it recognized complete religious freedom. The Generalissimo and Madame Chiang Kai-shek are both Protestant Christians. There are no accurate figures but it is estimated that there are over 2,600,000 Roman Catholics and about 618,600 Protestants in China.

Missionary Occupation

Christianity was first taken to China from the early eastern churches. During the 3rd and 4th centuries the Christian faith reached Persia and Central Asia. From the 8th to the 13th centuries the Nestorians had churches established from Mesopotamia to China and from South India to Mongolia. Christians from India may possibly have visited China in the 4th and 5th centuries. The more reliable records point to A. D. 635 as the date when the first Nestorian missionary arrived in the capital of China, but by the end of the 16th century the influence of Nestorian Christianity seems to have disappeared. In 1623 or 1625 workmen, excavating for the foundations of a building at Hsianfu, uncovered the famous monument erected in 781, inscribed with the history of Nestorianism in China. Other records which have come to light show that the Nestorians translated books and tracts into the Chinese language. Imperial edicts issued between the 7th and 9th centuries also contain references to Nestorianism. There were Nestorian churches in Yangchow and Nestorians in Yunnanfu, in Kansu and in Chihli, but many of those Nestorian Christians may have been foreigners and not Chinese.

The first Roman Catholic missionary known to have reached China was John of Montecorvine, a Franciscan who began his missionary journeys in 1272, went to India in 1291, and later entered China where, by 1305, he had baptized about 6,000 converts. No certain traces of the early work remained, but since the middle of the 16th century the work of the Roman Catholic Church in China has never been totally interrupted. In 1938 Roman Catholic communicants numbered 2,542,000; there were some 123 missions, and 4,109 Roman Catholic missionaries.

Protestant missions in China date from 1807 when Robert Morrison reached Canton. He had already begun the study of the Chinese language through the use of a manuscript in the British Museum. The East India Company was so hostile to missions that he could not get passage directly from England, so he came to America and sailed from New York, arriving in Canton in September, 1807. He continued the study of the Chinese language there with the help of two Chinese Roman Catholics, and in 1809 he became a translator for the same East India Company which had refused him passage on their ships two years before. It was 1814 before Morrison baptized his first Chinese convert. During the first 25 years of their work, he and the colleagues who had joined him baptized only ten Chinese. Morrison, with the aid of others, completed the translation of the entire Bible by the year 1819. The British and Foreign Bible Society helped with the publication of the translation and in 1836 they sent an agent to Macao. About 1822 the American Bible Society also began helping in the distribution of the Scriptures among the Chinese. The London Missionary Society had sent reinforcements to China and the Church Missionary Society sent its first missionary in 1836. Two missionaries from continental Europe arrived early in the 1830's.

America sent workers to China in 1829. David Abeel went as chaplain to the many American sailors in Chinese waters, and Elijah C. Bridgman, under the American Board, went to work among the Chinese. In 1836 the first Baptist missionaries arrived in Macao; the Protestant Episcopal Church sent workers in 1835; the Presbyterian Board in 1838, and the Methodists in 1847.

The China Inland Mission, founded by J. Hudson Taylor, began work in China in 1866. Mr. Taylor had already served in China, first under the Chinese Evangelization Society and then independently. At the time of his death the China Inland Mission had 828 missionaries in the country. Under the inspiration of the China Inland Mission other organizations were formed for work in China: the Swedish Mission and the German China Alliance sent workers in 1890; the Scandinavian Alliance Mission began work there two years later.

Chinese opposition to foreigners increased and reached its climax in the Boxer uprising of 1900, causing heavy loss to the missions and to Chinese Christians. The Roman Catholic martyrs during that period included 47 European missionaries and 30,000 Chinese Catholics, who were either killed or died from privation. About 134 Protestant missionaries and 52 children suffered martyrdom, of whom one-third were associated with the China Inland Mission, while 21 missionaries and 14 children were in The Christian and Missionary Alliance. The Chinese Protestant Christians who lost their lives for Christ's sake numbered about 1,912, including three Mongols.

Since the Treaty of Nanking in 1842 the work of Protestant missions in China has grown remarkably. Most of China's colleges and universities are Christian-founded, and modern medicine in China is also the result of Christian missions. Prior to 1937, Protestants in China had 1,130 mission stations, 19 colleges, 10,000 organized churches with over 500,000 members, and 239,655 were under Christian instruction. Data published by the International Missionary Council (1943) gives the following report for Protestant work in China:

	1911	1938
Protestant communicants	178,000	536,000
Protestant missionaries	4,197	5,747
National workers, ordained	513	2,135
National workers, others	11,595	9,527
Students in elementary schools .	55,000	173,000
Students in secondary schools ..	21,000	44,000

The British and Foreign Bible Society, the American Bible Society, and the National Bible Society of Scotland have united in China under an all-Chinese Advisory Council. During 1948 there were circulated in China by the joint work of these Societies, 98,842 Bibles, 111,686 New Testaments, and 2,726,154 Scripture portions, totalling 2,932,682 copies. Because of the paper shortage in China, the American Bible Society sent out, in 1948, 97 tons of Bible paper and 91 tons

of newsprint. The same Society estimates that China needs immediately over two million Scripture volumes, which will cost $77,000, and therefore the Society has increased its appropriation for China from $48,000 (1948) to $100,000 (1949).

The Christian and Missionary Alliance sent its first missionaries to China in 1888. Ten years later Alliance missionaries were witnessing for Christ in Anhwei, Hupeh, Hunan, the Tibetan frontier of Kansu, Shansi, Mongolia, Kwangsi and in the great cities of Peking, Shanghai, and Tientsin. Dr. Kenneth Latourette, in *A History of Christian Missions in China,* says: "With the exception of Anhwei and the three cities named, these districts, it will be noted, were among the most difficult in which to maintain missions. In Kwangsi the Alliance was apparently the first Protestant body to establish a permanent station, although that had been attempted by members of at least three other Societies. The prolonged effort to penetrate Tibet by way of Kansu was made in the face of almost continuous danger and entailed great heroism."

Under the Republic the Alliance had missions in Shanghai and seven interior provinces. Our active forces in China during those years averaged 85 missionaires and 225 native workers, while the church membership at the end of the period was over 8,000.

Now that Communism has spread over all China reports state that there are three stages in the attitude of the Communists toward Christianity. First, there is the stage of tolerance when notices are posted stating that mission property will be protected; second, there is the stage when notices appear warning the people that all religion is superstition; third, there is the stage of active opposition when churches are closed and foreign missionaries are ordered to leave. It has been found that the missionaries cannot function efficiently in Communist-controlled areas, especially in the evangelistic field. In some cases their very existence has been made miserable and they have been practically prisoners in their own residences or in that portion of the residence which the Communists let them continue to occupy. Christian schools have been permitted to continue but they have ere long ceased to be Christian. High schools have continued but with a teacher of Communism whom the Communists tried to require the missionaries to pay.

From the economic standpoint it has been found difficult and in most cases impossible to send money from America to the missionaries in Communist-held territory. Thus their position has been made untenable and The Christian and Missionary Alliance has considered that the wisest policy is for our missionaries not to remain where they would be inactive or merely marking time but to transfer to other open and needy Alliance fields for active service. Only a few have remained in China to keep as much contact as possible with the work behind the iron curtain and they are concentrated in Hongkong with an all-China office for Christian and Missionary Alliance fields.

When it became apparent that missionaries would be obliged to leave their stations the Alliance adopted the following policy. All first-term missionaries, being still young enough to learn a new language, were transferred to other fields permanently, except those who, having been born in China or having spent their youth there, had a background that made return to China advisable if and when possible. Missionaries who had spent one term on the field were transferred to other fields to fill out the balance of the present term with the understanding that, if and when China is again open, they should return to that country because of their experience and knowledge of the language. Older missionaries who had nearly completed another term of service were authorized to return home for an early furlough.

A recent visitor to China said, "Darkness threatens. . . . The ray of hope is the Christian student class." God's working among the student class has been especially marked since the close of the war. Missionaries have been invited to teach Bible classes on campuses which had never before allowed Christian teaching. A nation-wide conference was called in 1945, near Chungking, sponsored by Christian students, and with delegates from 40 different universities and colleges. A revival followed and as a result the Chinese Inter-Varsity Christian Fellowship was organized with Rev. Calvin Chao chosen as General Secretary. After three and a half years the China IVCF had some 30 workers, Chinese and missionary, who were ministering on more than 80 campuses. In the Nanking-Shanghai area alone, special evangelistic campaigns resulted in nearly one thousand inquirers seeking to know more about Christ. At a time when the people were never more hungry for the gospel, Satan is seeking to cut off missionary work and to bury China under the atheistic influence of Communism.

The China Alliance Press

In every portion of the Church throughout the world there is a growing recognition of the importance of the ministry of the printed page. Unfortunately the liberal and unorthodox sections and the false cults often show far more zeal in making use of this valuable agent for the promulgation of their doctrines than do the evangelical portions of the Church of Christ. We in The Christian and Missionary Alliance, with its precious truths of the four-fold gospel revealing the fulness of Christ, should be especially earnest and energetic in the increase of this ministry with its wonderful possibilities.

The printed page is more important than ever in missionary ministry in these days of world crisis. Missionaries may not be able to stay long in some of the lands but if the Church in those lands is well supplied with sound evangelical teaching through the printed page the Church will be greatly benefited and the work will progress more rapidly whether missionaries have to leave or not.

For more than a quarter of a century the late Dr. R. A. Jaffray edited and published the Bible Magazine in Chinese. His co-editor for many years was Rev. Wilson Wang. This effective collaboration in editorial ministry was sundered by the second world war and the editor died in an internment camp in Indonesia. However as soon as contacts could be made at the end of the war it was arranged that the Bible Magazine should be again published and the Chinese co-editor continues to faithfully carry on that responsible work in collaboration with a missionary editor, Rev. Paul H. Bartel.

The Bible Magazine has had a beneficial ministry in all sections of the Church in China and in neighboring lands where Chinese live. The able office secretary and manager who had conducted the work of distribution for many years prior to the world war and was interned in Shanghai during the world war, re-entered that city as soon as possible after the close of the second world war in order to resume the work of distribution of the Bible Magazine and other literature. With the coming of Communists to Central China and their threatened control of Shanghai the office was moved to Singapore as the center from which the China Bible Magazine will be mailed out to many lands in the Far East.

The China Alliance Press has recently opened an office in Kowloon, Hongkong, to care for the publication and distribution of other literature. Late in 1949 it was learned that it

might again be possible under the Communist regime in China to mail the Bible Magazine from certain large cities to subscribers throughout the land. Quantities of the Bible Magazine were therefore shipped to these cities and the result is awaited with much prayer and interest.

The work of the China Alliance Press as well as of the Alliance editorial and publication work in many other fields should be continually furthered by earnest prayer and supported by liberal giving.

KANSU-TIBETAN BORDER

The Province of Kansu in northwest China is bounded on the northwest by Sinkiang (Chinese Turkestan); on the north by Ningsia; on the east by Shensi; on the south by Szechwan; and on the west by Chinghai (Koko-Nor), all provinces of China. The Kansu-Tibetan Border Mission of The Christian and Missionary Alliance has as its sole responsibility the southwestern part of Kansu Province, that portion of the Sino-Tibetan marches that forms the boundary of the Chinese field, and also all that portion of northeast Tibet that extends in a westerly and southwesterly direction from the Chinese frontier to the limits of habitation where the central plateau rises to forbidding heights, or to those points along the trade routes where the central government of Lhasa has control. The location of the Alliance field in northwest China presents not only a heavy responsibility in a large Chinese and Moslem field, but also a most strategic position along the border of northeast Tibet—a wonderful opportunity that has resulted in the actual occupation of centers in Tibetan country. Northeast Tibet is a part of Outer Tibet which comprises the greater part of the Provinces of Chinghai and Sikang, both of which are claimed by the Chinese. Inner Tibet, or Tibet Proper, is still closed to the gospel. Its capital is Lhasa, and the western end of Tibet Proper, sometimes called Little Tibet, is more or less under Indian influence.

Area and Population

Kansu is one of China's largest provinces in area, but is one of the smallest in population. The China Year Book (estimates, 1944-45) gives the area as 152,922 square miles, and the population as 6,528,726. Distances in this part of China are great or short according to the method of travel. From the nearest railway terminal in Shensi to Lanchow, the capital of Kansu, the journey by mule requires eighteen days; by auto the trip is made in two or more days according to the condition of the roads; by airplane the distance is covered in three hours.

The Christian and Missionary Alliance area in Kansu and among the Tibetan tribes to the west has a population of about 3,500,000.

People and History

Living in the adjoining areas of the Kansu-Tibetan border are Chinese, Tibetans, Mongols, Salar Moslems and aborigines. The history of the Chinese portion of this interesting bit of borderland is a fairly continuous record from the time of the Chinese migration into the Yellow River basin over 4,000 years ago. The people of that period left in the loess interesting archeological traces that link their pottery and culture to similar discoveries in Central Asia, and to a source of culture in the Euphrates valley. By the second century B. C. the history of the Chinese field is quite authentic and detailed. It includes the story of the Ouigour Tartars, who finally accepted Islam and settled in the Tongsiang of Hochow, where as a distinct linguistic and racial group they constitute a responsibility and a challenge. The history includes the account of the arrival from Samarkand of the Salar Moslems; the subjugation and eventual absorption of the Tibetan tribes of the Minchow district; and the colonization of Taochow by military colonists from Nanking. The Tongsiang Moslems have won a reputation among the Chinese as thieves. The Salar Moslems have kept up their reputation as trouble makers, a reputation they had in Samarkand in the 12th century, when popular indignation drove them out to seek a new home. They settled in Kansu, and the Moslem rebellion there some 80 years ago, and again in 1928-30, began among the Salars.

Much less is known of the history of the Tibetan area. There are distinct traces both in archeological discoveries and in the language of Mongol dominance during the Yuan dynasty; and traces of later migratory movements from Central Tibet and Lhasa. The people of the greater part of our Tibetan field have no traditions extending back more than 250 years. It is therefore probable that most of the peoples of northeast Tibet took up their present locations less than 300 years ago. Recent history is largely made up of the record of inter-tribal warfare punctuated by several rather unsuccessful attempts on the part of the Chinese government to extend its authority over the liberty-loving Tibetans. Strange as it may seem, the brief dominance by Moslem military leaders of a portion of the field facilitated the occupation of Tibetan areas by missionaries. The Chinese had been content to let well enough alone, and to let the Tibetans in this border country do as they pleased, but the Moslem defense commissioner of the border set out to tax the trade of Tibetan country. After the Moslem victory over the Tibetans, and when they had established law and order among them, missionaries visited Amchok, and opened the lamasery centers of Labrang, Hehtso and Rongwu. Again and again during the period when Moslems were in power, their rebel leaders showed favor to the missionaries. The first-aid rendered by the missionaries to wounded Moslems may have contributed to this attitude. In the later Moslem rebellion of 1928-1930 the missionaries took advantage of the opportunity to go with fleeing Chinese into Tibetan country, and the suspicious Tibetans, believing them to be refugees, relaxed their suspicions and showed them hospitality. An entrance was thus gained into Samtsa Rong and Tebbu land.

Government

All of the Chinese section and some of the Tibetan area of this field is under the Chinese government, and full official protection and liberty of movement and work are accorded to the missionaries. Along the Kansu border there are certain areas where the Tibetan tribal rule still exists, largely dominated by Chinese control, however, and here the missionaries had a satisfactory official status as holding passports granted by the Chinese government. Such an area begins five miles west of Lintan Old City. There is a third region where Chinese control over the Tibetans is only nominal, and in such districts travel and residence is only possible when the local rulers, for reasons of friendship with the missionaries, give them permission and protection. Residence in such areas is no simple matter and there have been several rebuffs, yet God has graciously opened to the Alliance more ground than the Mission is able to occupy with the present force of missionaries. The local rulers may be either tribal chiefs, so-called kings, or lamasery authorities. There is no definite line of demarcation between areas wholly under Chinese control and those under Tibetan rule where Chinese authority is not acknowledged. The balance of power may depend on the strength of the local tribal or lamasery authorities.

Climate

The climate of the field varies out of all proportion to the variations in latitude. In the medium altitudes the climate is temperate and healthful. In the west border stations, in the higher altitudes, the winters are long, the winds are rough, and the mountain passes are often blocked with snow. The cycle of the seasons follows the changes of the solar year more nearly than in the States, making all the seasons earlier.

The Kansu summer temperatures may rise to 85 or 90 (depending on the altitude) but it is always cool at night. The winter temperature drops to zero but even then it is always hot in the sunshine, and children often remove their garments and stand naked in the sun to get warm. In Tibet the temperature drops to below zero in the winter, and the summers are cool.

Physical Features

"Only when one looks away to the majesty and grandeur of the mountains can he appreciate the name given to it by the Chinese," wrote a new missionary of the dust-like loess or "white earth" region of Kansu. The loess, a distinctive feature of North China, is found in Kansu chiefly north of the Peh Ling mountain range. Barren as a desert in the winter time, the loess-covered mountains and valleys become suddenly green and promising in the spring, for the soil is astonishingly fertile except in years of drought, and then famine stalks the land. Because of the great variety of grains, fruits and vegetables which it produces, the Chinese call the loess region the "blessed land."

South of the Peh Ling Mountains is beautiful mountain and forest country, but the soil is rocky, the frosts come early, and in these altitudes of 8,000 feet and more the people can be sure of only the barley crop. The compensation for the lack of garden produce and fruits is the abundance of beef, mutton and milk.

On the whole, Kansu is mountainous, starting with an elevation of 5,000 feet at the eastern boundary, and rising gradually to over 15,000 feet above sea level in the west. The Yellow River and its tributaries constitute the only waterways in the province. They are of little commercial importance since transportation by boats is practically impossible. The Alliance in Kansu is largely located in the basin of the Tao River, which unites with the Yellow River not far from Lanchow.

The Tibetan plateau beginning in the western part of the province is a mass of folding mountains ascending higher and higher to the west. In the Tibetan grasslands only the lower fringes are cultivated, the greater part being too high—11,000 to 13,000 feet—for any use except as pasture lands. Here in a setting of flower-bedecked meadows with a background of snow-capped mountains, are found the sprawling black tents of the nomadic Tibetans. This vast area with its roaming inhabitants is at once the greatest part of the Alliance potential field and the least worked.

Resources

Kansu produces wheat, barley, beans, peas, apricots, peaches, pears, and a poor grade of apples. In Northeast Tibet no fruit is produced and no grain in the higher altitudes among the nomad Tibetans. Along the border of Kansu there are sedentary Tibetans who raise grains and vegetables.

In Tibet are found antelope, musk-deer, the wapiti, blue mountain sheep and bears. The Tibetans export wool, cattle, and skins of wild animals, but keep most of the cattle hides for their own use.

Large deposits of gold, copper and coal are known to exist, but the inaccessibility of the region and the local difficulties of travel have thus far prevented the development of the immense mineral and agricultural resources of the province.

Progress

Although Kansu is chiefly a "province of transit," the means of communication are few and poor. Horses are commonly used for travel, but goods are transported for the most part on the backs of camels, mules and donkeys, and not infrequently on the backs of men. The transport animal of Tibet is still the yak. Although the rivers are not navigable they are often used for floating logs and log rafts from the Tibetan forests down to the Chinese cities.

During the latter part of 1935 the government at Nanking sent thousands of soldiers into Kansu ostensibly to protect the province from the hordes of Chinese Communists who were threatening to invade Kansu. With the coming of the soldiers there was a great impetus to road building and fairly good roads have been constructed between most of the important centers of the province. All of the towns or cities where the Alliance has Chinese churches and two of the Tibetan stations can now be reached by jeep or truck. Recently, within a year and a half, the Field Chairman traveled over 9,500 miles by auto, in 600 hours of actual travel, which was a great saving of time and strength in comparison with the old way of travel with mules or horses.

There is a fairly regular passenger truck service between Lanchow and Linsia, and also between Lanchow and Lintao, Lungsi and Minhsien. These trucks do not carry much freight except government supplies, but there are a number of auto-tired mule carts that haul a large tonnage of freight and grain over these same roads. There is excellent airplane service from Lanchow to Sian, Hankow and Shanghai. Instead of spending from one to three months to reach the Tibetan border from the coast, one can now fly the distance in seven or eight hours. Mail from the States used to require months to reach West China. Air mail now arrives in a week or ten days.

Education has made great progress during the past ten years. Every country village now has a good school, and in all the cities there are one or more elementary and high schools. In some of the schools the government furnishes books, clothing and food for the students. This is particularly true of the normal schools. The girls' schools are increasing in number and girls have equal advantages with the boys. The government has gone so far as to establish Chinese schools for Tibetans in some places along the border and beyond it.

Currency

For centuries the currency among the Chinese and Moslems of this field was silver bullion and copper cash. Later, silver dollars and small copper coins were used. For some years, except among the Tibetans in the distinctly border towns, Chinese National Currency has been in use. The depreciation in value of this worthless paper has forced many small merchants out of business. In most parts of Kansu all prices are now quoted in Chinese silver dollars, though payment may be accepted in paper money at the prevailing rate of exchange, and this latter may vary as much as 25 per cent in a single day. The Tibetans use only silver dollars, or else barter wool, skins, cattle and other Tibetan produce for flour, cloth and other necessities brought into the province by Chinese and Moslem traders.

(See also *Currency* under *China*.)

Languages and Races

There are four large and distinct language groups in the Kansu-Tibetan border field, viz., Chinese, Tibetan, Turki, and Mongolian. Arabic is taught in the Koranic schools and used in all Moslem religious exercises but few really understand it. In addition to the above there are two or three small language groups in little-known, out-of-the-way corners, while the still undefined southern border of the Tibetan field touches, if it does not include, some of the polyglot divisions of the Jarong or aboriginal tribes, speaking a dozen or more different languages.

The Chinese all speak Mandarin, which is now called the national language. In the written language the Mandarin script is used mostly, although the Chinese phonetic script is used by some.

The various Tibetan tribes are political units under different rulers, and not language groups; the clans are smaller divisions of the tribes. There is only one Tibetan language and one script, but there are slight variations of dialect.

The Moslems of Kansu represent three racial groups. There are the Chinese-speaking Moslems, found in various parts of the province. By intermarriage they have become more like the Chinese than the other Moslem groups, but they still show some traces of their descent from the Ta Shi (Arab) mercenaries who entered China centuries ago. Secondly, there are the Tongsiang Moslems of Tartar origin, who speak a corruption of the Mongolian language. Then there are the Salar Moslems, who speak a corrupt form of Central Asian Turki, though most of the men speak also Chinese or Tibetan. Although numerically the smallest Moslem group, the Salars are becoming increasingly important politically and religiously.

A foreigner is obliged to spend from two to three years in language study in order to get a good working knowledge of either the Tibetan or the Chinese language. Our missionaries use both the Tibetan and the Chinese in preaching the Gospel.

Religions

In the Chinese portion of the field the religion is largely the usual combination of Confucianism, adulterated with the polytheism of Taoism and the mysticism of Buddhism that is found throughout most of China. Yet as each of these three factors is found in varying proportions, so the different districts are more idolatrous or more materialistic in degree as the case may be.

The Tibetans are, almost without exception, the adherents of Lamaism—the Tibetan form of Buddhism—and are completely under the despotic religious rule of the Lamaist hierarchy. The monks are called lamas, and the city of Lhasa is to them the "place of the gods."

The three racial groups of Moslems are all intolerant, fanatical and warlike. Their fearlessness was put to good use in subjugating the Tibetans during the period of Moslem dominance. The Moslems first fiercely resisted Soviet aggression, but later the wealthy Moslem leaders made an emergency pilgrimage to Mecca and the Reds took the province unopposed.

(See *Religions,* under *China*.)

Missionary Occupation

The first missionaries to enter Kansu Province were two men of the China Inland Mission, who went there in 1872. The China Inland Mission headquarters for this field are in Lanchow, the capital of the province. Here they established a large, well-equipped hospital in addition to evangelistic and school work. Alliance missionaries entered Kansu in 1895. The Christian and Missionary Alliance field is located in the southwest of the province, the China Inland Mission in the southeast, center and northwest, and the Evangelical Alliance Mission (formerly called the Scandinavian Alliance) in the northeast. The Assemblies of God (Pentecostal), Seventh Day Adventists and Roman Catholics also have some work in Kansu.

The Christian and Missionary Alliance

The original purpose of our Kansu Mission was to enter the closed land of Tibet. It is impossible to enter that land from the north; the western and southern borders were already occupied by other Societies; but the entire Chinese-Tibetan border was unoccupied. Therefore the Alliance chose to approach Tibet from the Kansu side. Tangar and Taochow Old City were the two largest outlets from Northeastern Tibet, and the latter place was chosen as the base for Tibetan work. The two young men who opened the station of Taochow Old City in the spring of 1895 had sailed for China in 1892, but they did not try to rush unprepared into the task before them. For three years they studied the Tibetan language at the lama temple in Peking before starting on the journey of five months of laborious travel across China to Kansu. At that time the Alliance constituency in the homeland was not yet ten years old yet it had already established its oriental base in Central China and had begun work in South China. When Taochow was entered a foothold was gained in a city that is frequented by large numbers of nomadic Tibetans who come to trade; a city that is situated within a day's ride of lamaseries—the monasteries that dominate all Tibetan life.

In eastern Tibet there are no cities, towns, stores or inns. The work in this section must therefore be done by evangelistic itineration and this can only be accomplished by first entering into "traveling agreements" of friendship with the leading lamas, the chiefs of clans, village head-men or other influential persons. To establish the necessary friendships the missionaries provided at the mission station facilities for entertaining Tibetan guests, and open house was kept for man and beast. Tibetans who had been guests of the missionaries, in turn invited them to be their guests across the border. A remarkable result of such missionary tactics was the invitation extended to one of our missionaries to accompany the head Living Buddha of Labrang on a contemplated trip to Lhasa, a journey of five or six months. Unable to spare that much time the missionary accepted the invitation for a part of the journey, and during the long weeks of travel and camping in the retinue of the Living Buddha, many opportunities came to give literature to lamas of various monasteries and to speak freely of the gospel.

The plan of campaign of the Alliance Mission on the Tibetan border is to complete the occupation of a few leading lamasery towns along a line 80 miles from the border and 400 miles in length, working from these as centers while at the same time continuing to work also from the previously occupied centers of Chone, Lintan and Linsia. There is no restriction placed upon intercourse across the border. No other society is working in the area above indicated and the population there for which the Alliance is responsible is one-half million Tibetans, with a million more in the adjacent country to the west.

In describing our seven Kansu mission stations which were occupied up to the time of the evacuation in 1949, those relating to the Tibetan work are given first in the order of their opening, followed by those established for the carrying on of work among the Chinese. The new names given to certain Chinese cities are used, the old names being shown in parentheses.

Tibetan work has been carried on from three stations. There are no Tibetan churches as yet but there are a few converts who have openly confessed Christ, among them two women.

Lintan (Taochow) In 1895 this the first Alliance station
Old City in Kansu was opened. Although it is a Chinese city, there are large Tibetan communities on three sides of it at a distance of only a few miles. More Tibetans can be reached from Lintan than from most places across the border in Tibet, because great numbers of the nomads come to the city on business. There is a small Chinese church in this city.

Siaho Very early in their work the Kansu mission-
(Labrang) aries planned to have an evangelistic center in Labrang, where there are more than 3,000 priests in the greatest Tibetan monastery in all northeastern Tibet. An attempt to enter was repulsed but in 1919 the local power of Lamaism was broken by Moslem troops. Not long after, a house was rented and in 1922 missionaries took up residence there, witnessing steadily in the city and surrounding villages. Siaho is really twin cities—religious and commercial—for a few hundred yards downstream from the monastery is the trading village with its secular inhabitants, Chinese, Moslem and Tibetan. As the most influential religious, political and commercial center of northeast Tibet, Siaho has afforded remarkable opportunities for witnessing and for maintaining contacts with many Tibetan leaders in a way that has touched all of northeast Tibet. The guestroom work in this center has been greatly used in furthering these ends. On the other hand, the tyrannical power of the lamasery authorities is nowhere quite so great as in this district, and a number of secret believers are still too fearful to make open confession of faith.

There is a small but strong Chinese church in Siaho. Its members are mostly traders and officials from other places. As they have contributed generously they have been able to build an attractive chapel and it is in almost daily use.

Hehtso Another important station for Tibetan work is Hehtso, located midway between Lintan and Siaho. It is surrounded by an extensive and well-populated farming district with outlying nomadic clans, and it is the most easily worked district on the field, the periodic markets giving a splendid opportunity for evangelistic work while the village population is most encouragingly accessible. Work was begun here by Alliance missionaries in 1923 and the missionaries residing here have held services and witnessed throughout the district. A tribal monastery at Hehtso has 1,000 priests, the largest and ruling monastery of that area.

The two Tibetan towns of *Lhamo* and *Denga* stand empty and challenging. Formerly occupied by missionaries, and with mission property still there, no one has been available to reopen these closed stations.

Southwest of Lintan Old City about one hundred miles from the Chinese border, in the section called Stag-tsang-lhamo (Goddess of the Tiger's Den) are two lamaseries of considerable size, one on either side of the valley through which runs a small stream. After much prayer and negotiation with the lamasery authorities, the station here at *Lhamo* was opened in 1930, in the center of a large district of nomadic tribes. The population of Lhamo itself is about 2,000 but in the surrounding district are about 30,000 souls for whom the Alliance is responsible.

The lawlessness of the region greatly added to the difficulties and problems of life and work in this place, but a large number of tribes were reached by itineration and guestroom work, and Lhamo proved to be the gateway to further occupation of northeast Tibet. Contacts secured and maintained here resulted in a remarkable opportunity for entering the kingdom of Ngawa, five days to the southwest beyond the knee of the Yellow River. The rulers of that large princi-

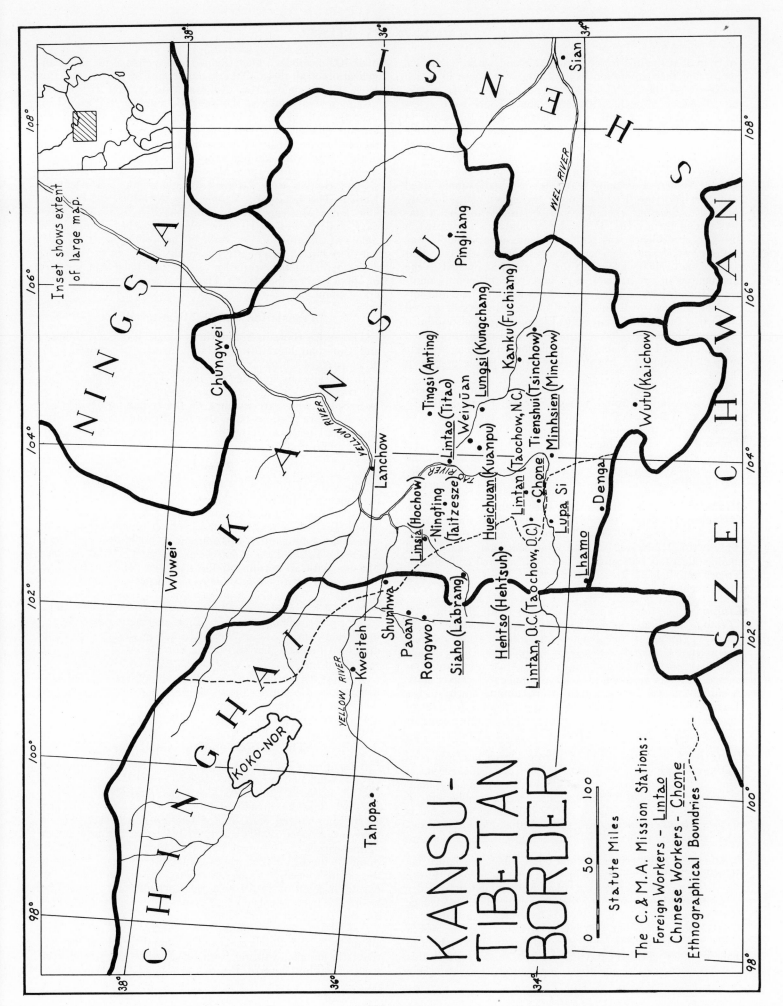

KANSU-
TIBETAN
BORDER

The C. & M.A. Mission Stations:
Foreign Workers – Lintao
Chinese Workers – Chone
Ethnographical Boundries

Statute Miles

0   50   100

Inset shows extent
of large map.

CHINGHAI

NINGSIA

KANSU

SHENSI

SZECHWAN

KOKO-NOR

YELLOW RIVER

YELLOW RIVER

TAO RIVER

WEI RIVER

Tahopa

Wuwei

Chungwei

Lanchow

Kweiteh

Shunhwa

Paoan

Rongwo

Siaho (Labrang)

Hehtso (Hehtsuh)

Lintan, O.C. (Taochow, O.C.)

Linsia (Hochow)

Ningting (Taitzesze)

Hueichuan (Kuanpu)

Lintan (Taochow, N.C.)

Chone

Lupa Si

Lhamo

Denga

Tingsi (Anting)

Lintao (Titao)

Weiyüan

Lungsi (Kungchang)

Kanku (Fuchiang)

Tienshui (Tsinchow)

Minhsien (Minchow)

Wutu (Kaichow)

Pingliang

Sian

pality invited the missionaries to reside and work in Ngawa, reinforcing their invitation by the offer of a house in which to live. Only the lack of workers kept the Mission from taking advantage of such an unusual offer. There were a few open professions of faith in connection with the work at Lhamo, and then to that lonely outpost came death and the closing of the station. The offer to go to Ngawa has never been accepted.

Between Lhamo and Lintan is the district of the fourteen clans of Tebbu. For many years the missionaries maintained contact with a few friends among the upper clans, looking forward to the time when it would be possible to open a station among them. In 1932 a plot of land was purchased, a missionary residence was built and a missionary couple was stationed at *Denga*. Life was not easy among the truculent clans of the Tebbu valley, but the district was opened to the missionaries in a remarkable way, and from this point a number of itinerations resulted in the knowledge of new and unreached sections—still unoccupied today. Raiders destroyed the Denga station and went on to Lhamo, hoping also to burn that station, but the local authorities at Lhamo prevented them and saved the home of the missionaries, who were far away at the time. It has not since been possible to reopen Denga.

Pao-an and Rongwu, also former Tibetan stations, were, by mission comity, turned over to Swedish Pentecostal missionaries. *Sungpan,* a Tibetan outpost in the Province of Szechwan, had to be closed because of the Sino-Japanese conflict, and it also is still unoccupied.

In the process of starting work among Tibetans on the border the Mission opened cities in Chinese territory also, and in this way work began among the Chinese in Kansu.

Minhsien In 1896, the year after opening the first Ti-
(Minchow) betan station at Taochow, the missionaries
established a Chinese station in the neighboring city of Minchow, later opening Tanchang and several smaller places as outstations. The first national church conference was held at Minchow in 1909. There is a thriving Chinese church here.

Lintao The next Chinese station was established in 1905
(Titao) at Titao, the first Christian and Missionary Alliance post one reaches after the long and dangerous journey overland from the railhead. The Central Bible School is located here and the work in this important Chinese center has resulted in a large number of conversions. A church of over 200 is active in proclaiming Christ in the district. The Sunday School has grown from a handful of children and adults until now the attendance often exceeds 1,000.

Lungsi This center of a large district having a pop-
(Kungchang) ulation of 25,000, was first opened as an outstation from Titao, but was made a main station in 1917. The Chinese Church has a membership of over 200, is developing along purely indigenous lines, and is marked by independence and virile faith. No missionaries were in residence here in 1949 at the time of the evacuation.

Linsia Formerly an outstation of Titao, Linsia became
(Hochow) a main station in 1917 and more recently the headquarters of the Kansu-Tibetan Border Mission and the residence of the Chairman. The importance of this city lies not only in its size as center of a district of 400,000 population, but also in the fact that it is the mecca of the Moslems in China, and a suitable point from which to make trips into adjacent territory. The Chinese work in this city has been fruitful and there is a church of considerably

over 100 members. The Alliance is responsible for the evangelization of all three of the racial groups of Moslems in this West China field. The Chinese Moslems are the largest group, several hundred thousand in number, and found all over the Alliance field, although the largest settlements are around Hochow. Seven-tenths of the large west country population are Moslem. Little intensive work has been done in this large group although they are the most intelligent and the most open of the three Moslem groups. Two of our missionary couples were assigned for work among Moslems in Kansu. The Tongsiang Moslems are found east of Hochow. The Salar Moslems are in Chinghai Province about three days' journey west of Hochow. Work was begun among the Salars at *Shunhua* on the banks of the Yellow River in 1927, but there have been no outward results except in the breaking down of individual prejudice on the one hand and increase of opposition on the other. There is a small group of believers at Shunhua.

Translation and Publication Work

The entire Bible in Mandarin is available for the Chinese, and Christian literature in Mandarin can be secured from other parts of China.

In the Tibetan language the entire Bible is now available. All translations in Tibetan have been made by missionaries of Societies which are working on the Indian border. Tracts and Scripture portions have also been printed in the Tibetan language, but there are no Bible commentaries and no devotional literature.

Schools

The Central Bible School located at Lintao (Titao) was first opened at the turn of the century. It was closed several times because of the necessary evacuations of the missionaries. In 1946 it was reopened by the Chinese Churches of the Alliance and other Missions as a Union Bible School. Since the fall of 1948 it has been operated by the Alliance Mission with an enrollment the past year of 19. The first Tibetan convert to enter Bible School attended the past year with his wife, who also is an earnest Christian. The need of the school is for more capable, consecrated Chinese teachers.

A primary school with daily Bible instruction was opened in 1948 at Linsia, and another at Lintao in 1949, for the children of Chinese Christians. The enrollment at each school was about forty.

The degree of literacy is now high among the younger generation of Chinese, for every village and hamlet has its school. Among the Tibetans only the priests or former priests know how to read, and many of them cannot read intelligently.

The Church and the Challenge

The ultimate goal of the Mission has ever been to establish an independent, indigenous church. In 1930 the Chinese Church in West China attained such a status, the missionaries acting in the capacity of advisors. The 13 organized and seven unorganized churches of Chinese Christians, with a total membership of 850 baptized believers, are now under native church government and are entirely self-supporting. Some of the Chinese churches contribute enough to care for the pastor's needs. Others give less and in such cases the pastor, in addition to his pastoral work, supports himself in business. There are 10 church centers, six of which are also mission stations; 12 full-time national workers, of whom six are ordained pastors, and one is a woman. The churches are administered by a chairman and a committee of representatives, the number varying from one to three representatives from each church according to the size of the membership.

The chairman is also the pastor of a church, but he receives in addition to his support some free-will offerings to help defray his traveling expenses. The Bible School has been operated by the Mission, not by the national church. The Sunday schools have a total enrollment of 350, but many more than that number attend. Most of the stations have conducted unorganized Sunday children's meetings at which the attendance has been anywhere from 300 to 1,000 each Sunday.

Chone, Lupasi, Lintan (Taochow) New City, and *Hwei-chuan (Kuanpu)* are now Chinese church centers. Three of them were formerly mission stations. Alliance missionaries began work in *Lintan New City* as early as 1899.

Hweichuan, first opened as an outstation from Titao, is important as a large market town in the center of a populous district.

Lupasi, opened about 1905, and originally called the Lela-cheur Memorial station, is situated on the south bank of the Tao River five miles from Lintan Old City, and is in the territory of the Chone Prince. There are a number of Tibetan Christians from near-by villages who regard the local Chinese church as their church home.

Chone is a Tibetan center, opened as a mission station in 1905. Situated on the north bank of the Tao River, 15 miles southeast of Lintan Old City, Chone is the seat of government of 48 clans of Tibetans.

In latter years the Mission has shifted the emphasis from Chinese to Tibetan and Moslem work. Of the 26 missionaries of the Kansu-Tibetan Border Mission, at home or on the field, at the beginning of 1949, ten were assigned to Chinese or to field administrative work; four were dedicated to Moslem work, and 12 to Tibetan work.

The history of this field is a story of political upheavals, danger, and repeated interruptions to normal missionary activity. Since the beginning of the work in 1895 there have been two Moslem rebellions, the Boxer uprising of 1900, the national revolution of 1911-12, the raids of the bandit chief, White Wolf, in 1914, the civil war of 1925-27, and the Communist invasion of Kansu besides many minor local disturbances. The entire missionary force has had to be evacuated five times—in 1900, 1911, 1927, 1934-35, and now in 1949. Three times the missionaries fled to the coast, and once to the provincial capital.

From 1924 to 1947 only one new missionary couple was added to our Kansu mission staff. Therefore a large number of the staff on the field at the beginning of 1949 were new missionaries necessarily devoting their time to language study. For some time after the Communists had occupied North and Central China it was hoped West China might escape. But even then supplies from the coast were cut off and funds were difficult to negotiate. Eventually the iron curtain closed in on even the far West and Kansu.

The greatest need for Kansu at present is for consecrated national workers, both men and women, who will carry the burden of leadership in the Chinese churches. The Chinese work is for the most part well established except for some unevangelized portions which can be taken care of by the Chinese Church. Among the 122 believers baptized in our Kansu Mission in the year 1948, were some second and even third-generation Christians. Moreover an unusual interest has been manifest among high school and college students and teachers also, and many of them have made definite decisions to follow Christ. Prayer is needed that many of these promising young people may hear and respond to God's call for Christian leaders in Kansu.

Among the Moslems there is still some interest, although fewer come to listen and converse than formerly. Several among them believe secretly but they have been forbidden to listen to the Christian message and they are afraid to confess Christ openly.

In spite of the tragedy of wars and death, the goal of sixty years ago for the Kansu-Tibetan border has been realized, for eastern Tibet is now open to the message of the Cross. Even yet it is not always safe to journey among the unbridled tribesmen of the plateau and mountains, but "the mission and those missionaries who have lived along the border and crossed the frontier hold in their hands a priceless key. That key has opened many communities to human friendships, and many hearts to the divine Lordship of Jesus Christ. As chaos and confusion sweep across China, threatening our Tibetan Mission, the Labrang General, brother of the Living Buddha, recently said to the missionary living at Siaho, 'As long as I have clothing, food and shelter, I will share them with and will protect you, even if we are forced to flee the town and live among the nomads.' This is the key which must not be lost!"

KWEICHOW-SZECHWAN

The Kweichow-Szechwan field of The Christian and Missionary Alliance occupies the northeastern corner of Kweichow Province and the southeastern corner of adjacent Szechwan Province. It is on the border of two other provinces also: on the northwest of Hunan, and on the southwest of Hupeh.

Area and Population

Below are the names of the 12 counties which the Kweichow-Szechwan Alliance Mission considers to be its field of responsibility, and in which it is the sole agency for the work of evangelization.

	Population	Number of Market Towns
Szechwan Province		
Siushan	410,000	66
Yuyang	490,000	105
Kienkiang	430,000	30
Pengshui	210,000	94
* Wulung	180,000	22
Kweichow Province		
Songtao	300,000	60
Szenan	280,000	37
Yinkiang	157,000	34
* Tehkiang	225,000	43
Yenho	100,000	23
* Wuchwan	175,000	30
* Chengan	350,000 (approx.)	50
	3,307,000	594

These counties are larger in area than the average county in the United States. It requires 14 days to travel on foot across the field from north to south, and 10 days from east to west. Lungtan, the Alliance Headquarters in this field, is about 1,200 miles inland from Shanghai.

Government

For years the two provinces were under a military form of government, the magistrates and all other officials being appointed by the military powers in the different provinces. The Central Government of China began some years ago the task of replacing the military with a civil government. Law and order are hard to enforce in this rugged mountain country but many of the bandits have surrendered to the government and there has been much less bloodshed than formerly.

After several magistrates had been killed by the people of

* As yet practically untouched.

the former Heoping County, the Provincial Government finally had to break up the county and divide its territory between the counties of Yenho, Wuchwan and Yuyang. The peasants of this ungovernable area carry small hatchets which they use disastrously in settling arguments.

No one likes to travel in sparsely-populated Tehkiang and Wuchwan Counties. In about 20 years only two evangelistic deputations have gone through these parts. People do not dare to travel except in large groups, and it is not wise to wear good clothing lest it be robbed from the wearer's back.

Climate

The climate is moderate. The winters are very mild, with temperatures below freezing for only a few weeks. The rainy season is in May and June. The summers are rather hot, reaching over 100 degrees in the shade, but the nights are usually cool. The temperature varies according to the altitude, and the higher ranges reach an altitude of over 4,000 feet. Lungtan is situated about 1,300 feet above sea level.

Physical Features

As a whole this section is mountainous. For the most part the country is well watered and, as the waterways provide the most inexpensive means of travel, the stations opened thus far are mostly along the rivers. The principal rivers flowing through this area are the Wu River (in parts called the Kungtan River) and the North River. The Wu River flows through Kweichow eastward and northward, joining the Yangtze River at Fowling about 100 miles east of Chungking. Pengshui and Szenan stations, though far apart, are both on the banks of the Wu River. The North River is the northern branch of the Yuan River which flows through Hunan. Siushan is situated on one branch of this river, Lungtan on another. A southern branch of the Yuan River flowing through Kweichow passes Songtao.

Resources

These districts are famous for the well-known tung oil (also called wood oil). The oil is pressed from the nuts of the tung tree and is used in making paints and varnishes as it is the most powerful drying oil known. It is produced throughout the whole district and is shipped in large quantities to foreign countries. The salt industry is also large. The wells farther west in Szechwan yield large quantities, which are carried through the neighboring provinces. There are also some coal mines. The agricultural products include rice, corn, wheat, oats, buckwheat, sweet potatoes and a variety of vegetables. Peaches, pears, persimmons and cherries are raised, and also tropical fruits, such as oranges, tangerines and pomelos.

Progress

Within the past ten years the means of communication in this field have been greatly improved by the building of motor highways. Most of our important mission centers are now linked by good, rock-surfaced roads. In 1935 the National Government built a highway from Changsha in Hunan to Chungking in Szechwan. This highway passes through our field and has facilitated travel and supervision of the work. During the Sino-Japanese war, most of the cargo that would formerly have been carried by boats on the Yangtze was transported by trucks over these roads. Journeys which formerly required about two weeks on foot or by sedan chair can now be made in two days.

Of special interest to the Mission is the highway that is being pushed from Szenan to Yinkiang over several inter-cepting mountains. Plans call for the road to be extended to connect with Songtao also, which would be a tremendous boon to our Mission. We were greatly benefited after the Mission acquired its own motor vehicles.

Telegraph and telephone services have been installed along the highways, so that most of our stations can now be contacted by wire. The mails are still carried by couriers traveling day and night, but this service is rather slow.

Currency

(See *Currency*, under *China*.)

Languages and Tribes

With the exception of a portion of Songtao County, Mandarin Chinese is spoken. The aboriginal Miao tribes in Songtao have no written language, and must learn Mandarin in order to read the Bible. Missionaries to the Miaos must learn the tribal language, however, to conduct services among them.

Religions

Buddhism, Taoism and Confucianism are the principal religions. Temples and shrines are numerous, but the government is now converting many of them into schools and offices. There is also a more primitive religion consisting of sacrifices to evil spirits, presided over by priests called Lao-Si. This religion is very prevalent, especially on the Kweichow side of the field.

Missionary Occupation

While there are a number of missionary Societies doing excellent work in other parts of these two provinces, the 12 counties of the Alliance field are without other missionary occupation.

The Christian and Missionary Alliance

At the Conference of our Central China Mission held in Hankow in December, 1922, it was decided that a committee should make a survey of the unoccupied districts in the extreme western portions of Hunan and Hupeh Provinces. The survey party, composed of two missionaries and two Chinese workers, left Changteh, Hunan, on March 10, 1923, and during a trip of two months surveyed not only the above-mentioned areas but also the southeastern section of Szechwan and the northeastern section of Kweichow. All these districts, comprising a total population of over three million, were unoccupied by any Mission. The findings of this Committee were reported at the Central China Conference in the summer of 1923, and it was decided to open two stations: Siushan in Szechwan and Songtao in Kweichow, both of which places could be reached by waterways. The party of six missionaries appointed to this new section, accompanied by two Chinese evangelists, two Bible women, two colporteurs, and a small Evangelistic Band arrived at their destination in December, 1923. They came from an older district in Hunan, under the protection of a military escort. The journey of 300 miles required a month's travel by boat. At the Annual Conference of 1934 it was decided to make this western field a separate Mission, to be called the Kweichow-Szechwan Mission.

Songtao This station in Kweichow was opened in December, 1923. Property was secured and there are now two chapels there, one for the Chinese and one for the Miao tribespeople. There is a splendid group of young people in the church. In the district witness is being borne by the members of seven churches in homes. There is growth

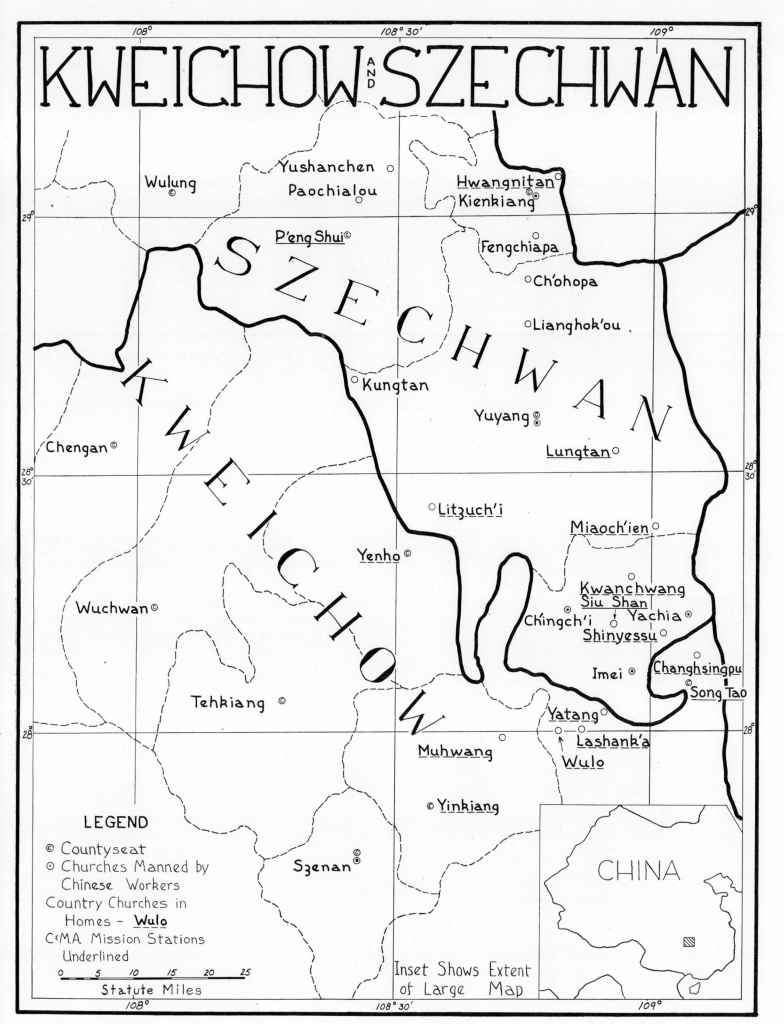

KWEICHOW AND SZECHWAN

Wulung

Yushanchen

Paochialou

Hwangnitan

Kienkiang

P'eng Shui

Fengchiapa

Ch'ohopa

Lianghok'ou

SZECHWAN

Kungtan

Yuyang

Chengan

Lungtan

Litzuch'i

Miaoch'ien

Yenho

Wuchwan

Kwanchwang

Siu Shan

Ch'ingch'i

Yachia

Shinyessu

Imei

Changhsingpu

Song Tao

Tehkiang

Yatang

Lashank'a

Muhwang

Wulo

Yinkiang

LEGEND

◎ Countyseat

⊙ Churches Manned by
   Chinese Workers

Country Churches in
   Homes – **Wulo**

C&M.A. Mission Stations
   Underlined

0   5   10   15   20   25
Statute Miles

Szenan

Inset Shows Extent
of Large Map

CHINA

especially in the Miao work in the country districts of Antangp'o and Ch'anghsingpu.

Siushan Also in December, 1923, property was purchased and a station opened in Siushan, Szechwan. In 1939, during a bombing raid, the property was wrecked and completely destroyed by fire. It has been partially rebuilt but is too small for the needs of the growing work. A new church is needed, leaving the present property as a missionary residence. In this district the country is more level and travel is less difficult. Church groups and preaching points have been established at Yachia, Kwanchwang, Shihyessu, Ch'ingch'ichang and Imei, several of the churches being in homes. About 100 believers have been baptized, which means that only one in 4,000 of the county population is a Christian. Some of the larger towns, among them Lungch'ih and Shilt'i, still have no gospel witness.

Lungtan In this, the busiest town in Yuyang County in the Province of Szechwan, a mission station was opened in the summer of 1932, and property was purchased. The firstfruits did not come until late in 1935, when two men were baptized. This station has been the Mission Headquarters for a number of years but tentative plans call for the moving of Headquarters to Yuyang, a town some 35 miles to the north.

Pengshui Property was acquired here and on the first day of the year 1932 a missionary couple began work in this town on the Wu River in Szechwan. The baptized Christians numbered 14 by the spring of 1935. This is one of the poorest of the districts and there are 16 dangerous rapids in the Wu River as it skirts and flows through this county, all of which adds to the difficulty of the work. The people are illiterate, making it difficult for them to understand the Gospel, and many false rumors have been circulated which have made the simple-hearted peasants afraid to come near the church. They have been told that those who believe in Jesus will have their hearts removed when they die. New life is now coming into the work under the ministry of the Chinese pastor, and all the market towns in the county have been visited. There was an outstation in Yushanchen for some years but through lack of workers and lack of response the work was dropped in 1943. The outstation in this large salt mining town was reopened in the summer of 1949. It was from Pengshui that a missionary was taken captive by a Communist band and held for about a month, until in answer to prayer he escaped.

Szenan This additional county in Kweichow was taken over from the China Inland Mission in 1940, and a missionary was in residence there for some time. Present plans call for the purchase of a permanent site and the development of the station with missionaries again located there. At present a Chinese evangelist is caring for the work. The Evangelistic Band labored here for a year and there are a few believers in the city and two country districts. There is a desire for the Gospel but due to lack of instruction and competent leadership there has not been growth. Szenan is a large business center located on the Wu River and on a motor highway linking it with Kwieyang and Chungking. From this point the work could be supervised in the three counties of Szenan, Yinkiang and Tehkiang.

Bible Schools

The Kweichow-Szechwan field coöperates with the Central China Mission in their Central Bible School at Wuchang. Short Term Bible Schools, with an average duration of 10 days, were conducted in 1948 in Lungtan, Pengshui, Kienkiang, Yuyang, Songtao and Litzuch'i, with a total enrollment of 150. Five Daily Vacation Bible Schools were held with a total enrollment of 300.

All schools are conducted in the Mandarin language. Some Miao tribespeople attend, but they must understand the Chinese. Miao Christians must study Mandarin in order to read the Bible for their own language is not written. The government is making a great effort to increase literacy among the tribespeople.

The Red Menace

For years there have been thousands of Chinese Reds and bandit groups in northwestern Hunan and portions of Szechwan and Kweichow Provinces. When other sections of China were being overrun by bandits only from time to time, the menace was almost continual in this section, despite the efforts of Chinese armies to subdue them. By the close of 1948 the Communist threat was so great that the U. S. Consul advised Americans to leave the area and remove to points of safety. Accordingly the women and children evacuated to Hongkong and Canton while the men remained at their stations until the summer of 1949.

The Church and the Challenge

The Christians have been taught from the beginning of the work that as soon as they are able to support their own work, the missionaries hope to move on to new territory. The Christians are active in assisting in the evangelistic program throughout the district. Even during the war years the substantial increase from year to year in field receipts has been encouraging. No foreign style buildings have been built in this field, and such remodeling as has been done is consistent with the expectation that soon the Chinese churches will be able to take over the work without too great a burden of upkeep. The progress in self-support was manifest at the Annual Chinese Conference of last year when a resolution was adopted to undertake the payment of one-tenth of the salaries of all official workers. This does not include the Evangelistic Band members or gatekeepers. A special offering taken each quarter and administered by the Chinese Central Committee is put into this fund. At the Chinese Conference the number of members on the Chinese Central Committee was increased. It is hoped that, should the missionaries be forced to retire from the field, this Committee will shoulder the administrative responsibilities of the field.

Reports for the year 1948 list 28 churches or groups, of which 12 are self-supporting. The four church centers are also mission stations. The ten Sunday schools have a total enrollment of 900. Several hundred children in attendance is common in certain of the Sunday schools and it has become a problem to accommodate them. Baptized church members number 435, and inquirers, 350. There were 92 believers baptized in 1948, the largest group to be received into the church in any single year on this field. Besides 23 full-time workers there are eight men engaged in Evangelistic Band work.

In earlier years it was customary to extend the work by opening outstations, each with its own mission-paid evangelist. This increased the financial responsibility of the Mission as the work expanded. In recent years the Evangelistic Bands have been doing an important work in opening new centers and there are now 24 outstations. Under present methods an Evangelistic Band enters a new center and carries on intensive work for a year. Every home in the district is visited and Scripture portions and tracts are distributed. When a nucleus of Christians has been formed, a local leader is chosen for that group, and he is responsible for the services and work in the area. Assistance is given from time to time by a Chinese pastor or missionary. In this way the work in the churches is self-supporting and self-propagating from the beginning. At present over a dozen of these churches are carrying on fruitful work for the Lord. Young people's groups, in addition to holding weekly meetings, are editing a Christian billboard newspaper; are sending evangelistic deputations to country churches; and are sponsoring reading rooms for students. Never before have so many open-hearted students in China studied the Word and searched for the Truth as now.

Here follow reports from some of the outstations in this field:

Kienkiang. In the fall of 1939 property was rented and an Evangelistic Band began work here. The Lord blessed their ministry, many were healed, and believers have been added to the church steadily. In 1944 a small property was purchased and another plot was added in 1948. The people are poorer here than in Yuyang or Siushan and many cannot afford to eat rice but must subsist on the cheaper cereals. Nevertheless, the church here has been a model for the other churches in spiritual life, generous giving and loyalty to Christ.

Thirty-two pupils, all from Christian homes, were enrolled in the Daily Vacation Bible School conducted recently. Not only is the Kienkiang Church growing, but also the near-by work at Hwangnitan on the Hupeh border.

Yenho. Evangelistic Band work began in 1938 in this county seat on the Wu River. A church was established in a home, where the group carried on well until the death of the owner of the home. The flock disintegrated because of lack of proper leadership. Visits have been made by missionaries and Chinese workers and they have been well received. An Evangelistic Band was sent again to this city early in 1949. Indications are that the work is again building up under leadership and instruction. About 99 per cent of the people of this county have not yet heard the Gospel. Many of them are addicted to opium and their hearts are hard.

Yinkiang. The Evangelistic Band worked here in 1940 and a number of believers were won. When the Band left, services were continued in a home, but there is a serious lack of spiritual vitality and leadership. The worker at Szenan visits Yinkiang periodically.

In Yuyang County where the Mission Headquarters are located, the three large towns are Yuyang, Lungtan and Kungtan. The Evangelistic Band labored in Yuyang in 1937 and established a work which was later suspended because of lack of workers and funds. Recently the Band worked there again and with gratifying results. Kungtan, situated near rapids of the same name, is an important trans-shipping point. In 1946 the Evangelistic Band was here for a year but the response was meager.

Wulung is a new county established within the last two years, a section formerly administered by Pengshui and Fowling Counties. Very little work has been done here. In Tehkiang and Wuchwan Counties there is still total ignorance of the gospel.

There is so much territory in the Kweichow-Szechwan field that, if our present staff should be multiplied by ten, there would still be insufficient personnel to proclaim the gospel adequately throughout the area. We have groups of believers in eight of the twelve counties in our field. We estimate that there is only one Christian in each 5,000 of the population. Four entire counties are still unreached and large portions of five others have not had an adequate witness of the Truth.

CENTRAL CHINA

The Christian and Missionary Alliance Central China Mission operates in the city of Shanghai and the provinces of Anhwei, Hupeh and Hunan. From eastern Anhwei to western Hunan, our field lies in the Yangtze River Valley and extends about 700 miles.

Area and Population

Province	Area	Population
Anhwei	54,952 sq. mi.	21,978,667
Hupeh	72,793 " "	24,658,988
Hunan	80,303 " "	28,165,981
Shanghai City		6,000,000

The figures given above for populations are 1944-45 estimates, the latest now available. Out of these totals, the Alliance, by inter-mission comity, is responsible for the spiritual welfare of six million souls in the three provinces and 10,000 in Shanghai and vicinity.

Government

The provinces of Anhwei, Hupeh and Hunan have enjoyed a more stable government than some other parts of China, and have been more closely allied with the Central authority. Each of these three provinces has long had a fully established provincial government. The city of Hankow, during the Republic, was one of six special municipalities under the direct control of the Executive Yuan in Nanking, the others being: Nanking, Shanghai, Tsingtao, Tientsin and Canton.

Climate

The climate of Central China compares favorably with that of other countries in similar latitudes. It is somewhat like the climate of the U. S. A., with four seasons corresponding approximately to ours, except that the summer is longer and the heat more oppressive due to great humidity. It is necessary for the missionaries to spend a month or more during the hot season at Kuling, Kikungshan or some other near-by mountain station. The higher altitudes provide a cooler, invigorating atmosphere in which the Annual Mission Conference is held.

The autumn weather is beautiful, cool and dry; but the winter is cold and damp. From late December through February there is much rain and some snow. The lowest temperature is about 14 degrees above zero. During the spring months rain falls abundantly, filling the rivers and irrigation canals. In this damp atmosphere everything molds, but the rice prospers. The heavy rains of summer often cause flash floods in small streams and raise the Yangtze to dangerous heights.

Physical Features

The Yangtze River flows across Hupeh and Anhwei Provinces and touches a corner of Hunan. Generally the area south of the Yangtze is mountainous, with fine forests and beautiful scenery. North of the river is an alluvial plain, rich in rice fields. When these plains are visited by drought or flood, severe famines often occur.

The western portion of Hupeh is also mountainous, while Hunan is six-tenths mountains, three-tenths plains and one-tenth water. The Siang River rises in Kwangsi and flows north through Hunan. The Yuan River rises in Kweichow and flows northeast through Hunan. Both of these streams and two others all empty into Tungting Lake and through it into the Yangtze River. During the spring and summer, these streams are flooded and expand Tungting Lake until it covers 4,000 square miles.

All Central China's rivers are highways of trade. Ocean steamers ascend the Yangtze 600 miles to Hankow. Smaller steam vessels penetrate into western Hupeh and northern Hunan. Junks carry trade up the Siang to South China, and up the Yuan to the West.

Resources

Our three Central China Provinces all produce rice, tea and silk, but Anhwei leads in the export of these items. Coal, antimony and wood oil are exported from Hunan as well as much of the lumber used in the lower Yangtze Valley.

Hupeh Province is very prosperous due to agriculture, commerce and industry. Its greatest metropolis is the Wuhan Center located at the junction of the Han River with the Yangtze, and composed of three cities: Hankow, the Chicago of China; Hanyang, the site of China's greatest iron works; and Wuchang, one of her most important educational centers.

Progress

The modern development of this area began under the Manchus with steamship travel up the Yangtze and was followed by the establishment of excellent postal and telegraph systems. These continued to function remarkably well through the many civil wars which plagued the Republic. Railroads followed early in this century, first from Shanghai to Nanking, then on to Peking, Peking to Hankow, and finally Hankow to Canton. Local railroads were built from Nanking to Wuhu and on southward. Before the conflict with Japan, extensive motor highways were developed. Although few of these are properly hard surfaced, yet they form important arteries of travel.

In education the Manchus encouraged private schools, but a real public school system appeared in the Republic. Each of these three provinces has many grade schools and a few high and normal schools. Colleges are located in Wuchang and Changsha. For many years the only important hospitals were missionary, but under the Republic the Chinese made considerable progress on this line also.

Currency

See *Currency,* under *China.*

Languages

The Chinese National Language, formerly called Mandarin, is usuable throughout our Central China field. Shanghai, being in the Wu Dialect area, uses Wu more than National, and South Anhwei Mountain counties have local dialects related to the Wu. The rest of Anhwei uses National tones similar to the North, while Hupeh and Hunan share tones similar to the West. In all public schools the National language is taught, but local dialects persist.

Religions

See paragraph on *Religion,* under *China.*

Missionary Occupation

In Shanghai and vicinity Protestant missions began more than a century ago. Hupeh led our three Central China provinces when the London Mission opened Hankow in 1861 and Wuchang in 1864. The Wesleyan Methodists entered Hankow in 1862, the Protestant Episcopals began work in Wuchang and Hankow in 1868, and the China Inland Mission in 1874. These and other societies soon extended their ministries by widespread evangelistic tours. The Alliance entered Wuchang in 1893.

In Anhwei Province the China Inland Mission opened a station at Anking in 1869 and three other cities in the next sixteen years during which that was the only Protestant mission in the province. The American Episcopal Mission was second to enter Anhwei, locating at Wuhu in 1885. Other societies now working in the province all entered before 1900, including the Alliance in 1888.

Hunan Province was visited by a Wesleyan missionary in 1865, and five years later two noted pioneers crossed northern Hunan en route to Szechwan. Between 1875 and 1886 several attempts were made to establish mission stations in Hunan, but rioting mobs soon drove the missionaries out. Among these were the American Presbyterians at Linwu in the extreme south where the first duly organized Protestant church in Hunan was founded in 1894.

The first missionaries to establish permanent residence in Hunan were two Alliance men who rented a house in Changteh in 1897 and were soon followed by the Cumberland Presbyterians. That same year the London Mission opened its first Hunan station at Yochow. The opening of Changsha by Rev. B. H. Alexander of the Christian and Missionary Alliance is described thus in "The Christian Occupation of China," the survey report of the China Continuation Committee:

He followed this visit (1898) by others, and later by regular residence on a boat just outside the west gate of the city, whence he made daily trips within the walls for preaching and bookselling. This steady, quiet work, combined with his persistent courage and unfailing courtesy, finally opened the gates of Changsha to all Protestant Missions.

In addition to extensive work by the Roman Catholics, about a dozen Protestant Societies are laboring in various parts of these three provinces. However, with the exception of four large cities, they have no missionaries in areas for which the Alliance is responsible.

The Christian and Missionary Alliance

The first Alliance missionaries to settle in Central China went in 1888 to Wuhu, 300 miles up the Yangtze River, two days travel by steamer from Shanghai. Native houses on a busy street constituted their missionary training home, and after a year or so of language study, two by two they began to open up mission stations in cities a few days journey farther inland, until five Anhwei centers had been established at Wuhu, Tatung, Tsingyang, Nanling and Wanchih. Meanwhile, in 1893 Dr. Simpson, making his memorable tour of the mission fields, visited Central China. That same year Wuchang was opened as a base for advance to Hunan and Tibet, and a few years later a superintend of all Christian and Missionary Alliance East Asia fields was appointed with headquarters at Wuhu, where a large receiving home was erected for training our Central and West China missionaries.

The advance into Hunan followed speedily, when, as already noted, Changteh was occupied in 1897, and the "siege of Changsha" began in 1898. A few years later a third station was opened at Hanshow. In 1900, while the Boxer Uprising stained North China with the blood of the martyrs, missionaries from Central China were obliged to seek the safety of the coastal cities. There some assisted in the beginnings of the new Shanghai work of the Woodberry family, themselves refugees from North China. Thus, the opening of the century found the Central China Alliance Mission operating in four provinces with a main station in the principal city of each and outstations scattered through the Yangtze River basin.

The men engaged in public evangelization. The ladies did home visitation. Day schools were opened on all the stations, and soon high schools were needed, so boarding middle

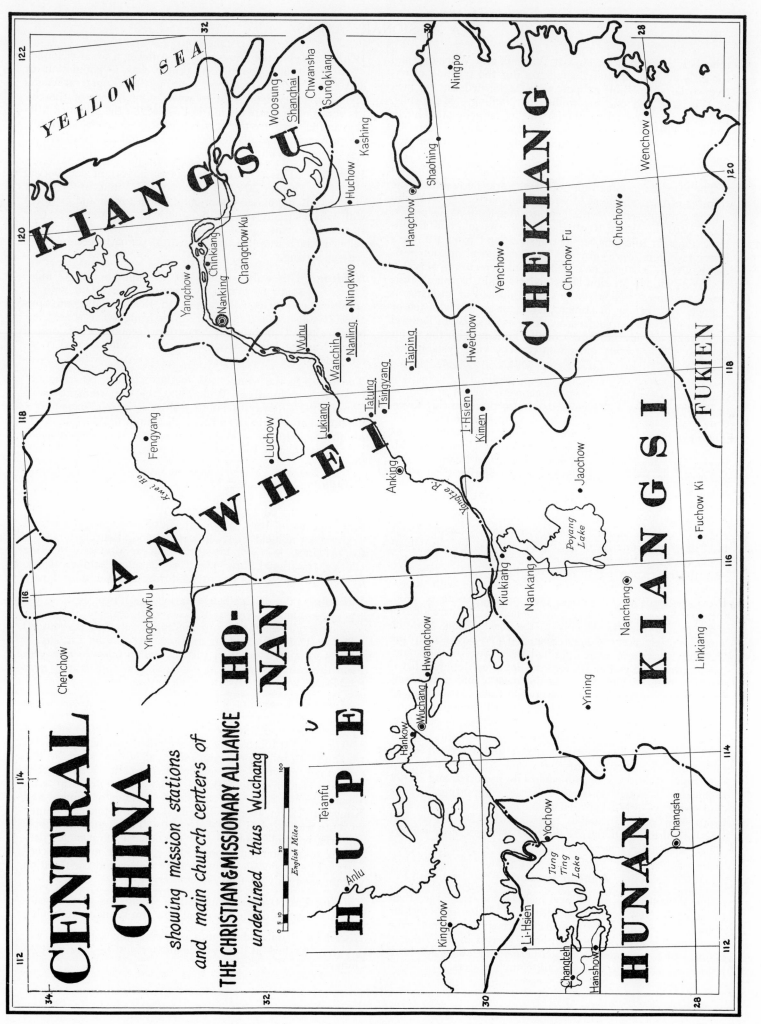

CENTRAL CHINA

showing mission stations
and main church centers of
THE CHRISTIAN & MISSIONARY ALLIANCE
underlined thus Wuchang

YELLOW SEA

KIANGSU

ANWHEI

HONAN

HUPEH

HUNAN

CHEKIANG

KIANGSI

FUKIEN

Woosung
Shanghai
Chwansha
Sungkiang
Ningpo

Huchow
Kashing

Shaohing
Hangchow
Wenchow

Yangchow
Chinkiang
Changchow-Ku
Nanking
Yenchow
Chuchow

Wuhu
Wanchih
Nanling.
Ningkwo
Taiping.
Hweichow
Chuchow Fu

Lukiang.
Tatung.
Tsingyang.
I-Hsien
Kimen

Fengyang
Luchow
Jaochow
Fuchow Ki

Anking
Yangtze R.
Poyang Lake

Yingchowfu
Kiukiang
Nankang
Nanchang

Chenchow
Linkiang

Yining

Teianfu
Hwangchow
Hankow
Wuchang

Anlu
Yochow
Changsha
Tung Ting Lake

Kingchow
Kwei Ho

Li-Hsien
Changteh
Hanshow

English Miles

109

schools were opened for boys at Wanchih and Wuchang, and for girls at Nanling and Changteh. For the training of native workers two Bible Schools were established, one for men at Wuchang and one for women at Nanling. Meanwhile, the need for purchasing and forwarding supplies to Hunan and our Tibetan Border Mission could no longer be met by a missionary at Wuchang, so a Business Department was opened in Hankow, the great trade center across the Yangtze.

The westward expansion of our work necessitated the transfer of Central China Mission Headquarters from Wuhu on the circumference of the field, to Wuchang at its center. So in 1910 the Wuhu Receiving Home was sold and accommodations for missionaries in transit to and from Anhwei's interior stations were provided in a large local mission residence. At Wuchang a new building was erected to serve as Receiving Home, Mission Headquarters and Chairman's residence combined. New stations were opened at Lukiang in Anhwei and Lichow in Hunan. Evangelistic bands of ten or a dozen men were organized, working extensively in Anhwei and intensively in Hanshow County, Hunan, with the result that more than twenty outstation churches were established.

Up to 1921, our Central China work had operated in the Yangtze Valley. Now surveys were made of the mountain hinterland, where three new stations were opened in Anhwei at Taiping, Ihsien and Kimen: and also three on the Kweichow-Szechwan border at Longtan, Siushan and Songtao. The opening of these additional stations was rendered possible by the closing of the older station of Changsha. Although our own persistent pioneer had opened Changsha, and although the ten societies now working among Changsha's half a million population would each be responsible for fifty thousand souls; yet the vision of the regions beyond inspired our Society to take this step as part of its pioneer ministry.

By 1933 the Central China Mission and Shanghai had a total of 47 missionaries operating 17 stations and 56 outstations, with a native church membership of 1,963. The next year the Kweichow-Szechwan work hived off as a separate mission, and three years later began the war with Japan. Previous disturbances, such as the Boxer Uprising of 1900, the Revolution of 1911 and the Communist Insurrection of 1927, caused withdrawal only to the coast. This time the Japanese early occupation of Shanghai and advance up the Yangtze River necessitated gradual withdrawal to the homeland, until by the end of 1944 all missionaries were evacuated from the field. After the Sino-Japanese conflict, the staff never again resumed its former proportions. By 1948, 15 had returned, but civil war again depleted their number until the Communist "Bamboo Curtain" closed down on only two.

The latest statistics available from Central China are for 1948 and list 14 church centers, named and described herein under their respective provinces, and 81 outstations not named. The church groups include 110 organized and 17 not organized, of which 11 were fully self-supporting. These churches have 3,172 baptized members, of whom 351 were baptized in 1948, 10 Sunday schools with 1,500 pupils, and 1,410 inquirers. Of the 72 full-time workers, 17 were ordained men and 11 were women.

Anhwei Province

The Alliance field in Anhwei includes an area larger than the State of New Jersey and with a population of over four million. The nine cities described herewith are among the largest in this area, six of them being located in the Yangtze plains and three among the southern mountains. All have been mission stations and are still church centers.

Wuhu Wuhu, the largest city in Anhwei, a great rice market and commercial center, has a population of 260,000. A tributary stream entering the Yangtze at Wuhu divides the city from east to west. One-fourth of the city lies south of that stream and in this section the Alliance Mission and Church are the only evangelical agencies. Logically, the provincial headquarters of Mission and Church have always been at Wuhu.

Wanchih This town of 5,000 is an important commercial center 30 miles southeast of Wuhu, in the midst of a densely populated plain, dotted with towns and crowded with villages easily reached by a network of waterways. Our station here was opened in 1896 and a strong church developed which was the first in Central China to become fully self-supporting.

Nanling This walled city of 20,000 population is 47 miles south of Wuhu in a county of 200,000 with an adjoining county equally large. In 1895 Alliance missionaries established a station here after being twice stoned out of the city. Our provincial boarding schools were located here. Nanling has a strong local church with several country groups.

Tatung On the south bank of the Yangtze, 60 miles upstream from Wuhu, lies the important town of Tatung, the gateway to South Anhwei. It was opened as a mission center in 1891 and a small church developed. During the Sino-Japanese War, the property was destroyed, but the importance of the location remains, and the work continues.

Tsingyang This city, 15 miles south of Tatung and 48 miles southwest of Nanling, has a population of 15,000 in a county of 200,000. It was opened as an Alliance station in 1896. A local church was developed and aggressive evangelization conducted among the pilgrims from five provinces who worship at the near-by Mountain of Nine Glories, traditional burial place of Guatama Buddha. Here, too, our property was destroyed during the war with Japan.

Lukiang is the only Alliance station in Anhwei north of the Yangtze River. It is a county seat and the center of a large alluvial plain surrounding a small lake about 70 miles west of Wuhu. Our missionaries opening the city in 1921 were rioted out and their rented property destroyed. Soon thereafter, however, a strong station and church were established with an outstation halfway to Wuhu.

Mountain Counties. The South Anhwei area, opened in 1922 and 1923, consists of the three counties listed below, each with a population of about 100,000 and a county seat of from 12,000 to 15,000. All are noted for their export of tea, and lie amid mountains of great scenic beauty. For more than ten years after our occupation they were reached only on foot over high passes. Just before the war with Japan a motor road was built from Tatung to Taiping and Kimen, and later a railroad from Hangchow touched Kimen en route westward. Local dialects are difficult and the people conservative and bigoted. Our missionaries first met hostility and opposition but soon gained confidence and won converts. After a decade of missionary occupation each station was manned only by Chinese workers.

Taiping lies 50 miles southeast of Tsingyang at the headwaters of the river that flows by Wanchih to Wuhu.

Ihsien is 60 miles due south of Tsingyang across the watershed at the source of a river flowing east to Hangchow.

Kimen is 20 miles southwest of Ihsien on a stream flowing west to the pottery country of Kiangsi and Poyang Lake.

Moling In addition to the above-named counties which were mission centers, there lies among the mountains, 40 miles south of Nanling, the large town of Moling, which during the war with Japan became a city of refuge and was made a church center and site of the temporary Anhwei Bible School.

Hupeh Province

The opening and development of Alliance work in this province have already been noted on previous pages. We now consider the cities concerned.

Wuchang This provincial capital is a great official and residential city and an important educational center. Logically, it was early made the headquarters of a number of missions for their work throughout the province and farther afield. Our mission station in Wuchang developed a large local church and eight other Alliance churches in country towns along the railroad southward. A large School for Blind Girls and another for Deaf and Dumb Boys and Girls were established independently and operated successfully by Mrs. Martin Ekvall.

In connection with the Wuchang Church, our missionaries maintained a reading room stocked with religious periodicals and books in both Chinese and English. Many college students frequented the reading room and attended Bible classes during the years between the war with Japan and the occupation by the Communists. In that period also the Church flourished under a consecrated young pastor from Shanghai. A strong stand was taken against modernism and worldliness. Prayer meetings and Bible classes multiplied, with a capacity attendance at all services.

Hankow, the "Chicago of China," is a natural metropolis of nation-wide trade by water, rail and road. Beginning early in the century, the Alliance operated a Business Department here for thirty years, serving our own missions in Central and West China and others as well. Eventually, the Lutheran Missions built a much larger Missionary Home and Agency, our Business Department was closed and our Manager missionary loaned to the Lutherans.

Hunan Province

This prosperous province is sometimes called the "Rice Bowl of China." Its haughty officialdom made it the last "Closed Province" to open to the Gospel. We have already described the important part played by Alliance missionaries in the opening of Hunan's two main cities.

Changteh This city of 200,000 people is the gateway to Western Hunan, famed for its export of wood oil. A strong Alliance church was developed here with a number of outstation chapels in the country. Changteh was also the site of our provincial Girls' School and Bible School for Hunan.

Hanshow This walled city was first opened as an outstation from Changteh by a zealous old idol-smashing evangelist. In 1913 it became a main station with resident foreigners and enjoyed a long and successful ministry of lady missionaries. The center of a large agricultural county, its many towns and villages were evangelized by the strong city church and missionaries until more than thirty branch churches were established.

Lihsien Sixty miles north of Changteh lies the city of Lihsien (also called Lichow), with a population of about 18,000 in a county of nearly half a million people. The Alliance opened a main station here in 1921, developing a church in the city and two others in the country.

Kiangsu Province

Shanghai, China's commercial and industrial capital and chief seaport, is located on the Huangpoo River 12 miles from where this small stream flows into the Yangtze's widening mouth. Large ocean steamers land at Shanghai and hitherto the port has enjoyed more than half of China's import trade and more than one-third of her exports. Under the Manchus and the Republic, Shanghai was divided into the Native City, the French Concession and the International Settlement, each with its own separate government. After the Sino-Japanese War, the three were combined into one Chinese municipality with a population of 6,000,000.

The principal Denominational Mission Boards made Shanghai an important base of operations shortly after the middle of the last century. It became also the base for three Bible Societies, the China Inland Mission and a number of faith or independent mission groups. The Door of Hope conducts a large and fruitful work for women and children in the city, and the Bible Seminary for Women is located at Kiangwan, about five miles from town.

As already noted, the Alliance began work in Shanghai in 1900. A few years later, Rev. and Mrs. John Woodberry purchased a valuable property in a strategic location and built up a large coeducational school offering a standard curriculum in the grades and junior high school with distinctly Christian instruction and spiritual atmosphere. Two churches were developed, one in the beautiful Ella M. Stewart Memorial built by Mr. Woodberry, and the other in rented property downtown. These churches in turn conducted two outstations in the country.

The Alliance work in Shanghai has been fruitful, especially among the progressive young people of that large city, hundreds of whom have made up its congregation throughout the past decade. The converts and graduates of these churches and schools are to be found in many parts of China and abroad. One missionary remained at our Shanghai work behind the "iron curtain" for some months; and, when forced to leave, brought good reports of the Chinese Alliance Christians' zeal and determination to carry on.

Translation and Publication Work

The China Alliance Press, which had been set up at Wuchow in 1913, was moved to Shanghai in 1932 for the publication and distribution of the Bible Magazine and many full gospel books and leaflets. During the Japanese occupation of Shanghai, the work of our Press was necessarily suspended. It was resumed in January, 1947, but nearly two years later the civil war made it necessary again to move the office and stocks to safer locations. Branch depots were opened at Wuchang in Central China, Chungking in the West and Liuchow in the South. In the summer of 1949 the head office was set up in Hongkong and the printing work transferred to Singapore.

Our most important publication is *The Bible Magazine,* founded thirty-eight years ago by the late Dr. R. A. Jaffray. Just the same age as the Chinese Republic, *The Bible Magazine* is the oldest Christian periodical in China. Edited jointly by missionary and Chinese workers, it is published bi-monthly and contains expository and missionary articles of devotional and inspirational value. A recent new publication is the *Alliance Quarterly,* designed to represent the interests of the Alliance work of all China, to help unify that work, and to proclaim a full Gospel testimony. The China Alliance Press reported the following output for the year 1948:

6 Issues of Bible Magazine	54,000	copies
Tracts	900,000	"
Sheet calendars	60,000	"
Books and booklets	342,000	"
Total number of pieces	1,356,000	
Total number of pages	14,754,000	

The above output reached not only the lost but also thousands of Christians in many denominational fellowships throughout China, Formosa, the Philippines, Malaya and other countries. Geographically, its range is from the Philippines to the borders of Tibet.

Central China Bible School

The Blackstone Bible Institute was opened at Wuchang in 1909 to train men from the three provinces of our Yangtze Valley field. It continued to operate successfully except for two intervals when political disturbances, rendering travel unsafe, made it difficult for students from the extremes of the field to reach the central location. During those intervals schools were conducted temporarily at Changteh and Hanshow in Hunan and Moling in Anhwei. This was the case during the Sino-Japanese conflict.

In February, 1949, the central school was reopened at Wuchang with an enlarged staff and continued to operate even after Communist occupation of the city. Our Home Board and the Central China Mission plan to continue the school under the administration of the Chinese Executive Committee, and to assist it financially as long as funds from abroad can be gotten through.

The Indigenous Church

From the very beginning, as stations were opened and converts gathered, churches were established. In 1911, the Mission Conference took action to consolidate these gains by a uniform local constitution. In 1917, in order to develop the indigenous church, its three Provincial Conferences, which hitherto had been only instructive and inspirational, were made representative and legislative. Finally in 1928, Chinese delegates from the three provinces drafted a complete constitution for the Alliance Church of the entire Central China field.

At first, self-support was stressed as a prerequisite for self-administration. A number of churches became fully self-supporting; and, just prior to the Sino-Japanese conflict, a program was adopted for all to become so in ten years by the gradual withdrawal of foreign subsidies. However, in the economic morass of war, self-support bogged down; and self-administration became an enforced reality when, for the first time in Central China's history, complete evacuation of all missionaries was necessitated by the same war.

Fortunately, in each of the four provinces, strong Chinese leaders had been developed, partly by the training of the missionaries, but even more by Divine preparation in the school of hardship through periods of revolution and unrest. During the Japanese occupation, these men rallied their weaker brethren and held the churches together in the long absence of the foreign missionaries. In Anhwei, realizing the great need for worker reinforcements, they organized and conducted a Bible School and held Provincial Conference in their mountain retreat at Moling.

After the close of the Sino-Japanese conflict, conferences were held in all three provinces, resulting in voluntary moves toward self-support and increased giving in the local churches. The returning missionaries also took new steps to develop autonomy. Beginning on July 1, 1948, the grants from the Home Board toward workers' salaries and all other expenses of church administration and evangelistic work were turned over to the Central China Executive Committee for disbursement.

In December of the same year the deeds for all properties in Central China used by the churches for their work and as residences for their workers were turned over to this same committee. The Alliance in China has not yet reached the state of incorporation. Only after incorporation will it be possible to make out suitable new deeds for these properties. In the meantime, the Chinese Executive Committee is responsible for the use and care of the properties. In all these arrangements, there has seemed to be a genuine desire on the part of the Chinese brethren for the missionaries to share with them in all their deliberations.

Early in 1948, duly authorized Chinese delegates from all four of our China fields met in conference at Wuchang and took the first steps towards the organization of an All-China Chinese Alliance. That conference drafted a tentative constitution which they referred for confirmation to the Church Conferences in the four fields concerned. Meanwhile, the Communistic flood engulfed the nation, cutting off the Chinese churches from the help and counsel of their missionary brethren. Courageously, the Chinese leaders have taken up the tasks which the missionaires have been forced to lay down. These men are superintending the work of the churches, the Provincial Conferences and the Bible School.

A dangerous responsibility is theirs in the extensive properties of Mission and Church which the Communists will covet and probably seize. But on them also rests the more serious burden of the spiritual welfare of the believers, looking to them for instruction and leadership, and of the millions still waiting for the Gospel message. The future is uncertain. Even the present is unknown. But it is certain and known that our Chinese brethren and sisters need our faithful support, by finance as far as may be possible, but still more by what is always possible, faithful prevailing prayer.

SOUTH CHINA

The South China Mission of The Christian and Missionary Alliance is located, with two exceptions, entirely in the province of Kwangsi in the extreme southern part of China. One exception is Iong-kiang, an outstation, in the province of Kweichow about fifty miles from the northern border of Kwangsi. The other exception is the port city of Hongkong. Here the South China Mission has a flourishing Chinese church, a hostel for missionaries' children and a business office.

Area and Population

The Kwangsi Government report for 1947 gives the area of Kwangsi province as approximately 80,000 square miles, and the population (estimated) as 14,545,528. The area is nearly equal to that of Pennsylvania and Ohio combined, and the population is slightly larger than that of the state of New York. The foreign population is small, approximately 160, and located principally in the larger cities.

History

Kwangsi meaning the broad, or extensive west, was one of the last provinces to be conquered by the Chinese. Because of its distance from the northern capital, and the ruggedness of its terrain as well as the stubborn resistance of its aboriginal inhabitants, it required centuries to bring this province under the Central Government. In fact at the beginning of the Chinese Republic in 1911 there were still some tribesmen in Kwangsi's mountain fastnesses who were not entirely subjugated.

Approximately a thousand years ago the famous General, Ti Chin, defeated the Kwangsi aboriginal General, Nong Tsz Koo. The victor's soldiers then settled in the province, exacting tribute for their Emperor. Since then Kwangsi has been known as a wild, dangerous province. This is due, no doubt, to the constant trouble between the Chinese and the aboriginal people, who are being pushed back by their conquerors deeper into the mountain fastnesses. The Emperor appointed a Viceroy, who represented him as ruler of the two provinces of Kwangsi and Kwangtung.

In 1911 Kwangsi joined with the other provinces in the revolution against the Manchus and, with the other provinces, established what was called a republican form of government. Since that date Kwangsi has several times been invaded by the troops of other provinces and on some occasions has sent her troops into neighboring provinces to attempt their conquest. Companies of bandits, sometimes numbering several thousand, have often infested the more mountainous regions, and sometimes looted whole cities. Kwangsi has had her quota of floods and famines and also her share of corrupt, civil and military officials. All these hindrances together with the struggle for existence in so unproductive a region, would seem to make survival impossible. Kwangsi has not only survived, but when she has had a few years of peace and a reasonably good government she has really prospered.

Government

Under the Republic, Kwangsi, like the other provinces of China, had a civil Governor who was appointed by the Central Government at the nation's capital. The provincial army, however, was not directly under the Governor's control, but under a leader, also appointed by the Central Government. The province was divided into ninety-nine counties or districts, each county presided over by a magistrate, appointed by, and responsible to, the provincial government. Each district was divided into townships, with their officials responsible to the district magistrate. Each township was divided into villages with an official under the township official. Each street in the village or town had its official, subject to the village officer. This was a good system when a fair degree of honesty prevailed among the officials, but it gave any corrupt officialdom that might exist a good opportunity to benefit at the expense of the people.

The recent period in China's history was supposed to be a time of tutelage when the people and their rulers would learn the art of democratic government, but little progress had been made in that direction. Since the formation of the Republic, Kwangsi's relationship to the Central Government has varied from that of friendliness to almost outbroken hostility. However, after the beginning of the Japanese invasion, Kwangsi's military officials cast in their lot with the Central Government, and became among the main supports of what was left of the National Government.

Although many of the business men of Kwangsi originally came from Kwangtung, and many of its artisans from Hunan, Kwangsi was quite "isolationist" in policy and largely managed its own affairs. However, since the Japanese War and the Communist advance from the north, great numbers of northerners and people from the coast have made their home in Kwangsi. While many of the people of Kwangsi treat these "outsiders" with coolness, yet their influx cannot fail to help toward cementing the unity between Kwangsi and the rest of China. Now, however, since the

8

Communist aggression has engulfed Kwangsi, who can say what turn the history of this province will take.

Climate

The climate of Kwangsi is tropical in the south, about one-third of the province lying within the Tropic of Cancer. Thus, the heat is excessive and the humidity great from May to September. In the north the climate is more moderate, although changes of temperature are sudden, and there is usually a little frost and snow each year. The most pleasant season of the year is from October to December, during which period most of the itinerating work in country districts is carried on. The damp dull weather begins in January, lasting through April, and is followed in the summer months by heavy tropical showers, which bring China's many rivers to flood tide.

Physical Features

Kwangsi is exceedingly mountainous. There are a few level areas in the eastern part of the province, but the western part, where the foothills of the Himalayan and Tibetan heights begin, is entirely mountainous. Many of the Kwangsi mountains are of limestone formation. They sometimes consist of cones of solid rock jutting up out of level ground and again they form serrated ranges which often assume fantastic shapes, making that part of Kwangsi justly famous for its scenic beauty. Some of the mountain ranges to the north are of granite formation and occasionally their slopes are covered with pine and camphor trees.

Kwangsi is well supplied with waterways. Near the eastern border of the province the West River divides into two branches and these branches again subdivide, making four rivers, which with their tributaries, penetrate to every part of the province. It is along these river valleys that we find most of the population of Kwangsi. For centuries these rivers have been the highways of transportation and travel in the province.

The mountains of Kwangsi have to a great extent been denuded of their trees and vegetation. Although some attempt has been made at reforestation, there is still so little to retain the heavy spring and summer rains that Kwangsi's rivers usually cause a disastrous flood each year.

Resources

Rice is Kwangsi's main agricultural product. Two crops a year are grown in the south and central part, while in the north one crop is grown annually. Corn and sugar are also grown extensively. The acreage planted in wheat, the greater part of which is grown in the northern part of the province, has been greatly increased in recent years. Sweet potatoes, peanuts, soybeans, cotton and hemp are also important agricultural products. Wood-oil and anise trees provide large quantities of wood-oil, anise oil and anise seed for export. Pine trees provide practically all the lumber for house building and other general purposes, while camphor wood is used for furniture and is also exported. There is a plentiful supply of bamboo with its hundred uses. Banyan trees are plentiful but are not useful in a practical sense. They are decorative, provide cool shade, and occasionally shelter an idol shrine.

Kwangsi's mineral resources have not been fully exploited owing to government monopolies and high taxes. However, coal of an inferior quality is being mined in several areas. Tin, antimony and manganese are being mined and exported. Gold, silver and copper are also found in small quantities.

Progress

Even though Kwangsi's many mountains and scarcity of fertile soil have not been conducive to progress, yet Kwangsi has progressed whenever she has a period of peace and a reasonably good government. But Kwangsi's times of peace have been very brief since the founding of the Republic, and have sometimes been marred by inefficient government.

During the twenty years immediately following the revolution, good motor roads were made, connecting all the principal cities of the province. A modern university was founded, and grade and high schools became much more numerous. Agricultural research was instituted; mining was promoted; many of the cities and towns widened their streets; and many other attempts at modernization were made, so that Kwangsi was considered to have outstripped many of the better endowed provinces. However, progress was at times hindered because the government imposed heavy taxes, and because it took over and managed poorly some projects such as mines and bus transportation.

Then came the Japanese War, which set Kwangsi's progress back many years, and from which she has never fully recovered. However there are many notable exceptions. Since the war Kwangsi's leather industry has improved immensely; many foreign vegetables have been introduced; more modern machinery for spinning and weaving has been brought into use; and all the schools are crowded far beyond capacity. One item of progress which the war brought to Kwangsi deserves special mention, namely, the railroad. As the Chinese troops retreated before the Japanese they took up the railroad tracks and moved them southward, and thus Kwangsi's railroad was built. It enters the province through Kweilin on the northeast, proceeds to Liuchow in the center, and extends over into Kweichow Province on the northwest.

Liuchow, situated in the center of Kwangsi, has made remarkable progress since the war. It now has a fine airport and motor roads radiating in all directions, with numerous trucks and busses carrying freight and passengers. There are fine banks and hospitals and good electric light and power plants supply the city day and night. All this is available in spite of a greatly inflated currency and other obstacles which would seem to be almost insurmountable.

Currency

The old silver currency which was formerly used in Kwangsi was comparatively steady in its market value, and yet the value of each of the three forms used was constantly varying in relationship to the value of the other two. Silver coins of the same denomination had a greater or lesser value according to their year of issue, and even the copper pennies varied in value from month to month.

In 1935 China issued a decree withdrawing all the old silver currency and substituting a paper currency. With the invasion of the Japanese the National currency began to lose its value. In 1947 it began to really "skyrocket" and by the autumn of 1948 became almost valueless. To pay even a small bill required a whole suitcase full of money which took hours to count. The government then issued the Gold Yuan, one of which was equal to three million of National currency. The Gold Yuan was officially pegged at one-quarter of an American dollar. Although severe punishment was threatened and several prominent business men were shot in an attempt to prevent inflation, the Gold Yuan inflation was more rapid than that of the National currency and in about six months it was of so little value as to be almost useless. Rice, the price of which had long been the

basis of business transactions, now became the medium of exchange, and practically all purchases, large and small, were paid for in rice. Some of the old silver currency which had been hidden away was brought out. In Wuchow and other places adjacent to Hongkong, Hongkong money was used, until finally the provincial government was compelled to go back to the old silver currency. (When silver currency is scarce and the demand great, its value rises and when the demand decreases its price drops.) The Mission keeps its accounts in U. S. and Hongkong currency and exchanges only as much as is needed from week to week.

Language and Tribes

The Chinese inhabitants of Kwangsi are divided into two main language groups, Mandarin, now called the National language, and Cantonese. The National language area, which is the larger of the two, is in the northern section of the province, while the Cantonese-speaking area is principally in the south. Many of the business men in the National language area have come from Kwangtung and use Cantonese in their homes and stores, while even in the Cantonese-speaking areas the National language predominates in official and educational circles, and is taught in all the public schools. Although the written language is practically the same in both the National language and Cantonese yet the pronunciation is entirely different.

The aboriginal inhabitants of Kwangsi, who comprise more than one-third of the total population, are to be found, for the greater part, in the northwest half of the province. They are almost entirely confined to the mountainous areas, where they were driven many years ago by their Chinese conquerors. Their language and religion are entirely different from those of the Chinese. Their dress and customs also are different. They have no written language and their spoken language, like their manner of life, is very simple and primitive. Where they have come into close contact with the Chinese, some of the men and a few of the women can speak the National language or Cantonese in addition to their own language. The Chinese Government has attempted, with varying measures of success, to open schools where the National language is taught, in some of the tribal centers.

There are four principal aboriginal tribes in Kwangsi: namely, Chwang, Yao, Tung and Miao.

The *Chwang* tribe is the most numerous of the Kwangsi tribes. They are a part of the great Thai race which is found also in Kweichow, Yunnan, Indo-China, Burma and Siam. It has been estimated that there are about three million Chwangs in Kwangsi. They have intermingled with the Chinese more than any other tribe. Where contacts have been close and continuous many are losing their identity as tribespeople, and are speaking the language and adopting the customs of the Chinese. However, in the rural and more remote areas no language is spoken or understood but their own, and their customs are practically untouched by outward influence.

Although none of our South China missionaries has fully mastered the Chwang language, yet because several of our Mission stations are in areas where Chwang tribespeople abound, work has been done among them by both missionaries and Chinese workers. In several districts great numbers have put away their heathen religion and turned to the Lord. In some villages the greater part of the inhabitants have turned to Christianity, and in many cases have built their own churches, although they more often meet to worship in the home of a local Christian.

The *Yao* tribe has more subdivisions than any other

Kwangsi tribe and is probably the most strongly "isolationist." They inhabit many of the highest mountains in the province. Extreme hardship is the common lot of the Yao people. Indeed it is a marvel that they have been able to maintain an existence through the centuries of their residence in Kwangsi.

Work among the Yaos has been carried on by the Chinese Conference in the Yao mountains north of Pingnam, but owing to difficulties met by the workers, and the disruption caused by the Japanese occupation the work has been allowed to lapse, so that the Yao people are at present practically unreached by the gospel.

The *Tung* tribe, estimated to number about 300,000 in Kwangsi, inhabits the wild mountain fastnesses of northern Kwangsi and southern Kweichow. Their tri-annual festival, when thousands gather in full native costume, is one of the most spectacular events in Kwangsi for the few who see them, and their obscure religious rites move the hearts of those who desire that the light of the gospel should reach their darkened hearts.

In 1931 the South China Mission appointed a missionary couple to the Tung work. After acquiring the language these missionaries not only lived in their midst, but also made visits to the tribespeople in their villages. They were encouraged by the interest with which many listened to the gospel message, and a number of the Tungs turned to the Lord from animism. Now because of the shortage of missionaries and the dislocation caused by the Japanese invasion, no missionary is working among them. While we cannot feel that we have by any means discharged our responsibility toward them, yet for the present the only way we can help them is by prayer.

The *Miao* tribe, the smallest of the four principal tribes of Kwangsi, is found in scattered areas throughout the north and west part of the province. Except on one or two occasions, when a tribesman has come out from his mountain home and heard and accepted the gospel, no definite work has been done for these tens of thousands of Miaos who are a part of the Alliance responsibility.

There are many other small tribes with their different languages, and many small communities with their local dialects who are still entirely unreached with the gospel.

Religions

The tide of materialism that has been sweeping over China in recent years had inundated Kwangsi, and all forms of the older religions have lost much of their influence over the people. Confucian, Buddhist and Taoist temples have been transformed into schools, barracks and hospitals; and many Moslem mosques are still in disrepair since the Japanese invasion. However, those four religions still influence a goodly number of the people of Kwangsi. Ancestor-worship, which stems largely from Confucianism, seems to be the last religious rite which the Chinese are willing to give up. The number of people, especially women, who have taken Buddhist vegetarian vows is still considerable, and not a few Taoist spiritualistic mediums and demon exorcists still carry on their practices. Many Moslems still abstain from eating pork or worshipping idols. A few of Kwangsi's millions have become atheists, but many have no particular interest in religion, in this time when they stand in great need of the comfort and hope that religion can bring.

The religion of the tribespeople of Kwangsi is animism. Although they often build crude little shrines with peculiarly shaped pieces of stone or other objects of veneration placed therein, they do not worship idols as do the Chinese, except in a few instances where they have come under Chinese influence. Many of them have peculiar and obscure religious rites about which little is known. The little enlightenment which has reached them from the outside world has, in many instances, caused their religion to lose its hold on the people, and where they have heard the gospel great numbers have turned to the Lord.

Missionary Occupation

For many years the people of Kwangsi met every attempt, made by missionaries, to settle in their midst, with determined opposition, and the missionaries were frequently mobbed and driven out. The Alliance and Southern Baptist missionaries were the first (1896) to secure a permanent residence in the province. Later the English Wesleyan church began work in Wuchow, and the Church Missionary Society in Kweilin. The Bible Churchmen's Missionary Society is also carrying on work in Nanning but in a different area from the Alliance. The Faith and Love Mission is working in Kweihsien, and the Pentecostal Mission has a station near the eastern border. The Boat Mission ordinarily has a missionary couple working in the province. French and American Roman Catholics are working in many sections of the province and some Seventh Day Adventists are working in one or two of the larger cities.

Kweilin, Wuchow, Nanning and (during the last few months) Liuchow are the only stations, occupied by Alliance missionaries, where missionaries of other Protestant organizations also reside.

The Christian and Missionary Alliance

In 1892 Dr. A. B. Simpson made a world-wide tour of mission fields and visited South China, calling at Canton and spending a few days in that city. His soul burned with a passion for China's unreached millions, especially for the near-by inland Province of Kwangsi—then unopened to the gospel. Upon his return to America a call for volunteers was made and a missionary couple sailed for China on October 25, 1892, and took up residence in Canton, ready to enter the closed province when God opened the way.

Two years later Dr. Simpson again visited China and advised that as soon as sufficient recruits arrived they should enter the still closed and hostile province of Kwangsi. By 1896 the little group of missionaries were ready for the venture of faith, the securing of a permanent residence in the forbidden province. Surveys had already been made and Wuchow was the city for which these intrepid pioneers set forth. After weeks of travel, the little boat finally reached Wuchow, and the Lord marvelously opened the way for the rental of a "haunted house." God was definitely leading, and this city proved to be a base from which the missionary activity of The Christian and Missionary Alliance has penetrated to the greater part of the province.

The objective of the South China Alliance has been the establishing of a strong Chinese Church in Kwangsi, and to this end the missionaries have worked with their Chinese colaborers in making exploration trips, undertaking evangelistic tours, carrying on regular and short term Bible schools, promoting Sunday school and young people's work, and in engaging in all kinds of church work in order to bring about the attainment of their united objective. For more than fifty years the missionaries and Chinese co-workers have proved God's faithfulness in the midst of many dangers and difficulties, and join in giving God all the glory for whatever fruit has been the result of their labors.

The following 12 stations until recently occupied, with one exception, by Alliance missionaries are described in the order of their opening.

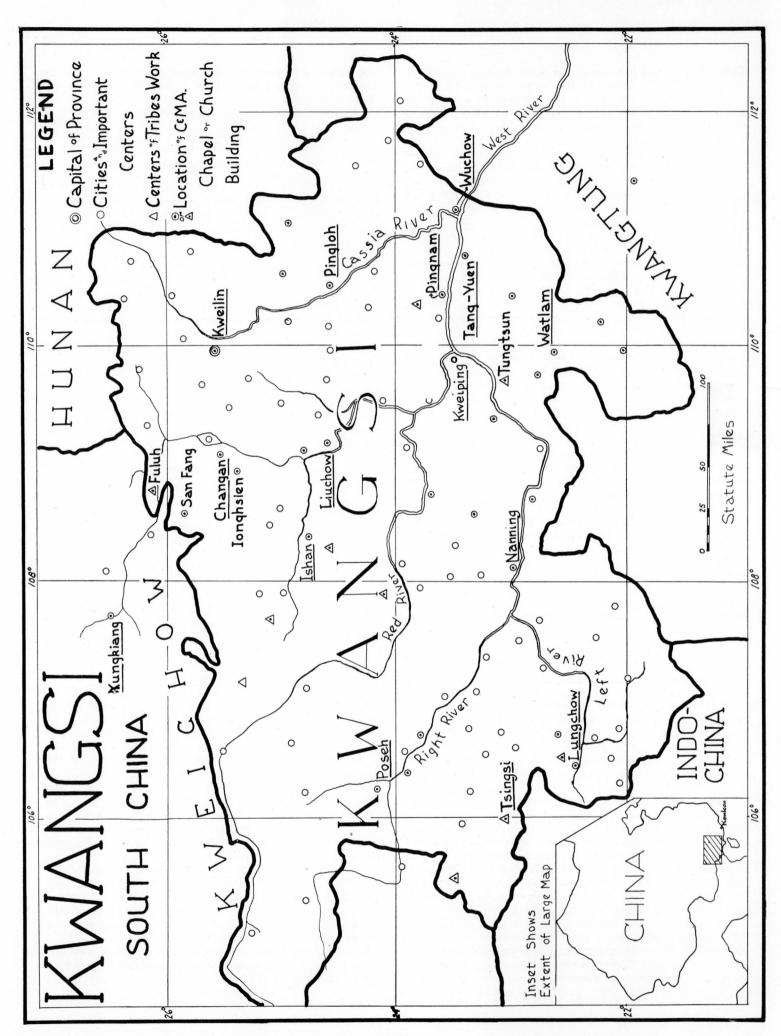

KWANGSI
SOUTH CHINA

LEGEND
◎ Capital of Province
○ Cities & Important Centers
△ Centers of Tribes Work
◎△ Location of C&MA.
△ Chapel or Church Building

HUNAN

KWEICHOW

KWANGSI

KWANGTUNG

Fuluh
San Fang
Changan
Ionghsien
Kungkiang
Ishan
Liuchow
Kweilin
Pingloh
Cassia River
Pingnam
Tang-Yuen
Kweiping
Tungtsun
Watlam
Wuchow
West River
Nanning
Red River
Right River
Poseh
Left River
Lungchow
Tsingsi

INDO-CHINA

Statute Miles
0 25 50 100

Inset Shows
Extent of Large Map

CHINA
Kowloon
INDO-CHINA

106° 108° 110° 112°
22° 24° 26°

Wuchow Situated at the junction of the West and Cassia Rivers, over 200 miles from Hongkong and Canton, is Wuchow, a city of 100,000 and the "gateway of the province." Built in A. D. 592, it is the oldest city in the province and was the seat of government until 1665 when the Government capital was transferred to Kweilin.

In 1896 the honor of having the first resident missionary within Kwangsi's hostile borders fell to Wuchow and to the Alliance Mission. Having secured living quarters, the base of our missionary operations was removed from Macao to Wuchow. The work thus started amidst great persecution and trial has never been abandoned. From a "haunted house" which was the first residence, the work has grown until now there is a church membership of approximately 250.

The Wuchow church was the first in the province to become entirely self-supporting and, in addition, for many years supported a worker among the near-by Yao tribesmen. Owing to financial difficulties and other hindrances consequent upon the Japanese invasion, the work among the Yaos was discontinued. The Wuchow church building and the two Bible school buildings were completely destroyed by fire and bombing, so that during the period of rehabilitation the church received financial aid from the Mission, but again it was the first church after the war to assume entire self-support.

The Wuchow church conducts a flourishing kindergarten, and has made a good start toward opening a full fledged primary school.

The Alliance Receiving Home, located on the hilltop across the river from Wuchow, was also destroyed during the Sino-Japanese War, but is now completely rehabilitated. Here resided the missionary staff of the Alliance Bible School, and here most of the new missionaries studying Cantonese have spent long months of hard language study preparatory to taking up work farther inland. Here also was located, for many years, the headquarters of the South China Alliance, which, since the Sino-Japanese War, has been removed to Liuchow.

The Alliance Bible School, located in the city prior to the war, has since been moved to the hilltop across the river where the quietness and fresh air are more conducive to study than the smoke and noise of the city.

Nanning Nanning, meaning "Peaceful South," is a city with a population of about 100,000, situated on the West River 360 miles west of Wuchow. It is an important center from which river and motor highways spread in all directions, several of them extending into other provinces. It first became important early in Kwangsi's history when the great aboriginal chief met his final defeat just north of the city. From 1907 until 1938 Nanning was the capital of the province. It has a college, a normal school and seven high schools, as well as numerous primary schools.

From the time of its opening as a mission station in 1897, great opposition was experienced, but the Lord overruled and the church has made steady progress. As a result of the anti-Christian campaign of 1925 the church suffered a loss of membership, but in 1933, with a membership of 50, it became entirely self-supporting. Both the church and missionary residence were severely damaged during the Sino-Japanese War, but have since been rehabilitated. Since the time of the Japanese occupation the church has been receiving financial assistance from the Mission, but expected to become fully self-supporting again before the end of 1949.

The Men's Short Term Bible School for the Cantonese area is conducted in Nanning for three months each year.

Nanning, including the Pinyang area, which has recently become a separate district, has nine outstations with an aggregate membership of about 450.

In the area along the lower reaches of the Red River there are still many unreached Chwang tribesmen.

Kwaiping This city, situated at the junction of the West and Willow Rivers, 140 miles west of Wuchow, was opened in 1897. The church at one time had a membership of over 90, and was the main station in a district with ten other churches having a total membership of about 325. This entire district had a most flourishing work but because of depleted ranks the missionaries had to be withdrawn, and during the recent war the work suffered a devastating blow. The property had not yet all been restored in 1949 for the church had been barely holding its own during those years of rehabilitation.

A self-supporting kindergarten has been carried on with an enrollment (1948) of about sixty, and the church hopes soon to establish a primary school.

Kweilin This city, the provincial capital, is situated in the northeastern section of the province on the Cassia River, about 250 miles north of Wuchow. It has a population of 150,000 and is nationally famous for its scenic beauty. It is also the educational center of the province, being the home of the Kwangsi University and numerous other educational institutions.

Opened as a mission station in 1898, it was the first station in the Mandarin area. Years of unusual blessing rested upon the Kweilin church and district. On April 26, 1924, the one used of God to open the work here was killed, shot by a stray bullet from a robber's rifle. During the anti-Christian campaign of 1925 the Kweilin church was severely tried, and during the Sino-Japanese War it suffered a total loss of buildings. The city church was rebuilt in 1943 with funds raised locally, and was preserved through the remaining years of the war. Later, a two-story building was erected as the national worker's residence. To accommodate the Mandarin Short Term Bible School, which is conducted three months in the year, a one-story brick building has been erected. The membership of the district churches is now about 350.

Pinglo, in the Mandarin area, was opened in 1904. Lying south of Kweilin on the Cassia River, it soon became a center for expansion, and a new district was formed which comprises two churches with a membership of about sixty. For nearly ten years no missionary resided here permanently, and the work has suffered tremendously from lack of proper supervision. During the war a bomb scored a direct hit on the church and residence building, partially destroying it. After the war a missionary couple took up residence here; the work was revived, and gives promise of fruitage.

Watlam In the southeastern corner of Kwangsi, situated in a fertile plain with a population of 50,000, lies the city of Watlam, which was opened as a mission station in 1904. During the first years the work was not encouraging, but in later years God worked mightily and this district now has a membership of almost 500. In 1933 the entire district of six churches assumed full self-support and as a district they became the model for the whole province. Not only did God teach them to trust Him for the supply of their running expenses, but they were also enabled to buy and repair church property. This district, however, suffered a setback financially because of the war and inflation, and at present is being subsidized by the Mission.

For the greater part of the year 1948-1949, two lady missionaries resided at Watlam and worked in the district. They were the first foreign missionaries to reside here since 1913.

We trust that this church will once more be able to assume full responsibility and go forward in this large district with a population of about half a million.

Liuchow In 1906 this strategic city in the center of the province was opened. It has a population of over 150,000 and is growing. It has become the center of communication, not only for Kwangsi, but for the whole of South China. From this city rivers, motor roads and railroads radiate through the province and into the neighboring Province of Kweichow. The railroad headquarters for South China are located here, and there is airplane service to various parts of China twice weekly.

The South China Mission Headquarters was located in Liuchow, and until recently when another Society entered, we were the only Mission operating here. This church, like many of the other churches, was severely tried in 1925, but at the present time there is a strong local church with a membership of from 250 to 300. Besides the English service and the evening evangelistic service, four services are held in various parts of the city on Sundays. Regular services are conducted in a chapel across the river in the newer section of the city. All that seems necessary to attract the people to the preaching of the gospel is to turn on the lights and open the church doors. Our central church cannot accommodate more than three hundred and therefore we are reaching only a fraction of those we should reach. Liuchow needs a building with a seating capacity of from one thousand to two thousand, and opportunities are just as great in almost all the large centers of the province.

Lungchow The city of Lungchow was opened to the gospel in 1906. It is an important city situated in the southwestern section of the province near the Indo-China border, and about 500 miles from Wuchow. While the people of the city are Chinese, seven-tenths of those residing in the district are either Chwang tribesmen or Annamese. This city has suffered much from revolutionary and communistic movements, and more recently from the Japanese invasion, at which time the church and residence were destroyed by fire. Many civilians evacuated from this area during the war, and the once large church membership has decreased to about 150 for the entire district. Buildings have been restored and the work is again showing signs of life, but various tribes in the mountain areas are still awaiting the entrance of the gospel.

Ishan This city of about 30,000 inhabitants is located *(Kinguen)* on the main national highway connecting the province with Chungking and Kunming. Not only is it located in the midst of a Chwang tribe area, but it is also the gateway to the northwest, where more than a million tribespeople, chiefly Chwang, reside.

It was opened as a mission station in 1918 and has seen both prosperity and adversity. At present there are approximately 120 church members and excellent opportunities for evangelistic service. Ishan was self-supporting for many years, but since the Japanese invasion, like all the other Kwangsi churches, it has received financial help from the Mission. Now, however, the believers here have decided to again assume entire self-support at the end of 1949.

God has worked in a marvelous way among the Chwang tribespeople in the district and great numbers have turned to the Lord. Two of the former outstations, Tungan and Hochi, have been recognized by the Joint Committee as main stations with their own outstations. In the Hochi area, with only one worker, four chapels have been built, two of them without financial help from the Mission or missionaries. Other centers are planning to build soon but, in the meantime, in eight-

een villages companies of believers meet regularly in homes to worship together on the Lord's day and souls are continually being saved. Apart from Ishan, a conservative estimate of the believers in this district is from 400 to 450.

Changan Situated seventy-five miles north of Liuchow, Changan is the gateway to the mountainous section inhabited by the Tung and Miao tribespeople. This, the terminus for launch and bus travel, is a busy distributing point for the tribesmen and Chinese living in the far interior. Since 1923 when missionaries first took up residence in the city, God has increased the little group of two or three inquirers to a congregation of earnest men and women who meet regularly in their own chapel. A property has recently been purchased and a church building erected in a better locality.

Two outstations have been opened from this center, one of them in an area largely occupied by Chwangs, where in four years the number of Christians has increased from four or five to more than one hundred. These earnest tribesmen have just completed the erection of their own chapel.

Tsingsi This far western, mountain-enclosed, walled town of about 11,000 inhabitants, most of whom are Chwang, is our most recently opened station. Practically its only connection with the outside world is the 175-mile long, poorly kept, motor road to Nanning. It is about 20 miles from the Indo-China border and 70 miles from the border of Yunnan Province. Tsingsi is the government and business center for Kwangsi's far west border region. It is also a center for tribal work and is the gateway to the mountainous backwoods area to the west where at least seven distinct classes of aboriginal tribes have their abode. Visits by both missionaries and national workers had been made to Tsingsi, but it was not occupied as a station until 1935.

From this place pioneer scouting and evangelistic tours have been carried on among the tribespeople with the result that there are now three self-governing and self-propagating churches in the district, with a total membership of well over one hundred, and the sphere of their influence is constantly increasing. It is hoped that the established churches will soon evangelize the tribes of the higher altitudes farther west.

Hongkong Missionaries of The Christian and Missionary *(Kowloon)* Alliance had used the port city of Hongkong (Fragrant Harbor) as an entrance for spearhead operations in the Province of Kwangtung and Kwangsi since 1892, but not until 1933 did our South China Mission open work in Kowloon (Nine Dragons). Kowloon is situated across the bay from Hongkong Island and is the mainland section of greater Hongkong. A missionary couple was stationed here to supervise a hostel for the children of Alliance missionaries. Children from South, Central and West China, from the Philippine Islands and from Indonesia have enjoyed the shelter of this home while attending the excellent English public schools in the city, for Hongkong and Kowloon are under British control. Since the war a house has been purchased and a small additional building erected in order to provide facilities for the hostel.

Seven years after the opening of the hostel, the missionary in charge opened a chapel in the neighborhood to meet the spiritual needs of the Chinese. One year later Hongkong surrendered to the Japanese, the missionaries were interned, and the little group of Chinese Christians were left on their own. When the missionaries returned to Hongkong after the war they found that, instead of dying out, the church in Kowloon had grown until the congregation was forced to seek larger quarters. Services are now conducted in both Cantonese and English with an attendance of some 400 at Sunday school and Sunday worship service. The church is entirely self-supporting and is planning to open several smaller places in order to spread the light farther among the two million people who make Hongkong their home.

In July, 1949, our Foreign Secretary, Dr. A. C. Snead, dedicated the ground for the new church building of the Kowloon Church.

The following centers were formerly mission stations but missionaries no longer reside in them.

Tangyuen Tangyuen, on the West river only thirty-five miles from Wuchow, was opened as a mission station in 1897. Here Dr. R. A. Jaffray and Dr. R. H. Glover began their missionary career. At present the church here is generally served by students from the Wuchow Bible Institute.

Pingnam Located about fifty miles farther up the river than Tangyuen, Pingnam was opened as a station in 1905. It is the natural gateway for work among the Yao tribes who live in the mountains to the north. At present Pingnam is a stronghold of the American Roman Catholic Church. The Alliance Church membership here at the present time is quite small.

Poseh Poseh, in the remote western part of the prov-
(Pakshik) ince about two hundred miles from Nanning, is accessible by motor road and small river motor boats.

Work was begun here in 1913 by a Standard Oil agent whose love for souls led him to give up selling oil and start out in faith to preach the gospel. God blessed his ministry and a number were won to the Lord. A few years later, ill health forced him to leave the field and The Christian and Missionary Alliance assumed full responsibility and sent missionaries to carry on the work. God has blessed the work and the growing church now has about fifty members. Various tribes of the Miao, and hundreds of Chwang villages are located in this district. There are three outstations but the greater part of the district still waits to be claimed for Christ.

Fuluh Fuluh, lying north of Changan and a few miles from the border of Kweichow Province, is an important market town on the Iong River where the Tung tribesmen bring their wares for barter with the Chinese. Fuluh became a mission station in February, 1932, but for more than five years the infant church has been without a missionary and is ministered to by the occasional visits of a national worker. There is, however, quite a strong Tung church across the border in Kweichow, so that there is promise of a harvest if only there were workers to reap.

Translation and Publication Work

In 1935 a new Chinese Alliance Hymnal was published with a view to furthering Scriptural truth and spiritual testimony in China. It is hoped that this hymnal may be enlarged to meet the need of our churches throughout the whole of China. In recent years the Alliance in South China has done little special publication work. The South China Alliance Tidings has been published only occasionally, in folded sheet form. South China, however, was the first home of the Alliance Press in China when a printing press was set up in Wuchow, in 1913, for publishing tracts and the Bible Magazine. The press was destroyed by fire on October 5, 1932, and the press headquarters were subsequently moved to Shanghai.

The China Alliance Press has recently opened an office in Kowloon, Hongkong, although the China Bible Magazine is now published in Singapore, where an editorial and circulation office has been opened.

This publication work is now doubly important, in view of the drastic curtailment of missionary work in China because of Communist control of the country.

See China Alliance Press under China (General) for further information.

Schools

The Alliance Bible School in Wuchow was the first Bible school to be opened by the Alliance on any of its mission fields. The Men's Bible School was opened in 1899 and two years later a separate school was opened for women.

During the fifty years of its operation, not only has the school supplied Kwangsi with workers, but many of its graduates are preaching the gospel in Kwangtung, in Hongkong, some in other provinces also, and even in other parts of the world. Its graduates represent many branches of the Christian Church.

After the Japanese occupation the school was reopened in 1946 as a co-educational institute with thirteen students in attendance. The attendance rapidly increased until, in 1949, there were seventy students enrolled.

Four courses are being taught: a Christian Workers' Course, a Preparatory Course, a Standard Bible Course, and a Theological Course.

Two Short Term Bible Schools are conducted annually, usually for men only. One is held in the Mandarin, and one in the Cantonese section of the province. Forty students attended these Short Term Bible Schools last year, and most of theme were Chwang tribesmen. Five former Short Term Bible School students are now studying in the Wuchow Bible School.

Two kindergartens were conducted by the Chinese churches last year.

The Bible School in Wuchow continues its work under full Chinese leadership since the Communists took control of Kwangsi Province.

The Church and the Challenge

The objective of the Alliance Mission in South China is the establishing of a Chinese Church that will be self-supporting, self-governing and self-propagating.

With this objective in view the missionaries are appointed to districts and are never in charge of local churches. Their ministry is largely spiritual and in the business affairs of the Chinese Church they act in an advisory capacity only.

The present organization of the South China Alliance was set up for the attainment of this objective. There are two legislative bodies, namely, the Chinese Conference and the Mission Conference, each with their executive committees acting on an equal basis, but in different spheres. The Chinese Conference and its Executive Committee are the sole authority on matters of purely Chinese business and finance, while the Mission Conference and its Committee deal with all matters concerning only missionaries and Mission finances. All matters which are partly Chinese and partly Mission are discussed by a Joint Committee consisting of both the Chinese and Mission Executive Committees. These Committees are responsible to their respective Conferences, but as a Joint Committee have power to act on certain matters which are more or less routine business. The object in having two Conferences is that the authority and responsibility of the Chinese Conference may gradually increase, and that of the Mission Conference gradually decrease without any weakening of the organization.

It was also decided that when a church becomes entirely self-supporting, or supplies six-tenths of its entire support and gives promise of becoming self-supporting within a few years, it shall be placed entirely under the jurisdiction of the Chinese Conference. Before the Sino-Japanese War eleven churches, under the blessing of God, met these conditions, ten of them being entirely self-supporting. Self-support has suffered a severe setback because the Japanese invasion rendered many Christians practically penniless and homeless. The currency inflation has caused added hardship, and the rehabilitation of church buildings has greatly increased the burden on the churches. Therefore, churches which were formerly self-supporting, as well as others, have received help from the Mission. Within the last few months, however, several churches have announced that they are again assuming self-support, and thus the authority and responsibility of the Chinese Conference has increased.

From all over the province come reports of unprecedented opportunities challenging the Alliance Church—crowded evangelistic meetings; large classes of interested high school students studying the Bible (often in English, but nevertheless studying God's Word); well attended Sunday schools and young people's meetings; deepened interest among university students; many Christians desiring Bible study; scores of tribespeople seeking the Lord; but a lamentable insufficiency of workers to buy up these marvelous opportunities. In some places there are only five or six workers including missionaries, for more than a million people. One Chinese evangelist has four organized churches and twenty smaller groups of believers to care for. One-half of the county seats in the province are still without any Christian meeting place. Several areas are entirely untouched and several tribes are still unreached.

Surrounded with these tremendous opportunities, the missionaries and national believers of South China watched with apprehension as the cloud of Communism rolled steadily southward. With many missionaries under the necessity of leaving China to labor in other fields since the iron curtain of Communism has enveloped South China, the entire responsibility of administering the work of the South China Alliance is now being handed over to the Chinese Conference. Will the Chinese Church, not yet fully recuperated from the suffering and ravages of the recent war, and bereft of the help of the Mission while faced with dangers and difficulties hitherto unknown, succumb to adverse influences and be exterminated? Will not the opposition and trials, through the grace of God, rather strengthen the church so that if and when the iron curtain is lifted, there will be found to remain a living Church still witnessing for Christ? The outcome will depend partly on the quality of work the missionaries have done; partly upon the stedfastness of the Chinese Church; and in no small measure upon the faithfulness of God's children throughout Christendom in supporting the Chinese Church by earnest believing prayer.

Youth Conference in Kweichow-Szechwan field, China

THE NEAR EAST

ISRAEL—HASHEMITE KINGDOM OF JORDAN—SYRIA

Situated at the crossroads of three continents, that which has been known as the Palestine-Arabian Border field comprises portions of the areas known as Israel, the Hashemite Kingdom of Jordan, and Syria from Damascus to the southern border. Israel is the name of the Jewish-held portion of what was formerly Palestine, while the Hashemite Kingdom of Jordan comprises the Arab-held portion of Palestine plus the Transjordan area.

On the west the field is bounded by the Mediterranean. To the north are Lebanon and Syria, and on the northeast is a narrow strip of Iraq. To the south are Sinai, Egypt, and Saudi Arabia. The boundaries between the Jewish and Arab-held areas west of the Jordan River had not been finally determined at the time of going to press.

Amman is the capital of the Hashemite Kingdom, and Tel Aviv the provisional capital of Israel, but the struggle is still going on (late 1949) between the Jews and the Arabs for the supremacy in Jerusalem. In October, 1949, the Israel government declared the former Arab city of Jaffa and the Jewish city Tel Aviv to be one city called Tel Aviv—Jaffa under united government.

Just before the General Assembly of the United Nations adjourned late in 1949 it voted to make all of Jerusalem an international city, under the control of a U. N. commission. This was opposed both by Israel and the Hashemite Kingdom of Jordan, which now control the city.

On Tuesday morning, December 13, in Tel Aviv Israel proclaimed Jerusalem its national capital. The Israel government will set up headquarters in the new city of Jerusalem, and Parliament voted to hold its next session during the week of December 18, 1949, in that city of present conflict, yet holy memories and prophetic import.

Area and Population

The territory formerly included under the name Palestine has an area of 10,429 square miles, and is about the size of Maryland. The population (estimated 1946) was 1,912,000. There are no accurate figures available for the Arab-held portion, but the area is about 4,500 square miles, with an approximate population of 804,000 Arabs and 10,000 Jews.

In 1919 there were only 57,000 Jews in Palestine. Today Israel has an area of about 5,500 square miles, and the population (November, 1948) was 782,000, of which 713,000 were Jews and 69,000 were Arabs and others. However, by March, 1949, the estimate for Israel was a total population of 950,000, as 24,000 Jewish immigrants are pouring into the country every month. The objective of Israel is one million Jewish immigrants within ten years.

During the latter half of 1949 several chartered planes were in almost daily flight bringing Jews from China and other far eastern lands, and then they engaged in a most remarkable project of transferring all the Jews from Yemen to Israel. The story of this twentieth century odyssey, by which tens of thousands of Jews are coming to their homeland after long wanderings, is full of humanitarian, historical, and prophetic interest. The ten-year goal of one million newcomers into Israel will probably be reached in a fraction of that time.

Except for Negev (also written Negeb), the new Republic of Israel covers only the areas which the Jews have settled and developed in the last 50 years or have recently con-

quered. The boundaries are not yet definitely settled but, by the 1947 partition resolution of the United Nations, Israel was assigned a large portion in southern Palestine, a smaller northern area, and a strip along the west coast. The Negev is a triangle of about 3,000 square miles, in the south of Israel, with its apex at Aqaba, at the head of the right arm of the Red Sea.

Transjordan is three times the size of all Palestine, yet it has a population of only about 340,000. Syria covers approximately 54,300 square miles and has a population estimated at more than three million.

History

This bridge between the East and the West has been a battleground of the nations. After the fall of Jerusalem to Rome in 70 A. D., Palestine had a checkered history for 1,500 years until it was conquered by the Turks. Turkey had full control of its destinies from 1517 until World War I when, on December 9, 1917, General Allenby (later Field Marshal Viscount Allenby) entered Jerusalem afoot, with head uncovered, as the leader of the conquering British Army. The land remained under British Military Administration until July 1, 1920, when a civil government was set up. After September 29, 1923, the country was governed by Great Britain under a mandate granted by the League of Nations. The Balfour Declaration (1917) expressed Great Britain's intention to establish a National Home for the Jewish people in Palestine. The Arabs have strenuously opposed the carrying out of the Balfour Declaration. In 1939 Britain issued the White Paper, suspending Jewish immigration in Palestine, and in 1944 Palestine was apportioned by Great Britain as follows: two-thirds of the population to be Arab, and one-third Jews.

The difficult Palestine question was submitted to the United Nations, and their General Assembly voted (November 29, 1947) to partition Palestine into independent Jewish and Arab states by October 1, 1948, with the formation of an enclave of Jerusalem, area 289 square miles, to be administered by the U. N. Trusteeship Council through a U. N. appointed Governor. The partition plan called for evacuation of British troops by August 1, 1948, but Great Britain requested that her mandate be ended by May 15, 1948, and she withdrew her forces by that date.

Internal strife began immediately following the vote for partition. By the end of 1947 it was evident that the trouble between the Jews and Arabs would be serious. Following the withdrawal of the British there was open war. The Arab countries—Egypt contending for the Negev—with Transjordan, Saudi Arabia, Iraq, Syria and Lebanon, all united against the new State of Israel. The United Nations issued a general cease-fire order July 15, 1948, but a formal cease-fire agreement was not signed until March 11, 1949. This agreement was a preliminary to a full armistice between Israel and Transjordan. By the end of March, 1949, Israel had signed an armistice with Lebanon, and was beginning negotiations with Syria. Israel requested the United Nations to order a plebiscite in Arab-held Palestine to decide whether it should remain a part of Palestine or be annexed to Transjordan.

In May, 1948, the British evacuated Palestine. Within a year the new Republic of Israel was established and held its first general election. Nobody knows the solution of the problems which are developing. It is true that recent events have already displaced a very large Arab population but, nevertheless, Arabs and Jews will doubtless learn to live with one another and to respect the admittedly high qualifications found in both groups of these children of Abraham. "Beyond the Arab politicians, one can find moderation . . . and innumerable friendship and non-aggression pacts between Arab and Israeli communities." At present both Arabs and Jews are experiencing the "growing pains of nationalism," but those who have lived long in the country predict that the two nations will be able to adjust their differences.

An Arab chauffeur taking the Foreign Secretary and two missionaries from Arab-held Jerusalem to Amman, August, 1949, said: "If the Government would only let us alone we Palestine Arabs could come to agreement with the Jews, and Arabs and Jews could live as peaceful neighbors in Palestine."

Transjordan was also formerly under British mandate, but by a separate treaty with Great Britain in 1946, Transjordan became an independent state, and its Emir Abdullah became King Abdullah in May of the same year. In 1949 Transjordan and Arab-held Palestine became by royal decree of King Abdullah, The Hashemite Kingdom of Jordan.

Syria comprises what was formerly the Turkish Empire Sanjaks (districts) of Damascus, Aleppo, Homs, Hama, Deir-Ezzor, Latakia, the Hauran, the Euphrates and Jezireh, and Jebel Druse. Syria became an independent state by the treaty of Sevres on August 10, 1920, and on September 1 of that year divided into the states of Syria and Greater Lebanon. Both were administered under a French mandate for the next 21 years. Syria was proclaimed a republic on September 16, 1941, by the occupying French authorities. The French troops were withdrawn in April, 1946, and both Lebanon and Syria became separate republics.

Syria, the Hashemite Kingdom of Jordan and Israel are each members of the United Nations and the two Arabic countries are also members of the Arab League.

Government

The first general election of the Republic of Israel was held January 25, 1949. Dr. Chaim Weizmann was elected the first President. Nearly 90 per cent of the eligible electorate voted, as compared with a little over 50 per cent in U. S. elections. The Constituent Assembly, meeting at Tel Aviv, has been elected for the specific purpose of writing a permanent constitution for the new Republic. The Assembly may be compared to our own Constitutional Convention held in Philadelphia in 1787.

Syria has an Assembly elected by direct vote. The President of Syria is elected by the Assembly, which also appoints the Premier and other high officers of the government. On Sunday morning, August 14, 1949, a few hours before the Foreign Secretary arrived on a deputation visit to our Mission, the President and the Premier of Syria were taken from their residences in Damascus, the capital, by a revolutionary group and were shot on the outskirts of Damascus. The country was under partial military rule for some time but later a constitutional government was resumed. Syria is negotiating treaties with certain of the Arab nations, hoping to establish a "greater Syria."

The Hashemite Kingdom of Jordan has its capital at Amman. Its king, Abdullah I, has been supported by Great Britain for a great many years. There is an assembly which is more or less representative of the population.

Climate

On the coastal plain and in the Jordan valley the summers are extremely hot. In the mountains and on the high plains of Syria and the Transjordan area, the heat is intense during the day but the nights are usually cool. From December to March, winter temperatures are not low, but in this, the rainy season, the dampness is disagreeable and often brings illness in those homes which are unheated.

Physical Features

Palestine's first High Commissioner once said: "The country offers, on the area of a province, the soil and conditions of a continent." The coastal plain, which is fertile and well watered, extends irregularly the whole length of the country, and is at places 15 miles wide. A mountain range, the plateau of Judea (altitude 2,000 to 3,000 feet), forms the high backbone of the country and is topped by majestic Hermon, whose peak is capped with snow most of the year. The small streams of the region are raging torrents in the winter but dry, stony valleys for the larger part of the year. East of the Judean mountains is the great rift of the Jordan River, reaching its lowest level at the Dead Sea, the surface of which is 1,292 feet below the level of the Mediterranean Sea. East of the Jordan the plateau region gradually becomes less and less fertile until it reaches the desert, where there can be no regular crops. However, between the Jordan and the Hejaz Railroad, Transjordan has a 30-mile strip of land with a high agricultural potential.

Resources

Investigation and development have shown that Palestine has great natural resources. Israel claims that the country can easily support four million inhabitants, or twice the present population. A concession to exploit the salts in the Dead Sea was granted in 1929. The value of the chemicals found there is estimated at four quadrillion dollars. The salinity is from four to five times as great as that of ocean water. Potash for fertilizer, bromides for medicines, and many salts used in treating nervous diseases are found there.

Sand wastes along the coastal plain have been irrigated and planted with citrus trees. In 1947, 17 million crates of citrus fruits were harvested. Claims have been made that there is oil in the country but no large scale development in this direction has been made. Wheat, fruits and olives are grown; sheep and goats are raised for local markets; and the chief exports are oranges, wine, olive oil and soap.

Syria has little mineral wealth but oil companies are prospecting in the Deir-Ezzor region. The principal industries are agriculture and cattle raising. Wheat, barley, tobacco, citrus fruit, olives, grapes, and sugar cane are the chief crops. Leather, wool and silk goods, and copper and brass utensils are manufactured.

Transjordan, now a part of the Hashemite Kingdom of Jordan, is largely desert. However, grain, fruits and vegetables are grown in the 30-mile strip east of the Jordan. Phosphate and potash deposits are being developed and surveys are being made for oil.

Progress

The progress in Palestine since the close of World War I has been almost phenomenal. The city of Tel Aviv has grown in less than 30 years from 2,000 to 184,000 Jewish inhabitants. A pipe line conveying crude oil from Mosul (Nineveh) in Iraq to the Mediterranean was completed in 1934. Oil tanks and refineries in Haifa process the petroleum. It is exported from both Haifa and Tripoli, Lebanon.

A railroad built for military purposes during World War I connects with the old Jaffa-Jerusalem Railway and, with the Hejaz Railway, gives direct service from the Suez Canal to Damascus and Stamboul. In another direction it provides service to Ma'an on the Moslem pilgrimage road. A more direct communication has been opened since the construction of a railroad between Haifa, where rail communications with Cairo end, and Tripoli, Lebanon, where rail connections with Ankara and Istanbul, Turkey, are resumed.

There is regular motor service to Baghdad and points in Iran; intercontinental airplanes stop in Israel and Syria; motor roads connect all cities. In Syria it is claimed that all villages also can be reached by automobile, in dry weather. Syria is much larger than Lebanon, but is less advanced. Syria is 70 per cent illiterate, but Lebanon is 70 per cent literate. The Hashemite Kingdom is making progress industrially. In Transjordan it is building hard surfaced roads, surveying petroleum deposits and developing potash and phosphate deposits. Socially the Transjordan area is backward. Although it is three times the size of Palestine, there are only 24 doctors and five dentists in the whole country.

Palestine has had a dual system of education, Arab and Hebrew, but it was not compulsory. All Jewish schools were privately financed even before the British withdrew, but while Britain was in control she sponsored the Arabic public schools. The Hebrew language is once more taking its place among the living languages of the world. Bookstores in Israel carry the works of Shakespeare and some by Victor Hugo, in Hebrew. Other secular, also scientific books are available in Hebrew. All these have been translated within the past 25 years. Hebrew University (opened 1925) on Mount Scopus in Jerusalem reported (1944-1945) a faculty of 159 teachers and 610 students.

Israel has a plan to harness the Jordan River. At an outlay of $250,000,000 dollars, at least 600,000 acres could be brought under cultivation, and supply yearly a billion units of hydroelectric power. The Jews have spent over half a billions dollars in reclaiming waste land and in building colonies, where Jews live on the land and raise farm products. In the Negev (a Hebrew word meaning "dry"), not even cactus will grow unless it is cultivated. It is land that has lain untilled for 1,500 years, yet in the last seven years over 23 Jewish colonies have been established there. The objective of Israel is to place a quarter million Jews there. Irrigation has proved that the land is suitable for all crops classed as "dry agriculture," and it is certain that oil is to be found there. Ezekiel 36:8-11 and Jeremiah 32:42-44 are being fulfilled literally today.

Currency

The Hashemite Kingdom of Jordan still uses the Palestinian pound, which is divided into 1,000 mills. Since the founding of the Republic of Israel, there is a distinctly Jewish currency, the Israeli pound. Both the Palestinian and the Israeli pound are valued at $2.81 in U. S. currency.

In Syria the Syrian pound is the principal monetary unit. Late in 1949 one dollar U. S. brought LS 3.33 (Syrian pounds).

Languages

Prior to the recent political disturbances, the general languages of the land of Palestine were three—English, Arabic, and Hebrew. All proclamations, all stamps, all coins, all street signs, etc., were in all three languages. Now in Israel the official language is Hebrew. The Jewish immigrant, with a score of languages at his command, immediately places his child in a Hebrew school and within a few weeks the child is teaching his parents the language of their ancestors. .

The official language in Syria and in the Hashemite Kingdom is Arabic and all of our workers use the Arabic language. Some native workers are able to witness in other languages such as Turkish, Armenian, and French.

Religions

Most of the inhabitants of Syria and the Hashemite Kingdom are Moslems of the Sunni group. There are, however, minority groups of various Christian sects, including the Roman Catholic church, the Greek Orthodox church, and some Protestant groups. In Israel the religion is Judaism. Originally the Zionists hoped for the return of the Messiah and they were gathering together in the homeland of Israel. Now some of them disavow mysticism and are depending not on a miracle but on their own efforts for the establishing of their homeland, while their leaders have gone so far as to say: "Our concept of the Messiah has undergone radical change. We no longer think of the Messiah as a person but as a golden age."

Jerusalem is considered a holy city to Moslems, Christians, and Jews. Prior to the recent disturbances there were large populations from all three of these religious divisions in the city of Jerusalem.

Missionary Occupation

Palestine and the Near East became a needy mission field because the Christian Church, from the third to the seventh century, became apostate. When the false prophet Mohammed challenged Christendom in the seventh century with his false teachings, the inhabitants were worshipping 375 gods and goddesses. Islam gained in power until today it is our chief challenge in this field.

American, British and European missionaries were in Palestine before the recent upheaval. Except in the larger cities, these groups were not often found in the same places. Educational work has been carried on, ranging from kindergarten to the American University of Beirut. Medical work has been conducted in well equipped city hospitals and in small village clinics. Some of the groups have a definite evangelistic message for the lost. There were more than 200 Protestant missionaries in Palestine before the recent evacuation, including many independent workers.

In 1949 it was again becoming possible for missionaries to return to Israel and some of our missionaries are finding a very profitable ministry in witnessing to the Jews in Jerusalem and in other parts of the republic of Israel.

Missionaries are also located in Syria and in the Hashemite Kingdom of Jordan. Because of American expressions of sympathy to the giving of Palestine over into the hands of the Jews and taking it from the Arabs, many of the Arabs have developed an antagonism to Americans which may be difficult for our missionaries to overcome. Traditionally the Arab people had been friendly to Americans for a great many decades.

The Christian and Missionary Alliance

The work of The Christian and Missionary Alliance began in Jerusalem, Hebron and Jaffa in the nineties. Early efforts were undertaken quietly and included visitation in the villages, meetings for women and children, and Sunday services in the homes of the missionaries.

The year 1948 closed with only three missionaries on the field: one woman in Jerusalem and one missionary couple in Damascus. In March, 1949, one missionary couple was able to return to Jerusalem. A few months later they were joined by another couple and a young woman who re-entered from Cyprus. In October one couple returned to the Transjordan section of the Hashemite Kingdom of Jordan.

Israel (Palestine)

Palestine is now divided between the Republic of Israel and the Hashemite Kingdom of Jordan.

NEAR EAST
ISRAEL-SYRIA-JORDAN

CYPRUS

MEDITERRANEAN SEA

SYRIA

• Beirut

• _Damascus_

Haifa •

ISRAEL

Deraa •   Sweida •
Ghasm • Tesia

• Mefrak

• Telaviv

• _Amman_

Jerusalem

TRANS-JORDAN
HASHEMITE KINGDOM of the JORDAN

• Bethlehem   • Madaba

Beersheba   • Kerak

IRAQ

EGYPT

NILE RIVER

SUEZ CANAL

SINAI

ARABIA

C&M.A. Mission
Stations Underlined

0   25   50   100
Statute Miles

124

Jerusalem Work was begun here in 1890. In 1913 a substantial stone building was erected which included a church auditorium, a Sunday school room, and a residence. This soon became Mission headquarters and the center of activity for work in the city and near-by villages. Some years ago a friend donated funds sufficient to purchase a lot and simple buildings to house the work among the Jews in Jerusalem. A reading room and a library have proved through the years to be an attraction that has yielded fruit. Another room is available as a place for public services conducted in Hebrew.

Early in December, 1947, it was evident that the trouble between the Jews and Arabs would be of a serious nature, and in January, 1948, all of our missionaries in Jerusalem, except one, evacuated to the Island of Cyprus, hoping to watch developments from there and return to Palestine at the earliest opportunity. The national pastor of the Jerusalem Church, with his family, evacuated to Damascus on the advice of the church board. Even before he left Jerusalem a large hotel only six yards from his house was bombed, completely wrecking the building. The windows of the pastor's house were shattered and bits of broken glass were scattered everywhere, yet not one of the family of five was harmed.

Our lady missionary, who remained in Jerusalem through all the months of warfare, wrote at the end of 1948: "As we look back over the past year, what impresses us most is not the days and nights of terror and the months of privation, but the miracles God has wrought. . . . We (in the Jewish section) were utterly cut off from all Arab Christians by the great gulf which had split the city into two armed camps. Only a dozen missionaries (of all Societies) and perhaps another dozen evangelical Christians remained in Jewish Jerusalem. . . . For some time the Jewish authorities viewed with suspicion the few foreigners left in their midst. . . . We underwent arrests and questionings until they were assured that we had no political motives whatever. Since then they have treated us with the utmost courtesy.

"Regarding inquirers, we have had a larger number than ever before in the same length of time. It has been one of the greatest privileges I have ever had in my life to put this Mission House at His disposal this past year and let Him bring into it for His glory missionaries and other Christians, war refugees and new immigrants. Our Mission House has been the center of Christian fellowship in the city this past year, every other mission property having been given over either largely or wholly to the Jewish community for secular uses. We had only one room which we could give up. It was occupied for five months by the Jewish Doctors' Association."

Beersheba, at one time a main mission station, has in later years been supervised from Jerusalem. The national worker (Bible woman) there was able to continue her work until October, 1948, which was more than five months longer than any other worker to the Arabs of Palestine was able to remain at his post in those months of turmoil. The Bible woman was unable to cash her allowance check and so was without income for eight months. Although subjected to indescribable dangers, she would have laid down her life rather than leave her work without authorization from the Mission. The Mission had tried to get word to her to leave but the letter never reached her. She left only when the Jewish bombs drove the Arabs from the town. After twelve days on the way she arrived in Transjordan without food or money, and with very little clothing.

In June, 1949, a reconnaissance trip to Beersheba revealed that our mission property remained intact in spite of the many bombs that had fallen in and around the town. Our property is being used by the government (summer, 1949), the town is being cleared of debris and shops are again doing business. Jewish families are settling in Beersheba.

A young missionary couple who are studying Hebrew in Jerusalem will go to Beersheba within a few months. Thus this city where work among Arabs was carried on for many years will soon be occupied as a center for work among the Jews.

Haifa is also supervised from Jerusalem. The Arab worker and his wife stayed at their post until the end of April, 1948. They were in almost constant danger long before they evacuated. The worker's health has been poor and the intense bombardment to which Haifa was subjected has been a setback to him physically. This couple now live in Deraa, Syria, and his health is much improved.

Although the history of Christian work among the Jews in many lands has borne evidence to the opposition in Jewry to those who accept Jesus Christ as Saviour and Lord, yet we are glad to report that the Israel government in Palestine is showing a very fine attitude toward missionary work in their midst. The Israel Consulate in New York has informed us that Israel is not discriminating against Christian Jews entering Palestine. For this we are grateful. May God grant that the Church shall be more faithful than ever in seeking to win Jews, both in Israel and in other lands, to the knowledge of Christ.

Hashemite Kingdom of Jordan (Transjordan)

Amman When the plans were being made for the return to Transjordan of our missionary couple it seemed advisable for their residence to be in Amman, the capital city of the Hashemite Kingdom of Jordan. Thus late in 1949 a house was rented, where the missionary couple is residing and where one room of the house will be open for gospel meetings as the opportunity is given. From Amman, the areas of which Madaba and Kerak are the centers, will be supervised and also surveys will be made of the missionary responsibilities in northern Transjordan.

Madaba was opened in 1921 and regular services have been held with the Oriental Christian groups. A large Sunday school meets regularly, women's meetings are conducted and visitation work is carried on. The national worker there reports that the past year has been his best year of service in Madaba.

Kerak was opened by the Alliance in 1923 and activities there have been along lines similar to those in Madaba. Itineration is carried on in the highlands and among the nomadic groups in the Dead Sea area. Kerak has been called the key city to northern Arabia as many Arabs come to this center on business. A national worker and his family served in Kerak during the first half of the year 1948. Finally the family was given forty-eight hours to leave the town and they evacuated to Damascus in June. The program of work at Kerak includes four regular weekly services and two Sunday schools, one for children from Christian homes and one on Friday for Moslem children. The Bible woman who had to flee from Beersheba has been appointed to Kerak.

Mefrak was entered by the Alliance in November, 1948, after an independent mission work had been turned over to our Society. A national worker has been placed at Mefrak and the work is going forward.

Syria

Damascus This city was entered as a mission station only since the close of World War II. Since that time the city has been bombed three times. God gave protection to His servants and the dangers have caused the local people to think seriously.

In June, 1948, a Prayer Conference for our Syrian evangelists was held here for the first time.

On Sunday, August 14, 1949, three candidates took the unprecedented step of being baptized by immersion. This day of the first baptismal service of our Mission in Damascus was also marked by the arrival of the Foreign Secretary, deputation from the Home Board, in time to take part in the service. Baptism by immersion has been practically unknown in Damascus and prayer is needed that more who profess to follow Christ may have the courage to take the step.

In the Hauran, *Ghasm* and *Tesia* are supervised from Damascus.

Deraa has recently been reopened. This town is the Edrei of the Old Testament, where Og, King of Bashan, once reigned. Day schools are carried on at Ghasm and Tesia.

In Djebel Druze, *Soueida, Kharaba, Jebaib* and *Ara* are supervised from Damascus. A day school is conducted at Kharaba. Ara is the home of the prince of the Druzes, and to this large community a national worker and his family have recently gone.

Translation and Publication Work

Through the British and Foreign Bible Society and the American Bible Society, Bibles are available in Arabic, Hebrew, Turkish, Armenian and many European languages which are used in witnessing to the Jews. Devotional, expository and doctrinal books are available in Arabic. Also available in Arabic are three of Dr. A. B. Simpson's books: *Christ Life, Wholly Sanctified,* and *Divine Healing. The Life of A. B. Simpson* has been translated into Arabic, but is still in manuscript form. Also still in manuscript form are translations into Arabic of two other books by Dr. Simpson, namely, *The Holy Spirit or Power from on High,* and *Christ in the Tabernacle.*

A former elder of our Jerusalem Alliance Arabic Church (which is now in Israel territory) and his wife are one of several families living in Arabic sections as refugees, receiving relief funds as they are available. He is devoting his time and energy to the translating of Dr. Simpson's writings for Arabic use.

Schools

The Bible School in Jerusalem was first opened in 1922. It was closed in 1934, reopened in 1946, and closed again in 1947. Three students graduated the last year of the school. This Bible School was for the training of Arabic Christian young men and women and should be reopened in an Arabic-speaking area whenever possible.

Day schools are conducted in Madaba, Ghasm, Tesia and Kharaba. Most of them have courses covering the first three elementary grades. The one at Madaba covers ten grades, and the enrollment there was 58 in 1948. The school has strengthened the work in Madaba. Ours was the only school in Tesia until 1948, when the government opened one, and thereafter many children who desired to attend our school were required to attend the government school. The enrollment for 1948 was 25 at Tesia and 49 at Kharaba. The Syrian government has required new permits for our three schools and when these permits are granted they will forbid us to give any Christian teaching to Moslem pupils who may attend.

The Church and the Challenge

The reports from our Palestine-Arabian Border field for the year 1948, although incomplete, listed eleven full-time workers, six organized and seven unorganized churches, and eleven Sunday schools with an enrollment of 600—all this in a land that has been going through blood and fire. Itineration reached beyond the border of our field into Lebanon, where national pastors were able to go to minister to scattered believers from our Jerusalem and Haifa churches. Members of our churches are scattered today in four countries: Israel, Lebanon, Syria, and the Hashemite Kingdom of Jordan, and most of them are without proper livelihood or spiritual advisors.

The responsibility of The Christian and Missionary Alliance in Israel, in the Hashemite Kingdom and in Syria is 700,000 souls. As to the prospects in Israel, there is now a more open spirit among the Jews. Trips and visits are possible which would not have been attempted ten or fifteen years ago. The reading room in Jerusalem has prepared the hearts of many for the working of the Holy Spirit. Services in both Arabic and Hebrew have brought in souls. In Tel Aviv and Jewish colonies, the Mission is not permitted to own property nor to conduct public meetings. However, visitation and personal work can be done. Much has been accomplished in this way in the past, and also by the distribution of literature.

Saudi Arabia has been an objective of the Alliance for many years. It is that section of the great Arabian Peninsula nearest to our Transjordan field, and formerly called Hejaz and Nejd. In Arabia, missionaries are working on the Persian Gulf Coast, in the British Protectorate of Aden and in other points near by, but the stronghold of the interior has never yielded. Trips into Arabia were made by Forder, Turnbull, Ward, Breaden, Rackett and Smalley, but no one was permitted to remain in Arabia or given opportunity for open witness for Christ. Rev. W. F. Smalley, for many years an Alliance missionary in Palestine, writes:

"One of the great trips of modern missions was taken by one of our missionaries, Rev. Archibald Forder, who traveled by camel to the desert city of El Jowf. . . . Later, in 1909, there was an effort to get into Yemen, South Arabia. . . . Other trips followed from time to time. The last of the visits of our missionaries into Arabia proper was made toward the end of 1927, when two of us started from Aqaba. After five days in Arabia proper, we were imprisoned and taken from one prison to another until finally, thirty-five days later, we were ignominiously ejected from the country, with the statement on our passports that it was forbidden for the bearer of that passport to enter that area again."

Every effort to get the gospel into the interior of Arabia has meant ill treatment, and in the end, refusal. This is the Holy Land and center of Islam; here King Ibn Saud has control of the lives and destinies of his desert subjects. Although it is forbidden to bring or send copies of the Bible into Saudi Arabia, copies have been taken and there is reason to believe that they have been read in the shadow of the *Kaaba*—the central point of Moslem pilgrimage.

Jerusalem—city of the Great King—is now marked by division and hatred. Most of the places sacred to Christians because of their Biblical relationship are in the section of Jerusalem under Arab control. The tomb where our Lord's body was probably laid for three days is on one side of a walled garden in Jerusalem which is in the hands of a Christian organization, but the Mount of Olives, and Gethsemane, and Calvaty are still in the hands of the followers of the false prophet. May God hasten the day when the word spoken concerning our Lord shall be fulfilled, "His feet shall stand in that day upon the Mount of Olives, which is before Jerusalem on the east—." Then Jerusalem will truly become the city of the Great King, for Christ enthroned in Jerusalem will rule over the whole earth. Wars shall cease and the knowledge of the Lord shall cover the earth as the waters cover the sea.

THE ISLAND WORLD

The islands of the world are so numerous, their location so widespread and their population so diverse as to race, language, habits and religion, as to make a treatment of the subject of the island world, in the limited space of these Atlas pages, an impossible task save for a few general statements.

Many of the principal islands of the world are intimately related geographically and politically to the continent which they adjoin. In historical and geographical descriptions, islands so located are usually considered a part of those continents close to whose coast they lie. In a study of missions, Japan, the Philippine Islands and Indonesia are usually linked with Asia; the Cape Verde and Madeira Islands, Madagascar and other islands off the coast of Africa are included with that continent; and the West Indies are usually linked with Latin America.

The islands of the Central and South Pacific Ocean are also known as the South Sea Islands, for the South Sea was the name first given to the Pacific when it was discovered in 1513. Oceania is a collective name for the lands of the Central Pacific and includes: Micronesia, Melanesia, Polynesia and sometimes Australia, New Zealand and the Malay Archipelago. The statistics in the following paragraphs as to population, number of Protestant foreign missionaries, and number of communicants or full church members, are taken from the *World Christian Handbook,* World Dominion Press, 1949.

Micronesia includes the Mariana, Caroline, Marshall, Gilbert and other islands east of the Philippines. The Carolines, Marshalls and Marianas (except Guam) were mandated territories held by Japan before World War II, but are now under United States Trusteeship. Their combined population is 102,519 (1935); they have six foreign missionaries and 11,575 communicants. The Gilbert Islands, together with the Ellice and Phoenix Islands (Polynesia) have a population of 32,529; nine foreign missionaries and 2,237 communicants.

Melanesia, northeast of Australia, comprises New Caledonia, the New Hebrides, Solomon, Fiji and Admiralty Islands, the Bismarck Archipelago, etc.

Solomons: population, 98,105; 99 foreign missionaries; 11,965 communicants.

New Hebrides: population, 48,914; 82 foreign missionaries; 1,886 communicants.

New Caledonia: population, 61,250; 11 foreign missionaries.

Fiji Islands: population, 259,638; 73 foreign missionaries; 32,364 communicants.

Polynesia, comprising the islands of the Central Pacific between 30° North and 47° South, includes islands all the way from New Zealand to Hawaii, and from the Samoas to French Oceania. The French Oceania group includes the Marquesas, Society, Gambier and Tubuai Islands and the Tuamotu Archipelago. Other islands included in Polynesia are: the Line, Cook, Tonga or Friendly Islands, Easter Island, Ellice or Lagoon, Tokelau or Union, Phoenix and Manihiki Islands, and Niue or Savage Island.

Hawaiian Islands: population, 423,330 (1940); 176 foreign missionaries; 26,011 communicants.

Tonga or Friendly Islands: population, 42,050; 13 foreign missionaries; 5,003 communicants.

Western and Eastern Samoa, with Swains: population, 82,103; 27 missionaries; 17,875 communicants.

Cook Islands with Niue: population, 18,341 (1945); nine foreign missionaries; 2,446 communicants.

French Oceania: population, 55,734; 20 foreign missionaries; 162 communicants.

During World War II, tens of thousands of native peoples of the South Pacific engaged in the struggle, some as fighters, others as laborers, and the islands suffered a great loss of life from actual fighting and from bombings. The result of the war on the Christian communities has been a sorting-out process. Some are noticeably more sceptical in matters of religion. As to church leadership, there is a decided tendency to place more responsibility on native leaders.

In February, 1948, the Southwest Pacific Conference met in Morpeth, New South Wales, and considered the lands of the Pacific south of the equator. About nineteen Australian and New Zealand societies were represented, convened by the National Missionary Councils of Australia and New Zealand. The island groups considered as wholly evangelized include French Oceania, Eastern and Western Samoa, Tonga, the Cook Islands, Savage Island, Naura, Fiji and others. Apart from minority groups in these islands, the population, generally speaking, is either Protestant or Roman Catholic. The Conference report stated that "the South Pacific is regarded as a major missionary obligation of the Australian and New Zealand churches. . . . These agencies are quite adequate to complete the task of evangelizing the native peoples of the South Seas, but the help of other bodies may be necessary before the Indian and other Oriental peoples now settled in the islands can be adequately reached with the gospel." As to minority groups, there are now about 120,000 Indians in Fiji and the Conference decided to suggest to the Missions working in the area, that the National Missionary Society of India be asked to coöperate in missionary effort in Fiji.

The record of the past one and a half centuries of missions in the South Pacific is marvelous. Few fields have shown a more ready response to the gospel. The entire native population of Fiji is now professedly Christian, yet when the first missionaries landed there in 1835, the people were entirely heathen. All denominations working in the South Seas have believed that a Bible in the vernacular languages was essential and, as a result of their convictions, the entire Bible or portions of it have been translated into some 160 languages of the Pacific area. Nineteen languages have the entire Bible, and thirty-four have the complete New Testament. Native Christians have shared with the missionaries in the translation task, and also in spreading the Scriptures throughout the various islands. Many self-supporting churches are now sending out their own people as missionaries to the surrounding islands.

In the larger islands many religious books as well as newspapers have been printed in the vernacular, but other areas still have very little Christian literature, and the percentage of illiterates in the smaller islands is still exceedingly high. The National Missionary Council of Australia has formed the Pacific Christian Literature Society to try to meet the literacy need of the area.

From this Atlas of Alliance Mission fields, the groups in that portion of the island world where Alliance missionary activity is carried on, either by foreign or national workers, are the only islands which will be treated with a somewhat detailed description. We have missionaries working in the Philippine Islands and in Indonesia. Although The Christian and Missionary Alliance has not re-entered Japan for active missionary service, two former missionaries of the Alliance, veterans in fruitful ministries in Japan, have returned to the field and are in official relation as associate missionaries. They represent our society among the Alliance churches in the Hiroshima and Matsuyama areas. In Puerto Rico the work is entirely indigenous, the churches being incorporated as The Christian and Missionary Alliance of Puerto Rico. An aggressive work of evangelism and Bible training is being carried on. The Alliance work in Jamaica has been transferred to the Missionary Church Association of Fort Wayne, Indiana.

Our field in the Philippines lies in the southern part of this extensive group, being chiefly in the Island of Mindanao, including Basilan and other near-by islands, and also in the Sulu Archipelago, especially the islands of Jolo and Siasi.

In the East Indian Archipelago, in a number of the islands of Indonesia, notably Borneo, Celebes, Lombok, Sumbawa, and Dutch New Guinea, as well as in some other smaller islands, our workers, both foreign and national, are carrying on an aggressive and increasingly fruitful ministry. The work in these island fields of the Alliance will be considered in the following pages.

PUERTO RICO

Puerto Rico is bounded on the north by the Atlantic Ocean and on the south by the Caribbean Sea. Santo Domingo is about 45 miles to the west, and St. Thomas 40 miles to the east. The islands of Culebra and Vieques to the east, and Mona to the west, form part of the territory.

Area and Population

Puerto Rico is the easternmost and fourth in size of the Greater Antilles. It is 95 miles long (from east to west) and 35 miles wide, with a coast line of over 300 miles. Its area is 3,435 square miles. The population (estimated 1945) is 2,094,000, of which about three-quarters are white, the remaining quarter Negro. San Juan, the capital, has a population of 169,247.

History and Government

Puerto Rico was discovered and named by Columbus in 1493. Ponce de Leon conquered it for Spain in 1509-11. It was conquered by Major General Miles in the Spanish-American War and ceded to the United States by the Treaty of Paris, December 10, 1898. Puerto Rico is administered under the Organic Act of Puerto Rico (March 2, 1917), which with its amendments granted Puerto Ricans American citizenship and unrestricted suffrage. On August 5, 1947, President Truman signed a bill giving Puerto Rico the right to choose its chief executive, the Governor, by popular vote. The Legislature—a Senate of 19 members and a House of Representatives of 39—is elected for four years by direct vote. The Executive Council consists of the seven heads of the seven executive departments: Justice, Finance, Interior, Education, Agriculture and Commerce, Labor, and Health. The island elects for a term of four years, a Resident Commissioner at Washington with a voice, but no vote, in the House of Representatives.

Climate and Physical Features

The climate is the most healthful of the Western Hemisphere in the tropics. The temperature is moderated by the Northeast Trade Winds. At San Juan the temperature varies little—from 76.5° during January and February to 83.2° during July and August.

Through the middle of the island, from east to west, runs little—from 76.5° during January and February to 83.2° feet, cultivable to the summit.

Resources

The soil is extremely fertile and largely under cultivation. The lower lands to the north are well watered, but irrigation is needed in the south; an extensive system has been constructed by the Government. Sugar production, under modern methods, increased from 35,000 tons in 1899 to one million tons in 1947. The chief exports are sugar, citrus fruits, coconuts, tobacco, coffee, rum, molasses and needlework. Many minerals, including gold, silver, iron, copper, platinum and nickel are found in the island but the only established industry in minerals is that of manganese ore. There are very productive salt works.

Progress

A successful program for industrializing Puerto Rico is being carried on under a government corporation. By offering twelve-year tax exemptions to industries which give promise of being permanent on the island, mainland American businessmen are being enticed to open plants there. Several textile manufacturing plants, a milling firm and a china corporation from the States have already taken advantage of the opportunity to manufacture consumer goods free of all taxes. In 1940 Puerto Rico began a program of hydroelectric power expansion and 23 new electric power plants have been constructed.

Education is free and compulsory. In 1946 there were 364,944 pupils enrolled in public and private schools. The University of Puerto Rico is in Rio Piedras; the Polytechnic Institute in San German.

Although in recent years the United States has invested large sums in Puerto Rico, both in the establishing of strategic military bases and in the building of hundreds of homes and other aid to the people, the results have not been entirely beneficial. Prices and cost of living has increased seriously and large numbers of the people are living in abject poverty and find no satisfactory method of increasing their income or bettering their condition.

Currency and Languages

United States currency is used exclusively.

Spanish is the popular language but most of the people also speak English and the Insular Government fosters intensive instruction in English in the public schools.

Religions and Missionary Occupation

The Roman Catholic religion is dominant but a number of Protestant denominations are established throughout the island. At least twelve United States Societies besides The Christian and Missionary Alliance are working in Puerto Rico.

Because of the widespread poverty among the people and the abnormally high cost of living many churches find it very difficult to adequately support their pastors and few are able to build suitable church buildings without help from the churches in the United States.

Among the larger denominations in Puerto Rico are the Baptists, who in 50 years of ministry have established 44 churches with a membership of 6,000, who now provide about $8,000 a year for the support of the work. However, they and several other denominations have during the years expended large sums of money from the States to build up the work in Puerto Rico. Even today these subsidies are continuing in part to aid in the training of workers and in equipping them for more effective ministries.

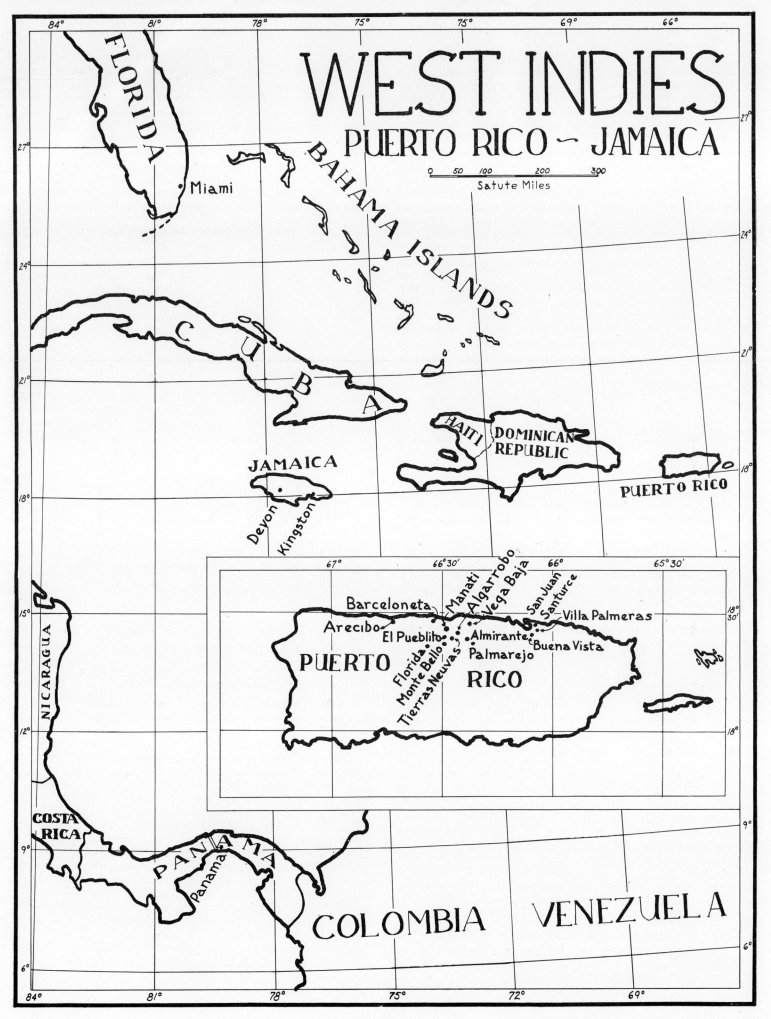

WEST INDIES
PUERTO RICO ~ JAMAICA

FLORIDA

• Miami

BAHAMA ISLANDS

0 50 100   200   300
Satute Miles

C U B A

JAMAICA

HAITI DOMINICAN REPUBLIC

PUERTO RICO

Devon Kingston

NICARAGUA

COSTA RICA

PANAMA

Panama

COLOMBIA VENEZUELA

Barceloneta

Arecibo

Manati Algarrobo Vega Baja

San Juan Santurce Villa Palmeras

El Pueblito Almirante Buena Vista

PUERTO Palmarejo

Florida Monte Bello RICO

Tierras Neuvas

The Protestant churches in Puerto Rico have formed an Association of Evangelical Churches of Puerto Rico. The 16th annual assembly of this association was held in November, 1949. The Christian and Missionary Alliance of Puerto Rico holds membership in this evangelical association.

The Christian and Missionary Alliance

In January, 1900, the work of the Alliance began in this island under unique circumstances. A former priest in the parish of Barceloneta went to Venezuela and was converted there. After God had given him the light of the knowledge of Christ, he returned to Barceloneta and, from a room in his own house opening on the street, delivered his first message. After bitter opposition, his faithful ministry was used of God to the conversion of many, and from this work grew the Puerto Rico Mission of The Christian and Missionary Alliance.

Through all the years the Alliance work in Puerto Rico has been very steadfast and true to the Fourfold Gospel message and ministry. The work has grown under the manifest blessing of God, souls are being saved and new centers are being opened. The loyalty of the pastors and the people to the Alliance message and movement and the self-sacrificing zeal of the pastors, who are for the most part very poorly supported because of the poverty of the majority of the church members, is not exceeded, we believe, in our world-wide work.

The Alliance in Puerto Rico is incorporated under the name of *Alianza Cristiana Y Misionera de Puerto Rico*. There are 13 church centers and 34 other preaching points, with a total responsibility of about 50,000 population. There are nine full-time workers, six of whom are ordained pastors. The principal churches are located in Santurce, Villa Palmeras, Barceloneta, Arecibo, Manati and Vega Baja.

In 1947 a Bible School was opened in Barceloneta, and ten students were enrolled in 1948. A new church called Buena Vista has recently been founded on the Bible School property in the outskirts of Barceloneta. The total membership of Alliance churches in Puerto Rico is about 600, of whom 74 were baptized in 1948. More than 1,200 pupils are enrolled in the 25 Sunday Schools. The church offerings for 1948 totaled nearly $13,000. However, this amount was not sufficient to give the pastors a proper living wage after paying the other operating expenses.

The Alliance in Puerto Rico has weekly radio broadcasts which proclaim the full gospel message.

In earlier years workers were sent down from the States to conduct a Bible School, but after a few years this was discontinued. Three years ago the Puerto Rico Alliance opened the present Bible Institute of which the President of the Alliance is the Superintendent. Ten young men are attending the school and teachers and students are working hard to help erect a concrete block school building on land given to the Alliance for the purpose by the former President before his death. Some funds are being provided through our treasury in New York to aid in the erection of this greatly needed school building. The Alliance in Puerto Rico is seeking a closer bond with the pastors in the States and are asking especially that spiritual leadership be given.

We join with our Puerto Rican co-members in the body of Christ and in the Alliance movement, praying according to the request of their Chairman that "the daily anointing of the Holy Spirit may rest upon every pastor, every Christian, every church, every student, and every teacher."

Translation and Publication Work

Since the work in Puerto Rico is conducted entirely in Spanish there is little need for extensive translation work. However, one of the pastors is aiding in the Spanish editing of the Manual of Visual Teaching, which is published by our publishing company, Christian Publications, Inc., in Harrisburg, Pennsylvania, for sale throughout our churches in Spanish-speaking lands. The churches are active in the distribution of tracts and in the circulation of Spanish editions of Dr. A. B. Simpson's writings and other helpful publications.

The periodical, *El Misionero,* first published by the Alliance in Puerto Rico in 1908, now has a circulation of 1,000. It is evangelistic and doctrinal in content, and also contains news of the work of the churches.

The Church and the Challenge

Other denominations in Puerto Rico whose churches are given goodly financial help from their denominations in the States, seeing the poverty of the Alliance pastors, have offered to take over the work and give it adequate support. The Alliance pastors and churches, however, feel the call of God to the proclamation of the Fourfold Gospel and to continue as an integral part of the Alliance movement throughout the world.

The Fourfold Gospel message has had and is having a worthwhile influence not only in the regular ministries in the Alliance churches but among many of the churches and Christians in the Island. There is need for the building up of the churches and the Bible Institute so that their fruitful ministries can be more widespread and many of the towns and areas now without the evangelical message may be entered with this glorious truth of the all-sufficient Christ.

JAPAN

Japan lies in the north Pacific Ocean, separated from the coast of China and Korea by the Sea of Japan. The terms which ended World War II forced Japan to surrender Manchuria (Manchukuo), Korea, and other seized lands, leaving her four islands: Honshu, Hokkaido, Kyushu and Shikoku.

Area and Population

The four islands now constituting Japan have an area of 147,690 square miles. The fast-growing population numbers over 81 millions, more than half that of the United States, yet Japan's population is crowded into an area about the size of California.

History and Government

The Japanese claim that Emperor Jimmu Tenno founded their empire in 660 B. C. Temporal power was contended for by rival families of *shoguns,* military governors, until 1192 A. D., when the family Minamoto monopolized the title. The office of shogun was abolished by the revolution of 1867-1868, and imperial power was restored through the Emperor Meiji. The fall of feudalism in 1871 abolished the rights of the *samurai,* a class of military retainers of the feudal barons, and this date marked the rise of the upper middle classes. The nineteenth century also saw the reopening of Japan's doors to contacts with the western nations.

By the terms of Japan's surrender in World War II there was to be established a new order of peace, with a democratic government. General Douglas MacArthur was appointed Supreme Commander for the Allied Powers and occupied Japan. No time limit was set for the occupation—it was to continue until democratic objectives had been attained.

A new Constitution, approved by General MacArthur, went into effect May 3, 1947, on which day the General restored the Rising Sun flag to the Japanese people. The new charter opens with a preamble in which the Japanese people "renounce forever" the right to wage war or maintain armed forces. The Constitution strips the Emperor of all pretensions to "divinity" but states that he derives his position from the sovereign will of the people, and reaffirms his line of direct succession within his family. The new Constitution creates a parliamentary regime and establishes a bill of rights for the people, guaranteeing them due process of law without fear of despotic police methods.

Climate

There are frequently heavy snows on the Japan Sea slopes of the mountains of Hokkaido, while the Pacific side, warmed by the Japan Current, enjoys a mild winter. The climate varies considerably; the air temperature on land is high in the summer; rainfall is abundant.

Physical Features and Resources

Volcanic mountains occupy about four-fifths of Japan's area. Sixty miles west of Tokyo the majestic, sacred Fujiyama lifts its white cone to an altitude of 12,425 feet. The Japanese coastline is deeply indented, measuring more than 17,000 miles, and few places are far removed from the mountains or really distant from the sea. Separating the islands of Shikoku and Kyushu from Honshu, the mainland, is the Inland Sea with 700 miles of coastline, and opening both into the Sea of Japan and the Pacific.

More than half of the arable land is devoted to growing rice. Wheat, barley, rye, tobacco, tea, beans and fruits are also grown. Because of the mountains much of the land cannot be cultivated and population experts have variously estimated that if Japan had to depend entirely on indigenous natural resources, the land could probably support not more than 40 or 50 million people on a reasonable standard of living. The mineral supply includes gold, silver, copper, lead, zinc, iron and coal. Prior to World War II the exports in their order of importance were: cotton tissues, raw silk, rayon cloth, machinery, canned goods, silk tissues, knitted goods, potteries, wrought iron, cotton yarns, toys and vegetable oil.

Progress

Japan had made rapid material progress up to the time of the outbreak of World War II. In normal times there were 67 ports open to foreign trade. In spite of the stupendous economic problems of the postwar era, exports from Japan increased from a total of $103,000,000 in 1946 to $258,-000,000 in 1948. The coal output expanded from 20,376,000 metric tons in 1946 to 33,720,000 metric tons in 1948.

Elementary education was and is compulsory, and well over 90 per cent of the people are literate. English is the language of commerce and a required subject in the high schools.

Currency and Language

The monetary unit is the yen, worth 27.7 cents in U. S. currency.

With the exception of the Luchu Islands, no other country claims relationship to the Japanese language, which is difficult to learn and contains many Chinese characters.

Religions

Shinto. This ancient religion, native to Japan, and meaning literally "the way of the gods," was partially dormant after Buddhism was introduced into the country, but it was revived and strengthened when the Imperial House was re-stored in 1868. For many years there was absolute religious freedom in Japan, but for some time prior to World War II Shinto was the recognized national cult and shrine worship was required of all loyal subjects. It was declared to be a patriotic duty and the law placed Christians in all Japanese-held territories in a difficult position. Under the present military occupation, support of Shintoism is prohibited, all faiths are tolerated, and there is freedom of thought and conscience.

The Japanese people have modified and adapted to their own customs the imported religions of Buddhism and Confucianism. At one time both Shinto and Buddhist priests presided over the same altars. The faiths were later officially separated but the people still practice both. (See *Buddhism*, under *Religions, India,* and *Confucianism,* under *Religions, China.*)

Many thousands of Shintoists are also counted as Buddhists, which makes statistics unreliable. However, the Religious Division Headquarters of the Civilian Information and Education section of the Army of Occupation lists the population by religions as follows:

Buddhists	40,000,000
Shintoists (claim)	
Sects	10,000,000
Shrine Shintoists	20,000,000
Catholic adherents	120,000
Protestant adherents	200,000

Missionary Occupation

The Japan Christian Year Book for 1932 listed a total foreign missionary staff of 1,176 and a national staff of 5,779, with over 2,000 organized churches. However, while practically all the denominations were represented, prior to the war, in the larger cities, and some in the smaller cities and towns, the country districts were largely neglected, and it was reported that there were preaching places in only 610 out of the 9,737 villages of Japan. The small area of the country helped to offset this, putting even the remotest villages into fairly close proximity to organized mission work.

Postwar conditions reveal that rural Japan is still largely unserved, that the rural districts are the most open and are therefore a target for Communist propaganda. Latest statistics from the Religious Division Headquarters of the Army of Occupation list 1,200 Catholic missionaries in Japan, and 800 Protestant missionaries, representing the Lutheran and Episcopal Churches, Kyodan (United Church), and miscellaneous groups and societies. Among the latter is the Evangelical Alliance Mission (formerly The Scandinavian Alliance), which has been ministering in Japan since 1891 and which at present has work in a number of districts in central Honshu and neighboring small islands. The Christian and Missionary Alliance opened work in Japan about 1891. The Far Eastern Gospel Crusade is a newer effort, organized in 1947 by ex-Gi's and former Chaplains who had served in the Far East during the war. In April, 1949, this Crusade, in coöperation with four other mission boards, opened the Japan Bible Institute at Higashe Kurume on property that was formerly the private dairy farm of the Emperor.

General MacArthur has been deeply interested in having missionaries come to Japan and in having a widespread distribution of the Scriptures throughout the land. In the fall of 1949 in conversation with Dr. Eric M. North, General Secretary of the American Bible Society, General MacArthur told Dr. North that while he greatly appreciated and valued the distribution in 1949 of nearly four million copies of the Scriptures, including the Bible, New Testament and Scripture portions, he had hoped that thirty million copies might be distributed within a very few years. General Mac-

Arthur is still urging Protestant churches to send large numbers of evangelical missionaries to Japan. Dr. North and many other leaders declare Japan is one of the most strategic centers for missionary service at the present time.

The Christian and Missionary Alliance

From the beginning of the work, about 1891, the principal areas of Alliance ministry have been in the southern portion of the mainland (Island of Honshu), and on the Island of Shikoku. The headquarters of the work was located for many years at Hiroshima. In 1931 was organized the Japan Alliance, an entirely autonomous body. It was agreed that all subsidy from the Mission should cease not later than the close of 1939. The Christian and Missionary Alliance has supported no foreign missionaries in Japan since 1936.

At the time of its inception the Japan Alliance had 20 Japanese workers, 14 organized churches and about 13 unorganized groups. Reports from the field, received in the summer of 1949, listed 17 churches and 21 outstations, with a total of 840 church members. Eleven of the churches are on the Island of Shikoku, and on the mainland are four churches in Hiroshima Province and two in Shimane Province. The Japan Alliance has a parish of 1,500,000 souls in Hiroshima Province, 800,000 in Shimane Province, and 1,300,000 in Ehime Province, Shikoku.

Missionaries working in affiliation with Alliance indigenous churches in Japan write: "We have spoken to far more people in the past four years than in all the other 36 years that we have been here. . . . It is a tremendous hour, a spiritual vacuum, but oh, the reaching out for something durable and true. . . . At the close of the war the Japanese people felt that their gods had failed them. Many have told us, 'I have never felt like folding my hands to them in prayer since.' . . . False cults are springing up in numbers, especially forms of spiritism, and Catholics are increasing rapidly. Buddhism has a hold on the hearts of older people but not on the young. Shintoism and Buddhism are both losing their hold on the people but unless they hear of Christ this leaves them atheists."

In 1948 the Board of Managers of The Christian and Missionary Alliance re-established the official relationship of the two veteran missionaries who had served with devotion and zeal in Japan for years as Alliance missionaries and later on an independent basis. These consecrated women had remained in Japan during the second world war and continued in service after the war ended. Their knowledge of Japan and their Spirit-filled lives and ministries gave them almost unlimited opportunities for witness for Christ among multitudes of hungry-hearted Japanese. During their brief furlough in 1948 they were appointed to represent the Society on their return to Japan among the churches in the area of which Hiroshima and Matsuyama are the centers. There is urgent need in Japan now for many more truly evangelical missionaries to enter the wide-open doors and take Christ to the people and lead many of the people to Christ.

PHILIPPINE ISLANDS

The Philippine Islands are the largest group in the Malay Archipelago. They lie about 200 miles directly east of Indo-China, between 21° 10' and 4° 40' north latitude, and between 116° 40' and 126° 34' east longitude. When it is 9:00 A. M. Monday in San Francisco, it is 1:00 A. M. Tuesday in the Philippines. The Republic of the Philippines comprises a number of groups of islands, including the Sulu Archipelago in the south which reaches almost to Borneo.

Area and Population

The Philippines are a large and strategic island group. There are 7,083 islands extending 1,152 miles from north to south and 682 miles from east to west. Of this number 462 islands have an area of one square mile and over; 11 have an area of more than 1,000 square miles each; 2,441 are named, and 4,642 are unnamed. The largest island, Luzon, contains 40,814 square miles, and Mindanao, the next in size, 36,906 square miles. The total land area of this group is less than 115,000 square miles.

A census taken prior to World War II accounted for a population of almost 18 million, but the figures are not accurate as the tribesmen in the far interior are seldom reached. In 1947 the population was estimated at 19,500,000, as against 10,300,000 in 1918. The cities with their populations are: Manila (623,362); Cebu (142,912); Davao (95,444); Iloilo (88,203); Zamboanga (80,000); Bacolod (57,703); Basilan (57,000); and Baguio (24,122). Quezon City, suburb of Manila, was made the official capital July 17, 1948.

People and History

The peoples of the Philippine Islands are difficult to classify. The inferred history of unknown date is that the land was originally sparsely populated by the ancestors of the present Negritos, few in number and of Pygmy statute. Tradition points to an invasion or succession of invasions by Malay peoples, who drove the Pygmies back into the mountains of the interior. These Negritos or "little blacks" may number today between 30,000 and 50,000. A second invasion of Malays seems to have, in turn, driven the first invaders back into the interior. Later, the Moslem Malays carried on marauding expeditions against their northern neighbors and might have overwhelmed them had not Spain appeared on the scene.

The principal language groups in the Philippines are the Tagalogs, the Cebuano and Illongo Visayans, and the Ilocanos. The Tagalogs are dominant in Luzon and the well-known, copper-colored Igorots are found in the northern interior of that island. Filipino is the name applied to the greater part of the population, which is of mixed race and speech, with evidences of Malay, Papuan, and Mongolian blood. Some of the people are brown, some quite light.

The authentic history of the Philippines begins with their discovery by Magellan in 1521. About 1525 Joffre de Loaisa led an expedition from Spain which reached Mindanao Island and entered either Polloc or some other place in Illana Bay. From that time on the Spaniards made partly successful attempts to gain a foothold in a number of places along the Cotabato River. They had many bloody fights with the Moros (as Moslems are called in the Philippines) up to the latter part of the 19th century, but were not able to subjugate the Maguindanao and Joloano Moros. The only success was the establishment of stone forts or guardhouses in a number of places. In 1570 Manila was captured and made the seat of government by Spain, and in 1810 the Philippine Islands were given representation in the Spanish courts. In April, 1898, war was declared between the United States and Spain, and by treaty of Paris, December 10, 1898, Spain ceded the Philippine Islands to the United States, which agreed to pay 20,000,000 dollars for them.

The islands enjoyed American control in varying degrees until 1942 when the Japanese occupied the country. At that time President Quezon of the Philippine Commowealth, with several members of his Cabinet, went to Washington, D. C., where they established a Government-in-exile. On July 5, 1945, General MacArthur announced that the entire group of the Philippine Islands had been liberated from the Japanese. Representative government was resumed June 9, 1945. On July 4, 1946, the independent Republic of the Philippines was proclaimed in accordance with the act passed by the United States Congress in 1934, providing for Philippine independence by that date. President Truman formally recognized the Philippines as a separate and self-governing nation, announcing the withdrawal and surrender by the United States of all rights of possession, supervision, jurisdiction, control, or sovereignty over the new Republic's territory and people.

Manuel A. Roxas was elected first President of the Republic on April 23, 1946. On the death of President Roxas, President Quirino succeeded to the office on April 15, 1948.

On March 14, 1947, the Philippines and the United States signed a 99-year agreement for American military and naval bases in the islands. The agreement provides that, in the interest of international security, any of the bases may be made available to the Security Council of the United Nations.

Government

For many years the head of the government of the Philippine Islands was a Governor-General appointed by the President of the United States. On November 15, 1935, the Philippine Commonwealth Government was inaugurated. It took the Philippine Islands from under the provision of the Jones Law, passed by the United States Congress in 1916, and made effective a new Constitution of the Commonwealth. The American High Commissioner, appointed by the President of the United States, became the representative of the United States Government in the Philippines, while the Commonwealth elected its own President, Vice-President and Legislature.

Since independence was gained in 1946, the Constitution of the Republic of the Philippines provides for a legislative body called the Congress, with a Senate of 24 members and a House of Representatives which has a theoretical membership of 120, but actually 96 members. The President and Vice-President are elected for a term of four years, and the President may be re-elected for one additional term only. The Cabinet consists of 13 members.

Freedom of the press, religion and right of assembly are guaranteed in the Bill of Rights. Women have suffrage on equal terms with the men. The development and exploitation of forces of potential energy and other natural resources is under the control of the State, and is limited to citizens of the Philippines or to corporations of which 60 per cent of the capital is owned by such citizens. However, by an amendment to the Constitution, the right to own and operate public utilities, for a limited period, was extended to citizens of the United States.

Climate

The climate throughout these islands is tropical. The average temperature ranges from 72° to 96° Fahrenheit. The dry season of the southern islands of the group is from December to the middle of April. While the nights are not excessively hot, yet their temperature seldom falls below 70 degrees. The rains in the northern islands are heaviest in July, August and September, and lightest in February and March. Typhoons occur frequently in the summer but are mostly confined to the northern half of the group, the southern part being seldom visited. Warnings are sent out from Manila when storms are approaching.

Physical Features

The geographer's description of the coastal plains of the Philippines is brief: Between the mountains in the center

and the sea, lie great fertile, well-watered tropical plains with numerous and swift rivers which are navigable for small steamers. The missionary, on the spot, writes: "A small boat took us into shallow water, but it was necessary to wade through 300 yards of muck and eel grass. Ashore, we followed a narrow trail past crocodile-infested swamps, snake-infested thickets, and saw-grass that slashed our shins."

The topography of the islands is magnificent viewed from the air. The mountains in the interior of the larger islands rise to a height of from 5,000 to 10,000 feet above sea level. There are 20 more or less active volcanoes. Mount Apo, 9,610 feet, in Mindanao, and Mayan Volcano, 7,943 feet, in Albay, are the most famous. The Philippines have a coast line of 14,407 miles, greater than that of the entire United States.

Resources

About 39,657,000 acres, or 65 per cent of the total area of the islands, are suitable for cultivation, but less than 40 per cent of this area is actually under cultivation. There are approximately 46 million acres of forests, which provide cabinet and construction lumber as well as large quantities of gums, resins, vegetable oils, bamboo, dyebarks and dyewoods. Rubber is being cultivated, also the Cinchona tree for quinine.

The chief agricultural products are rice, Manila hemp, copra, sugar cane, corn and tobacco. The principal fruit is pineapple and other tropical fruits are also grown.

There are about 75 square miles of coal fields and the islands are rich in other minerals also: namely, gold, silver, lead, zinc, copper, iron, asbestos, petroleum, chromite and manganese. Pearl fishing is engaged in in several localities.

Progress

The Philippines have 21 fine harbors and eight land-locked straits. The ports of entry are Manila, Iloilo, Zamboanga, Jolo and Davao. Manila Bay, with an area of 770 square miles and a circumference of 120 miles, is the finest harbor in the Far East.

Education is free, and is conducted in English. Government institutions include: the Normal School, the School of Arts and Trades, the Nautical School, and the Central Luzon Agricultural School. There are also provincial trade schools. There are 10 universities in Manila, one of them restricted for women. Among those in Manila are the State-supported University of the Philippines, and the Dominican University of Santo Tomas, founded in 1611. The Silliman University at Dumaguete, established by the Presbyterians, is now maintained by the coöperative support of several Protestant societies. In 1903 the literacy rate was 10 per cent; in 1939 it had reached 48.8 per cent. Since the close of World War II, private high schools have been opened everywhere, and the institutions of higher learning find it difficult to adequately care for the increased enrollments. Newspapers are published in many languages and dialects including English, Tagalog, Ilocano, and Chinese.

Under the supervision of American advisors a definite road system has been established to develop a national system of trunk highways and a network of roads feeding them. The war years left the country with much to do in repairing roads and bridges and it will take time to realize all the plans for improvement. One missionary wrote of traveling over a so-called improved road, but the ruts in it were a foot deep and it was not yet bridged at the rivers.

Currency

The monetary unit is the peso, worth 49.7 cents in U. S. currency. The peso is divided into pesetas and centavos;

20 centavos to one peseta; 100 centavos to one peso. Coins are minted in Manila and treasury certificates and bank notes are issued in denominations of from one to five hundred pesos. For all practical purposes the value of the peso is 50 cents U. S., that is $1.00 U. S. equals 2 pesos.

Languages and Tribes

The national language is Tagalog (a Malayan dialect), but the teaching of English is compulsory and it is the common language of both government and private schools, being spoken by about five million of the people. Spanish was formerly the official language but today only about 500,000 of the people speak it. However, by Congressional action Spanish is again to be taught in the secondary schools. In all, 87 distinct languages and dialects are spoken in the islands. The Moros of the Sulu Archipelago have a native literature, and several of their dialects are said to show a certain affinity to the Sanskrit language, which has led to the theory that the ancestors of these proud, fierce Moslems may have come from North India.

Of the provinces where the Alliance is working, 11 dialects are spoken in Zamboanga Province; 13 in Cotabato Province; eight in Davao Province, and five dialects in Sulu Province. Alliance missionaries and national workers use the following languages: English, Cebuano, Ilongo, Maguindanao Moro, Manobo, Subanun, Tausug Moro, and Yakan Moro. Additional languages used only by national workers include: Atao, Bagobo, Bajao Moro, Bilaan, Ilocano, Kalibugan, Maruri, Samal Moro, Tagabili, Tiruray, Tagalog, Tuboy and Zamboangueño.

Religions

The religion of Islam and Islamic culture was brought to the Philippine Islands in the 14th century by Raja Bayinda and Makdum, an Arabian scholar, who are believed to have landed in Buansa, west of Jolo, in the year 1380. Some years later, other Moslem leaders came and pushed on with their work to near-by islands and provinces. Sariph Mohammed Kabungsuan introduced Islam to Cotabato Province more than a generation before Magellan discovered the Philippines. These leaders rapidly made converts among the native pagans, and Islam spread throughout Mindanao and Sulu. (See *Islam,* under *India.*)

Of the many pagan tribes, each has its own dialect and distinctive customs, but all of them are animists. (See *Animism,* under *Africa.*)

The Roman Catholic religion, introduced into the islands in 1571 by Franciscan monks and Jesuit missionaries, with methods that often approached coercion, now has a firm hold upon two-thirds of the total population of the islands. The Independent Filipino Church was founded in 1902 by Father Gregorio Aglipay. His followers are called Aglipayans. They claim that science is superior to Biblical tradition, deny the possibility of miracles, and conceive God as the invisible Father, with one essence and as a single Person. Their ritual resembles that of the Roman Church. (See *Roman Catholicism,* under *Latin America.*)

Several Protestant denominations and societies are working in the Philippines, and some of them coöperate in maintaining the Union Theological Seminary. Seventh Day Adventists and Jehovah's Witnesses are also working in the islands.

The Philippine government considers the inhabitants under two categories only: non-Christians, which include both pagans and Moslems; and *Cristianos,* including both Catholics and Protestants.

The following table gives the latest estimate of the population by religions:

Roman Catholics	13,500,000
Aglipayans	3,500,000
Protestants	600,000
Moslems	600,000
Pagans	500,000
Buddhists and Shintoists	100,000
Others	700,000

Missionary Occupation

The Protestant missionaries in the Philippines represent some fifteen societies and include the following: Baptists, Presbyterians, Congregationalists, Episcopalians, Lutherans, Mennonites, Methodists, Pentecostal Societies, the Salvation Army, the United Brethren, the Church of God, the United Missionary Society and The Christian and Missionary Alliance. Chaplains and Christian soldiers in the U. S. Army who were stationed in the Philippines during World War II became interested in the opportunities for service for the Lord in the islands. Since the close of the war they have organized definite missionary work here and in Japan. Their society is the Far Eastern Gospel Crusade, and "Febias" the name of their school in the Philippines, this name being formed from the initial letters of the full name—Far Eastern Bible Institute and Seminary. At the beginning of the 20th century there were but a few members of Protestant churches. Today Protestant adherents in the Philippines number about 600,000. The national churches, notably those of the Alliance, have developed the spirit of evangelism to a marked degree.

The effort to merge all Protestant churches in the Philippines dates back to 1901 when American missionaries set up an association known as the Evangelical Union. The Union accomplished little in the way of church unification, but it defined areas in which the denominations were to work; the Alliance going to Mindanao and Sulu. In 1924 another group known as the United Church of Manila was formed by American missionaries and Filipino Christian leaders. This was followed by the formation of the National Christian Council, another attempt at union. In 1929 the churches of the United Brethren, Presbyterian, and Congregational Missions became the United Evangelical Church of the Philippine Islands. In 1939 the Philippine Federation of Evangelical Churches was formed. In April, 1948, still another attempt at union was made, called The United Church of Christ in the Philippines. Three groups merged to form this new union: namely, the United Evangelical Church of the Philippines, the Philippine Methodist Church, and the Evangelical Church in the Philippines. The union includes the following denominations: Presbyterian, United Brethren, Congregational, Church of Christ (Disciples), Methodist, United Church and Iglesia Evangelica Unida de Cristo.

The Christian and Missionary Alliance

The Christian and Missionary Alliance opened work in the Philippine Islands in 1902 on the Island of Mindanao, the second largest island of the Archipelago. In August of 1903 the work was suddenly suspended when the only missionary died of cholera. In 1908 the work was again begun on the island in the city of Zamboanga. For several years two married couples were the only missionaries of the Alliance here, but from 1923 until the outbreak of World War II, reinforcements were added from year to year, bringing the total number of missionaries up to 19 in 1940. When conditions became disturbed in Indo-China early in the war, some of the newer missionaries there were transferred to assist in the Philippines, making a staff of 30 adults who, with their

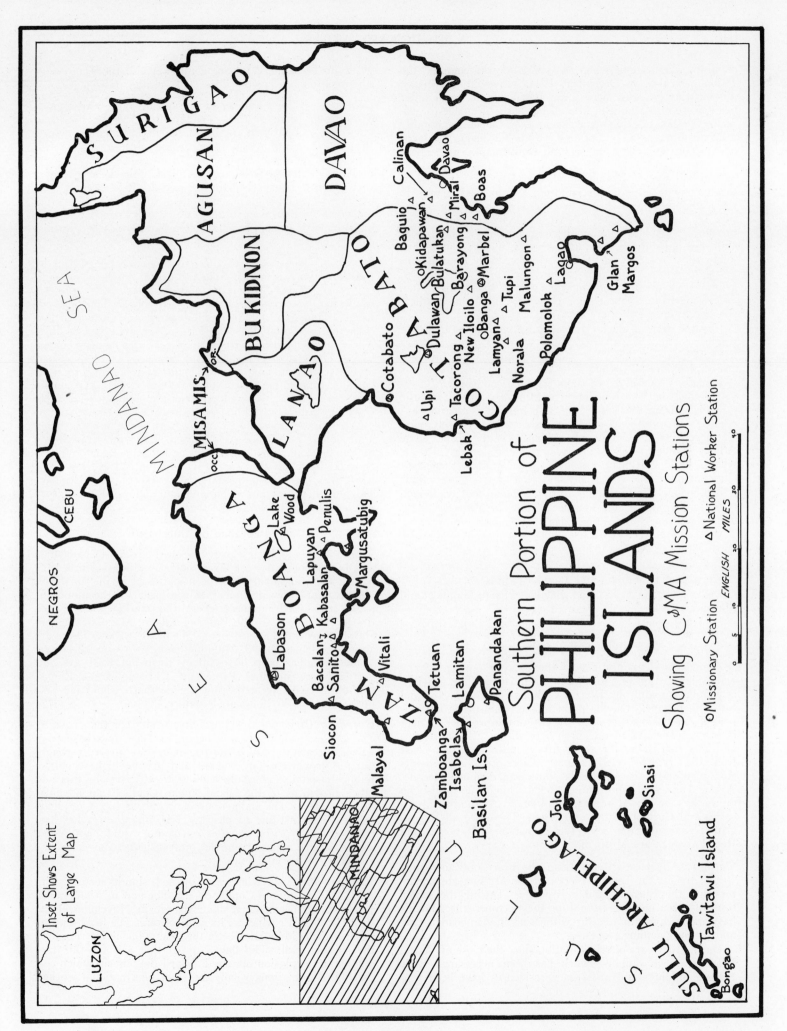

Southern Portion of
PHILIPPINE ISLANDS

Showing C$MA Mission Stations

○Missionary Station   △National Worker Station

ENGLISH MILES

Inset Shows Extent of Large Map

LUZON

MINDANAO

SURIGAO

AGUSAN

DAVAO

BUKIDNON

MISAMIS OR.
OCC.

LANAO

COTABATO

Calinan
Baguio
Davao
Miral
Boas
Okidapawan
Dulawan
Bulatukan
Barayong
New Iloilo
Banga ○Marbel
Tacorong
Lamyan
Tupi
Malungon
Norala
Polomolok
Lagao
Glan
Margos
○Cotabato
Upi
Lebak

SULU SEA

MINDANAO SEA

NEGROS

CEBU

ZAMBOANGA
Lake Wood
Lapuyan
Penulis
Margusatubig
Labason
Bacalan
Kabasalan
Sanito
Vitali
Tetuan
Lamitan
Panandakan
Zamboanga
Isabela
Basilan Is.
Siocon
Malayal

MINDANAO

SULU ARCHIPELAGO
Jolo
Siasi
Tawitawi Island
Bongao

children, were caught when the storm of war engulfed the Philippines also, in December, 1941. Five other Alliance missionaries en route across the Pacific, to or from other fields, were also caught in Manila Harbor and unable to proceed. All but one missionary couple of the entire number went through the horrors of long internment during the Japanese occupation. The one couple who escaped internment remained successfully hidden deep in the jungle, cared for by the tribespeople among whom they labored. In spite of the harrowing experiences endured, all our missionaries in the Philippines were spared to experience the joy of liberation. By the close of 1948 our staff in the islands had reached the number of 28, including those on furlough. There were eight mission stations, 49 church centers, and 260 outstations (only 138 outstations in 1947). More recently the missionary staff has been still further reinforced by the addition of a number of missionaries allocated to the Philippines when evacuation from China became necessary. This has made it possible to open still more stations.

In some parts of northern Mindanao, and at one point in southeast Mindanao, the American Board (Congregational) has missionaries. The Association of Baptists has missionaries in Bukidnon Province; the Episcopal Church maintains two stations, one in Zamboanga Province and one in Cotabato Province. The remainder of Mindanao Island and the other islands to the south, with a combined population exceeding one and one-half million, are dependent largely upon The Christian and Missionary Alliance for the gospel. The Alliance field divides naturally into the following districts where, besides Roman Catholics and nominal Protestant Christians, the following pagan and Moslem tribes are found:

Zamboanga West: pagans of the Subanun and Kalibugan tribes; also Yakan and Tausug Moros (Moslems).

Margosatubig: Subanun and Tuboy pagans.

West Cotabato: Tagabili and Tiruray pagans; Maguindanao Moros.

Koronadal-Ala Valleys: Bilaan pagans.

Kidapawan: Manobo and Bagobo pagans.

Davao: pagans of the Atao, Bagobo, Bilaan, Mandaya and Mansaca tribes.

Sulu: Moslems of the Tausug, Samal and Bajao tribes.

Province of Zamboanga

Zamboanga Province lies in the western portion of the peninsular section of the island of Mindanao. The province is populated mainly by Roman Catholics, Yakan Moros and Subanun pagans. On the point of the peninsula is the seaport of Zamboanga, the principal city of the province. There is an organized Alliance Church here with a Filipino pastor. Work is carried on for about fifteen miles up either coast from this city. Travel is by auto. There are 12 main points from which work is conducted: Baliwasan, Sinonoc, Recodo, Ayala, Talisayan, San Ramon Penal Colony, and Busugan on the west coast; Mercedes, Taluksangay, Catumbal, Monicahan and Curuan on the east coast. These are all Roman Catholic communities with the exception of Sinonoc and Recodo, which are Moslem.

Tetuan About two miles from the heart of Zamboanga City, in Tetuan, is located the Mission Headquarters and the Ebenezer Bible Institute. During the school term of seven months, from June to December, the students have many opportunities for witnessing in Zamboanga City and the surrounding places.

During the years of rehabilitation since the close of World War II, much building work has been necessary. Bible School buildings and missionary residences have been pro-

vided in Tetuan. With some mission aid, the Zamboanga congregation has erected a new chapel and parsonage.

Labason, Sindangan For a number of years prior to the war, a graduate of the Bible Institute was stationed in Labason in northern Zamboanga Province. Because of limited missionary personnel, the urgent calls for a resident missionary couple had to go unheeded until early in 1947. Labason is important: first, it is the center of a vast pagan territory (Subanun); second, it is a center from which to work among the multitude of incoming settlers from the northern provinces; third, a privately-owned Christian high school is located here with its doors wide open to missionary endeavor.

Lamitan, Basilan The island of this name is two hours' run by motor launch from the city of Zamboanga southward. By an act of Congress in 1948, the city of Basilan was created, including the entire island and adjacent islands, and taking in the former municipality of Isabella and the municipal districts of Lamitan and Maluso. These municipalities were formerly a part of Zamboanga City. The seat of government of the new city of Basilan is in the former municipality of Isabella. Basilan City now has an estimated population of 57,000, about 30,000 of whom are Yakan Moros. The remainder of the population is largely Cristiano with a sprinkling of Tausug Moros from Sulu.

Work among the Yakan Moros was begun in 1937 when a missionary couple entered Lamitan. Later they transferred to Panandakan, a Yakan center, and a school for boys was opened. Through the war years and until July, 1948, the work was carried on by national workers. A missionary couple is now stationed at Panandakan and a girls' dormitory has been added to the school there.

Province of Cotabato

Cotabato is the largest province on the island of Mindanao and has a population of about half a million. Until 1929 no Alliance missionary had been stationed in this province, but there are now a number of stations. Of the numerous pagan tribes, each numbers several thousand people and each has its own dialect. The Bagobo, Bilaan, Manobo, Tagabili and Tiruray are the most important of the tribes. There are approximately 150,000 Maguindanao Moros in this area. Some work has been done among them but with few converts. Many nominal Protestant Christians and Roman Catholics have migrated from the northern islands to take up homesteads in Cotabato Province.

Cotabato City In this port city, capital of the province, work was begun in 1929 as a base from which to reach the Moro and pagan tribes scattered throughout the province. Government and private high schools, a public hospital, and roads leading to all parts of this and other provinces of the island, make Cotabato an advantageous center. The indigenous church here has a graduate of the Bible Institute as pastor. His ministry reaches hospital patients, prison inmates, elementary and high school students, and a large number of transients who carry the gospel back to their homes.

Kidapawan This work was opened simultaneously with that of Cotabato City. The new mission launch, just arrived, began its maiden voyage in November, 1929, with Cotabato Province as its destination. The head-hunting pagans of the Manobo tribe in the forests of the interior were the specific goal. The day after setting sail for this new outpost, an explosion occurred aboard the launch, which cost the life of a missionary lady and that of a national worker, besides the loss of the launch. However, three weeks after the tragedy, an entrance was made into the Manobo tribe. Within a year the gospel had reached many interior villages. An adjoining tribe had also heard and welcomed the message. Manobo converts trudged over mountain trails through the dense forests to carry the Good News beyond their provincial boundary to the pagan Ataos of Davao. They believed God with simple faith and signs of healing and deliverance followed. The gospel spread rapidly throughout most of the pagan areas in both Cotabato Province and Davao. Hundreds were saved and baptized. Testings came,—sickness, death, drought, famine, the recent war and wicked lawlessness. Out of the fires have come true, noble Christians. The Kidapawan district is linked with the Davao district and the whole is subdivided into five sub-districts for geographical, linguistic and practical convenience.

Marbel, A mission residence was built here in 1948, and
Koronadal there is a nucleus of a promising church.
Marbel presents a unique opportunity among the 1,000 young people who come from various towns to attend the two high schools here. Of the 150 to 175 people who attend the church services, at least two-thirds are young people.

Marbel is in the Koronadal Valley. From Cotabato City the national highway passes through Dulawan and cuts a southeastern course to Dadiangas on Sarangani Bay. The southern two-thirds of the area served by this highway is known as the Koronadal Valley. Southeast from Marbel, about nine miles, one is ushered into the Ala Valley. In 1940 the Koronadal-Ala Valleys were opened by the government to home seekers from the northern islands. They have become a melting pot for thousands of Cristianos. In 1940 one of our missionary ladies, stationed in Glan on Sarangani Bay, began making frequent, hazardous trips across the stormy bay to penetrate the valleys and reach their shepherdless immigrants. In 1941 missionaries entered the valleys from Dulawan. A Filipino pastor was placed in Lagao, near Dadiangas, and the valleys teeming with homesteaders were his responsibility. Missionaries gave him aid from time to time. The war broke, but nevertheless some of the Filipino pastors and deaconesses toiled all through those terrible years, working in the valleys despite much suffering. The number of established churches there today are the fruit of their labors.

Banga, Banga was occupied as a mission station in
Ala Valley 1949. The practically unreached Tagabili tribe is the immediate goal of the workers here. The National Land Development Company and the Philippine Economic Progress Association are pioneering from Banga into new territory, and a trail leads from Banga to Lamyan in the heart of the vast Tagabili pagan area.

Dulawan Dulawan, a distance of four hours by motor launch up the Cotobato River from Cotabato City, is the center of the Maguindanao Moro tribe. Little was done toward evangelizing this tribe until 1938 when a missionary couple was placed here. A foothold was secured and a national pastor was called. Only a small portion of the congregation was Moro, but the chapel stood as a lighthouse in a Moslem stronghold, up to the outbreak of the war. After the close of the war a Filipino pastor and his wife were stationed here. They were the only gospel messengers for this entire tribe until a missionary couple, transferred from China, was appointed here in 1949. The Gospel of John in the Maguindanao Moro dialect was published in 1946.

Lagao, Buayan Another missionary couple, transferred from China, opened Lagao as a mission station in the fall of 1949. There is a church here which has been recognized as the mother church of the Koronadal and Ala Valleys, a church from which the light has gone out to many other towns. Located near Dadiangas, Lagao will be a center for Short Term Bible School work in addition to other ministries.

Sulu Archipelago

The population of the Sulu Archipelago, according to the census of 1939, was 247,000. In 1948 it was estimated at 270,000. Of this number 263,000 are Moslems; 4,000 are Cristianos; 3,000 are Chinese, and there are about a dozen Americans.

Jolo The estimated population of Jolo Island is 130,000, and of Jolo City, 20,000. The first resident missionary came to Jolo about 1923. A chapel was erected in 1934. Two missionary families and three Filipino pastors are now laboring in this area. The largest baptismal service in Sulu history was held in Jolo in April, 1948, when 26 believers took this step. There are approximately 250 baptized believers in the province. More than 50 of them live in remote regions.

Siasi This island, opened as a mission station some years prior to World War II, was reoccupied as a station in 1949. Siasi District has a population of 30,000 and Siasi Town, 3,500. To the south are many other islands, the largest of which is Tawi Tawi. A newly acquired mission launch, to replace the one lost as a result of the war, will help to speed the gospel to those islands of the Sulu Archipelago, where commercial launches do not call. The population of this area is predominantly Moslem, with a few Roman Catholics. The local dialect of Siasi is Samal, which is somewhat different from the Joloano dialect. English is largely used in Siasi proper. Many of the Samals mingle a kind of ancestor-worship with the religion of Islam. Some have professed faith in Christ but cannot seem to forsake their Moslem and pagan practices, apparently thinking they can follow more than one religion at a time. In North Ubian, a rather remote district, there has been a remarkable turning to God recently and several have been baptized and dedicated their children to God. These people were all strong Moslems, and this is the greatest turning to God yet seen among Moslems in the Philippines.

Province of Davao

Believers of the Manobo tribe who had heard the gospel for the first time only one year before, visited Baguio in Davao Province in 1930. In 1934, as a result of their witness, the first three were baptized there. The three withstood ridicule and persecution, and when an epidemic struck the region, they responded to the call of the pagans to pray for their sick. The sick were healed, the people wondered at the power of God, and from that time on there was interest in the Gospel. In 1935 there were 26 baptized there. A woman blind for nine years was healed in answer to prayer, and thereafter about 200 people gathered together regularly to hear more about God.

Davao City After the war (1948), a missionary couple was stationed here with a view to reaching the untouched tribes to the north. The work in the city itself is presenting unlimited opportunities to reach young people. The various Sunday schools conducted throughout the city are overflowing their quarters, and the Chinese population in Davao is presenting wide open doors for evangelism.

Translation and Publication Work

The entire Bible is available in Spanish, Cebuano, Ilongo, Tagalog, Ilocano, Bicol and Pangasinan, and is being sold by Alliance workers in all of these languages except Pangasinan. The New Testament has been translated in Pampangan and Samareno but very few who speak these dialects are found in the areas where the Alliance is working. Our missionaries have translated the following portions, which the American Bible Society has published: Gospel of Luke in Tausug Moro (Joloano) dialect, both in Romanized and Arabic script; Gospel of Luke and selected passages in the Manobo dialect; Gospel of Luke in the Subanun dialect; Gospel of John in Maguindanao Moro dialect.

Some 5,000 copies of Luke in the Tausug Moro dialect were distributed before the war. Since the war new editions of the Gospel of Luke both in the Romanized and Arabic script have been printed. A book of thirty Joloano hymns printed before the war has been republished. There is a great need for the entire New Testament in Joloano and for at least a Gospel in the Samal Moro dialect.

The Ebenezer Book Room at Zamboanga has done a large volume of business in both English and Spanish literature. Bibles in English and the dialects, hymnbooks, commentaries, concordances and Christian fiction have all been sold. A small printing press has been secured to take care of the demand for tracts. Two national believers have translated several tracts into the Ilocano and Visayan dialects and these have been widely circulated. As a Professor in a Near East University said, "No other agency can penetrate so deeply, witness so daringly, abide so persistently, and influence so irresistibly as the printed page."

Schools and Literacy Campaigns

The Ebenezer Bible Institute, located in Tetuan near the city of Zamboanga, was opened in 1928, being organized from the Ebenezer Schools. Because of the war it was closed in 1942, but was reopened in 1946. In 1947 there were 95 students enrolled, but limited accommodations have made it necessary to reduce the number of admissions. In 1948 the enrollment was 57, with a faculty of five missionary and four national teachers. Since 1930, 94 students have graduated from the school. A good percentage of them are in active Christian service in the Mission and are supported chiefly by national church funds. Throughout the five months' vacation period, undergraduates are urged to seek opportunities for service and many villages have been reached through their ministry. The student body organized, in 1946, the Ebenezer Missionary Society, which has met weekly to make the students acquainted with the needs in their own country and in other fields. This Society financed four undergraduates who were out in service during the vacation months, and it has also supported a field evangelist.

Three primary schools were conducted last year with a total enrollment of 125. A dormitory for Yakan Moslem girls has been opened at Panandakan in order that Yakan girls as well as boys may attend the Mission school there. Yakan parents are willing to send their boys to the school as day pupils, but it is difficult to get the girls. Yakan boys who have gone from this school to Ebenezer Bible Institute have had little chance for Christian marriage within their own tribe. The Yakan girls' dormitory will tend to correct this situation.

Literacy campaigns are being carried on in the various districts systematically and a body of believers who are able to study the Word for themselves is being built up.

The largest enrollments and the speediest results have been seen in the Short Term Bible Schools and the Daily Vacation Bible Schools which together minister to both adults and children. In 1948, 34 Short Term Bible Schools, with an average of 11 days' duration each, were conducted in six different languages and had a total enrollment of 2,474, as against an enrollment of 850 the preceding year. The courses taught included Bible, Doctrine, Personal Evangelism, and Teacher Training. The Daily Vacation Bible Schools numbered 36, with a total enrollment of 1,449.

The Church and the Challenge

Within ten years after the gospel had entered one area of pagan head-hunters in the Philippines, that district had become fully self-supporting. Immediately after World War II, conditions on the field were such that it was necessary for all the national pastors and deaconesses to receive mission aid. In spite of all the Filipino church had suffered, the believers were looking forward to a National Church that would be supported by national offerings. Before the close of 1946 a number of churches had again become self-supporting and others followed in 1947. In February, 1947, the National Workers' Conference was organized, composed of all pastors and deaconesses supported by national funds. From the reopening of the work in 1945 to the close of 1947, approximately two-thirds of the Bible School graduates, who were actively engaged in Christian work, were being supported by national funds.

Reports for the year 1948 listed 56 organized and 98 unorganized churches; 146 Sunday schools with a total enrollment of 8,380; a total church membership of 4,349 baptized believers; 2,770 inquirers; church offerings that totaled the equivalent of $20,656.51 in U. S. money. There were 57 full-time national workers, of whom 15 were women. At least forty places in the Alliance areas were manned by Filipino workers.

Workers trained in the Ebenezer Bible Institute are manning the Zamboanga coastal towns of *Siocon, Malayal* and *Limpapa* on the west coast; and *Vitali, Sanito, Bakalan, Titay* and *Kabasalan* on the east coast. These workers are ministering to nominal Christians, Roman Catholics and Subanun pagans. Between Zamboanga City and these points are hundreds of settlements where thousands of Subanuns and Samal Moros are still unreached.

On *Basilan Island* a student-pastor took charge of the work in *Lamitan* in 1946. A 5,000-peso chapel was erected in 1948, the people themselves paying most of the cost. In December, 1947, a teacher-pastor from the Bible Institute was stationed in *Isabella,* a former United States naval base. This is a strong Roman Catholic center, but the response of the people is good. A substantial chapel and parsonage have been erected. *Maluso,* a third Cristiano town on the island, has been manned since the close of the war by national workers. The present missionary personnel, American and national, on Basilan Island, is inadequate to properly evangelize the Yakan Moros and the colonies of immigrants from the northern islands.

Margosatubig is the name of both a district and a town. The town, located on Margosatubig Bay, is a center for work among the pagan Subanuns and Roman Catholics. The station was opened in 1914 by a missionary couple who continued their ministry there during the war, as long as was possible. At the close of 1947 there were 21 churches in the district, most of them under lay leaders supported by the local churches or by their own labors. At the beginning of 1948, in addition to the faithful lay preachers, there were seven appointed national workers, three of them supported by national district funds.

Another advance was made in the district in December,

1947, when a worker was stationed in *Lake Wood*, deep in the mountains among the Subanun tribe, of whom few in that area have ever heard the gospel.

In the Margosatubig district, the annual Camp Meeting and Short Term Bible School are eagerly anticipated by hundreds of believers. For four weeks daily classes are held, with evangelistic services each night. The erection of a new district chapel is now being planned.

In *Cotabato Province* the town of *Parang*, north of Cotabato City, is in charge of a Bible School graduate, who from here can reach the Visayan and Ilocano tribes as well as the Maguindanao and Maranao Moros. *Lebak*, to the south of Cotabato City, has an established church, and the national worker here has unusual opportunities for reaching large groups of pagan Manobos. *Kling*, still farther south, is manned by Bible School students during the vacation months. The people here are nominal Christians and Roman Catholics. *Upi* in a mountainous district has a church and a national worker who reaches not only a colony of homesteaders here, but also has access from here to 17,000 of the pagan Tiruray tribe.

Baguer, Salunayan, Maganoy, Labolabo and *Lambayang* are outstations of the mission station of Dulawan.

Down on the Sarangani Bay, the port of Dadiangas serves the *Koronadal* and *Ala Valleys*. In 1948 this growing city became the seat of government for the newly-created municipality of Buayan, which includes Glan across the bay, and the Koronadal Valley up to and including Tupi. *Glan* and *Margos*, both on the same side of Sarangani Bay, are manned by men and women from the Bible Institute. Roman Catholics and Bilaan pagans can be reached from these two centers. Growing churches are in both places and several smaller churches are in the outlying districts of Margos. From the mission station of Lagao the gospel is carried to the outstations of *Dadiangas, Bula, Silway, Klinan* and *Upper Klinan*, in each of which is an unorganized church.

Malungan, about 21 miles from Lagao in the hills of southern Cotabato, has a church in the Bilaan pagan tribe, and with the help of lay leaders, the national worker is seeing church groups spring up far in the interior. The gaps are being filled up between our districts, for the pastor here, in evangelizing northward, has contacted outstations of our Kidapawan pastors who are working southward from their district. The Kidapawan workers among the Manobos, and the Malungan workers among the Bilaans, have now penetrated the Tagacola pagan tribe. Regular services are being held in that and another new tribe, the Kalagan. *Polomoloc* has shown an unprecedented openness to the Gospel since the war, and a Bible Institute graduate is stationed in this Roman Catholic center which previously resisted the message. *Tupi* was occupied by a missionary couple in 1941, but the war prevented their plans for supervising the district. In 1947 a missionary lady and a national deaconess took up the work here, and in 1948 a second missionary lady was added to the staff. A large number of young people from the two local high schools have been won to the Lord and there is a growing church besides work in the four outstations of *Polunoling, Kipalbig, Sulit,* and *Palkan*. However, because of increased opportunities in Marbel, the two missionaries were transferred to that place and a national worker is continuing in Tupi.

National pastors are located in *Norala, Lamyan*, and *Tacarong*. Norala is a growing agricultural center, and Tacarong on the national highway is on the crossroads leading to Koronadal Valley, Ala Valley, and to Buluan and Dulawan among the Maguindanao Moros.

In the Kidapawan-Davao district, national workers occupy the following centers: *Miral, Kidapawan, Bulatukan, Goma, Baracatan, Baguio, Calinan, Tomayong,* and *Baraiong*. More than a hundred other points in the district are reached by lay workers. The lay workers meet for monthly instruction classes and continue their volunteer services with unabated interest as from the beginning, 18 years ago. This district is fully self-supporting. The local churches bear the entire burden of supporting the twelve national workers located here. Allowances for the workers have been increased from 100 to 200 per cent, and now two additional workers, making a total of 14, have been appointed to this district, and definite plans are being made to enter two unoccupied pagan tribes.

In the Sulu Archipelago, the Jolo Church has been self-supporting since 1936 except for one year after the recent war when mission help was needed. In *Siasi* a permanent chapel was built in 1925 and burned by the Japanese in 1942. Plans have been made to rebuild this chapel. The Siasi Church hopes to be self-supporting this year (1949). Jolo and Siasi are mission stations; Sisangat has a national worker. Sunday schools are conducted in the Jolo City suburbs of San Raymundo, Tulay and Tindalaud; and in Musu and Sibalang, near Sisangat. The total attendance in the Sunday schools of this area is about 450. The prospects for advance in Sulu are splendid, but more workers are needed. Instead of two missionary families and three Filipino pastors, there should be at least four missionary couples and many national workers. The second great need is for further translations of the Scriptures, and also for proper marine transportation among the islands. A Christian dormitory in Jolo is needed for high school students who come from the outlying districts.

New opportunities have arisen throughout the areas for which the Alliance is responsible. Tens of thousands of Cristiano colonists—Roman Catholics and nominal Protestant Christians—have migrated from the northern islands to the island of Mindanao. This is a result of the National Land Settlement Administration Act which went into effect in 1936. The immigrants have taken up homesteads in the various provinces of the island, and their entrance into these pagan and Moslem areas has greatly multiplied the problems and responsibilities of missionary work.

Unparalleled opportunities for widespread evangelism and Bible conference ministries in English as well as in certain tribal languages make this a momentous hour in our southern Philippine field. The missionary staff was reinforced in 1949 by the transfer of 16 missionaries from the China fields. A great door and effectual is open to us in Mindanao and in the Sulu Archipelago. In humble dependence upon God for His utmost enabling we should buy up these opportunities and aid the Mission and the Church in this Alliance field to press forward into the fulfillment of the task that a people gathered out of all the tribes shall be ready for the return of Christ Jesus our Lord.

INDONESIA

Indonesia is the name now applied to the island empire which was formerly called the Dutch East Indies, and later the Netherlands East Indies. The island group includes most of the East Indies Archipelago, known also as the Malay Archipelago. The term Indonesia was first used by a German scholar in a book written many years ago, and the name has been adopted by the nationalists who desire to make the islands a united whole. The Archipelago lies between the continents of Asia and Australia in that stretch of sea which connects the Indian Ocean with the Pacific Ocean, and is situated between longitude 95° east and 141° east, and between latitude 6° north and 11° south.

Area and Population

The vast extent of the Indonesian Archipelago is a matter of surprise to many. The distance between the extreme westerly part of Sumatra and the most easterly point of New Guinea is greater than that from Los Angeles to New York.

There are thousands of islands in this group. Many of them are small and practically uninhabited, but three of them rank among the six largest in the world: namely, New Guinea, second only to Greenland; Borneo, third, and Sumatra, sixth in size among the islands of the world. Java and Celebes are also large and important islands. The total land area of the almost countless islands of Indonesia is 733,296 square miles, or an area about one-quarter of that of the United States.

No census was organized in 1940 because of the war, but recent official estimates of the population suggest the following figures: Java and Madura, 48,416,000; Outer Provinces, 22,060,000, making a total population of 70,476,000. Some official estimates give a total of from 72,000,000 to 76,000,000. If these estimates are correct this would give Java a population density of well over 900 people to the square mile. About two-thirds of the total population of Indonesia live in Java.

The Republic of Indonesia laid claim to an area of over 50,700 square miles in portions of Java and Madura, an area with a population of over 47,000,000; it also claimed about 163,500 square miles in Sumatra (total area of Sumatra, 167,620 square miles), with a population of 7,500,000.

The area and population of the Federal Territories—those still under control of the Netherlands Government—were estimated (January, 1949) as follows, but no boundaries are yet definitely established either in the Republic or in Federal Territories:

	Area (sq. mi.)	Population
Riau-Lingga Archipelago	12,506	298,329
Bangka	4,549	205,433
Billiton	1,873	73,429
Borneo (Netherlands portion) .	208,286	2,169,000
Island of Celebes		
Celebes	38,786	4,232,000
Menado	34,200	1,139,251
Moluccas (including Dutch New		
Guinea)	191,682	894,000
Timor Archipelago (Netherlands		
portion)	24,450	1,657,000
Bali and Lombok	5,231	2,402,227

People and History

There are several theories concerning the early inhabitants of Indonesia but most anthropologists distinguish two groups from which the Malay races sprang. The first group, now thought to be the ancestors of perhaps all the Malay-Polynesian peoples, is believed to have come from southern China or northern India. The Alas and Gajo races of southern Sumatra, and the Torajas of the Celebes belong to this group. The second group is believed to have come from northern Indo-China about B. C. 200-300, and all the remaining races of Indonesia, except the Papuans of New Guinea and adjacent islands, are believed to have sprung from this group. New racial groups have been formed as a result of frequent intermarriages with later immigrants. One or two reports from Chinese sources of the first and second century A. D. indicate that there was communication between China and Indonesia at that early date.

About the eighth century A. D. the immigration of Hindus from India began and extended over a period of seven centuries. This immigration strongly influenced the culture of the Indonesian races, primarily those of Java and Sumatra. During this Hindu-Indonesian period a number of small kingdoms flourished in Java, and later became the empire of Majapahit in the 13th and 14th centuries. The cultural influence of this Hindu period is evidenced in the remains of many temples, among them the Buddhist temple of Borobudur and the Shiva temple of Prambana, both located in Java.

The Venetian, Marco Polo, visited North Sumatra in 1292. In the first decade of the 15th century Moslem influence, brought to the islands by merchants from Gujarat in India, began moving eastward and Malakka was converted to Islam. The religion spread rapidly to Sumatra, Java and the Moluccas, following the trading and shipping routes of Southeast Asia. Since Islam justifies the propagation of its faith by the sword, it appears that success was largely due to the traders, who felt that piety and piracy were expedients admirably suited to their ends.

In 1509 the Portuguese came, and did much to develop the spice trade in the Moluccas, a trade which later gave these islands a wide reputation. The Dutch arrived on the scene in 1596 and after a few years drove out the Portuguese. In 1602 the Dutch East India Company was formed, by which medium the Dutch, during the next 200 years, consolidated, governed and extended their island empire. Lombok came under Dutch rule in 1894. Hindus from the neighboring island of Bali had settled in Lombok and were the dominating group though not the majority. When they became too oppressive, the Sasak Moslems of the islands implored the Dutch government for help and an expeditionary force was sent to quell the disturbances. Lombok, which had previously been ruled by native kings, was from this time on under Dutch rule.

Except for a short period from 1811 to 1816 when Napoleon overran the Netherlands in Europe, and the British invaded and took Java, the Dutch exercised uninterrupted control of the East Indian Archipelago until the Japanese invasion in 1941. During this period the Dutch colonial government may be said to have been both good and bad. Although much has been done to develop the islands, and although the population has increased and benefited because of improved living conditions, there are some dark years in the history of this period when a policy of extortion and cruel tyranny was exercised.

The growing urge of the Indonesians for independence began with the Budi Utomo (Noble Endeavor) Movement as early as 1908; it recurred in 1920 under the Communist party and received a further stimulus during the four years of Japanese occupation in the recent war. The Netherlands Government-in-Exile, foreseeing this reaction, took the necessary steps and made a proclamation from London in 1942, promising the Indonesians a large measure of independence, comparable to Dominion status.

Since the close of the war, the Republic of Indonesia has been formed, following a 19-month rebellion against the Netherlands. The independence of the Republic was recognized in the Cheribon Agreement signed in Batavia, Java, March 25, 1947. The Netherlands promised the new Republic full independence and co-equal status with the Dutch in a projected Netherlands-Indonesian Union by the tentative date of January 1, 1949. Plans were drawn up for the U. S. I.—the United States of Indonesia—to be patterned after the United States of America. Four states are envisioned: Java, Sumatra, Borneo and East Indonesia.

Guerrilla warfare on the part of Republicans, parleys and deadlocks between the Indonesians and the Dutch were still complicating matters early in 1949. The dispute between the Indonesians and the Dutch is in some respects the same as that between the thirteen American colonies and the British Crown. The Dutch affirm that the Netherlands Government desires to hold free elections and establish independence of the U. S. I. The Indonesians have been incensed because Dutch forces remained in Republican territory. A round-table conference at The Hague has been held and a definite agreement has been reached as to the form of the United States of Indonesia.

Government

After the dissolution of the Dutch East India Company in 1798, the government of the East Indies was administered from Holland through the Ministry of Colonies, and a Governor-General in Batavia who was appointed by the Queen. In the Indies there were two main branches of administration: the Government of the Interior and the Native Administration. The islands were divided into 36 provinces or residences, usually headed by residents, but with governors over the three most important ones. Under them were lesser district officials who worked in close relationship with native government officials called regents, men who were usually of noble stock. In Java there were 70 regencies, but in a number of the Outer Provinces such as Borneo, Sumatra and Ternate, the government worked through the native sultans. Under this old order, all of the Dyak Christians in Alliance areas in Borneo were subjects of such sultans.

For administrative purposes the Island of Celebes is divided into two main parts: the Government of Celebes and dependencies; and the Residency of Menado. In Borneo the highest official is the Governor who, prior to the war, resided in the capital city of Banjermasin. He is assisted by residents, assistant-residents and district officers, of whom the latter carry the bulk of the responsibility of administration.

Since the war the Netherlands Government has been giving the nationals of Borneo as much administrative responsibility as they can take, in preparation for independence and the formation of that new State. The national officials are nominally under the sultans of the various districts. Already native Administrative District Councils have been formed in West and East Borneo and titular heads have been appointed. Because of their primitive culture the Dyak population is poorly represented in these councils. It is to be hoped that in the not too distant future their representation will be in proportion to the population. The nationals have renamed the island Kalimantan.

In New Guinea, prior to the war, the Netherlands portion was administered by the Resident of the Moluccas, with headquarters at Ambon. He was assisted by three assistant-residents: one at Merauke on the south coast; one at Fak Fak near the western tip of the island; and one at Manokwari on the north coast. Since the war the entire Dutch area is under a Resident who lives in Hollandia on the north coast. The Moluccas were formerly a part of the Great East, comprising all the islands east of Java and Borneo, and administered under a governor. In December, 1946, all this area, with the exception of New Guinea, was united in an autonomous state called East Indonesia. New Guinea has the status of a colony of the Netherlands.

In January, 1950, in Amsterdam's Royal Palace, Juliana, Queen of the Netherlands, proclaimed the 340 years of Dutch rule in Indonesia to be ended. Next day two C-47s bearing Indonesian President Soekarno and his official party arrived in Jakarta (as the city of Batavia, Java, will now be known). Four years ago Soekarno had been driven from Batavia (now Jakarta) by the Dutch. Now President Soekarno spoke over the public address system to a great multitude of Indonesians in the mile-wide Koningsplein in front of the palace. "We are one nation, and we pray we may live as a single free na-

tion. . . . We want to build a strong nation, prosperous and orderly."

Dutch New Guinea remains a colony of the Netherlands, at least for the present.

The rest of the great expanse of islands known for centuries as the Netherlands East Indies has become the United States of Indonesia (U. S. I.).

Borneo is divided into five sections, East Borneo and West Borneo being the areas where most of the Alliance work is located.

Celebes, Lombok, Sumbawa and Bali, also centers of Alliance labor and interest, are in the State of East Indonesia.

Climate

Indonesia is pre-eminently tropical, but some of its islands are north of the equator and some are south of the equator and the conditions of those two groups vary greatly. The Archipelago covers such an extensive area and has such variations in altitude that there are many different types of climate. From snow-capped mountains one can descend to lowlands where the temperatures are high, accompanied by great humidity, for in the lowlands there is abundant rainfall and little wind. However, on several of the islands dry winds have a bad effect. The islands lie directly in the regions of the monsoons, those periodic winds which cause important climatic variations; and the equator is the region of convergence for the Northeast and Southeast Trade Winds. Great regularity exists in daily weather changes and in the alteration of the winds.

In the Alliance fields in Indonesia, except in New Guinea, the climate is tropical with little variation throughout the year. The equator crosses the central part of Borneo, Sumatra, and the northern arm of Celebes, yet the average temperature is only 79 degrees Fahrenheit. The climate, generally speaking, is humid, but the nights are usually cool. The only marked change in the weather is the rainy season.

In Borneo the average temperature throughout the year is 86 degrees. The seasons are not distinctly divided. During most of the year there are frequent electrical storms with heavy downpours of rain lasting from two to three hours at a time. In the Bulongan districts there are several floods annually, causing many prolonged delays in travel up the swollen rivers. The rainfall in Borneo varies from 150 to 200 inches per year. The climate is humid and trying, and there is much malaria.

In southern Celebes the rainy season usually begins in December and lasts through March. The heat is tempered by the sea breezes and the monsoons, for all parts of Celebes are near the sea due to the unusual shape of the island.

The coastal areas of New Guinea also are affected by the monsoons and have a rainy season, but the mission stations in the Wissel Lakes region are in the central mountains where the rainfall is quite evenly distributed throughout the year. In this fairly healthful mountain area the temperatures are moderate, ranging from 60° at night to 80° during the day. Because of its altitude of 6,000 feet the Wissel Lakes area has a semi-tropical climate. Many of the vegetables which are grown in the United States can be raised there.

Physical Features

Of the many mountains in Borneo, the highest peak is in British North Borneo, Mount Kinibalu, with an elevation of 13,750 feet. The mountainous islands of Lombok and Bali have volcanic peaks rising to between 10,000 and 12,000 feet above sea level. In the central and northern parts of Celebes there are several active volcanoes, and one peak in the south, Mount Lompobattang, is about 10,000 feet high. In the southeastern part of New Guinea, the Owen Stanley range has peaks rising to 13,250 feet high, while in the northern section of Dutch New Guinea there are several snow-capped peaks, the highest, Carstensz Peak, having an altitude of 16,400 feet. In the Dutch portion of Borneo there are many small mountains in the Bulongan district of East Borneo, ranging around 2,000 feet in elevation and making travel slow and difficult. In the Mahakam district of East Borneo, and also in West Borneo, there is some open country but most of the area is covered by a dense jungle growth.

Borneo is the best watered country in the world, with 40 rivers emptying into the sea. The largest is the Barito in the south, rising in the interior and flowing south into the Java Sea. The Kapuas River rises in the center of the island and flows west into the China Sea. A missionary wrote of this river: "The Kapuas is the very life of West Borneo. It is the people's home, their drinking fountain, their bathroom, their dishpan, their laundry, their mail carrier, their market and their amusement place." The Mahakam, Kayan and Sesayap Rivers all flow eastward into the Celebes Sea. The Mahakam, the Barito and the Kapuas are navigable for launches for hundreds of miles. Small steamers can travel up the Kayan as far as Tanjongselor, 30 miles from the coast. Above that point the rapids permit only Dyak canoes. River steamers can travel up the Sesayap as far as Malinau, 90 miles from the coast.

The Island of Celebes, shaped like a starfish, or an octopus, lies for the most part south of the equator. No large wild animals are to be found, but there are many species of birds and butterflies peculiar to the island. Some of the finest scenery in Indonesia is to be found in the forests, lakes, volcanoes and rivers of Celebes. The two principal rivers are the Sadang, 250 miles long, and the Bonor Solo, 150 miles long.

New Guinea's irregular form resembles somewhat a bird. Its broad central plateau descends into two narrow peninsulas, one in the northwest and the other in the southeast. The coast line is broken by many indentations, the most important ones being the McCluer Inlet and Geelvink Bay at the northwest end of the island; Astrolabe Bay and the Huon Gulf on the northern side; and the Gulf of Papua on the southeast. The chief rivers of New Guinea are the Memberamo, the Sepik and the Rami in the north; and the Digul, the Fly and the Markham in the south. New Guinea has few indigenous mammals, its fauna consisting mainly of marsupials, similar to those of Australia, and the many wild pigs that roam the jungle. The island abounds in birds, among them the famous bird of paradise.

Resources

When Indonesia was cut off from the rest of the world by the Japanese occupation, quinine became almost unprocurable, for Java has supplied 91 per cent of the world's supply, the first cinchona trees having been taken there from Bolivia. Besides raising sufficient food for their own dense population, Java and Madura export coffee, tea, cocoa, indigo, spices, tobacco, rubber and copra.

Sumatra also is fertile, producing large quantities of rubber, coffee and sugar, and it has valuable oil resources. The main product of the Moluccas or Spice Islands is copra. Bangka and Billiton, off the coast of Sumatra, have large tin mines.

Before the war Indonesia supplied 77 per cent of the world's supply of kapok, 92 per cent of the pepper, 40 per cent of the rubber and 19 per cent of the tea. War damage to areas under cultivation has greatly reduced production. Indonesia's sugar production, once so important, is now almost nothing. Minerals produced include tin, silver, gold,

petroleum and coal. The last three are found in good quantities in Borneo, as are also diamonds, but Borneo's mineral wealth will no doubt prove to be the large oil wells on the east coast. The port of Tarakan is famous for its oil deposits. The crude oil found here is of such good quality that it can be pumped directly from the wells to tankers at the dock, and used without refining. Borneo's main exports are copra, rubber, rattan cane for furniture, reptile skins and resins. The island has extensive forests with a large variety of both hard and soft woods, and in the future these may become its main exports. The Dyaks live mainly on rice, raised for their own use but not for export.

The most important rice producing regions in the State of East Indonesia are South Celebes, Sumbawa, Bali and Lombok. Prior to the war East Indonesia produced about one million tons of rice. During the war this production was reduced by probably 25 per cent or more, but it was anticipated that by 1948 most regions would be again self-sufficient.

Very little is exported from Dutch New Guinea at present, but it is believed that it has large oil resources, and the Northern New Guinea Petroleum Company has long been at work on the island. Some spices are exported. The coastal people live mainly on sago, which is found in abundance.

Progress

Up to the outbreak of the war the Netherlands Government had accomplished much in Indonesia. In addition to commercial development, much has been done to improve the health and living conditions of the populace. Hospitals are maintained in the principal districts and a good school system has been developed throughout the principal islands. Even in the heart of Borneo schools have been conducted, and in later years Dyak teachers have been used as well as Menadonese and Ambonese teachers. The Dyak schools have the first three elementary grades, and pupils can go on to the fifth grade at government expense in schools in the larger towns. In important centers like Makassar, there are high schools.

A well-ordered system of inter-island steamship service connects Indonesia from the extreme west of Sumatra to the most easterly possession of New Guinea. Some of the principal coastal cities are ports of call for many steamship lines running to all parts of the world.

As to transportation facilities in the islands, the principal construction of railways has been in Java and Sumatra. By the end of 1938 there were 3,380 miles of railways in Java, 1,130 miles in Sumatra, and 29 miles in southern Celebes. In 1938 Indonesia had about 40,600 miles of highways and roads, of which nearly 35,000 miles were either asphalted or metalled. In Bali and some of the other islands bus service was maintained between the main points. All roads are now in poor condition as there is a shortage of repair material since the war. Horses are used in some parts of the islands but in many regions walking is the only means of land travel. In islands like Borneo, the rivers are the popular thoroughfares.

The number of motor vehicles in the islands in 1947 included 6,100 passenger cars and jeeps, and 9,600 trucks. The number of aircraft in the islands increased from 41 in 1941 to about 50 in 1947, with some 3,000 flying hours monthly.

Currency

The guilder or florin is the unit of currency, and has been on a gold basis since April, 1925. It has about the same foreign exchange valuation as the guilder of the Netherlands, which at present is worth 26.3 cents in U. S. currency (old par 40.20 cents). Although the legal rate for the U. S. dollar is 3.80 florin or guilders, the true commercial value is much higher.

In the Wissel Lakes region of New Guinea the medium of exchange is the cowrie shell, no bigger than a grain of popped corn. The money cowrie (C. moneta), found in the Pacific and the Eastern seas, is used also in some parts of Africa as a basis of barter. (See *Currency*, under *French West Africa*.)

Languages and Tribes

The universal language of the islands is Malay which, since the war, is called the Indonesian language. Together with Dutch it may be termed the commercial language of the islands, and is used in all the port cities. Although it has many variations yet, for general purposes, what is known as low or market Malay is the popular language. It has long been the medium of teaching in the elementary schools up to the sixth grade, and it is now also being taught in the secondary schools. In keeping with the present nationalistic aspirations, plans are being made to improve the Indonesian language so as to give it greater usefulness and to make it the official language of the archipelago.

Apart from the Indonesian language, the native languages and dialects of this island world are legion. Even many of the smaller islands have their own dialects or languages. This constitutes a serious problem in missionary work, though the wide use of the Indonesian language has simplified the task to some extent. Among the Dyaks of Borneo, as among the primitive peoples in New Guinea and in some of the other islands of the archipelago, there are many languages which have not yet been reduced to writing. In the interior it is necessary for the missionary to master the dominant language of the area where he is working, as the people of the remote regions usually understand only their native dialects.

Among the larger and more important Malay races may be mentioned the following: in Java, the Javanese and Sudanese; in Madura, the Madurese; in Sumatra, the Bataks, Achinese and Minangkabaus; in Borneo, the Dyaks and the Banjarese. In Celebes there are six races: the Menadonese and Gorontalese in the north; the Toala people, who are fairly well scattered throughout the island and who are thought to be the original inhabitants; the Torajas in the central, southern and eastern parts; and the Buginese and Makassarese in the southwestern peninsula. The last two and the Gorontalese are Moslem races, and there is a growing Moslem element among the Toalas. In Bali are the Balinese, and in Lombok are the Moslem Sasaks and some Balinese. In the extreme eastern part of the archipelago there are the Papuan races, who are of Polynesian origin and quite different in many ways from the other Indonesian races.

In the interior of the larger islands, notably Sumatra, Borneo, Celebes and New Guinea, aboriginal mountain tribes are still to be found. Of these the Dyaks of Borneo are among the most important, and they in turn may be divided into various tribes, such as the Sea Dyaks, the Gypsy Dyaks, and the Mountain Dyaks.

Everywhere in this vast island world, in all the port cities and even in the far interior, there is a large Chinese population. In many cases after a few generations the Chinese are assimilated by the native tribes and their language is lost. In 1930 the population of Indonesia was composed of 97 per cent Indonesians; two per cent Chinese; and the remainder, Europeans and those given the same status, as well as a few orientals of foreign origin.

The languages used by Alliance missionaries and national workers include the following: Malay (Indonesian), and Sasak; the Dyak languages: Murut, Kenya and Mualang; the New Guinea dialects: Ekari (Kapauku), and Moni. Additional languages used only by national workers include,

among the Dyaks: the Lepo Tau, Lepo Kulit, and in the Mahakam district, the Tunjung; the South Celebes languages: Makassar, Bugis, Muna and Buton; the Balinese language; the Sumbawa languages: Bima and Donggo. The Alliance is the only gospel agency in all the above mentioned languages, except in the Makassar and Balinese languages.

More detailed information concerning the tribes in Indonesia is given in connection with the description of our missionary work in the various islands.

Religions

From the eighth century to the fourteenth century A. D. the dominant religions of most of the islands in the western and central sections of Indonesia were Hinduism and Buddhism. At the end of that period Islam, whose entrance first became apparent about the twelfth century, came more and more to the fore. Merchants from India established themselves on the coast and in the harbor towns of Java and Sumatra. They intermarried with the natives and thus brought into being the Moslem colonies, which gained adherents until they became small kingdoms. Marco Polo in his travels at the end of the thirteenth century, found that Islam had gained a firm footing on the northeast coast of Sumatra, and soon thereafter on the northeast coast of Java. The parts of the archipelago which first went over to Islam were Atjeh and Palembang in Sumatra, and also the Moluccas and parts of Java. Islam continued to grow until now it is conservatively estimated that at least 85 per cent of the total population is Moslem. Only one island seems to have successfully resisted the Moslem invasion, the little island of Bali, which still clings to its own form of Hinduism. Many of the interior tribes of the Indonesian Archipelago have not yet fully embraced Islam, and as a consequence are more open to the gospel. The Moslems of Indonesia, though ignorant and bigoted, are probably less fanatical than in other parts of the world. As a matter of fact there have been more converts to Christ from Islam in Java than in any other part of the world. The Moslems of Makassar and its surrounding areas are ignorant but bigoted also. They have shown little interest in the gospel. (See *Islam*, under *Religions, India*.)

The Dyaks and other wild tribes of the interior jungles are animists, steeped in gross superstitions and engaging in demon worship. (See *Animism*, under *Religions of Africa*.) The religion of the Dyaks makes countless demands on them and affects their life and activities from early morning until they retire at night. A Dyak would not think of going on a journey or doing any work without consulting the Great Spirit, who is believed to have many spirits and servants abroad in the earth. The Dyaks also believe in and greatly fear the Great Evil Spirit, to whom they offer blood-sacrifices.

Roman Catholic Missions entered the Indonesian Archipelago in the sixteenth century and in 1934 they had over 400,000 adherents.

Owing to the long occupation of the islands by the Dutch, who are predominantly Protestant, a number of Protestant denominations have done extensive work in Java, Celebes, New Guinea and others of the islands. In 1936, official statistics for Indonesia gave 1,571,157 as the total number of Protestant Christians. Efforts are being made by Dutch leaders to unite all Protestant groups in a National Christian Council for the whole of Indonesia.

Missionary Occupation

The missionary roll of Indonesia contains a formidable list of martyrs, and the history of missions in this archipelago has some unique distinctions. The largest group of converts from Islam in the world is to be found in Java, and one of the most fruitful mission fields anywhere is that of the Batak Church in Sumatra. Including their believers on the island of Nias, this church has a membership of between 550,000 and 600,000. Most of the work in Indonesia has been carried on by Dutch missionary societies, and although not strongly evangelistic, they are predominantly orthodox. They have engaged in considerable educational and medical work, which has in most cases been marked by a spiritual emphasis.

As early as the seventeenth century ministers of the gospel came to the Indies under the auspices of the East India Company. Most of their work was done in the Sangir Islands north of Celebes, and in the Moluccas. The missionary fervor which began with Carey in England was carried to Holland by a Dutch medical student and resulted, in 1797, in the formation of the Netherlands Missionary Society, the first society of its kind on the continent. Not until 1814, however, did the group turn its attention to the East Indies, when 21 missionaries were sent to Java and one to the Moluccas. In 1831 two men were sent to Menado in North Celebes, and by 1848 this society had sent 84 missionaries to the Moluccas and the Timor group of islands. The Utrecht Missionary Society sent its first missionaries to the north coast of New Guinea in 1855, and to the island of Halmahera in 1865. In 1890 the Netherlands Missionary Society sent a representative to the west coast of Sumatra, and the next year they began work among the Toraja people of Central Celebes. A Lutheran Mission has been laboring in the Batu Islands off the coast of Sumatra since 1899. The Reformed Church has done fine work in Central Java and on the island of Sumatra. The Salvation Army, besides conducting several leprosariums and doing some social work, carries on work in Central Java and in Central Celebes.

Among the non-Dutch missionary organizations working in Indonesia is the Rhenish Missionary Society (German), which began work among the Dyaks of South Borneo in 1836, but because of financial difficulties after World War I, this responsibility was given over to the Basle Mission (Swiss) in 1925. Their Dyak church now has 17,000 members and 235 national workers. The Rhenish Mission began work also among the Batak people of Sumatra in 1866. By 1910 they had 70 missionaries on the field to care for their fast growing church, which now has a membership of more than 500,000. The Methodist Episcopal Church has conducted work mainly among the Chinese in the neighborhood of Batavia, Java, and in the larger cities on the east coast of Sumatra.

The Roman Catholics entered Indonesia with the Portuguese colonization early in the sixteenth century, and before the end of that century claimed 200,000 converts in the various islands. With the fall of Portuguese power in the archipelago, the Roman Catholic work there collapsed. It again became active in 1808 when priests arrived from Holland, but by 1902 there were only 51,000 adherents on 16 stations manned by 32 priests. The Roman Catholics have been working for a number of years on the south coast of New Guinea. They also have work in the Mahakam district of East Borneo and in certain sections of West Borneo, where they have about 120 priests. With the growth of the Catholic Church in Holland there came a corresponding growth of that church in Indonesia, and in 1934 they had 417,785 members and 36,323 catechumens in the islands. In the same year, 124,198 pupils attended Catholic schools; the church maintained 26 hospitals, 23 dispensaries and two leprosariums; and they issued 32 periodicals in the Dutch, Malay and Javanese languages. Such figures show the importance of providing for a definite increase in evangelical work in Indonesia.

A number of Chinese Christians who had formerly been students in the Alliance Bible School in Wuchow, South China, but who were not working for our society, felt the call of the South Sea Islands and, in 1928, under the leadership of Dr. R. A. Jaffray, organized The Chinese Foreign Missionary Union. That same year their first Chinese missionary sailed from his native land to take up residence in Makassar. By 1933 there were four missionary couples and three young men on the field. The areas occupied by this society were the Mahakam River district in East Borneo, the Island of Bangka, and Makassar. The Chinese Foreign Missionary Union looked to Dr. Jaffray, until his death, as its chief leader, and the funds for the support of the work under this new organization were secured largely in the United States and Canada through Dr. Jaffray's efforts. Now, however, the organization has Chinese churches in Indonesia which are supporting their own pastors and helping in the support of others. The Alliance Mission in Indonesia has advised that hereafter all support for the C. F. M. U. should come chiefly from Chinese churches in Indonesia and Southeast Asia.

Although the greater part of Indonesia has long been occupied by Protestant missionaries, the Alliance is the only Protestant society in East Borneo at present, and until we entered the Wissel Lakes region in the interior of Dutch New Guinea, the peoples of that hinterland had had no contact whatever with the gospel. Alliance missionaries entered Borneo in 1929 and opened their first station in New Guinea in 1939.

In southern Sumatra considerable work had been done by the Courier Mission among the degraded jungle people, the Kubus, but because missionaries of that Society have not returned since the close of the war, the Alliance Mission has been assuming some responsibility for this field.

The total results of the missionary work of all societies in Indonesia are phenomenal. No accurate figures are at present available, but the latest estimates of the membership of the larger churches are as follows: Batak (Sumatra), 450,000; Nias (off the coast of Sumatra), 100,000; Minahasa (North Celebes), 311,000; Sangihe and Talaud (North Celebes), 175,000; Molucca Islands, 200,000; Timor, 175,000; Toraja (Celebes), 60,000; Dyak (South Borneo), 17,000, and (East and West Borneo), 16,000; Java, 50,000; Papuan (New Guinea), 100,000. Six Dutch societies, the Salvation Army and The Christian and Missionary Alliance carry on missionary work in Celebes. The Menadonese in the northern peninsula and the Sangir and Talaud Islands to the north are almost wholly evangelized. The preceding statistics do not include the many European, Indo-European and Chinese Christians, and therefore it is estimated that the total number of Protestant Christians in the archipelago now approaches two million.

The Christian and Missionary Alliance

The late Dr. R. A. Jaffray, then a missionary in South China, made the first trip of investigation for the Alliance to the Netherlands East Indies in 1928. The earliest missionaries sent out from the United States to reside there did not reach the field until July, 1929. The first party consisted of five missionaries, and they occupied the following areas: two points in East Dutch Borneo—one on the Mahakam and the other on the Bulongan River—entered for the purpose of reaching the Dyaks of the interior; and one station on the Island of Lombok east of Java. The port city of Makassar, Celebes, was selected as the headquarters of the Mission. Reinforcements came, and by 1935 the missionary staff numbered 21. Three years later there were 38 missionaries on the field. These increases made it possible to open new fields, among them the Sesayap district farther north in East

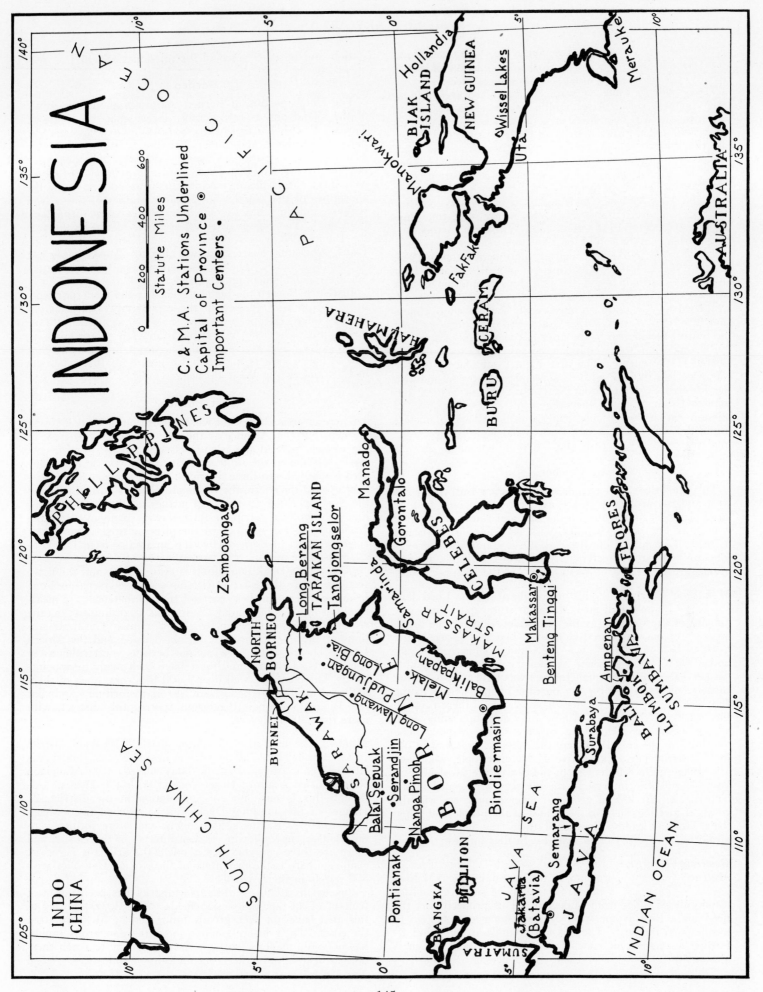

INDONESIA

Statute Miles
0 200 400 600

C. & M.A. Stations Underlined
Capital of Province ⊙
Important Centers •

PACIFIC OCEAN

PHILIPPINES

Zamboanga

SOUTH CHINA SEA

INDO CHINA

NORTH BORNEO

BRUNEI

SARAWAK

Long Berang
TARAKAN ISLAND
Tandjongselor

Samarinda

Balikpapan

Melak
Long Bia

Long Nawang

Pudjungan

BORNEO

Balai Sepuak
Serandjin
Nanga Pinoh

Pontianak

BANGKA

BILLITON

Bindjermasin

JAVA SEA

Semarang

Surabaya

Jakarta (Batavia)

JAVA

SUMATRA

INDIAN OCEAN

Manado

Gorontalo

CELEBES

MAKASSAR STRAIT

Makassar ⊙

Benteng Tinggi

Ampenan

BALI

LOMBOK

SUMBAWA

FLORES

HALMAHERA

BURU

CERAM

FakFak

Manokwari

BIAK ISLAND

Hollandia

NEW GUINEA

Wissel Lakes

Uta

Merauke

AUSTRALIA

140° 135° 130° 125° 120° 115° 110° 105°

10° 5° 0° 5° 10°

Borneo, and the Wissel Lakes region in New Guinea. Efforts were also made to reach the Moslem population of South Celebes, comprising the Makassar and Bugis races.

Then suddenly came the war. As the tidal wave of Japanese conquest rolled closer, individual missionaries had to take measures for their safety on short notice. Some through great peril and the sure mercies of God were rescued to live out the duration in Australia or the States. Some were herded into filthy internment camps, the horror of which can never be understood by those who have not experienced it. With heavy hearts we mention a third group—the martyrs. Rev. and Mrs. Andrew Sande and their infant son, and Rev. Fred Jackson were murdered by the enemy some time during the summer of 1942. Rev. John Willfinger surrendered to the enemy in December of the same year and was executed. Rev. C. R. Deibler died in internment camp in 1943, and Dr. R. A. Jaffray, Chairman of our Netherlands East Indies work, succumbed to the hardships of internment just two weeks before hostilities ceased. Rev. W. E. Presswood, weakened by the years of internment, succumbed to illness shortly after the war. Miss Grace Dittmar, after reaching the States, succumbed to the after-effects of her escape.

Rehabilitation began in Indonesia as soon as the land was cleared of the enemy. The first Field Conference after the war was held in 1947 with 21 missionaries present and also the Foreign Secretary from New York, whose counsel and ministry brought much encouragement. There are now 12 mission stations and 50 missionaries of the Alliance ministering in the islands of Celebes, Borneo and New Guinea. Our total responsibility there is about five million souls.

Celebes

This starfish-shaped island, lying between Borneo on the west and the Moluccas on the east, consists mainly of four large peninsulas stretching to the east and south, which give it a shore line of 3,500 miles, with no point on the island more than 70 miles from the sea. Of its population of over four millions, the greater portion are the Buginese and Makassarese in the southwestern arm of the island.

Makassar   Early in the history of the work the Lord definitely indicated Makassar, the capital and largest city of the Celebes, as the logical location for the headquarters of our work in Indonesia. The first phase of the work to be opened there was the Chinese Church, in 1928, under the Chinese Foreign Missionary Union. In 1932 a Gospel Tabernacle, "Kemah Indjil," was built with a seating capacity of about 500 for the purpose of ministering to the Indonesians. Regular services have been held there through the years and the church is now fully self-supporting, with a membership of 500, and a Sunday school of 400. The offerings for the year 1948 were the equivalent of over $3,700 in U. S. currency. The native Makassar people, who have a language quite different from the Malay are Moslems and have shown little interest in the message proclaimed in the Tabernacle. In 1933 a group of sincere inquirers was the result of meetings held in the homes of the people, but when their Moslem leaders threatened them, the inquirers were afraid to be baptized or to manifest further interest.

Benteng Tinggi,   In 1934 God provided a fine piece of
Malino   property in the mountains near Malino, about 3,000 feet above sea level, and located only 45 miles from Makassar. This property met the need for a Rest Home where the missionaries could go to escape from the heat. The mission grounds are on a hill affording a magnificent view of Mt. Lompobattang, which is almost 10,000 feet high. Field conferences are held at this

station and in 1948 a school for missionaries' children was opened here.

Borneo

The Dutch portion of Borneo comprises about two-thirds of the island and is considerably larger than the State of Texas. British North Borneo, Sarawak and Brunei are the portions of the island under British control. The entire island has a population of nearly 3,000,000, and the Dutch portion, over 2,000,000. There are three main classes of inhabitants: the Dyaks of the interior, who were probably the aborigines of the island; the Moslem Malays of the coastal regions, and the Chinese, who are well scattered throughout the island. The classes or tribal divisions of the Dyaks are: the Punans, Kenyas, Kayans, Muruts, Klemantans and the Ibans. Our missionaries are working in all except the last two of these tribes. The Dyaks were originally head-hunters but are now subdued and civilized.

In Dutch Borneo the highest official is the Governor who, prior to the war, resided in the capital city, Banjermasin. He has many European assistants as well as native officials under him. There are no railroads and few motor roads in the country. The rivers are the highway into the interior. The Alliance area is in Dutch Borneo, with three districts in East and two in West Borneo.

East Borneo

There is some Protestant work carried on in British North Borneo, but the Alliance is the only Protestant Society in the eastern part of the island between the territory of the Basle Mission in the south and British North Borneo. Our area is divided into three districts: the *Mahakam River District* toward the south, the *Bulongan District* north of it, and the *Sesayap River District* still farther north. When the initial reconnoitering trip to Borneo was made in 1928, the *Mahakam* district was one of the places visited. This is our largest district in Borneo, covering an area of from 15,000 to 20,000 square miles. It is twice the size of the state of New Jersey, yet its Dyak population is only 69,000, and the three sections where there are Christians are widely separated one from the other. In these parts of Borneo distances are measured not in miles but in days and weeks according to the time required to travel between two given points. The three sections of the district are the Melak, Tabang and the Muara Lawa. The response here has not been as spectacular as in some parts of Borneo and there have been many disappointments, but there are well over 1,000 believers, most of them gathered in organized churches. From a spiritual standpoint the Tabang section is the bright spot of this district, with more than 400 believers.

Melak   The first mission station in the Mahakam district was located at Samarinda near the coast, but it was later moved to Melak, a small Malay village on the Mahakam River, so as to afford closer contact with the Dyaks. Although this is our only mission station in the district, 23 villages of the Tunjung Dyaks can be reached from Melak by footpaths. In this section many who were formerly indifferent are now showing a keen interest in the Gospel and there are three churches and about 200 Christians here. A challenge here is the proximity of the Roman Catholics with 800 pupils in their schools.

Opened in 1929, the *Bulongan* district has been the most fruitful of all our Indonesian fields. The 30,000 Dyaks of this area have not been greatly influenced by Moslems from the coast. Their inaccessibility, above the dangerous rapids, has not only made it hard for the missionary to reach them but has also served to keep out undesirable influences. A real break came among the Dyaks in 1931 when the King of the Pujungan district, Jalong Ipoy, was converted. Soon after, 225 of his people accepted Christ, and by the end of the year the number had risen to 278. The next year there were 700 conversions, including 130 from the Apo Kayan district. In 1933, 500 more were converted and in 1934, 1,100 of the Dyaks were baptized. By 1938 the number of believers, most of whom were from the Pujungan district, was about 4,000. A number of churches were organized and manned by national workers of whom a fair proportion were Dyaks. Some of the national evangelists have done outstanding work.

The airplane has played an important part in the work of the Bulongan district. The first hydroplane secured for Indonesia arrived in 1939 and was put to immediate use. In this district nine trips were made in one year with the plane, where formerly not more than two or three trips could possibly have been made, to say nothing of the discomfort and risks incurred in ascending the rapids in a canoe. The first plane, lost in the war but permanently preserved in memory, has been replaced by a new hydroplane, subscribed to by Christian business men. The new plane, in six months, covered 18,000 miles and carried 20,000 pounds of missionary equipment. Missionaries can be transported by air from Tanjongselor or Long Bia to Long Nawang in the Apo Kayan area in about two hours. In Dyak canoes the same trip would usually require from five to seven weeks.

There are now four mission stations in the Bulongan district: Tanjongselor, Long Bia, Pujungan and Long Nawang.

Tanjongselor Tarakan is the port of entry to this district, but after living there a few months, the first missionary moved to Tanjongselor, about 50 miles inland. This village of 3,000 inhabitants is the home of a Dutch District Officer and of the sultan, the native regent of the area. It is the gateway to the Dyak population of this section, still unreached with the gospel.

Pujungan This station is about 160 miles up the river from Tanjongselor, above the worst of the rapids. There were 437 believers baptized there recently, and there is a total of 2,500 baptized Christians in this area.

Long Bia This point, 40 miles from Tanjongselor, is the home of the East Borneo Bible School. Radiating from here one finds 10 groups of Christians in the area in a population of about 6,500 Dyaks. A call for teachers has come from the Berau River Valley, about three days' journey south of Long Bia.

Long Nawang This town, the most important in the Apo Kayan region, was opened as a mission station in June, 1948. It was from this region that the Netherlands government official sent the following telegram to our Mission: "At meeting of village chiefs it was decided that after next rice harvest, in all the Apo Kayan, their fetish worship would be abolished. Therefore a great turning to Christianity can be expected. We request you to place preachers in every village and missionaries in Long Nawang."

Actually only two villages turned to Christ after the rice harvest in question, but on a recent tour of 22 villages, 553 believers were baptized, making a total of 1,314 Christians. The movement toward God in this area began during the war years and gathered momentum, until now there are some 5,000 inquirers. We believe that this is the seed sown by our martyred brethren, now coming to fruition.

North of the Bulongan district lies the *Sesayap* district, with a population of 27,000 Dyaks, most of whom belong to the Murut tribe. The native name for this section is *Tee-dong,* meaning mountain country, and indeed the mountains and rapids make traveling difficult and dangerous. Though it has a landing field the present mission hydroplane cannot serve this mountainous district—a twin-motored amphibian plane is therefore needed.

Long Berang The one mission station of the Sesayap district was formerly located in the small Malay village of Malinau, 90 miles from Tarakan, but is now located at Long Berang in the heart of Dyak territory. Like the Dyaks of the Bulongan district, the people here have also responded heartily to the gospel. Six months after the district was opened in 1932, the missionaries, on a reconnoitering trip in the interior, received an enthusiastic welcome. Some of the Dyaks told of dreams in which they had been urged to accept the white messenger and his message. Many traveled from 80 to 100 miles to hear the missionary; others waited at an appointed place from three to four days, and meetings sometimes lasted eleven hours. By 1936 there were 946 baptized Christians and a large number of inquirers. By 1941 the church membership had increased to approximately 3,500. The besetting sin of the Dyaks, before their conversion, was drunkenness. The genuineness of their faith was evidenced by the fact that they were completely delivered from this habit. During the war a British officer entered the district to organize the Dyaks for guerrilla warfare against the Japanese. He encouraged the Christians to return to their drinking. His advice was followed to some extent, but since the return of the missionary, the number of those who yielded to the temptation has been conspicuously reduced.

Not until the fall of 1947 was it possible to send anyone back to this district, which meant that for five long war years it had been without missionary supervision. It was from this district that John Willfinger left to surrender himself to the Japanese. They had threatened with death any native who might hide a white man, and John Willfinger chose death rather than run the risk of compromising his native brethren. He wrote his decision as follows, to an official: "If I hide, naturally the saints will be forced to lie and disobey orders if they shelter me. I would drag them into sin." When he left to give himself up he asked one of our ordained Indonesian workers to take charge of the work, and this brother was the instrument in the Lord's hands of holding the church together through those trying years.

West Borneo

The Alliance work in West Borneo is divided into two districts, the *Belitang* and the *Melawi.* Our missionaries first entered West Borneo in 1933. Two student-evangelists from the Makassar Bible School felt called of God to work in the *Belitang* district and they were greatly used. The work of the Spirit began there in 1934, and the station at Balai Sepuak is the outgrowth of that awakening.

Balai Sepuak In the latter part of 1935 the missionary visited the point near Balai Sepuak where the national evangelists were working, and found 2,000 people genuinely interested in the Gospel. After examining the candidates as to their faith in Christ, 508 were found to be ready for baptism. All of these were Dyaks except two Chinese. By the end of 1936 the churches in West Borneo had a membership of 2,589. In 1936 alone, 1,673 were baptized. Since that time the growth of the church has been less phenomenal but there has been steady progress. By 1940, eight churches with more than 3,500 members were fully self-supporting. They built their own churches, supported their pastors, and financed some of their young men who were attending the Makassar Bible School. Describing that glorious awakening in West Borneo, the missionary wrote:

"What a joy comes to the heart in climbing up the notched log ladder into the long house, to see 500 or more people gathered. At 7:30 in the morning the service starts and except for short intervals for eating, we are teaching, singing and telling them the most wonderful news that has ever come to their ears, until midnight. . . . The signs which accompanied this awakening were as follows: human skulls were taken from long houses and buried; drunkenness ceased among the believers; men returned to their wives from whom they had been separated; men, women and children were healed, some of them having been at death's door; the fame of our Lord Jesus Christ is spreading throughout the whole district."

During the war years this young church experienced great trials. The national pastors were able to continue their ministry without interference during 1942 and 1943, but the following year trouble began. The Japanese accused the workers of hiding things belonging to the missionaries, and they were suspicious that the meetings were being held for political ends. As a result several of the national workers were arrested and one was later killed. The others were released but were forbidden to hold any meetings and the churches remained closed for more than a year. This gave the enemy a chance to work among the Christians and many of them gradually returned to their old habits of smoking, drinking and gambling. The churches were reopened in April, 1945, but the attendance had fallen off considerably. However, most of the believers have now been restored. Since missionaries are again in residence there, further progress has been made, and at the close of the year 1948, there were eight national workers and eight self-supporting churches in the district.

West Borneo represents a large unoccupied mission field, and although the Belitang River district has been entered, there are other areas with a considerable Dyak population still without a witness of Christ. Consequently, in 1938, work was begun in the *Melawi district* where there are 70,000 Dyaks. Two mission stations have been opened.

The Bible School for West Borneo was opened in Seranjin early in 1949. Later in the year the plantation at Seranjin was sold, making it necessary to move the Bible School to Balai Sepuak where it reopened with an enrollment of 32 students.

Nanga Pinoh This town of 3,000 inhabitants is situated 150 miles upstream from Sintang. At first the response was not encouraging, but in 1939 while the missionaries were visiting villages on the Keninjal River, 17 Dyaks were converted. The group grew, built their own chapel, and a church was organized in 1941 with 52 baptized members. Up to the time of the war this was the most receptive section of the Melawi district, with about 500 baptized Christians. In Nanga Pinoh are quite a few Chinese, and there have been good results among them also. A Chinese worker went to labor among them and soon they also had an organized church.

The war had its effect here as elsewhere. The Christians were threatened and intimidated until finally all religious services were stopped and were not resumed until April, 1945. Only three national workers were still at their posts when peace came, but the church has since made a good recovery. There has been an unusual response in a number of Dyak villages in the sector known as the Pinoh country, and there are now about 2,000 earnest inquirers there, although only 13 of them have been baptized so far.

New Guinea

New Guinea, the second largest island in the world, is 1,500 miles long and 400 miles wide at its broadest point. The western part, approximately half of the total area, is under the control of the Netherlands, while the eastern half is under Australia. Prewar maps of New Guinea showed large white spaces covering the interior of the island, for the mountain areas there had never been explored, although the island was discovered only a few years after Columbus landed in America. In 1936 the Wissel Lakes region of New Guinea was spotted by chance when a pilot employed by an oil company was making an aerial survey over the heart of the island. The pilot reported his discovery, the government sent in a plane, and people called Kapaukus or Ekaris, were found there who were still living in the Stone Age and who had had no contact whatever with the outside world. In 1937 the government sent a reconnaissance party to the lakes from the coast, and in 1938 a government post was established in that remote spot.

Wisselmeren Three years after the discovery of the lakes, The Christian and Missionary Alliance opened a mission station at the Wissel Lakes, or Wisselmeren. Two missionaries and three national Christians went in from the coast on foot, reaching the lakes after eighteen strenuous days on the trail. The early days at the station were spent in laying the necessary groundwork of housebuilding, learning the language of the people, gaining their confidence, and in keeping the party supplied with food. This last was the most difficult problem. The diet was meager enough—rice, split peas and dried fish—but it had to be carried for eight days over a difficult mountain trail at a cost of approximately $1.66 per pound.

When a sufficient vocabulary had been acquired, simple religious services were begun, but all efforts were brought to an abrupt end when the government, menaced by war, closed its post at the lakes in 1940 and requested the Mission to do the same. When the government post was again opened in March, 1941, eight national workers went in with the returning missionaries. These workers were placed at various points in the vicinity of Lake Paniai and at each point the Gospel was preached. By the time the war reached the Far East, interest had increased and about 1,000 Ekaris (or Kapaukus) were regularly attending the services. At first the war with the Japanese did not seriously affect this interior post. Indeed on the very day Pearl Harbor was attacked (December 7, 1941), another missionary arrived to reinforce the Wissel Lakes staff, and he later opened a station among the Moni people. As the war advanced the position of this isolated post became more precarious, and in May, 1943, almost the entire post was evacuated—just two days before a Japanese company arrived. At that time about 16 Ekaris had declared that they were ready to accept Christ as their Saviour.

New Guinea was the last of the Pacific Isles to be evacuated by our missionaries. The last couple to leave withdrew to Australia in order that they might be able to re-enter at the first possible moment after the close of the war. During much of the time they were absent, they served with the Netherlands East Indies Government-in-Exile in Australia. When the war ended, this couple was called upon to return to Makassar, where the man was appointed our Board's representative, and later chairman of the field, despite the urge of these missionaries to return to New Guinea.

After Japan's defeat, one missionary and four national brethren returned, in October, 1946, to rebuild the station at Wissel Lakes. This time, however, the missionary and his supplies were flown in by plane. A missionary family went in later to relieve him, and they held the post, out of touch with the outside world for seventh months at a time. Progress was slow and again much time had to be spent in housebuilding. Another difficulty was that the natives had moved to another locality, and in some places they were hostile, thinking that perhaps the white man would again be followed by the Japanese, whom the Kapaukus had learned to dislike. The missionary party was in danger on several occasions, particularly in January, 1947, when the situation became really tense. However, not long after this, the firstfruits of the Lord's harvest in New Guinea were gathered in, for, by the beginning of 1948, about 17 had professed conversion and were baptized. Thirty-one have been converted to date and the gospel is being preached regularly in 12 villages. The national workers have been placed in villages around the lakes, with each worker responsible for two villages. Two young Kapaukus have been attending the Makassar Bible School.

Kemandora Valley In June of 1949 a missionary proceeded from Wisselmeren to the Kemandora Valley with supplies for two months. The mission station there has not been re-established and work begun among the Moni people. Villages are being visited and people showing friendliness come to the mission house. The language must be reduced to writing before the scriptures can be given to the people in their own tongue.

At the close of 1949 there were eight missionaries in New Guinea, one of these being especially trained at the Wycliffe Institute of Linguistics for language reduction and translation work.

Reinforcements have now been sent to Wissel Lakes and the Kapauku and Moni tribes are being reached. It is hoped that soon a center may be opened in the large Dani tribe of 150,000 or more in the Baliem and Swart Valleys. One of these valleys was the scene of an air tragedy during the war, when only one woman and two men were left alive after a plane crashed into a mountain side. Rescuers were dropped by parachutes and the world waited tensely until the news came that the survivors had been brought out by glider. If the interior of New Guinea is to be made accessible, a twin-motored plane is necessary. Government restrictions prevent the use of the present mission plane on flights to New Guinea, as experience has shown that ocean and mountain flying can be done more safely with a twin-motored plane.

In September, 1949, the Board of Managers of The Christian and Missionary Alliance approved the purchase of a twin-engine plane for use in Indonesia as soon as funds should be available for this purpose. After careful research it was decided that a twin-engine amphibian plane, manufactured in Belfast, Ireland, called the Short Sealand, was the plane best adapted for our use in Borneo and New Guinea. On December 8 the Board approved the purchase of this plane whenever the money was available, in expectation of having the plane in operation on the field in the spring of 1950. The use of this plane under the blessing of God will not only save much time in missionary travel but will greatly aid in the transport of their supplies. The cost for the transportation of people and goods will be lower than would be possible without the plane.

Sumbawa

Bima Another of the Lesser Sunda Islands (the group between Java and Timor) is Sumbawa, directly east of Lombok. It is larger than either Lombok or Bali, but the population is only a little over 300,000. One group of the people there resembles the Sasaks of Lombok, and in the eastern part there are a few small tribes: the Donggo, the Bima and the Dompo. There are many people from Celebes living in Sumbawa, and apart from the pagan tribes, most of the inhabitants are Moslems. In the past our work-

ers have done some colportage work in Sumbawa, and student-evangelists working under the National Bible Society of Scotland have sold and distributed a great amount of Christian literature, but the island has been barren soil for the seed of the gospel. In 1936 there were a few converts among the Chinese in the city of Bima but not until work was begun among the pagan Donggo people was there much response. In 1939 fifteen of these simple-hearted folk were baptized, and at the outbreak of the war, the number of Christians had increased to 86. After the war, in 1946, when a Chinese worker visited them, 43 more were baptized. There has since come a more definite break, with 300 converts baptized in 1947. The believers have been under the care of a wise, consecrated national worker, and in 1949 the city of Bima was opened as a mission station, with a new missionary couple in residence. The total number of Donggo believers now exceeds 800; there are 120 inquirers and seven churches.

Other Islands

Although at present there are no missionaries of The Christian and Missionary Alliance residing on other islands of Indonesia than those already mentioned, yet by God's grace, some of the national workers of the Alliance and of the Chinese Foreign Missionary Union are being enabled to carry the gospel to other islands and sections where the Light had not penetrated.

Lombok Before the Alliance came to the East Indies in 1929, no missionary work had been done in Lombok, a small island east of Java and southwest of Celebes. A missionary couple was placed there in 1929. The work was more difficult than and very different from the work in Borneo. Two-thirds of the total population of 750,000 or more are Moslem Sasaks. The remaining third is the Balinese population which has overflowed into Lombok from Bali, and they are Hindus. In spite of the difficulties, six converts were baptized in 1933, including one Balinese, two Moslems, two Chinese young men, and one Menadonese woman. At the end of about six years, the little church near Ampenan had grown to a membership of 30, and by 1937 there were 55 Christians. The next year there was a break among the Moslems, with even a hadji (a pilgrim who has been to Mecca) among those baptized. In 1940 there were no less than eight outstations in the island, manned by national workers. Some of the Christians died as a result of the torture and beatings they received during the war. Two of the national workers were beaten, burned and cast into a pit. It is a marvel that they are still alive. Because of the persecutions, many of the Christians moved away, some recanted, others died, and thus most of the groups were broken up or scattered. Two groups remained at the close of the war: the Balinese Church at Negara Sakah and a remnant of the Moslem converts in East Lombok. These groups have been visited; a National Church Council for Lombok has been organized; and the new missionary couple recently appointed to Sumbawa will also supervise the work in Lombok.

Bali Between Java and Lombok lies the small but important island of Bali, with a population of over one million. It is different from all the other islands of Indonesia in that it resisted the Moslem invasion and has retained the Hindu religion. Its picturesque setting, culture and customs have made it a popular tourist resort. The religious life of the Balinese is so closely interwoven with their social and community life that the introduction of Christianity would certainly disturb the peace and order of the community as it now obtains. The government, apprehensive of difficulty, has therefore not permitted missionary work among the Balinese. However, in 1932, the government gave permission to our Field Chairman to send to Bali a Chinese missionary of the Chinese Foreign Missionary Union for the purpose of working among the Chinese on the island. It so happened that the Balinese wives of some of the Chinese converts also believed on Christ and witnessed to their Balinese relatives. They too began to accept Christ and a difficult situation arose, causing some local but no serious disturbances. Nevertheless the government demanded, in 1935, that The Christian and Missionary Alliance cease its missionary activity in Bali. By that time the Christians there numbered 800, and they were committed to the oversight of the East Java Church. Converts from Bali were no longer permitted to attend the Makassar Bible School, but a number had already received two years of training there and they were able to minister the Word to the Balinese converts and also to win new converts. During the Japanese occupation from 300 to 400 more were added to the church in Bali. Within the last few years the Balinese Church leaders have organized the Balinese Christian Protestant Union, and this body is making slow but steady progress.

Two Balinese young men, graduates of our Makassar Bible School, were appointed by the Mission to work among the Balinese in the Island of Lombok. Later, each of them was led to return to Bali, and one was for a time with the Dutch Church there, but he later resigned. Both of these workers are now in independent church work, shepherding groups of Balinese Christians, the one in North Bali, the other in South Bali. Thus the full gospel message is being proclaimed in Bali and we are praying that the doors may reopen for definite Alliance ministries there in God's own time.

Bangka and **Billiton**   These two small islands off the eastern coast of Sumatra, southwest of Borneo, have a population made up largely of Malays from Sumatra and of Chinese from the Province of Kwangtung. Most of the Chinese are employed in the tin mines. The Malays here are a very ignorant class.

For a number of years the Chinese Foreign Missionary Union has had a missionary stationed in Billiton, aided by student-evangelists, and excellent work has been done. In 1948 a second Chinese missionary arrived to take over the work in Bangka, where the church has been without a pastor for some years. The church in Billiton is self-supporting, has a membership of about 300, and carries on work on three outstations. The Bangka Church has about 100 members and is also doing work in the outlying areas.

Sumatra   The Alliance did some work in southern Sumatra, prior to the war, among the Moslems and Chinese in the cities, and also among the primitive Kubu nomads of the jungle. Since the close of the war, the political unrest has prevented the reopening of this work, although one national teacher is still working among the Kubu Christians, who are now settled in villages. They are in that part of the island which is in the hands of the Republicans, and therefore it has not been possible to make contact with the national worker there.

Translation and Publication Work

Much of Dr. Jaffray's life work can be summed up in two words, pioneering and publishing. Since no memorial for him could be more suitable than a fund that would insure the continuance of the work that was dearest to him, an appeal has gone out for a "Robert A. Jaffray Memorial Fund," to be allocated as follows:

Indonesia Publication Work, $5,000 per year
   for three years $15,000.00
China Publication Work, $5,000 per year for
   three years 15,000.00
Indo-China Press and Publication Work 14,000.00
Pioneer Work in New Guinea, $2,000 per year
   for three years 6,000.00

Total $50,000.00

The paucity of Christian literature at present is appalling. The entire Bible is translated into the Malay language but the supply is still limited. Copies of the New Testament are available in sufficient quantities to meet only the most urgent needs. Only small quantities of the Old Testament have been distributed thus far since the war.

The Netherlands Bible Society, the British and Foreign Bible Society and the National Bible Society of Scotland have united their efforts in Indonesia, as in other countries also, and Scripture translation and distribution are being done jointly by the three Societies.

With the thirst for education growing, and in view of the efforts of the government to make the country literate, the need for publishing and distributing Christian literature cannot be emphasized too strongly. Before the war The Christian and Missionary Alliance had already made an appreciable contribution towards meeting this need by publishing a Bible Magazine in Malay, the *Kalam Hidup,* which was started by Dr. Jaffray in 1930. It now has 1,500 subscribers, the largest circulation in its history.

The postwar Mission Book Room sales have exceeded all previous records, with 31,298 books and tracts sold in 1948. *The Christ Life,* by Dr. A. B. Simpson, is ready for printing. A Malay translation of Dr. Jaffray's Bible expositions is being reprinted, with the fourth volume of Genesis and an exposition of Revelation now ready.

Since the policy of the government is to make Malay, now called Indonesian, the official language of this archipelago, little translation work has been done in other languages. For the Dyaks in the Sesayap district of East Borneo, the Gospels of Matthew and John have been translated in their own dialect. For Lombok, the Gospel of John has been published in the Sasak language. Gospel portions are available in the Balinese, Bugis and Makassar languages. In the Wissel Lakes region of New Guinea, where Malay is unknown, a primer, hymnbook and collection of Old Testament stories are now translated and in use in the Kapauku language.

Schools and Literacy Campaigns

The first phase of our missionary task in Indonesia, an intensive evangelistic ministry, is now passing and the second phase has begun. The missionary must concentrate on the building up of the existing churches, and on the instruction and training of both lay Christians and national workers.

The Bible School in Makassar has in the past trained many of the Dyak workers for Borneo. It was first opened in 1932 with 20 students. The enrollment increased year by year until, by 1939-1940, there were more than 150 students in attendance. The enrollment is less now since two Bible schools have been opened in Borneo. In 1948 the Makassar Bible School had an enrollment of 52, with 35 students graduating. The opening of Bible schools in East and West Borneo and in New Guinea will have a definite effect upon the future of the Makassar school. The best interests of our work in Indonesia call for the training of Dyak workers in Borneo, and of workers from the New Guinea tribes in New Guinea. Hence the scope of the Makassar Bible School will be restricted, but there are possibilities of continued fruitful and far-reaching ministries, especially if the school continues to accept students from other Christian Churches throughout Indonesia.

To meet the need for a larger number of trained Dyak workers, the East Borneo Bible School was opened in 1947 at Long Bia, 40 miles upstream from Tanjongselor. The following year there were 21 students enrolled, besides 80 in the preparatory school. A Bible school was opened in West Borneo at Seranjin, in the Melawi district, in 1949, with 20 students enrolled.

Throughout the field, during the year 1948, 14 primary schools were conducted with a total enrollment of 557. These schools generally run for nine months of the year, and are conducted in the Malay language. Some of the schools cover the first three grades, and the Bible is a part of the daily curriculum in all of them. In the school in the Wissel Lakes region, 25 young people were enrolled, learning to read in order that they might study the Scriptures for themselves.

Six million of Indonesia's 70 million people are now literate, and the growing desire for education will soon increase this number. Villages are asking for teachers in many parts of Borneo and the new Dyak generation is gradually breaking away from many of the old heathen traditions. The witch doctors are finding it difficult to secure apprentices to learn their trade. Christian schools are essential, not only to develop a Bible-reading body of believers, but also to meet the mental hunger of the people with a knowledge that leads to Christ.

The Church and the Challenge

Within less than six years after the Alliance entered Indonesia, in 1929, 29 churches had been established in Borneo, with nearly 8,000 baptized believers; two churches had been established in Makassar, Celebes; four in Bali (but with no official association with the Alliance because of government restrictions); and one small church in Lombok. The total church membership was over 8,300, with an additional 7,000 listed as inquirers.

The present task is threefold: to consolidate the work already begun by establishing the organized churches on an indigenous basis; to meet the needs of expanding work in fields already occupied, particularly in Borneo and Sumbawa; and lastly to concentrate our major pioneer effort on New Guinea and on unoccupied areas in Borneo.

Considering the fact that Indonesia is one of our youngest mission fields, and only 20 years old, it is no small step to undertake to establish the churches on an indigenous basis, but good progress is being made. At the close of 1948, besides the 12 mission stations, there were six church centers and 165 outstations; 70 out of a total of 133 national workers were being supported by the national churches. Of the 123 organized and 25 unorganized churches, 53 were fully self-supporting. The total church membership was 16,754, besides 1,000 members of the churches of the Chinese Foreign Missionary Union. The believers baptized during the year numbered 1,698, and there were 6,859 inquirers. Over 3,000 pupils were enrolled in the 62 Sunday schools. The total church offerings for the year amounted to the equivalent of nearly $23,000 in U. S. currency.

The spiritual need of the churches is great. In the Belitang district of West Borneo, it was rumored during the war that the Japanese would take most of the unmarried young people. This threat led to hasty marriages and later, divorces and remarriages, creating a serious problem of divorce in the church. In the Bulongan district of East Borneo the church needs a spiritual quickening and a greater urge toward self-support. In South Celebes, in the area of Buton and Muna, the Christians are standing true, but this is a Moslem area and there has been renewed opposition.

Among the Balinese there is a growing feeling that their Hindu religion is not sufficient to cope with the problems of this postwar era, and there are signs of disintegration in their worship. The Balinese are facing a crisis—will they turn to Islam or to Christ?

The present political situation has not greatly affected our missionary work, but this may be due to the fact that most of our work is in territory still controlled by the Netherlands, where the conditions are more settled than they are in Java and Sumatra. Eighty-five per cent or more of the Indonesians are Moslems, and if nationalistic aspirations are realized, this will mean that Moslems will have the deciding voice in matters of government. Already Moslem leaders are envisioning an Islamic state. Another menace is Communism, which is growing in influence here as throughout the Far East. A Communistic victory would bode no good for missionary effort. Prayer is needed that the doors in Indonesia may remain open until the task is finished among the five million souls who are our responsibility in this field.

Bible School, Makassar, Indonesia, oldest of the four Bible Schools in Indonesia

THE UNFINISHED TASK

The early reports of The Christian and Missionary Alliance clearly present the objective of entering various fields which were almost, if not altogether, without missionary laborers. Among the places mentioned in the published report of 1892 are: The Island of Borneo; Peru and Ecuador in South America; Szechwan, South and West China, and Tibet; and French Indo-China. In 1893 the purpose of extension in the Congo field was stated, and the Mission in Sierra Leone was recognized as the gateway to the French Soudan. All of these fields have been entered by the Alliance, some in the early days, others later. But our task is not finished, because, within these expansive fields there remain many areas yet untouched. Among the 79,839,000 souls for whom we are responsible, there are many millions yet without Christ. And lying just beyond are other areas whose peoples are still without a witness of the Light of Life.

Among the peoples yet unreached in our Alliance foreign mission fields are many tribes—probably 100 to 200 in number—in whose languages and dialects the gospel message has not yet been preached. There are also millions of people in the parishes of our responsibility in many fields, the largest being in French Indo-China, Siam, and French West Africa. However under the grace of God and the resultant loyalty and liberality of the Alliance constituency in the United States and Canada, steady progress is being made. Nearly 250 new missionaries have gone to the fields in the last five years and 30 more are under appointment to sail, D.V., in 1950.

When the founder of the Alliance movement, Dr. A. B. Simpson, died in 1919 missionaries and native Christians in our foreign fields were witnessing for Christ in 24 languages and principal dialects. By 1941, when the second world war broke out, the number had risen to a little more than 110. In 1949 in the 20 mission fields of the Alliance the life-giving message of salvation through Christ alone is being proclaimed in 151 languages and principal dialects. While rejoicing in this increase let us be earnest in prayer and intercession that we may press forward with great zeal and devotion to finish the task God has granted to us under the Great Commission. It would be well for us to study anew this Great Commission in Matthew 28:18-20. As we contemplate the victory of the "Unfinished Task" we see in the Scriptures three outstanding things:

The GO of an Eternal Passion—The LOVE of God.

The GOAL of an Eternal Purpose—The CHURCH of God.

The GLORY of an Eternal Presence—The CHRIST of God.

Closed Lands

The greatest unreached area in the world today is in *Central Asia* where *Russian Turkestan, Afghanistan, Inner Tibet, Nepal, Bhutan* and *Outer Mongolia* have kept their doors tightly closed against the entrance of the gospel message, and where Sinkiang (Chinese Turkestan) and Inner Mongolia, enthralled by Islam and Buddhism, have made missionary work difficult, and at times impossible. Shut in by snow-capped mountain ranges and vast desert areas these countries rest ignorantly content in their exclusive isolation.

Inner Tibet, also called Tibet Proper, is closed, but Outer Tibet, that portion under Chinese rule, is open to the gospel. Wide areas of Tibet are unexplored, and estimates of its population vary from a low of 700,000 to a high of 6,000,000, but the usual estimate is about 3,000,000. The elaborate hierarchy of Lamaism is in control, and the religious leaders have successfully frustrated attempts to carry the Christian message into the land. Lhasa, the capital, at an altitude of nearly 12,000 feet above sea level, remains in lofty, forbidding seclusion.

Several missionary societies, including the China Inland Mission and The Christian and Missionary Alliance, are laboring on the borders of Tibet on the China side, occupying advantageous points among Tibetan tribes who live in territory nominally governed by China. Other Missions are working from the India side, trying to reach Inner Tibet from points on the border. The Moravian inn at Leh has proved to be an excellent means of contact with Tibetan travelers who come down through the mountain passes into India to trade. The little Tibetan Frontier Mission, now united with the Evangelical Alliance Mission (formerly called the Scandinavian Alliance), has carried on for years where India, Nepal and Tibet meet. Other missionaries are laboring farther east in the neighborhood of Darjeeling. Reports have come of two or more Indian Christians who entered Tibet as witnesses for Christ, and became martyrs to His cause.

Afghanistan, a rugged, mountainous country inhabited by 12 million fearless, warlike peoples, has been called "the land of rocks and stones and sanguinary feuds." It borders Russian Turkestan on the north but has not been greatly influenced as yet by Communistic propaganda; on the west it is bounded by Iran; and on the east and south by parts of India and Pakistan. No missionaries travel over the seven important trade routes that cross the country, for the Moslem rulers and people not only forbid the messengers of Christ to enter their land, but also make it an offense punishable by death to profess the Christian faith.

Various Missions have tried to penetrate Afghanistan from the Indian side. From the Persian side the American Presbyterians are attempting to enter, and in 1924, four of their missionaries were permitted to visit Herat to dispense medical aid. A few European traders and some technicians have been permitted to work in Afghanistan, but the walls of this Moslem Jericho have not yet begun to crack before the brave soldiers of the Cross who are circling it with their testimony.

The countries of *Nepal* (estimated population, 5,600,000) and *Bhutan* (estimated population, 300,000), lying south of Tibet in the north of India, have been closed not only to Christian missionaries but to all Europeans. Nepal is now becoming more lenient, and Americans who can give technical aid to the government have been invited to enter the country. Nepal has long been ruled by Hindu Rajputs, but Buddhism seems to be the dominant religion, as it is in Bhutan also. A number of Nepalese living just outside their country have been converted, but are not permitted to re-enter and live in Nepal. The Scottish Mission in Sikkim has been much used in reaching both Bhutanese and Nepalese outside their own countries.

Missionary work is forbidden within the vast territories of the *Union of Soviet Socialist Republics,* covering one-sixth of the earth's land surface, with a total population of over 211,000,000. However, thousands of Christians within the U. S. S. R. are bearing witness for Christ, and many agencies are seeking opportunities to get the Scriptures into the hands of the people in various parts of the Union.

Russian Turkestan, population 16,600,000, comprising five Soviet republics in Central Asia, was once witnessed to by Nestorian Christians. Today it is totally unoccupied for

Christ. Soviet influence is also very strong in Sinkiang (Chinese Turkestan), and in Mongolia. Sinkiang is accessible from China and work has been done there by a Swedish Mission and by the China Inland Mission, but with periods of interruption, evacuation and imprisonment.

Outer Mongolia, now the Mongolian People's Republic, has its independence guaranteed by the U. S. S. R. under the terms of a pact signed in 1936. Although its area is 622,744 square miles, or about one-fifth of that of continental United States, its estimated population is only 850,000, for the Gobi desert covers 200,000 square miles of its area. The Evangelical Alliance, other smaller Missions, and some independent workers have labored in a section of Inner Mongolia which comprises several provinces under Chinese rule. Outer Mongolia is closed to the gospel but the people have a written language and this fact makes the ministry of the printed Word an urgent challenge.

Arabia, with an estimated population of 10 millions, is still closed to the followers of Christ, except for a few points on the Persian Gulf Coast, in the British Protectorate of Aden, and in other points near-by. No missionaries are permitted in the interior.

Inadequately Occupied Lands

The greatest number of unevangelized people, in the vast continent of Asia, may still be found in already occupied fields, among them India, China, Indo-China and Siam. There, valiant soldiers of the Cross are winning thousands to Christ, but there are still millions and tens of millions who will have no proper opportunity within their lifetime to hear the story of salvation unless the Church of Christ at home and abroad is inspired with greatly increased missionary zeal.

The Islands need more adequate occupation. A chart appearing in *Christian Life* magazine indicates that 45 per cent of the population in the island world is still unevangelized. There is still great need for pioneer effort in the southern Philippines and in the interior of some of the islands of Indonesia. The large Dani tribe (100,000 or more) in the interior of Dutch New Guinea should have a gospel witness. Some islands can and are being evangelized by the Christian churches in other islands of the same general area. (See pages on *The Island World.*)

Africa is for the most part open to missionary effort. The doubtful areas are Italy's former colonies, Libya, Eritrea and Italian Somaliland, where Catholic influence long hindered Protestant missions. Now that the future status of those territories is in the hands of the four powers—Britain, France, the United States and the U. S. S. R.—who are working on the problem in conjunction with the United Nations, it may be that there will be more tolerance shown to Protestant missionary effort.

Although numerous new tribes in Africa are being reached by witnesses for Christ, there remain millions of people and a large number of tribes and language groups who have not yet heard the gospel.

In *Latin America* the populations of the Indian tribes are not large compared with the vast numbers of unreached peoples in other lands, but their spiritual destitution is a great challenge. According to some estimates the Indians of the continent of South America number about 15 millions. Other estimates state seven millions. No one knows, for no census has ever been taken in some parts of the jungles, and in fact no one dares to even enter the territory of some tribes such as the Aukas in Ecuador, where a white man would be killed on sight. Over five million Indians of the continent live in mountain areas where they are subject to the civil government of the country, and some of them speak the Spanish language, at least in a measure. However, most of the Indian tribes must be evangelized in their own tongue, and there are some 500 different languages spoken by the Indians of all Latin America. Within the last thirty years definite advance has been made in carrying the gospel to the Indians of Central and South America, but fruit has been exceedingly meager. In his book, *Under the Southern Cross,* R. B. Clark writes:

God has today, working among these peoples His witnesses, . . . but they are few in number and battling against fearful odds. An army must be organized and an advance called, if the Indian race is to be evangelized. . . . This citadel will fall only to heavy artillery, and surrender only at the sound of the marching of a host!

The Bible in Every Tongue

Horace Greeley once said, "It is impossible to mentally or socially enslave a Bible-reading people. The principles of the Bible are the groundwork of human freedom." Now is the time to distribute the Book, the panacea for bewildered, restless spirits, throughout the lands where a growing spirit of nationalism and insurrection is causing confusion and bloodshed.

The nations were never more ready for the printed Word. Russia, in the past 20 years, has taught 100 millions to read; India hopes to teach 150 millions to read within the next three years; China's difficult language can now be read by 135 millions of her people and millions more are learning to read each year.

Bible Societies of the various countries are the principal agencies in the world for the publication and distribution of the Scriptures. Within the last three years they have joined forces as the United Bible Societies in order to consolidate and further their work in the many lands where they have representatives. Besides the larger, better known Bible Societies such as the British and Foreign, American, National (Scotland), and the Netherlands Bible Societies, the United Bible Societies include the Bible Society of India, Pakistan and Ceylon, the Bible Society of Brazil, and a long list of societies in other countries as well.

The work of translating the Scriptures in the languages of peoples and tribes is an essential part of missionary ministry. It means not hours but years of exacting labor, "hemmed in by book-heaps piled around," but the Church of Christ cannot be established without it. The entire Bible has been published in 188 languages, the New Testament alone in 243 more, and Scripture portions—a Gospel or other book or books, in 585 others. Some part of the Bible is now available in 1,108 languages and dialects. The Bible has been translated into more languages than any other book, yet there are hundreds of languages in which there is still no portion of Scripture translated, and many more have but one or two gospels. The Pioneer Mission Agency has stated, "Of the 5,000 languages and dialects which are spoken by mankind, . . . 3,000 are unimportant and hardly demand attention." But with the entire Bible, or at least the New Testament, available in a total of less than 500 languages, the remaining portion of the 2,000 important languages surely needs more of the Scriptures translated than a few portions.

Religion or politics may close certain countries to missionaries, but into those closed lands is going the Word of God in the hearts and hands of pilgrims and traders who have ventured outside their isolated countries and have been met by messengers of Christ, alert and ready for just such opportunities. A Swedish Mission, which was expelled from Kashgar, is revising the Bible in the Turki language so that it can re-enter Chinese Turkestan. In Lahore, Pakistan, the Bible is being printed in Tibetan for circulation across the border.

The Bible in the Pushtu language has recently been revised and is being sold along the Afghan border.

"Thy Word shall leap the barriers, and the Light
Shall sweep these lands; and Faith and Love and Hope
Shall win for Christ these strongholds of the night."

The World Challenge

Islam, Buddhism, Roman Catholicism and Communism are more formidable foes of the gospel than the animism of primitive peoples. Of the 20 million Communists in the world (United Press survey, 1947), only six million are in the U. S. S. R. boundaries. Eleven million of them are in other parts of Europe and two million are in China. It is estimated that the menace has now reached more than 800 million persons, the number living today in countries definitely under Communist influence. Besides the threat of Communism, there is the resurgence of Roman Catholicism, and the strength of Islam with its total of nearly 221 million followers.

It is true that there are more Christians in Korea today than there were in the entire Roman Empire at the close of the first century, but the world's population is increasing by at least 50 additions every minute, and out of a total world population of over 2 billion, 300 million (most recent estimate) the number of Christians, both Protestant and Catholic, has been estimated at from 600 million to 700 million at the most. Between 50 and 60 per cent of the peoples of earth still wait to hear the gospel message, while in the United States there is said to be an average of one pastor for every 500 or 600 people.

If Christ's commission to go and teach all nations is to be carried out, we must send and support a much larger staff of missionaries than we now have. American Christians give generously to the missionary cause, but a large number of them still possess enough to enable them to live on a much more comfortable scale than do most of the people of Europe. May God give us a passion for souls that will cause us to give prodigally and go gladly, guarding against the deadening influence of that which Kahlil Gibran characterizes as "Comfort, that stealthy thing that enters the house as guest, and then becomes a host, and then master. Ay, and it becomes a tamer, and with hook and scourge makes puppets of your larger desires."

God so loved the world that He gave His only begotten Son to die in the agony of Calvary that the world might be saved through believing on His Name. Christ loved the Church, which was to be built of living stones—the lives of the redeemed—and in this love gave Himself for the Church. Yet even this marvelous fullness of love, the love of God the Father and the love of God the Son, will not bring to a sin-cursed world in our generation the message and privilege of salvation unless that two-fold love for souls and the Church is shed abroad in our hearts and in the hearts of all who belong to Christ by God the Holy Spirit. This infilling and outflowing love will cause us to so faithfully serve God and our fellowmen that we will count no cost too great, no hardship too severe, and no sacrifice too costly if we may but, by God's enabling, fulfill our ministry in obeying the Great Commission and giving to all men everywhere a chance to hear the gospel, accept the Saviour and obey the Lord.

Red Bobo Workers, Sanekui, French West Africa

Tribes Bible School, Banmethuot, Indo-China

POPULATIONS AND LANGUAGES
OF THE MISSION FIELDS OF
THE CHRISTIAN AND MISSIONARY ALLIANCE

Field	Population for which the Alliance is responsible	Languages and Principal Dialects used in Alliance Fields by Missionaries, Native Workers and Native Christians			
India	5,000,000	Gujarati	Hindi	Marathi	Urdu
French West Africa	5,000,000	Agni Andos Arabic Ashanti Appoloni Bambara Baouli Black Bobo	Dioula Dyimini Fanti Foula French Gberese Gouro Habbe	Kissi Kuranko Maninka Marka Mianka Nounouma Pana Red Bobo	Samogo Sankaran Sonhrai Tamachek Toma Yalounka Yokouba
Congo	500,000	French	Kifioti	Portuguese	
Gabon	300,000	Djiwoumvou French Getsogo	Gichira Yibongo Yindjavi	Yingomo Yipounou Yissango	Yivarama Yivoungou
French Indo-China	27,300,000	Bahnar Cambodian Cantonese Cham Chil French	Hdrung Jarai Katu Kha Mhu Khamoo Koho	Krung Laotian Mnong Budang Mnong Gar Mnong Preh Pnong	Raday Sre Thai Tho Viet-Namese
Siam	6,617,000	French Lao-Kao	Lao-Putai Lao-Wiengohan	Lao-Yaw Mandarin	Swatow dialect
Colombia	1,642,000	Guambiano	Huitoto	Paez	Spanish
Ecuador	2,500,000	Jivaro	Quechua	Spanish	
Peru	700,000	Spanish			
Chile	1,000,000	Araucanian	German	Spanish	
Argentina	1,000,000	Spanish			
Kansu Tibetan Border	3,500,000	Arabic	Mandarin	Salar	Tibetan Tongsiang
Kweichow-Szechwan	3,000,000	Mandarin	Miao		
Central China	6,000,000	Mandarin	Shanghai dialect		
South China	9,000,000	Cantonese Chuang	Ma Lao Mandarin	Peh Hsin Tung	Yao
Israel	300,000	Armenian Bulgarian	Dutch English	French German	Hebrew Russian Yiddish
Syria-Jordan	400,000	Arabic	English	French	Turkish
Philippine Islands	1,000,000	Atao Bagobo Bajao Moro Bilaan Cantonese Cebuano	English Ilocano Ilongo Kalibugan Maguindanao Moro Mandaya	Manobo Mansaca Maruri Samal Moro Subanun Tagabili	Tagacola Tagalog Tausug Moro Tiruray Tuboy Yakan Moro Zamboangueno
Indonesia	5,000,000	Abai Air Taboen Bali Benua Bima Boegis Boeton	Donggo Ekari Kayan Kenya Lepo Bem Lepo Koelit Lepo Taoe	Long Ilau Makassar Malay Modan Moealang Moena Moeroet	Moni Oeloe Kerayan Oema Alim Poetoek Sasak Toendjoeng
Puerto Rico	50,000	English	Spanish		
TOTAL RESPONSIBILITY	79,809,000	TOTAL LANGUAGES AND DIALECTS USED		151	